# CCNP Enterprise Design
## ENSLD 300-420

## Official Cert Guide: Designing Cisco Enterprise Networks

**ANTHONY BRUNO,** CCIE No. 2738

**STEVE JORDAN,** CCIE No. 11293

**Cisco Press**
Hoboken, New Jersey

# CCNP Enterprise Design ENSLD 300-420 Official Cert Guide: Designing Cisco Enterprise Networks

Anthony Bruno, CCIE No. 2738
Steve Jordan, CCIE No. 11293

Copyright© 2021 Cisco Systems, Inc.

Published by:
Cisco Press

1 2020

Library of Congress Control Number: 2020906746

ISBN-13: 978-0-13-657519-1

ISBN-10: 0-13-657519-6

## Warning and Disclaimer

This book is designed to provide information about the CCNP Enterprise Design ENSLD 300-420 exam. Every effort has been made to make this book as complete and as accurate as possible, but no warranty or fitness is implied.

The information is provided on an "as is" basis. The authors, Cisco Press, and Cisco Systems, Inc. shall have neither liability nor responsibility to any person or entity with respect to any loss or damages arising from the information contained in this book or from the use of the discs or programs that may accompany it.

The opinions expressed in this book belong to the author and are not necessarily those of Cisco Systems, Inc.

## Trademark Acknowledgments

All terms mentioned in this book that are known to be trademarks or service marks have been appropriately capitalized. Cisco Press or Cisco Systems, Inc., cannot attest to the accuracy of this information. Use of a term in this book should not be regarded as affecting the validity of any trademark or service mark.

## Special Sales

For information about buying this title in bulk quantities, or for special sales opportunities (which may include electronic versions; custom cover designs; and content particular to your business, training goals, marketing focus, or branding interests), please contact our corporate sales department at corpsales@pearsoned.com or (800) 382-3419.

For government sales inquiries, please contact governmentsales@pearsoned.com.

For questions about sales outside the U.S., please contact intlcs@pearson.com.

## Feedback Information

At Cisco Press, our goal is to create in-depth technical books of the highest quality and value. Each book is crafted with care and precision, undergoing rigorous development that involves the unique expertise of members from the professional technical community.

Readers' feedback is a natural continuation of this process. If you have any comments regarding how we could improve the quality of this book, or otherwise alter it to better suit your needs, you can contact us through email at feedback@ciscopress.com. Please make sure to include the book title and ISBN in your message.

We greatly appreciate your assistance.

**Editor-in-Chief:** Mark Taub

**Alliances Manager, Cisco Press:** Arezou Gol

**Director, ITP Product Management:** Brett Bartow

**Executive Editor:** Nancy Davis

**Managing Editor:** Sandra Schroeder

**Development Editor:** Ellie Bru

**Project Editor:** Mandie Frank

**Copy Editor:** Kitty Wilson

**Technical Editors:** Kevin Yudong Wu, James Hill

**Editorial Assistant:** Cindy Teeters

**Designer:** Chuti Prasertsith

**Composition:** codeMantra

**Indexer:** Ken Johnson

**Proofreader:** Gill Editorial Services

| Americas Headquarters | Asia Pacific Headquarters | Europe Headquarters |
|---|---|---|
| Cisco Systems, Inc. | Cisco Systems (USA) Pte. Ltd. | Cisco Systems International BV Amsterdam, |
| San Jose, CA | Singapore | The Netherlands |

Cisco has more than 200 offices worldwide. Addresses, phone numbers, and fax numbers are listed on the Cisco Website at **www.cisco.com/go/offices**.

# About the Authors

**Anthony Bruno**, CCIE No. 2738, is an architect and technical resource manager with British Telecom (BT) with more than 27 years of experience in the internetworking field. Previously, he worked for International Network Services (INS) and Lucent Technologies, and he was a captain in the U.S. Air Force. He has consulted for many enterprise and service provider customers in the design, implementation, and optimization of large-scale networks. Anthony leads architecture and design teams in building next-generation networks for customers.

Anthony completed a master of science degree in electrical engineering at the University of Missouri–Rolla in 1994 and a bachelor of science in electrical engineering at the University of Puerto Rico–Mayaguez in 1990. For the past 20 years, he has coauthored five editions of the *CCDA Official Cert Guide* for Cisco Press.

Outside work, Anthony enjoys running marathons and Spartan obstacle races, and he has finished seven Ironman distance triathlons. He is also an avid genealogist and ancestry tree researcher. Anthony also enjoys piloting his Mavic Pro drone during trips.

**Steve Jordan**, CCIE No. 11293, is a Principal Architect with J. Network Architects and has 23 years of experience in the field of internetworking. For the last 13 years, Steve has specialized in data center and network security architectures involving compute, network, security, storage, and virtualization. Over the years, Steve has consulted with many enterprise and service provider customers in both pre-sales and post-sales engineering and architecture roles, along with working at several Cisco Gold Partners. He has extensive experience in data center and security architecture design and has implemented solutions in many financial, energy, retail, healthcare, education, and telecommunications industries. Steve is a 15-Year triple CCIE in the tracks of Routing & Switching, Storage Networking, and Data Center. His other certifications include CCNA, CCNP Enterprise, VMware VCIX6-NV, and VCP6-NV.

Steve lives in Houston, Texas; and when he is not working on technology, Steve can be found traveling to new places, homebrewing, and trading stocks.

For the past 14 years, Steve was also the coauthor for three editions of the *CCDA Official Cert Guide*.

# About the Technical Reviewers

**Kevin Yudong Wu**, CCIE No. 10697 (Routing & Switching and Security), is a senior consultant at AT&T Consulting. He has been engaged as a leading engineer in various network design projects, including LAN, WLAN, data center, and network security. Before joining AT&T, Kevin worked as a senior consultant at British Telecom (BT) and customer support engineer at Cisco High Touch Technical Support (HTTS) where he supported both Cisco LAN switching and security products. He holds master's degrees in both computer science (University of Texas at Arlington, 2003) and materials engineering (Beijing University of Aeronautics and Astronautics, 1995).

**James Hill**, CCIE No. 29455, CISSP, is a highly respected security professional with a career spanning 25 years in the field of IT. Currently, he is the co-owner of H5 Strategic Alliances, LLC, an IT consulting firm, and serves as the chief technology officer. H5 is committed to providing an "intelligent IT" mindset while providing expert-level professional services. H5's focuses include cybersecurity, network access control, architectural design, implementation, and support. James has designed and implemented infrastructure and security solutions at several Fortune 500 companies within the United States. James has held the CISSP certification since 2004 and CCIE Security certification since 2011.

# Dedications

Anthony Bruno:

This book is dedicated to my wife of 29 years, Yvonne Bruno, Ph.D., and to our daughters, Joanne and Dianne. Thanks for all of your support during the development of this book. And to my mom, Iris Bruno: Thank you for being a wonderful mother.

Steve Jordan:

This book is dedicated to my daughter, Blake, and my two sons, Lance and Miles, for always supporting me during the development of this book. I also want to dedicate this book to my mother, Frances Brennan, and my good friend David Carswell Jr. for supporting me and providing encouragement during the writing of this book.

# Icons Used in This Book

vBond

Switch

Server

VSS

Laptop

vManage

Router

File Server

Route Switch
Processor

WWW Server

vSmart

vEdge

Cloud

Wireless Router

# Command Syntax Conventions

The conventions used to present command syntax in this book are the same conventions used in the IOS Command Reference. The Command Reference describes these conventions as follows:

- **Boldface** indicates commands and keywords that are entered literally as shown. In actual configuration examples and output (not general command syntax), boldface indicates commands that are manually input by the user (such as a **show** command).

- *Italic* indicates arguments for which you supply actual values.

- Vertical bars (|) separate alternative, mutually exclusive elements.

- Square brackets ([ ]) indicate an optional element.

- Braces ({ }) indicate a required choice.

- Braces within brackets ([{ }]) indicate a required choice within an optional element.

# Introduction

Congratulations! If you are reading this Introduction, then you have probably decided to obtain a Cisco certification. Obtaining a Cisco certification will ensure that you have a solid understanding of common industry protocols along with Cisco's device architecture and configuration. Cisco has a high network infrastructure market share of routers, switches, and firewalls, and a global footprint.

Professional certifications have been an important part of the computing industry for many years and will continue to become more important. Many reasons exist for these certifications, but the most popularly cited reason is that they show the holder's credibility. All other factors being equal, a certified employee/consultant/job candidate is considered more valuable than one who is not certified.

Cisco provides three levels of certifications: Cisco Certified Network Associate (CCNA), Cisco Certified Network Professional (CCNP), and Cisco Certified Internetwork Expert (CCIE). Cisco made changes to all three certifications, effective February 2020. The following are the most notable of the many changes:

- The exams now include additional topics, such as programming.

- The CCNA certification is no longer a prerequisite for obtaining the CCNP certification.

- CCNA specializations are not being offered anymore.

- The exams test a candidate's ability to configure and troubleshoot network devices in addition to the candidate's ability to answer multiple-choice questions.

- The CCNP is obtained by taking and passing a Core exam and a Concentration exam.

- The CCIE certification requires candidates to pass the Core written exam before the CCIE lab can be scheduled.

CCNP Enterprise candidates need to take and pass the Implementing and Operating Cisco Enterprise Network Core Technologies ENCOR 350-401 examination. Then they need to take and pass one of the following Concentration exams to obtain their CCNP Enterprise certification:

- **300-410 ENARSI:** Implementing Cisco Enterprise Advanced Routing and Services

- **300-415 ENSDWI:** Implementing Cisco SD-WAN Solutions

- **300-420 ENSLD:** Designing Cisco Enterprise Networks

- **300-425 ENWLSD:** Designing Cisco Enterprise Wireless Networks

- **300-430 ENWLSI:** Implementing Cisco Enterprise Wireless Networks

- **300-435 ENAUTO:** Implementing Automation for Cisco Enterprise Solutions

This book helps you study for the Designing Cisco Enterprise Networks (ENSLD 300-420) exam. When you take the exam, you are allowed 90 minutes to complete about 60 questions. Testing is done at Pearson VUE testing centers or via Cisco online testing.

Be sure to visit www.cisco.com to find the latest information on CCNP Concentration requirements and to keep up to date on any new Concentration exams that are announced.

## Goals and Methods

The most important and somewhat obvious goal of this book is to help you pass the ENSLD 300-420 exam. In fact, if the primary objective of this book were different, then the book's title would be misleading; however, the methods used in this book to help you pass the ENSLD 300-420 exam are designed to also make you much more knowledgeable about how to do your job. While this book and the companion website together have more than enough questions to help you prepare for the actual exam, our goal is not simply to make you memorize as many questions and answers as you possibly can. One key methodology used in this book is to help you discover the exam topics that you need to review in more depth, to help you fully understand and remember those details, and to help you prove to yourself that you have retained your knowledge of those topics. So, this book does not try to help you pass by memorization but helps you truly learn and understand the topics. Designing Enterprise Networks is one of the concentration areas you can focus on to obtain the CCNP certification, and the knowledge tested in the ENSLD 300-420 exam is vitally important for a truly skilled enterprise network designer. This book would do you a disservice if it didn't attempt to help you learn the material.

This book will help you pass the ENSLD 300-420 exam by using the following methods:

- Helping you discover which test topics you have not mastered

- Providing explanations and information to fill in your knowledge gaps

- Supplying exercises and scenarios that enhance your ability to recall and deduce the answers to test questions

## Who Should Read This Book?

This book is not designed to be a general networking topics book, although it can be used for that purpose. This book is intended to tremendously increase your chances of passing the ENSLD 300-420 CCNP exam. Although other objectives can be achieved by using this book, the book is written to help you pass the exam.

So why should you want to pass the ENSLD 300-420 CCNP exam? Because it's one of the milestones toward getting the CCNP certification. Getting this certification might translate to a raise, a promotion, and recognition. It would certainly enhance your resume. It would demonstrate that you are serious about continuing the learning process and that you're not content to rest on your laurels. It might also please your employer, which may need more certified employees.

# Strategies for Exam Preparation

The strategy you use to study for the ENSLD 300-420 exam might be slightly different than strategies used by other readers, depending on the skills, knowledge, and experience you already have obtained. For instance, if you have attended the ENSLD course, then you might take a different approach than someone who has learned enterprise design through on-the-job experience.

Regardless of the strategy you use or the background you have, this book is designed to help you get to the point where you can pass the exam in the least amount of time. For instance, there is no need to practice or read about IP addressing and subnetting if you fully understand it already. However, many people like to make sure that they truly know a topic and thus read over material that they already know. Some readers might want to jump into new technologies, such as SD-Access, SD-WAN, and automation. Several book features will help you gain the confidence you need to be convinced that you know some material already and will help you know what topics you need to study more.

# The Companion Website for Online Content Review

All the electronic review elements, as well as other electronic components of the book, exist on this book's companion website.

## How to Access the Companion Website

To access the companion website, which gives you access to the electronic content provided with this book, start by establishing a login at www.ciscopress.com and registering your book. To do so, simply go to www.ciscopress.com/register and enter the ISBN of the print book: 9780136575191. After you have registered your book, go to your account page and click the Registered Products tab. From there, click the Access Bonus Content link to get access to the book's companion website.

Note that if you buy the Premium Edition eBook and Practice Test version of this book from Cisco Press, your book will automatically be registered on your account page. Simply go to your account page, click the Registered Products tab, and select Access Bonus Content to access the book's companion website.

## How to Access the Pearson Test Prep (PTP) App

You have two options for installing and using the Pearson Test Prep application: a web app and a desktop app. To use the Pearson Test Prep application, start by finding the registration code that comes with the book. You can find the code in these ways:

- **Print book:** Look in the cardboard sleeve in the back of the book for a piece of paper with your book's unique PTP code.

- **Premium Edition:** If you purchase the Premium Edition eBook and Practice Test directly from the Cisco Press website, the code will be populated on your account page after purchase. Just log in at www.ciscopress.com, click Account to see details of your account, and click the Digital Purchases tab.

■ **Amazon Kindle:** For those who purchase a Kindle edition from Amazon, the access code will be supplied directly by Amazon.

■ **Other bookseller E-books:** If you purchase an e-book version from any source other than Cisco, Pearson, or Amazon, the practice test is not included because other vendors to date have not chosen to provide the required unique access codes.

**NOTE**    Do not lose the activation code because it is the only means by which you can access the extra content that comes with the book.

Once you have the access code, to find instructions about both the PTP web app and the desktop app, follow these steps:

**Step 1.**    Open this book's companion website, as just described.

**Step 2.**    Click the Practice Exams button.

**Step 3.**    Follow the instructions provided both for installing the desktop app and for using the web app.

Note that if you want to use the web app only at this point, just navigate to www. pearsontestprep.com, log in or establish a free login if you do not already have one, and register this book's practice tests using the registration code you just found. The process should take only a couple of minutes.

**NOTE**    If you purchase a Kindle e-book version of this book from Amazon, note that it is easy to miss Amazon's email that lists your PTP access code. Soon after you purchase the Kindle e-book, Amazon should send an email. However, the email uses very generic text and makes no specific mention of PTP or practice exams. To find your code, read every email from Amazon after you purchase the book. Also do the usual checks (such as in your spam folder) to ensure that you get the email.

**NOTE**    As mentioned earlier, as of the time of publication, only Cisco, Pearson, and Amazon supply PTP access codes when you purchase their e-book editions of this book.

## How This Book Is Organized

Although this book could be read cover to cover, it is designed to be flexible and allow you to easily move between chapters and sections of chapters to cover just the material that you need to work with further. Chapters 1 through 5 cover IPv4, IPv6, EIGRP, OSPF, IS-IS, BGP, multicast, and network management. Chapters 6 and 7 cover enterprise LAN campus design. Chapters 8 and 9 cover WAN design. Chapters 10, 11, and 12 cover newer technologies, including SD-Access, SD-WAN, and automation. If you intend to read all the chapters, the order in the book is an excellent sequence to use.

The core chapters, Chapters 1 through 12, cover the following topics:

- **Chapter 1, "Internet Protocol Version 4 (IPv4) Design":** This chapter discusses the IPv4 header, addressing, subnet design, and protocols used by IPv4.

- **Chapter 2, "Internet Protocol Version 6 (IPv6) Design":** This chapter covers the IPv6 header, addressing, design best practices, and migration strategies.

- **Chapter 3, "Routing Protocol Characteristics, EIGRP, and IS-IS":** This chapter discusses metrics, design, and operation for EIGRP and IS-IS routing protocols.

- **Chapter 4, "OSPF, BGP, and Route Manipulation":** This chapter discusses OSPF and BGP routing protocols and summarization, redistribution, and manipulation of routing information.

- **Chapter 5, "IP Multicast and Network Management":** This chapter discusses multicast routing concepts, multicast services, and network management techniques.

- **Chapter 6, "Enterprise LAN Design and Technologies":** This chapter covers the design of Layer 2 infrastructures, hierarchical network models, LAN media, and STP design considerations.

- **Chapter 7, "Advanced Enterprise Campus Design":** This chapter discusses campus LAN design and best practices, first-hop redundancy protocols, and high availability design.

- **Chapter 8, "WAN for the Enterprise":** This chapter discusses WANs, WAN transport technologies, and site-to-site VPN design.

- **Chapter 9, "WAN Availability and QoS":** This chapter discusses WAN design methodologies, high availability, Internet connectivity, backup connectivity, and quality of service.

- **Chapter 10, "SD-Access Design":** This chapter discusses SD-Access architecture and SD-Access fabric design considerations for both wired and wireless access.

- **Chapter 11, "SD-WAN Design":** This chapter discusses SD-WAN architecture, the orchestration plane, the control plane and overlay design, scalability, security, and design considerations.

- **Chapter 12, "Automation":** This chapter discusses network APIs, YANG, NETCONF, RESTCONF, and model-driven telemetry.

## Certification Exam Topics and This Book

The questions for each certification exam are a closely guarded secret. However, we do know which topics you must know to *successfully* complete this exam. Cisco publishes them as an exam blueprint for the Designing Cisco Enterprise Networks ENSLD 300-420 exam. Table I-1 lists the exam topics listed in the blueprint and provides a reference to the book chapter that covers each topic. These are the topics you should be proficient in when designing Cisco enterprise networks in the real world.

**Table I-1** ENSLD 300-420 Exam Topics and Chapter References

| ENSLD 300-420 Exam Topic | Chapter(s) in Which Topic Is Covered |
|---|---|
| **1.0 Advanced Addressing and Routing Solutions** | |
| *1.1 Create structured addressing plans for IPv4 and IPv6* | 1, 2 |
| 1.2 Create stable, secure, and scalable routing designs for IS-IS | 3 |
| 1.3 Create stable, secure, and scalable routing designs for EIGRP | 3 |
| 1.4 Create stable, secure, and scalable routing designs for OSPF | 4 |
| 1.5 Create stable, secure, and scalable routing designs for BGP | 4 |
| 1.5.a Address families | 4 |
| 1.5.b Basic route filtering | 4 |
| 1.5.c Attributes for path preference | 4 |
| 1.5.d Route reflectors | 4 |
| 1.5.e Load sharing | 4 |
| 1.6 Determine IPv6 migration strategies | 2 |
| 1.6.a Overlay (tunneling) | 2 |
| 1.6.b Native (dual-stacking) | 2 |
| 1.6.c Boundaries (IPv4/IPv6 translations) | 2 |
| **2.0 Advanced Addressing and Routing Solutions** | |
| 2.1 Design campus networks for high availability | 7 |
| 2.1.a First Hop Redundancy Protocols | 7 |
| 2.1.b Platform abstraction techniques | 12 |
| 2.1.c Graceful restart | 4 |
| 2.1.d BFD | 4 |
| 2.2 Design campus Layer 2 infrastructures | 6 |
| 2.2a STP scalability | 6 |
| 2.2.b Fast convergence | 6 |
| 2.2.c Loop-free topologies | 6 |
| 2.2.d PoE and WoL | 6 |
| 2.3 Design multicampus Layer 3 infrastructures | 7 |
| 2.3.a Convergence | 7 |
| 2.3.b Load sharing | 7 |
| 2.3.c Route summarization | 7, 4 |
| 2.3.d Route filtering | 7, 4 |
| 2.3.e VRFs | 4 |
| 2.3.f Optimal topologies | 7 |
| 2.3.g Redistribution | 4 |
| 2.4 Describe SD-Access architecture (underlay, overlay, control and data plane, automation, wireless, and security) | 10 |

| ENSLD 300-420 Exam Topic | Chapter(s) in Which Topic Is Covered |
|---|---|
| 2.5 Describe SD-Access fabric design considerations for wired and wireless access (overlay fabric design, control plane design, border design, segmentation, virtual networks, scalability, over the top and fabric for wireless, multicast) | 10 |
| **3.0 WAN for Enterprise Networks** | |
| 3.1 Compare WAN connectivity options | 8 |
| 3.1.a Layer 2 VPN | 8 |
| 3.1.b MPLS Layer 3 VPN | 8 |
| 3.1.c Metro Ethernet | 8 |
| 3.1.d DWDM | 8 |
| 3.1.e 4G/5G | 8 |
| 3.1.f SD-WAN customer edge | 8, 11 |
| 3.2 Design site-to-site VPN | 8 |
| 3.2.a Dynamic Multipoint VPN (DMVPN) | 8 |
| 3.2.b Layer 2 VPN | 8 |
| 3.2.c MPLS Layer 3 VPN | 8 |
| 3.2.d IPsec | 8 |
| 3.2.e Generic Routing Encapsulation (GRE) | 8 |
| 3.2.f Group Encrypted Transport VPN (GET VPN) | 8 |
| 3.3 Design high availability for enterprise WAN | 9 |
| 3.3.a Single-homed | 9 |
| 3.3.b Multihomed | 9 |
| 3.3.c Backup connectivity | 9 |
| 3.3.d Failover | 9 |
| 3.4 Describe Cisco SD-WAN Architecture (orchestration plane, management plane, control plane, data plane, on-boarding, and provisioning, security) | 11 |
| 3.5 Describe Cisco SD-WAN design considerations (control plane design, overlay design, LAN design, high availability, redundancy, scalability, security design, QoS and multicast over SD-WAN fabric) | 11 |
| **4.0 Network Services** | |
| 4.1 Select appropriate QoS strategies to meet customer requirements (DiffServ, IntServ) | 9 |
| 4.2 Design end-to-end QoS policies | 9 |
| 4.2.a Classification and marking | 9 |
| 4.2.b Shaping | 9 |
| 4.2.c Policing | 9 |
| 4.2.d Queuing | 9 |
| 4.3 Design network management techniques | 5 |

| ENSLD 300-420 Exam Topic | Chapter(s) in Which Topic Is Covered |
|---|---|
| 4.3.a In-band vs. out-of-band | 5 |
| 4.3.b Segmented management networks | 5 |
| 4.3.c Prioritizing network management traffic | 5 |
| 4.4 Describe multicast routing concepts (source trees, shared trees, RPF, rendezvous points) | 5 |
| 4.5 Design multicast services (SSM, PIM directional, MSDP) | 5 |
| 5.0 Automation | |
| 5.1 Choose the correct YANG data model set based on requirements | 12 |
| 5.2 Differentiate between IETF, Openconfig, and Cisco native YANG models | 12 |
| 5.3 Differentiate between NETCONF and RESTCONF | 12 |
| 5.4 Describe the impact of model-driven telemetry on the network | 12 |
| 5.4.a Periodic publication | 12 |
| 5.4.b On-change publication | 12 |
| 5.5 Compare dial-in and dial-out approaches to model-driven telemetry | 12 |

Each version of the exam can have topics that emphasize different functions or features, and some topics are rather broad and generalized. The goal of this book is to provide comprehensive coverage to ensure that you are well prepared for the exam. Although some chapters might not address specific exam topics, they provide a foundation that is necessary for a clear understanding of important topics. Your short-term goal might be to pass this exam, but your long-term goal should be to become a qualified CCNP enterprise designer.

It is also important to understand that this book is a static reference, whereas the exam topics are dynamic. Cisco can and does change the topics covered on certification exams often.

This book should not be your only reference when preparing for the certification exam. You can find a wealth of information at Cisco.com that covers each topic in great detail. If you think that you need more detailed information on a specific topic, read the Cisco documentation that focuses on that topic.

Note that as CCNP enterprise network technologies continue to evolve, Cisco reserves the right to change the exam topics without notice. Although you can refer to the list of exam topics in Table I-1, always check Cisco.com to verify the actual list of topics to ensure that you are prepared before taking the exam. You can view the current exam topics on any current Cisco certification exam by visiting the Cisco.com website, choosing More, choosing Training & Events, choosing Certifications, and selecting the appropriate certification. Note also that, if needed, Cisco Press might post additional preparatory content on the web page associated with this book, at http://www.ciscopress.com/title/9780136575191. It's a good idea to check the website a couple weeks before taking your exam to be sure that you have up-to-date content.

## CHAPTER 1

# Internet Protocol Version 4 (IPv4) Design

**This chapter covers the following subjects:**

**IPv4 Header:** This section describes the fields in the IPv4 header.

**IPv4 Addressing:** This section covers the format of IP addresses.

**IP Address Subnets:** This section discusses how to divide IP address space into subnets.

**IP Addressing Design:** This section shows how to fully design the IP addressing for regions, a campus, buildings, floors, and VLANs.

**Address Assignment and Name Resolution:** This section describes how to assign IPv4 addresses to devices and groups and fully qualified domain names.

This chapter covers concepts and terminology related to Internet Protocol Version 4 (IPv4) address design. It provides an overview of IPv4 address structures and IPv4 address types. IPv4 is the version of the protocol that the Internet has used since the initial allocation of IPv4 addresses in 1981. In those days, the size of the enterprise determined the address class that was allocated. This chapter covers the IPv4 header to give you an understanding of IPv4 characteristics. The mid-1990s saw the implementation of classless interdomain routing (CIDR), Network Address Translation (NAT), and private address space to prevent the apparent exhaustion of the IPv4 address space. Companies implement variable-length subnet masking (VLSM) in their networks to provide intelligent address assignment and summarization. Separate IP subnets are used for IP phones and wireless LANs to segregate this traffic from wired data traffic. In 2011, the Internet Assigned Numbers Authority (IANA) allocated the last remaining address blocks of the IPv4 address space, thus depleting the free pool of IPv4 address space. Furthermore, in 2015, the American Registry for Internet Numbers (ARIN) issued the final IPv4 addresses in its free pool. Careful allocation of available IPv4 address space must be part of network design. A CCNP enterprise designer needs to have a deep understanding of all these concepts in order to create structured addressing plans for IPv4 addressing for a network.

This chapter covers the following objective from the ENSLD 300-420 exam:

■ Create structured addressing plans for IPv4

## "Do I Know This Already?" Quiz

The "Do I Know This Already?" quiz helps you identify your strengths and deficiencies in this chapter's topics. This quiz, derived from the major sections in the "Foundation Topics" portion of the chapter, helps you determine how to spend your limited study time. Table 1-1 outlines the major topics discussed in this chapter and the "Do I Know This Already?" quiz questions that correspond to those topics. You can find the answers in Appendix A, "Answers to the 'Do I Know This Already?' Quiz Questions Q&A Questions."

**Table 1-1** "Do I Know This Already?" Foundation Topics Section-to-Question Mapping

| Foundation Topics Section | Questions |
|---|---|
| IPv4 Header | 4, 10 |
| IPv4 Addressing | 1, 5, 9 |
| IPv4 Address Subnets | 2–3, 6–7 |
| Address Assignment and Name Resolution | 8 |

1. Which of the following addresses is an IPv4 private address?
   a. 198.176.1.1
   b. 172.31.16.1
   c. 191.168.1.1
   d. 224.130.1.1

2. How many IP addresses are available for hosts in the subnet 198.10.100.64/27?
   a. 14
   b. 30
   c. 62
   d. 126

3. What subnet mask should you use in loopback addresses?
   a. 255.255.255.252
   b. 255.255.255.254
   c. 255.255.255.0
   d. 255.255.255.255

4. In what IPv4 field are the precedence bits located?
   a. Priority field
   b. IP Protocol field
   c. Type of Service field
   d. IP Options field

5. What type of address is 225.10.1.1?
   a. Unicast
   b. Multicast
   c. Broadcast
   d. Anycast

6. Which subnetworks are summarized by the summary route 150.10.192.0/21?
   a. 150.10.192.0/24, 150.10.193.0/24
   b. 150.10.192.0/22, 150.10.196.0/23, 150.10.197.0/24
   c. 150.10.192.0/22, 150.10.199.0/22
   d. 150.10.192.0/23, 150.10.194.0/23, 150.10.196.0/23, 150.10.199.0/24, 150.10.198.0/24

7. What type of network and subnet mask would you use to save address space in a point-to-point WAN link?

   a. 100.100.10.16/26

   b. 100.100.10.16/28

   c. 100.100.10.16/29

   d. 100.100.10.16/30

8. What protocol is used to automatically assign IP addresses?

   a. Dynamic Host Control Protocol

   b. Dedicated Host Configuration Protocol

   c. Dynamic Host Configuration Protocol

   d. Automatic Host Configuration Protocol

9. A company needs to use public IP addresses so that four network servers are accessible from the Internet. What technology is used to meet this requirement?

   a. DNS

   b. IPsec

   c. Static NAT

   d. Dynamic NAT

10. The DS field of DSCP is capable of how many codepoints?

    a. 8

    b. 32

    c. 64

    d. 128

## Foundation Topics

This chapter reviews IPv4 headers, address classes, and assignment methods.

IP is the network layer protocol in TCP/IP. It contains logical addressing and information for routing packets throughout the internetwork. IP is described in RFC 791, which was prepared for the Defense Advanced Research Projects Agency (DARPA) in September 1981.

IP provides for the transmission of blocks of data, called *datagrams* or *packets*, from a source to a destination. The sources and destinations are identified by 32-bit IP addresses. The source and destination devices are workstations, servers, printers, sensors, cameras, IP phones, firewalls, and routers. A CCNP candidate must understand IPv4 logical address classes and assignment. The IPv4 protocol also provides for the fragmentation and reassembly of large packets for transport over networks with small maximum transmission units (MTUs). A CCNP candidate must have a good understanding of this packet fragmentation and reassembly.

Appendix C, "OSI Model, TCP/IP Architecture, and Numeric Conversion," provides an overview of the TCP/IP architecture and how it compares with the OSI model. It also reviews binary numbers and numeric conversion (to decimal), which is a skill needed to understand IP addresses and subnetting.

# IPv4 Header

The best way to understand IPv4 is to know the IPv4 header and all its fields. Segments from Transmission Control Protocol (TCP) or User Datagram Protocol (UDP) are passed on to IP for processing. The IP header is appended to the TCP or UDP segment. The TCP or UDP segment then becomes the IP data. The IPv4 header is 20 bytes in length when it uses no optional fields. The IP header includes the addresses of the sending host and the destination host. It also includes the upper-layer protocol, a field for prioritization, and a field for fragmentation. Figure 1-1 shows the IP header format.

| Version | IHL | Type of Service | | Total Length | |
|---|---|---|---|---|---|
| Identification | | | flags | Fragment Offset | |
| Time to Live | | Protocol | | Header Checksum | |
| Source Address | | | | | |
| Destination Address | | | | | |
| IP Options Field | | | | Padding | |

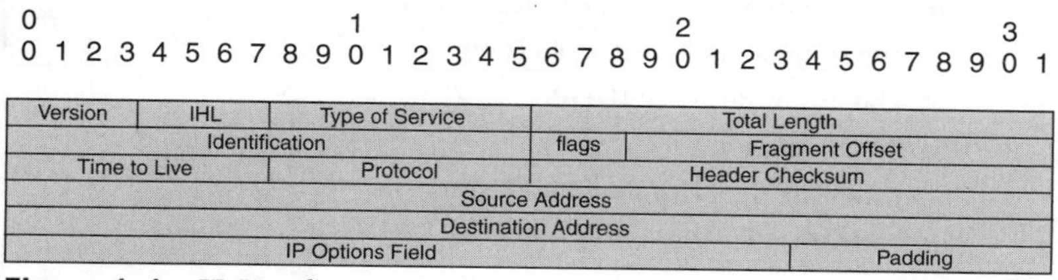

**Figure 1-1**  *IP Header*

The following is a description of each field in the IP header:

- **Version:** This field is 4 bits in length. It indicates the IP header's format, based on the version number. Version 4 is the current version, and this field is set to 0100 (4 in binary) for IPv4 packets. The Version field is set to 0110 (6 in binary) in IPv6 networks.

- **IHL (Internet Header Length):** This field is 4 bits in length. It indicates the length of the header in 32-bit words (4 bytes) so that the beginning of the data can be found in the IP header. The minimum value for a valid header is 5 (0101) for five 32-bit words.

- **ToS (Type of Service):** This field is 8 bits in length. Quality of service (QoS) parameters such as IP precedence and DSCP are found in this field. (These concepts are explained later in this chapter.)

- **Total Length:** This field is 16 bits in length. It represents the length of the datagram, or packet, in bytes, including the header and data. The maximum length of an IP packet can be $2^{16} - 1 = 65,535$ bytes. Routers use this field to determine whether fragmentation is necessary by comparing the total length with the outgoing MTU.

- **Identification:** This field is 16 bits in length. It is a unique identifier that denotes fragments for reassembly into an original IP packet.

- **Flags:** This field is 3 bits in length. It indicates whether the packet can be fragmented and whether more fragments follow. Bit 0 is reserved and set to 0. Bit 1 indicates May Fragment (0) or Do Not Fragment (1). Bit 2 indicates Last Fragment (0) or More Fragments to Follow (1).

- **Fragment Offset:** This field is 13 bits in length. It indicates (in bytes) where in the packet this fragment belongs. The first fragment has an offset of 0.

- **Time to Live:** This field is 8 bits in length. It indicates the maximum time the packet is to remain on the network. Each router decrements this field by 1 for loop avoidance. If this field is 0, the packet must be discarded. This scheme permits routers to discard undeliverable packets.

- **Protocol:** This field is 8 bits in length. It indicates the upper-layer protocol. The Internet Assigned Numbers Authority (IANA) is responsible for assigning IP protocol values. Table 1-2 shows some key protocol numbers. You can find a full list at www.iana.org/assignments/protocol-numbers.

**Table 1-2   IP Protocol Numbers**

| Protocol Number | IP Protocol |
|---|---|
| 1 | Internet Control Message Protocol (ICMP) |
| 2 | Internet Group Management Protocol (IGMP) |
| 6 | Transmission Control Protocol (TCP) |
| 17 | User Datagram Protocol (UDP) |
| 41 | IPv6 encapsulation |
| 50 | Encapsulating Security Payload (ESP) |
| 51 | Authentication Header (AH) |
| 58 | ICMPv6 |
| 88 | Enhanced Interior Gateway Routing Protocol (EIGRP) |
| 89 | Open Shortest Path First (OSPF) |
| 103 | Protocol-Independent Multicast (PIM) |
| 112 | Virtual Router Redundancy Protocol (VRRP) |

- **Header Checksum:** This field is 16 bits in length. The checksum does not include the data portion of the packet in the calculation. The checksum is verified and recomputed at each point the IP header is processed.

- **Source Address:** This field is 32 bits in length. It is the sender's IP address.

- **Destination Address:** This field is 32 bits in length. It is the receiver's IP address.

- **IP Options:** This field is variable in length. The options provide for control functions that are useful in some situations but unnecessary for the most common communications. Specific options are security, loose source routing, strict source routing, record route, and timestamp.

- **Padding:** This field is variable in length. It ensures that the IP header ends on a 32-bit boundary.

Table 1-3 summarizes the fields of the IP header.

**Table 1-3   IPv4 Header Fields**

| Field | Length | Description |
|---|---|---|
| Version | 4 bits | Indicates the IP header's format, based on the version number. Set to 0100 for IPv4. |
| IHL | 4 bits | Length of the header, in 32-bit words. |
| ToS | 8 bits | QoS parameters. |
| Total Length | 16 bits | Length of the packet, in bytes, including header and data. |

| Field | Length | Description |
|-------|--------|-------------|
| Identification | 16 bits | Identifies a fragment. |
| Flags | 3 bits | Indicates whether a packet is fragmented and whether more fragments follow. |
| Fragment Offset | 13 bits | Location of the fragment in the total packet. |
| Time to Live | 8 bits | Decremented by 1 by each router. When this is 0, the router discards the packet. |
| Protocol | 8 bits | Indicates the upper-layer protocol. |
| Header Checksum | 16 bits | Checksum of the IP header; does not include the data portion. |
| Source Address | 32 bits | IP address of the sending host. |
| Destination Address | 32 bits | IP address of the destination host. |
| IP Options | Variable | Options for security, loose source routing, record route, and timestamp. |
| Padding | Variable | Added to ensure that the header ends in a 32-bit boundary. |

## ToS

The ToS field of the IP header is used to specify QoS parameters. Routers and Layer 3 switches look at the ToS field to apply policies, such as priority, to IP packets based on the markings. An example is a router prioritizing time-sensitive IP packets over regular data traffic such as web or email, which is not time sensitive.

The ToS field has undergone several definitions since RFC 791. Figure 1-2 shows the several formats of the ToS service field, based on the evolution of RFCs 791 (1981), 1349 (1992), 2474 (1998), and 3168 (2001). The following paragraphs describe this evolution.

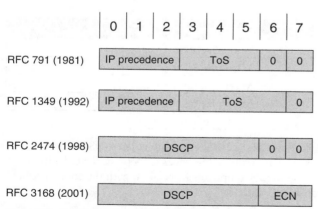

**Figure 1-2**  *Evolution of the IPv4 ToS Field*

The first 3 (leftmost) bits are the IP precedence bits. These bits define values that are used by QoS methods. The precedence bits especially help in marking packets to give them differentiated treatment with different priorities. For example, Voice over IP (VoIP) packets can get preferential treatment over regular data packets. RFC 791 describes the precedence bits as shown in Table 1-4.

**Table 1-4**   IP Precedence Bit Values

| Decimal | Binary | IP Precedence Description |
|---------|--------|--------------------------|
| 0 | 000 | Routine |
| 1 | 001 | Priority |
| 2 | 010 | Immediate |
| 3 | 011 | Flash |
| 4 | 100 | Flash override |
| 5 | 101 | Critical |
| 6 | 110 | Internetwork control |
| 7 | 111 | Network control |

All default traffic is set with 000 in the precedence bits. Voice traffic is usually set to 101 (critical) to give it priority over normal traffic. An application such as FTP is assigned a normal priority because it tolerates network latency and packet loss. Packet retransmissions are typically acceptable for normal traffic.

**Note**   It is common to see voice traffic classified as IP precedence 5, video traffic classified as IP precedence 4, and voice and video signaling classified as IP precedence 3. Default traffic remains as IP precedence 0.

RFC 1349 redefined bits 3 and 6 (expanding for ToS bits) to reflect a desired type of service optimization. Table 1-5 shows the ToS field values that indicate service parameters to use for IP packets.

**Table 1-5**   ToS Field Values

| ToS Bits 3 to 6 | Description |
|-----------------|-------------|
| 0000 | Normal service |
| 1000 | Minimize delay |
| 0100 | Maximize throughput |
| 0010 | Maximize reliability |
| 0001 | Minimize monetary cost |

In 1998, RFC 2474 redefined the ToS octet as the Differentiated Services (DS) field and further specified bits 0 through 5 as the Differentiated Services Codepoint (DSCP) bits to support differentiated services. RFC 3168 (2001) updates RFC 2474, with the specification of an Explicit Congestion Notification (ECN) field.

The DS field takes the form shown in Figure 1-2. The DS field provides more granular levels of packet classification by using 6 bits for packet marking. DS has $2^6 = 64$ levels of classification, which is significantly higher than the eight levels of the IP precedence bits. These 64 levels are called codepoints, and they have been defined to be backward compatible with IP precedence values. RFCs 2474, 3246, and 3260 define three sets of PHBs: Class Selector (CS), Assured Forwarding (AF), and Expedited Forwarding (EF). The CS PHB set is for DSCP values that are compatible with IP precedence bits. The AF PHB set is used for queuing and congestion avoidance. The EF PHB set is used for premium service. The CS per-hop behaviors (PHB), in the form of xxx000, make it backward compatible with IP precedence.

A network designer uses DSCP to give priority to IP packets using Cisco routers. Routers should be configured to map these codepoints to PHBs with queuing or other bandwidth-management techniques. Table 1-6 compares DSCP and IP precedence values used to assign priority and apply policies to IP packets.

**Table 1-6**  DSCP and IP Precedence Values

| IP Precedence | Limitation | | DSCP | | |
|---|---|---|---|---|---|
| Service Type | Decimal | Binary | Class | Decimal | Codepoint |
| Routine | 0 | 000 | Best effort | 0 | 000000 |
| Priority | 1 | 001 | Assured Forwarding (AF) Class 1 | 8 to 14 | 001xxx |
| Immediate | 2 | 010 | AF Class 2 | 16 to 22 | 010xxx |
| Flash | 3 | 011 | AF Class 3 | 24 to 30 | 011xxx |
| Flash override | 4 | 100 | AF Class 4 | 32 to 38 | 100xxx |
| Critical | 5 | 101 | Expedited Forwarding (EF) | 40 to 46 | 101xxx |
| Internetwork control | 6 | 110 | Control | 48 | 110xxx |
| Network control | 7 | 111 | Control | 56 | 111xxx |

RFC 2597 defines recommended values for AF codepoints with low, medium, and high packet-drop precedence. Table 1-7 shows the recommended AF codepoint values.

**Table 1-7**  DSCP AF Packet-Drop Precedence Values

| Precedence | AF Class 1 | AF Class 2 | AF Class 3 | AF Class 4 |
|---|---|---|---|---|
| Low drop precedence | 001010 | 010010 | 011010 | 100010 |
| Medium drop precedence | 001100 | 010100 | 011100 | 100100 |
| High drop precedence | 001110 | 010110 | 011110 | 100110 |

RFC 2598 defines the EF PHB for low loss, loss latency, and assured bandwidth types of traffic. This is considered a premium service. Traffic such as VoIP is classified as EF. The codepoint for EF is 101110, which corresponds to a DSCP value of 46.

When you are configuring Cisco routers, some options are preconfigured and summarize the defined values for DSCP (see Table 1-8).

**Table 1-8**  IP DSCP Values

| DSCP Class | DSCP Codepoint Value | DSCP Decimal |
|---|---|---|
| Default | 000000 | 0 |
| CS1 | 001000 | 8 |
| AF11 | 001010 | 10 |

| DSCP Class | DSCP Codepoint Value | DSCP Decimal |
|---|---|---|
| AF12 | 001100 | 12 |
| AF13 | 001110 | 14 |
| CS2 | 010000 | 16 |
| AF21 | 010010 | 18 |
| AF22 | 010100 | 20 |
| AF23 | 010110 | 22 |
| CS3 | 011000 | 24 |
| AF31 | 011010 | 26 |
| AF32 | 011100 | 28 |
| AF33 | 011110 | 30 |
| CS4 | 100000 | 32 |
| AF41 | 100010 | 34 |
| AF42 | 100100 | 36 |
| AF43 | 100110 | 38 |
| CS5 | 101000 | 40 |
| EF | 101110 | 46 |
| CS6 | 110000 | 48 |
| CS7 | 111000 | 56 |

### IPv4 Fragmentation

One key characteristic of IPv4 is fragmentation and reassembly. Although the maximum length of an IP packet is 65,535 bytes, most of the common lower-layer protocols do not support such large MTUs. For example, the MTU for Ethernet is approximately 1518 bytes. When the IP layer receives a packet to send, it first queries the outgoing interface to get its MTU. If the packet's size is greater than the interface's MTU, the layer fragments the packet.

When a packet is fragmented, it is not reassembled until it reaches the destination IP layer. The destination IP layer performs the reassembly. Any router in the path can fragment a packet, and any router in the path can fragment a fragmented packet again. Each fragmented packet receives its own IP header and identifier, and it is routed independently from other packets. Routers and Layer 3 switches in the path do not reassemble the fragments. The destination host performs the reassembly and places the fragments in the correct order by looking at the Identification and Fragment Offset fields.

If one or more fragments are lost, the entire packet must be retransmitted. Retransmission is the responsibility of a higher-layer protocol (such as TCP). Also, you can set the Flags field in the IP header to Do Not Fragment; in this case, the packet is discarded if the outgoing MTU is smaller than the packet.

## IPv4 Addressing

This section covers the IPv4 address classes, private addressing, and NAT. The IPv4 address space was initially divided into five classes. Each IP address class is identified by the initial bits of the address. Classes A, B, and C are unicast IP addresses, meaning that the destination is a single host. IP Class D addresses are multicast addresses, which are sent to multiple hosts. IP Class E addresses are reserved. This section introduces IPv4 private addresses, which are selected address ranges that are reserved for use by companies in their private networks. These private addresses are not routed on the Internet. NAT translates between private and public addresses.

An IP address is a unique logical number to a network device or interface. An IP address is 32 bits in length. To make the number easier to read, the dotted-decimal format is used. The bits are combined into four 8-bit groups, each converted into decimal numbers (for example, 10.1.1.1). If you are not familiar with binary numbers, see Appendix C, which provides a review of binary and hexadecimal number manipulation.

Consider an example involving the binary IP address 01101110 00110010 11110010 00001010. Convert each byte into decimal.

Convert the first octet as follows:

| 0 | 1 | 1 | 0 | 1 | 1 | 1 | 0 |
|---|---|---|---|---|---|---|---|
| 0 | +64 | +32 | +0 | +8 | +4 | +2 | +0 = 110 |

01101110 = 110

Convert the second octet as follows:

| 0 | 0 | 1 | 1 | 0 | 0 | 1 | 0 |
|---|---|---|---|---|---|---|---|
| 0 | +0 | +32 | +16 | +0 | +0 | +2 | +0 = 50 |

00110010 = 50

Convert the third octet as follows:

| 1 | 1 | 1 | 1 | 0 | 0 | 1 | 0 |
|---|---|---|---|---|---|---|---|
| 128 | +64 | +32 | +16 | +0 | +0 | +2 | +0 = 242 |

11110010 = 242

Convert the fourth octet as follows:

| 0 | 0 | 0 | 0 | 1 | 0 | 1 | 0 |
|---|---|---|---|---|---|---|---|
| 0 | +0 | +0 | +0 | +8 | +0 | +2 | +0 = 10 |

00001010 = 10

The IP address in decimal is 110.50.242.10.

## IPv4 Address Classes

IPv4 addresses have five classes: A, B, C, D, and E. In classful addressing, the most significant bits of the first byte determine the address class of the IP address. Table 1-9 shows the high-order bits of each IP address class.

**Table 1-9**    High-Order Bits of IPv4 Address Classes

| Address Class | High-Order Bits |
|---|---|
| A | 0xxxxxxx |
| B | 10xxxxxx |
| C | 110xxxxx |
| D | 1110xxxx |
| E | 1111xxxx |

Again, the IPv4 Class A, B, and C addresses are unicast addresses. Such an address represents a single destination. Class D is for multicast addresses. Packets sent to a multicast address are sent to a group of hosts. Class E addresses are reserved for experimental use. IANA allocates the IPv4 address space. IANA delegates regional assignments to the five Regional Internet Registries (RIR):

- **ARIN (American Registry for Internet Numbers):** Covers USA, Canada, and some Caribbean Islands

- **RIPE NCC (Reseaux IP Europeens Network Control Center):** Covers Europe, the Middle East, and Central Asia

- **APNIC (Asia Pacific Network Information Center):** Covers the Asia Pacific Region

- **LACNIC (Latin America and Caribbean Network Information Center):** Covers Latin America and some Caribbean Islands

- **AfriNIC (African Network Information Centre):** Covers Africa

Updates to the IPv4 address space can be found at https://www.iana.org/assignments/ipv4-address-space/ipv4-address-space.xhtml.

The following sections discuss each of these classes in detail.

## Class A Addresses

Class A addresses range from 0 (00000000) to 127 (01111111) in the first byte. Network numbers available for assignment to organizations are from 1.0.0.0 to 126.0.0.0. Networks 0 and 127 are reserved. For example, 127.0.0.1 is reserved for the local host or host loopback. A packet sent to a local host address is sent to the local machine.

By default, for Class A addresses, the first byte is the network number, and the three remaining bytes are the host number. The format is *N.H.H.H*, where *N* is the network part and *H* is the host part. With 24 bits available, there are $2^{24} - 2 = 16,777,214$ IP addresses for host assignment per Class A network. We subtract 2 for the network number (all 0s) and broadcast address (all 1s). A network with this many hosts will surely not work with so many hosts attempting to broadcast on the network. As discussed later in this chapter, subnetting can be used to define smaller networks within a larger network address.

## Class B Addresses

Class B addresses range from 128 (10000000) to 191 (10111111) in the first byte. Network numbers assigned to companies or other organizations are from 128.0.0.0 to 191.255.0.0. This section discusses the 16 networks reserved for private use later.

By default, for Class B addresses, the first 2 bytes are the network number, and the remaining 2 bytes are the host number. The format is *N.N.H.H*. With 16 bits available, there are $2^{16} - 2 = 65,534$ IP addresses for host assignment per Class B network. As with Class A addresses, having a segment with more than 65,000 hosts broadcasting will surely not work; you resolve this issue with subnetting.

## Class C Addresses

Class C addresses range from 192 (11000000) to 223 (11011111) in the first byte. Network numbers assigned to companies are from 192.0.0.0 to 223.255.255.0. The format is *N.N.N.H*. With 8 bits available, there are $2^8 - 2 = 254$ IP addresses for host assignment per Class C network. *H* = 0 is the network number; *H* = 255 is the broadcast address.

## Class D Addresses

Class D addresses range from 224 (11100000) to 239 (11101111) in the first byte. Network numbers assigned to multicast groups range from 224.0.0.1 to 239.255.255.255. These addresses do not have a host or network part. Some multicast addresses are already assigned; for example, routers running EIGRP use 224.0.0.10. You can find a full list of assigned multicast addresses at www.iana.org/assignments/multicast-addresses.

## Class E Addresses

Class E addresses range from 240 (11110000) to 254 (11111110) in the first byte. These addresses are reserved for experimental networks. Network 255 is reserved for the broadcast address, such as 255.255.255.255. Table 1-10 summarizes the IPv4 address classes. Again, each address class can be uniquely identified in binary by the high-order bits.

**Table 1-10**   IPv4 Address Classes

| Address Class | High-Order Bits | Network Numbers |
|---|---|---|
| A | 0xxxxxxx | 1.0.0.0 to 126.0.0.0* |
| B | 10xxxxxx | 128.0.0.0 to 191.255.0.0 |
| C | 110xxxxx | 192.0.0.0 to 223.255.255.0 |
| D | 1110xxxx | 224.0.0.1 to 239.255.255.255 |
| E | 1111xxxx | 240.0.0.0 to 254.255.255.255 |

*Networks 0.0.0.0 and 127.0.0.0 are reserved as special-use addresses.

# IPv4 Address Types

IPv4 addresses can be classified as one of three types:

- Unicast

- Broadcast

- Multicast

A unicast address represents a single interface of a host (PC, router, or server). It can be a source or destination IP address. A broadcast address is a destination IP address that is set to all other devices in a given address range; normally it is sent to all devices in the IP subnet. A multicast address is a destination IP address sent to a specific set of hosts. Table 1-11 summarizes IPv4 address types.

**Table 1-11**   IPv4 Address Type

| IPv4 Address Type | Description |
|---|---|
| Unicast | The IP address of an interface on a single host. It can be a source address or a destination address. |
| Broadcast | An IP address that reaches all hosts in an address range. It is only a destination address. |
| Multicast | An IP address that reaches a group of hosts. It is only a destination address. |

## IPv4 Private Addresses

Some network numbers in the IPv4 address space are reserved for private use. These numbers are not routed on the Internet, so there is no way to reach them over an Internet connection. Many organizations today use private addresses in their internal networks with NAT to access the Internet. (NAT is covered later in this chapter.) Private addresses are explained in RFC 1918: *Address Allocation for Private Internets*, published in 1996. Creating private addresses was one of the first steps in dealing with the concern that the globally unique IPv4 address space would become exhausted. The availability of private addresses combined with NAT reduces the need for organizations to carefully define subnets to minimize the waste of assigned public global IP addresses.

The IP network address space reserved for private internetworks is 10/8, 172.16/12, and 192.168/16. It includes one Class A network, 16 Class B networks, and 256 Class C networks. Table 1-12 summarizes private address space. Large organizations can use network 10.0.0.0/8 to assign address space throughout the enterprise. Midsize organizations can use one of the Class B private networks 172.16.0.0/16 through 172.31.0.0/16 for IP addresses. The smaller Class C addresses, which begin with 192.168, can be used by corporations and are commonly used in home routers.

**Table 1-12**   IPv4 Private Address Space

| Class Type | Start Address | End Address |
|---|---|---|
| Class A | 10.0.0.0 | 10.255.255.255 |
| Class B | 172.16.0.0 | 172.31.255.255 |
| Class C | 192.168.0.0 | 192.168.255.255 |

## NAT

Network Address Translation (NAT) devices convert IP address space into globally unique IP addresses. NAT was originally specified by RFC 1631; the current specification is RFC 3022. It is common for companies to use NAT to translate internal private addresses to public addresses and vice versa, although it can also translate public IP addresses to public IP addresses.

The translation can be from many private addresses to a single public address or from many private addresses to a range of public addresses. When NAT performs a many-to-one translation, the process is called Port Address Translation (PAT) because different port numbers identify translations.

As shown in Figure 1-3, the source addresses for outgoing IP packets are converted to globally unique IP addresses. The conversion can be configured statically, or it can be done dynamically, using a global pool of addresses.

NAT has several forms:

- **Static NAT:** Maps an unregistered or private IP address to a registered IP address; it is configured manually. It is commonly used to assign a network device with an internal private IP address a unique public address so that it can be accessed from the Internet.

- **Dynamic NAT:** Dynamically maps an unregistered or private IP address to a registered IP address from a pool (group) of registered addresses. The two subsets of dynamic NAT are overloading and overlapping:

  - **Overloading:** Maps multiple unregistered or private IP addresses to a single registered IP address by using different ports. This is also known as PAT, single-address NAT, or port-level multiplexed NAT. The number of PAT translations is limited. Since the port number is a 16-bit integer number, one single registered IP address can support a maximum of 65,535 internal hosts via PAT.

  - **Overlapping:** Overlapping networks result when you assign an IP address to a device on your network that is already legally owned and assigned to a different device on the Internet or outside network. Overlapping networks also result when two companies, both of which use RFC 1918 IP addresses in their networks, merge. These two networks need to communicate, preferably without having to readdress all their devices.

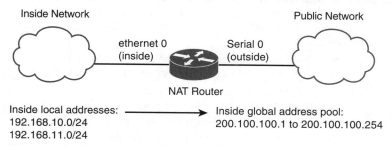

**Figure 1-3**  *Network Address Translation*

When designing for NAT, you should understand the following terminology:

- **Stub domain:** The internal network that might be using private IP addresses.

- **Public network:** The network outside the stub domain, which resides in the Internet. Addresses in the public network can be reached from the Internet.

- **Inside local address:** The real IP address of the device that resides in the internal network. This address is used in the stub domain.

- **Inside global address:** The translated IP address of the device that resides in the internal network. This address is used in the public network.

- **Outside global address:** The real IP address of a device that resides in the Internet, outside the stub domain.

- **Outside local address:** The translated IP address of the device that resides in the Internet. This address is used inside the stub domain.

Figure 1-4 illustrates the terms described in this list. The real IP address of the host in the stub network is 192.168.10.100; it is the inside local address. The NAT router translates the inside local address into the inside global address (200.100.10.100). Hosts located on the Internet have their real IP addresses (outside global addresses) translated; in the figure 30.100.2.50 is translated into the outside local address 192.168.100.50.

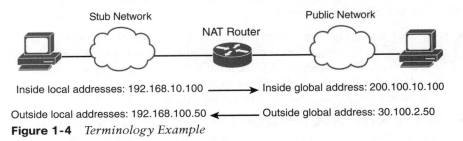

Inside local addresses: 192.168.10.100 ⟶ Inside global address: 200.100.10.100

Outside local addresses: 192.168.100.50 ⟵ Outside global address: 30.100.2.50

**Figure 1-4**   *Terminology Example*

Table 1-13 summarizes the NAT concepts.

**Table 1-13**   NAT Concepts

| NAT Address Type | Description |
|---|---|
| Static NAT | Commonly used to assign a network device with an internal private IP address a unique public address so that it can be accessed from the Internet. |
| Dynamic NAT | Dynamically maps an unregistered or private IP address to a registered IP address from a pool (group) of registered addresses. |
| PAT | Maps multiple unregistered or private IP addresses to a single registered IP address by using different ports. |
| Inside local address | The real IP address of a device that resides in the internal network. This address is used in the stub domain. |
| Inside global address | The translated IP address of the device that resides in the internal network. This address is used in the public network. |
| Outside global address | The real IP address of a device that resides on the Internet, outside the stub domain. |
| Outside local address | The translated IP address of a device that resides on the Internet. This address is used inside the stub domain. |

# IPv4 Address Subnets

Subnetting plays an important part in IPv4 addressing. The subnet mask helps determine the network, subnetwork, and host part of an IP address. A network architect uses subnetting to manipulate the default mask to create subnetworks for LAN and WAN segments. These subnetworks provide enough addresses for LANs of different sizes. Point-to-point WAN links usually get a subnet mask that allows for only two hosts because only two routers are present in the point-to-point WAN link. You should become familiar with determining subnetwork numbers, broadcast addresses, and host address ranges, given an IP address and mask.

Subnet masks are used for Class A, B, and C addresses only. Multicast addresses do not use subnet masks. A subnet mask is a 32-bit number in which bits are set to 1 to identify the network portion of the address, and a 0 is the host part of the address. The mask's bits set to 1 are contiguous on the left portion of the mask; the bits set to 0 are contiguous on the right portion of the mask. Table 1-14 shows the default masks for Class A, B, and C addresses. This section addresses various ways to represent IP subnet masks. Understanding these ways is significant because the representation of a network and its mask can appear differently in Cisco documentation or on the command-line interface.

**Table 1-14**   IPv4 Default Network Address Masks

| Class | Binary Mask | Dotted-Decimal Mask |
|-------|-------------|---------------------|
| A | 11111111 00000000 00000000 00000000 | 255.0.0.0 |
| B | 11111111 11111111 00000000 00000000 | 255.255.0.0 |
| C | 11111111 11111111 11111111 00000000 | 255.255.255.0 |

## Mask Nomenclature

There are several ways to represent IP subnet masks. A mask can be binary, hexadecimal, dotted decimal, or a prefix "bit mask." Historically, the most common representation was the dotted-decimal format (255.255.255.0). The prefix bit mask format is now more popular. This format represents the mask by using a slash followed by the number of leading address bits that must be set to 1 for the mask. It is also referred to as classless interdomain routing (CIDR) prefix notation. For example, 255.255.0.0 is represented as /16. Table 1-15 shows most of the mask representations. The /24 mask is common on LAN segments. The /30 mask is common for WAN point-to-point links, and /32 is used for router loopback addresses.

**Table 1-15**   Subnet Masks

| Dotted Decimal | Bit Mask | Hexadecimal |
|----------------|----------|-------------|
| 255.0.0.0 | /8 | FF000000 |
| 255.192.0.0 | /10 | FFC00000 |
| 255.255.0.0 | /16 | FFFF0000 |
| 255.255.224.0 | /19 | FFFFE000 |
| 255.255.240.0 | /20 | FFFFF000 |
| 255.255.255.0 | /24 | FFFFFF00 |
| 255.255.255.128 | /25 | FFFFFF80 |
| 255.255.255.192 | /26 | FFFFFFC0 |
| 255.255.255.224 | /27 | FFFFFFE0 |
| 255.255.255.240 | /28 | FFFFFFF0 |
| 255.255.255.248 | /29 | FFFFFFF8 |
| 255.255.255.252 | /30 | FFFFFFFC |
| 255.255.255.255 | /32 | FFFFFFFF |

## IP Address Subnet Design Example

The development of an IP address plan or IP address subnet design is an important concept for a network designer. You should be capable of creating an IP address plan based on many factors, including the following:

- Number of locations

- Number of devices per location

- IP addressing requirements for each individual location or building

  - Number of devices to be supported in each communication closet

  - Site requirements, including VoIP devices, wireless LAN, and video

- Subnet size

Let's look at an example of subnetting for a small company. Suppose the company has 200 hosts and is assigned the Class C network 195.10.1.0/24. The 200 hosts need to be in six different LANs.

You can subnet the Class C network using the mask 255.255.255.224. Look at the mask in binary: 11111111 11111111 11111111 11100000. The first 3 bytes are the network part, the first 3 bits of the fourth byte determine the subnets, and the 5 remaining 0 bits are for host addressing.

Table 1-16 shows the subnetworks created with the mask 255.255.255.224. Using this mask, $2n$ subnets are created, where $n$ is the number of bits taken from the host part for the subnet mask. This example uses 3 bits, so $2^3 = 8$ subnets. The first column of the table lists the LANs. The second column shows the binary of the fourth byte of the IP address. The third column shows the subnet number, and the fourth and fifth columns show the first host and broadcast address of the subnet.

**Table 1-16**   Subnets for Network 195.1.1.0

| LAN | Fourth Byte | Subnet Number | First Host | Broadcast Address |
|-----|-------------|---------------|------------|-------------------|
| LAN 0 | 00000000 | 195.10.1.0 | 195.10.1.1 | 195.10.1.31 |
| LAN 1 | 00100000 | 195.10.1.32 | 195.10.1.33 | 195.10.1.63 |
| LAN 2 | 01000000 | 195.10.1.64 | 195.10.1.65 | 195.10.1.95 |
| LAN 3 | 01100000 | 195.10.1.96 | 195.10.1.97 | 195.10.1.127 |
| LAN 4 | 10000000 | 195.10.1.128 | 195.10.1.129 | 195.10.1.159 |
| LAN 5 | 10100000 | 195.10.1.160 | 195.10.1.161 | 195.10.1.191 |
| LAN 6 | 11000000 | 195.10.1.192 | 195.10.1.193 | 195.10.1.223 |
| LAN 7 | 11100000 | 195.10.1.224 | 195.10.1.225 | 195.10.1.255 |

We use the formula $2^n - 2$ to calculate the number of hosts per subnet, where $n$ is the number of bits for the host portion. The preceding example has 5 bits in the fourth byte for host addresses. With $n = 5$, there are $2^5 - 2 = 30$ hosts. For LAN 1, host addresses range from 195.10.1.33 to 195.10.1.62 (30 addresses). The broadcast address for the subnet is 195.10.1.63. Each LAN repeats this pattern, with 30 hosts in each subnet.

## Determining the Network Portion of an IP Address

Given an address and a mask, you can determine the classful network, the subnetwork, and the subnetwork's broadcast number. You do so with a logical AND operation between the IP address and subnet mask. You obtain the broadcast address by taking the subnet number and making the host portion all 1s. Table 1-17 shows the logical AND operation. Notice that the AND operation is similar to multiplying bit 1 and bit 2; if any 0 is present, the result is 0.

**Table 1-17**   AND Logical Operation

| Bit 1 | Bit 2 | AND |
|-------|-------|-----|
| 0 | 0 | 0 |
| 0 | 1 | 0 |
| 1 | 0 | 0 |
| 1 | 1 | 1 |

As an example, take the IP address 150.85.1.70 with subnet mask 255.255.255.224, as shown in Table 1-18. Notice the 3 bold bits in the subnet mask. These bits extend the default Class C prefix (/24) 3 bits to a mask of /27. As shown in Table 1-18, you perform an AND operation of the IP address with the subnet mask to obtain the subnetwork. You obtain the broadcast number by making all the host bits 1. As shown in bold, the subnet mask reaches 3 bits in the fourth octet. The subnetwork is identified by the five rightmost 0s in the fourth octet, and the broadcast is identified by all 1s in the 5 rightmost bits.

**Table 1-18**   Subnetwork of IP Address 150.85.1.70

| | Binary First, Second, and Third Octets | Binary Fourth Octet | | Dotted-Decimal IP |
|---|---|---|---|---|
| IP address | 10010110 01010101 00000001 | 010 | 00110 | 150.85.1.70 |
| Subnet mask | 11111111 11111111 11111111 | **111** | 00000 | 255.255.255.224 |
| Subnetwork | 10010110 01010101 00000001 | 010 | **00000** | 150.85.1.64 |
| | **Major Network Portion** | **Subnet** | **Host** | |
| Broadcast address | 10010110 01010101 00000001 | 010 | **11111** | 150.85.1.95 |

## Variable-Length Subnet Masking

Variable-length subnet masking (VLSM) is a process used to divide a network into subnets of various sizes to prevent wasting IP addresses. If a Class C network uses 255.255.255.240 as a subnet mask, 16 subnets are available, each with 14 IP addresses. If a point-to-point link only needs 2 IP addresses, 12 IP addresses are wasted. This problem scales further with Class B and Class A address spaces. With VLSM, small LANs can use /28 subnets with 14 hosts, and larger LANs can use /23 and /22 masks with 510 and 1022 hosts, respectively. Point-to-point networks use a /30 mask, which supports 2 hosts.

There isn't one way to subdivide a network, so there is no single correct way to create subnets. The best practice is to divide large networks into smaller subnets that can be assigned to sites. Then you can further divide each site subnet into smaller subnets for data, VoIP, wireless LAN, and other subnets to be used in site VLANs. Furthermore, WAN and point-to-point links, router, and switch loopback addresses are allocated IP subnets.

### VLSM Address Assignment: Example 1

Let's look at a VLSM IP address assignment example involving the Class B network 130.20.0.0/16. Using a /20 mask produces 16 subnetworks, as shown in Table 1-19. With the /20 subnet mask, the first 4 bits of the third byte determine the subnets.

**Table 1-19**   Subnets with the /20 Mask

| Third Byte | Subnetwork |
|---|---|
| 0000 0000 | 130.20.0.0/20 |
| 0001 0000 | 130.20.16.0/20 |
| 0010 0000 | 130.20.32.0/20 |
| 0011 0000 | 130.20.48.0/20 |
| 0100 0000 | 130.20.64.0/20 |
| 0101 0000 | 130.20.80.0/20 |
| 0110 0000 | 130.20.96.0/20 |
| 0111 0000 | 130.20.112.0/20 |
| 1000 0000 | 130.20.128.0/20 |
| 1001 0000 | 130.20.144.0/20 |
| 1010 0000 | 130.20.160.0/20 |
| 1011 0000 | 130.20.176.0/20 |
| 1100 0000 | 130.20.192.0/20 |
| 1101 0000 | 130.20.208.0/20 |
| 1110 0000 | 130.20.224.0/20 |
| 1111 0000 | 130.20.240.0/20 |

With fixed-length subnet masks, the network supports only 16 networks. Any LAN or WAN link has to use a /20 subnet. In this scenario, if the sites involved vary in size, this "one net-work size fits all" solution might be a waste of address space and therefore be inefficient. With VLSM, you can further subnet the /20 subnets.

For example, say that you want to subdivide 130.20.64.0/20 to support LANs with about 500 hosts. A /23 mask has 9 bits for hosts, producing $2^9 - 2 = 510$ IP addresses for hosts. Table 1-20 shows the subnetworks for LANs within a specified subnet.

**Table 1-20**   Subnetworks for 130.20.64.0/20

| Third Byte | Subnetwork |
|---|---|
| 0100 0000 | 130.20.64.0/23 |
| 0100 0010 | 130.20.66.0/23 |
| 0100 0100 | 130.20.68.0/23 |
| 0100 0110 | 130.20.70.0/23 |
| 0100 1000 | 130.20.72.0/23 |
| 0100 1010 | 130.20.74.0/23 |
| 0100 1100 | 130.20.76.0/23 |
| 0100 1110 | 130.20.78.0/23 |

With VLSM, you can further subdivide these subnetworks of subnetworks. Say that you want to use subnetwork 130.20.76.0/23 for two LANs that have fewer than 250 hosts. This subdivision produces subnetworks 130.20.76.0/24 and 130.20.77.0/24. You can also subdivide 130.20.78.0/23 for serial links. Because each point-to-point serial link needs only two IP addresses, you can use a /30 mask. Table 1-21 shows the subnetworks produced.

**Table 1-21**   Serial-Link Subnetworks

| Third Byte | Fourth Byte | Subnetwork |
|---|---|---|
| 01001110 | 00000000 | 130.20.78.0/30 |
| 01001110 | 00000100 | 130.20.78.4/30 |
| 01001110 | 00001000 | 130.20.78.8/30 |
| 01001110 | 00001100 | 130.20.78.12/30 |
| ... | ... | ... |
| 01001111 | 11110100 | 130.20.79.244/30 |
| 01001111 | 11111000 | 130.20.79.248/30 |
| 01001111 | 11111100 | 130.20.79.252/30 |

Each /30 subnetwork includes the subnetwork number, two IP addresses, and a broadcast address. Table 1-22 shows the bits for 130.20.78.8/30.

**Table 1-22**   Addresses Within Subnetwork 110.20.78.8/30

| Binary Address | IP Address | Function |
|---|---|---|
| 10000010 00010100 01001110 00001000 | 130.20.78.8 | Subnetwork |
| 10000010 00010100 01001110 00001001 | 130.20.78.9 | IP address 1 |
| 10000010 00010100 01001110 00001010 | 130.20.78.10 | IP address 2 |
| 10000010 00010100 01001110 00001011 | 130.20.78.11 | Broadcast address |

## Loopback Addresses

You can reserve a subnet for router loopback addresses. There are several reasons to use loopback addresses:

- A loopback address provides an always-up interface to use for router-management connectivity.

- A loopback address can serve as the router ID for some routing protocols.

- A loopback address is reachable even if a single interface goes down on a device that has multiple interfaces.

- They are used for IP telephony (for example, in the configuration of dial peers).

- A loopback address is used as the source IP address for network management and monitoring.

The loopback address is a single IP address with a 32-bit mask. In the previous example, network 130.20.75.0/24 could provide 256 loopback addresses for network devices, starting with 130.20.75.0/32 and ending with 130.20.75.255/32.

## IP Telephony Networks

You should reserve separate subnets for LANs using IP phones. IP phones are normally placed in a VLAN that is in a logical segment separate from that of the user workstations. Separating voice and data on different subnets or VLANs also aids in providing QoS for voice traffic with regard to classifying, queuing, and buffering. This design rule also facilitates troubleshooting.

Table 1-23 shows an example of allocating IP addresses for a small network for a company located within three buildings. Notice that separate VLANs are used for the VoIP devices.

**Table 1-23**   IP Address Allocation for VoIP Networks

| Building Floor/Function | VLAN Number | IP Subnet |
|---|---|---|
| First-floor data | VLAN 11 | 172.16.11.0/24 |
| Second-floor data | VLAN 12 | 172.16.12.0/24 |
| Third-floor data | VLAN 13 | 172.16.13.0/24 |
| First-floor VoIP | VLAN 111 | 172.16.111.0/24 |
| Second-floor VoIP | VLAN 112 | 172.16.112.0/24 |
| Third-floor VoIP | VLAN 113 | 172.16.113.0/24 |

Overlay subnets can be used where IP subnets have already been allocated and no spare subnets are available. A different class of private address can be used. This solves the scalability issues with the addressing plan. Table 1-24 shows an example similar to that in Table 1-23 but using overlay subnets.

**Table 1-24**   Overlay IP Address Allocation for VoIP Networks

| Building Floor/Function | VLAN Number | IP Subnet |
|---|---|---|
| First-floor data | VLAN 11 | 172.16.11.0/24 |
| Second-floor data | VLAN 12 | 172.16.12.0/24 |
| Third-floor data | VLAN 13 | 172.16.13.0/24 |
| First-floor VoIP | VLAN 111 | 10.16.11.0/24 |
| Second-floor VoIP | VLAN 112 | 10.16.12.0/24 |
| Third-floor VoIP | VLAN 113 | 10.16.13.0/24 |

## VLSM Address Assignment: Example 2

Because this is an important topic, here is another example of a VLSM design, this time involving network 10.0.0.0/8, which is commonly used by companies in their internal networks because this is private IP address space.

Global companies divide this address space into continental regions for the Americas, Europe/Middle East, Africa, and Asia/Pacific. An example is shown in Table 1-25, where the address space has been divided into four major blocks:

- 10.0.0.0 to 10.63.0.0 is reserved.

- 10.64.0.0 to 10.127.0.0 is for the Americas.

- 10.128.0.0 to 10.191.0.0 is for Europe, Middle East, and Africa.

- 10.192.0.0 to 10.254.0.0 is for Asia Pacific.

**Table 1-25**   Global IP Address Allocation

| Region | Network |
|--------|---------|
| Reserved | 10.0.0.0/10 |
| Americas | 10.64.0.0/10 |
| South America | 10.96.0.0/11 *part of the Americas network above |
| Europe/Middle East | 10.128.0.0/10 |
| Africa | 10.160.0.0/11 *part of the Europe/Middle East network above |
| Asia Pacific | 10.192.0.0/10 |

From each of these regions, address blocks can be allocated to company sites. Large sites may require 4, 8, or 16 Class C equivalent (/24) subnets to assign to data, voice, wireless, and management VLANs. Table 1-26 shows an example. The large site is allocated network 10.64.16.0/20. The first four /24 subnets are assigned for data VLANs, the second four /24 subnets are assigned for voice VLANs, and the third four /24 subnets are assigned for wireless VLANs. Other subnets are used for router and switch interfaces, point-to-point links, and network management devices.

**Table 1-26**   IP Address Allocation in a Large Site

| Function | IP Subnet |
|----------|-----------|
| Data VLAN 1 | 10.64.16.0/24 |
| Data VLAN 2 | 10.64.17.0/24 |
| Data VLAN 3 | 10.64.18.0/24 |
| Data VLAN 4 | 10.64.19.0.24 |
| Voice VLAN 1 | 10.64.20.0/24 |
| Voice VLAN 2 | 10.64.21.0/24 |
| Voice VLAN 3 | 10.64.22.0/24 |
| Voice VLAN 4 | 10.64.23.0/24 |
| Wireless VLAN 1 | 10.64.24.0/24 |
| Wireless VLAN 2 | 10.64.25.0/24 |
| Wireless VLAN 3 | 10.64.26.0/24 |
| Wireless VLAN 4 | 10.64.27.0/24 |
| Reserved | 10.64.28.0/24 |
| Reserved | 10.64.29.0/24 |
| Router/switch loopbacks | 10.64.30.0/24 |
| P2P links, misc. | 10.64.31.0/24 |

# IPv4 Addressing Design

This section covers IPv4 design topics that a CCNP candidate should be aware of. There is no perfect way to address a network, and each company will have a unique set of requirements that will drive the allocation and subnetting of the IPv4 address space.

## Goals of IPv4 Address Design

What is the goal of IPv4 addressing? As a designer, you want to provide enough address capacity to address all nodes in the network and allow for future growth. You want to allow enough IPv4 subnets for data networks, wireless LANs, IP telephony (IPT) networks, video/CCTV networks, access control systems, network management, server farms, and router/switch loopback addresses. You want to allow communications via the network's applications and to and from the Internet.

With your addressing, you want to assign specific subnets that allow you to easily segment communications between different traffic types—for example, assigning 192.168.x.x subnets for data and 172.16.x.x for IPT at a particular site. This makes it easier to configure filters that prevent nodes on 192.168.x.x from attempting to connect to 172.16.x.x devices, thus protecting your IP phones.

## Planning for Future Use of IPv4 Addresses

When assigning subnets for a site or perhaps a floor of a building, do not assign subnets that are too small. You want to assign subnets that allow for growth. Many applications and services get added to your "data-only" network, such as VoIP, security cameras, access control systems, and video conferencing systems.

For example, if a floor has a requirement for 50 users, do you assign a /26 subnet (which allows 62 addressable nodes)? Or do you assign a /25 subnet, which allows up to 126 nodes? You need to balance between the scalability of the address space and the efficiency of its use. Assigning a subnet that is too large will prevent you from having other subnets for IPT and video conferencing.

> **Note**   I recently had a project for a large headquarters building where, in addition to the standard data, voice, and wireless subnets for each floor, we allocated IP subnets for access control systems (Badge), CCTV, security cameras, digital name displays, telepresence, Cisco Spark devices, IPTV, conference room schedulers, and power CPU.

The company might make an acquisition of another company. Although a new address design would be the cleanest solution, the recommendation is to avoid re-addressing of networks. Here are some other options:

- If you use 10.0.0.0/8 as your network, use the other private IP addresses for the additions.

- Use NAT as a workaround.

## Performing Route Summarization

As a network designer, you will want to allocate IPv4 address space to allow for route summarization. Large networks can grow quickly from 500 routes to 1000 and higher. Route summarization reduces the size of the routing table and, as a result, reduces the amount of route update traffic on the network. Route summarization allows the network address space to scale as the company grows.

As an example, suppose a company has assigned the following subnets to a site:

- 10.10.130.0/24 to 10.10.140.0/24 for data networks

- 10.10.146.0/24 to 10.10.156.0/24 for VoIP networks

- 10.10.160.0/24 to 10.10.166/24 for wireless networks

- 10.10.170.0/29 for access control systems

- 10.10.176.0/28 for server farm and other systems

Instead of announcing each and every subnet of this network to the WAN, the recommendation is to summarize the site with a 10.10.128.0/18 route. This subnet encompasses networks from 10.10.128.0/24 to 10.10.191.0/24, so this address block would be assigned to this site.

## Planning for a Hierarchical IP Address Network

When IPv4 addressing for a companywide network, recommended practice dictates that you allocate contiguous address blocks to regions of the network. Hierarchical IPv4 addressing enables summarization, which makes the network easier to manage and troubleshoot.

As an example, consider the IPv4 deployment shown in Figure 1-5. Network subnets cannot be aggregated because /24 subnets from many different networks are deployed in different areas of the network. For example, subnets under 10.10.0.0/16 are deployed in Asia (10.10.4.0/24), the Americas (10.10.6.0/24), and Europe (10.10.8.0/24). The same occurs with networks 10.70.0.0/16 and 10.128.0.0/16. This lack of summarization in the network increases the size of the routing table, making it less efficient. It also makes it harder for network engineers to troubleshoot because it is not obvious in which part of the world a particular subnet is located.

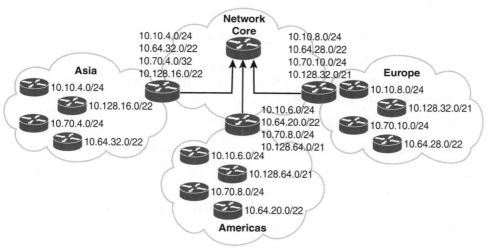

**Figure 1-5**  *Network That Is Not Summarized*

By contrast, Figure 1-6 shows a network that allocates a high-level block to each region:

- 10.0.0.0/18 for Asia Pacific networks

- 10.64.0.0/18 for Americas networks

- 10.128.0.0/18 for European/Middle East networks

This solution provides for summarization of regional networks at area borders and improves control over the growth of the routing table.

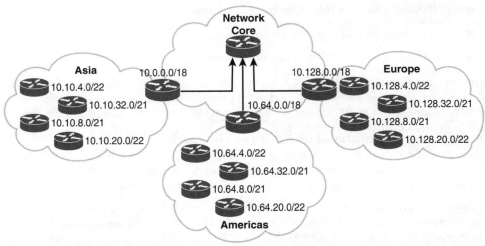

**Figure 1-6** *Summarized Network*

## Private and Public IP Address and NAT Guidelines

Use public IPv4 addresses on external-facing devices that require connectivity to the Internet and external organizations. Examples include the following:

- Internet connectivity module, such as publicly accessible web and DNS servers

- E-commerce or cloud module

- Remote access and virtual private network (VPN) module, where public IP addresses are used for selected connections

The following are some public/private IP addressing best practices:

- Use private IP addresses throughout the internal enterprise network.

- Use NAT and PAT as needed to translate between private internal IP addresses and public external addresses.

- Use one private address to one public address NAT when servers on the internal network need to be visible from the public network. In firewalls, this is a static NAT configuration.

- Use PAT for many private address translations to one public address translation for end systems that need to access the public network.

Table 1-27 provides examples of where public or private IP addresses should be used in the Cisco network architecture.

**Table 1-27**    Public Versus Private IP Addresses

| Network Location | Public or Private Address |
| --- | --- |
| E-commerce module | Public |
| Intranet website | Private |
| External DNS servers | Public |

| Network Location | Public or Private Address |
|---|---|
| Remote-access/VPN module | Public |
| Inside global address | Public |
| Real IP address of a web server located in internal network | Private |

## Steps for Creating an IPv4 Address Plan

A CCNP Enterprise Design candidate needs to know how to create an IPv4 address plan. These are the basic steps:

**Step 1.** Define addressing standards.

**Step 2.** Plan the IPv4 range and allocate it.

**Step 3.** Document the IPv4 addressing plan.

Addressing standards vary from company to company and in different situation. Define the standards that you want to use for your network, use them, and document them. Using standards will make it easier for operations to troubleshoot any network issue. Here are some examples of standards:

- Use .1 or .254 (in the last octet) as the default gateway of the subnet.

- Match the VLAN ID number with the third octet of an IP address. (For example, the IP subnet 10.10.150.0/25 is assigned to VLAN 150.)

- Reserve .1 to .15 of a subnet for static assignments and .16 to .239 for the DHCP pool.

For the allocation of IPv4 subnets, stick to the following best practices:

- Use private addresses for internal networks.

- Allocate /24 subnets for user devices (such as laptops and PCs).

- Allocate a parallel /24 subset for VoIP devices (IP phones).

- Allocate subnets for access control systems and video conferencing systems.

- Reserve subnets for future use.

- Use /30 subnets for point-to-point links.

- Use /32 for loopback addresses.

- Allocate subnets for remote access and network management.

- Use public addresses for the public-facing network.

## Case Study: IP Address Subnet Allocation

Consider a company that has users in several buildings in a campus network. Building A has four floors, and building B has two floors, with the address requirements shown in Table 1-28.

**Table 1-28**   Building Address Requirements

| Network Location | Addresses Required |
|---|---|
| Building A: Floor 1 | 40 |
| Building A: Floor 2 | 70 |
| Building A: Floor 3 | 30 |
| Building A: Floor 4 | 90 |
| Building B: Floor 1 | 80 |
| Building B: Floor 2 | 120 |

As shown in Figure 1-7, the building's Layer 3 switches will be connected via a dual-fiber link between switch A and switch B. Both switches will connect to the WAN router R1. Assume that you have been allocated network 10.10.0.0/17 for this campus and that IP phones will be used.

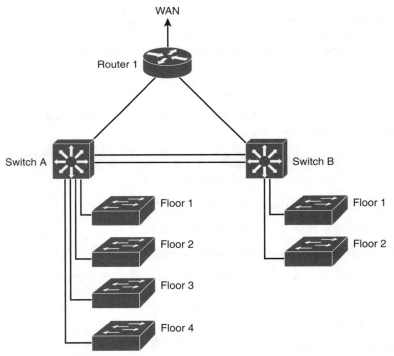

**Figure 1-7**   *Campus Network Connectivity*

Many possible solutions meet the requirements for IPv4 address assignment. Table 1-29 shows one solution.

**Table 1-29**   Building IPv4 Address Allocation

| Network Location | Addresses Required | Subnet Size | VLANs | Addresses Assigned |
|---|---|---|---|---|
| Building A: Floor 1 | 40 | /24 | 11 | 10.10.11.0/24 |
| Building A: Floor 2 | 70 | /24 | 12 | 10.10.12.0/24 |
| Building A: Floor 3 | 30 | /24 | 13 | 10.10.13.0/24 |
| Building A: Floor 4 | 90 | /24 | 14 | 10.10.14.0/24 |
| Building B: Floor 1 | 80 | /24 | 21 | 10.10.21.0/24 |
| Building B: Floor 2 | 120 | /24 | 22 | 10.10.22.0/24 |
| Switch A–switch B links | | /30 | | 10.10.2.4/30 and 10.10.2.8/30 |
| Switch A R1 link | | /30 | | 10.10.2.12/30 |
| Switch B R1 link | | /30 | | 10.10.2.16/30 |
| R1 Loopback | | /32 | | 10.10.1.1/32 |
| Switch A loopback | | /32 | | 10.10.1.2/32 |
| Switch B loopback | | /32 | | 10.10.1.4/32 |
| Building A: Floor 1 IPT | 40 | /24 | 111 | 10.10.111.0/24 |
| Building A: Floor 2 IPT | 70 | /24 | 112 | 10.10.112.0/24 |
| Building A: Floor 3 IPT | 30 | /24 | 113 | 10.10.113.0/24 |
| Building A: Floor 4 IPT | 90 | /24 | 114 | 10.10.114.0/24 |
| Building B: Floor 1 | 80 | /24 | 121 | 10.10.121.0/24 |
| Building B: Floor 2 | 120 | /24 | 122 | 10.10.122.0/24 |
| Access control system | 40 | /24 | 300 | 10.10.3.0/24 |

Data subnets are assigned starting with IP subnet 10.10.11.0/24 for floor 1 in building A. Notice that the VLAN number matches the third octet of the IP subnet. The second floor is assigned VLAN 12 and IP subnet 10.10.12.0/24. For building B, VLAN numbers in the 20s are used, with floor 1 having a VLAN of 21 assigned with IP subnet 10.10.21.0/24.

VLANs for IP telephony (IPT) are similar to data VLANs, with the correlation of using numbers in the 100s. For example, floor 1 of building A uses VLAN 11 for data and VLAN 111 for voice, and the corresponding IP subnets are 10.10.11.0/24 (data) and 10.10.111.0.24 (voice). This is repeated for all floors.

This solution uses /30 subnets for point-to-point links from the 10.10.2.0/24 subnet. Loopback addresses are taken from the 10.10.1.0/24 network starting with 10.10.1.1/32 for the WAN router. Subnet 10.10.3.0/24 is reserved for the building access control system.

# Address Assignment and Name Resolution

Device network configuration parameters such as IP addresses, subnet masks, default gateways, and DNS server IP addresses can be assigned statically by an administrator or dynamically by DHCP or BOOTP servers. You should statically assign most shared network systems, such as routers and servers, but dynamically assign most client systems, such as end-user PCs and laptops. This section covers the protocols you use to dynamically assign IP address parameters to a host, which are the Bootstrap Protocol (BOOTP) and the Dynamic Host Configuration Protocol (DHCP). This section also covers Domain Name System (DNS) and Address Resolution Protocol (ARP), which are two significant protocols in IP networks. DNS maps domain names to IP addresses, and ARP resolves IP addresses to MAC addresses. These protocols are important in TCP/IP networks because they simplify the methods of address assignment and resolution.

## Recommended Practices of IP Address Assignment

IP addresses can be assigned statically (manual configuration) or dynamically:

- Use static IP address assignment for network infrastructure devices.
- Use dynamic IP address assignment for end-user devices.

Use static IP address assignment for routers, switches, printers, and servers. These static IP addresses are assigned in the network infrastructure, data center modules, and in modules of the enterprise edge and WAN. You need to manage and monitor these systems, so you must access them via a stable IP address.

You should dynamically assign end-client workstations to reduce the configuration tasks required to connect these systems to the network. Cisco IP phones and mobile devices are also assigned IP addresses dynamically. Wireless access points also learn their IP addresses and the IP addresses of the wireless controllers via DHCP. When you assign client workstation characteristics dynamically, a system automatically learns which network segment it is assigned to and how to reach its default gateway as the network is discovered. One of the first methods used to dynamically assign IP addresses was BOOTP. The current method to assign IP addresses is DHCP.

## BOOTP

BOOTP was first defined in RFC 951. It has been updated by RFC 1497 and RFC 1542. BOOTP is a protocol that allows a booting host to configure itself by dynamically obtaining its IP address, IP gateway, and other information from a remote server. You can use a single server to centrally manage numerous network hosts without having to configure each host independently.

BOOTP is an application layer protocol that uses UDP/IP for transport. The BOOTP server port is UDP port 67. The client port is UDP port 68. Clients send BOOTP requests to the BOOTP server, and the server responds to UDP port 68 to send messages to the client. The destination IP address of the BOOTP requests uses the all-hosts address (255.255.255.255), which the router does not forward. If the BOOTP server is one or more router hops from the subnet, you must configure the local default gateway router to forward the BOOTP requests.

BOOTP requires that you build a MAC address–to–IP address table on the server. You must obtain every device's MAC address, which is a time-consuming effort. BOOTP has been replaced by the more sophisticated DHCP.

## DHCP

Dynamic Host Configuration Protocol (DHCP) provides a way to dynamically configure hosts on a network. Based on BOOTP, it is defined in RFC 2131 and adds the capability to reuse network addresses and additional configuration options. DHCP improves on BOOTP by using a "lease" for IP addresses and providing the client with all the IP configuration parameters needed to operate in the network.

DHCP servers dynamically allocate network addresses and deliver configuration parameters to hosts. With DHCP, a computer can obtain its configuration information—IP address, subnet mask, IP default gateway, DNS servers, WINS servers, and so on—when needed. DHCP also includes other optional parameters that you can assign to clients. The configuration information is managed centrally on a DHCP server.

Routers act as relay agents by passing DHCP messages between DHCP clients and servers. Because DHCP is an extension of BOOTP, it uses the message format defined in RFC 951 for BOOTP. It uses the same ports as BOOTP: DHCP servers use UDP port 67, and DHCP clients use UDP port 68.

DHCP has three address allocation mechanisms:

- **Manual:** In manual allocation, DHCP is used to dispatch a preallocated IP address to a specific MAC address.

- **Automatic:** For automatic allocation, IP addresses are permanently assigned to a host. The IP address does not expire.

- **Dynamic:** For dynamic allocation, an IP address is assigned for a limited time or until the host explicitly releases the address. This dynamic allocation mechanism can reuse the IP address after the lease expires.

An IP address is assigned as follows:

**Step 1.**  The client sends a DHCPDISCOVER message to the local network using a 255.255.255.255 broadcast.

**Step 2.**  DHCP relay agents (routers and switches) can forward the DHCPDISCOVER message to the DHCP server in another subnet.

**Step 3.**  The server sends a DHCPOFFER message to respond to the client, offering IP address, lease expiration, and other DHCP option information.

**Step 4.**  Using DHCPREQUEST, the client can request additional options or an extension on its lease of an IP address. This message also confirms that the client is accepting the DHCP offer.

**Step 5.**  The server sends a DHCPACK (acknowledgment) message that confirms the lease and contains all the pertinent IP configuration parameters.

**Step 6.**  If the server is out of addresses or determines that the client request is invalid, it sends a DHCPNAK message to the client.

One important note for a CCNP to remember is to place DHCP servers in the enterprise campus data center/server farm module and the enterprise branch of the enterprise campus architecture.

Table 1-30 summarizes DHCP allocation mechanisms.

**Table 1-30**   DHCP Allocation Mechanisms

| Address Allocation Mechanism | Description |
| --- | --- |
| Dynamic | Reuses an IP address after the lease expires. |
| Manual | Dispatches an IP address allocated to a specific MAC address. |
| Automatic | Permanently assigns allocations of IP addresses to a host. |

## DNS

Domain Name System (DNS) is an Internet-based directory system that returns a destination IP address, given a domain name (such as www.cisco.com). DNS is a distributed database. Separate, independent organizations administer their assigned domain name spaces and can break their domains into a number of subdomains. For example, given www.cisco.com, DNS returns the IP address 198.133.219.25. DNS was first specified in RFCs 882 and 883. The current specifications are provided in RFCs 1034 and 1035. DNS has also been updated by RFCs 1101, 1122, 1183, 1706, 1876, 1982, 1995, 1996, 2136, 2137, 2181, 2308, 2535, 2782, 2845, 3425, 3658, 3755, 4033, 4034, 4035, 6014, and 6840. As you can see, a lot of work has gone into making DNS efficient and secure.

Figure 1-8 shows a simplified view of the DNS process for name resolution. The client device queries its configured DNS server (the resolver) for the IP address of a fully qualified domain name (FQDN; for example, www.cisco.com). The resolver in turn queries the DNS server of the foreign or remote DNS server, which responds with the IP address of www.cisco.com. This response is stored in cache on the resolver so that it can be used for future queries. The resolver provides the response to the client machine, which can then communicate via the IP address to the destination.

**Figure 1-8**   *DNS Name Resolution*

DNS was implemented to overcome the limitations of managing a single text host table. Imagine creating and maintaining text files with the names and IP addresses of all the hosts on the Internet! DNS scales hostname-to-IP-address translation by distributing responsibility for the domain name space. DNS follows a reverse tree structure for domain name space, as shown in Figure 1-9. IANA (www.iana.org) manages the tree's root.

DNS data is called resource records (RR). Resource records are the data within a DNS zone. Table 1-31 lists some common resource records.

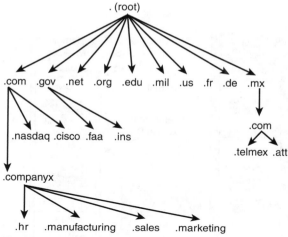

**Figure 1-9**   *DNS Tree*

**Table 1-31**   DNS Resource Records

| DNS RR | Description |
|--------|-------------|
| A | Address. Provides the name-to-address mapping. It contains the IP address in dotted-decimal form. |
| AAAA | Secure IPv6 address. |
| CNAME | Canonical name. Used for aliases or nicknames. |
| MX | Mail Exchanger. Specifies the IP of the server where mail should be delivered. |
| NS | Name server. Specifies the name of the device that provides DNS for a particular domain. |
| PTR | Pointer. Used for reverse mapping from the translation of IP addresses to names. |
| SOA | Start of Authority. Designates the start of a zone. This is the device that is the master of DNS data for a zone. |

DNS uses TCP and UDP port 53. UDP is the recommended transport protocol for DNS queries. TCP is the recommended protocol for zone transfers between DNS servers. A zone transfer occurs when you place a secondary server in the domain and transfer the DNS information from the primary DNS server to the secondary server. A DNS query searches for the IP address of an FQDN, such as www.cnn.com.

One important note for the CCNP to remember is to place DNS servers in the enterprise campus server farm module and enterprise branch of the enterprise campus architecture (see Figure 1-10).

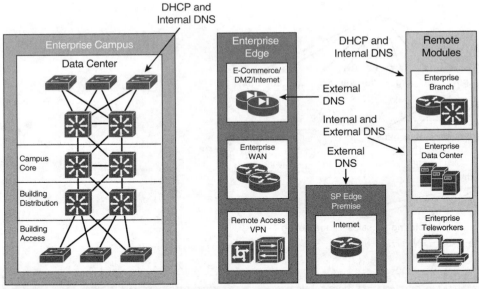

**Figure 1-10**   *DHCP and DNS Servers in the Network*

Table 1-32 summarizes the placement of DHCP and DNS servers on a Cisco enterprise network.

**Table 1-32**   DHCP and DNS Servers

| Network Location | Server Type |
|---|---|
| Campus data center | DHCP and internal DNS |
| Enterprise branch | DHCP and internal DNS |
| E-commerce | External DNS |
| Internet | External DNS |
| SP edge premises | External DNS |
| Remote enterprise data center | Internal and external DNS |

## ARP

When an IP host needs to send an IP packet over an Ethernet network, it needs to find out what 48-bit MAC physical address to send the frame to. Given the destination IP address, Address Resolution Protocol (ARP) obtains the destination MAC address. The destination MAC address can be a local host or the gateway router's MAC address if the destination IP address is across the routed network. ARP is described in RFC 826. The local host maintains an ARP table with a list relating IP addresses to MAC addresses.

ARP operates by having the sender broadcast an ARP request. Figure 1-11 shows an example of an ARP request and reply. Suppose a router with the IP address 10.1.1.1 has a packet to send to 10.1.1.10 but does not have the destination MAC address in its ARP table. It broadcasts an ARP request to all hosts in a subnet. The ARP request contains the sender's IP and MAC address and the target IP address. All nodes in the broadcast domain receive the ARP request and process it. The device with the target IP address sends an ARP reply to the sender with its MAC address information; the ARP reply is a unicast message sent to 10.1.1.1. The sender now has the target MAC address in its ARP cache and sends the frame.

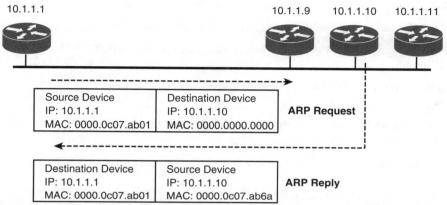

**Figure 1-11**  *ARP Request and Reply*

# References and Recommended Readings

RFC 791: *Internet Protocol*, www.ietf.org/rfc.

RFC 826: *Ethernet Address Resolution Protocol: Or Converting Network Protocol Addresses to 48-Bit Ethernet Address for Transmission on Ethernet Hardware*, www.ietf.org/rfc.

RFC 951: *Bootstrap Protocol (BOOTP)*, www.ietf.org/rfc.

RFC 1034: *Domain Names—Concepts and Facilities*, www.ietf.org/rfc.

RFC 1035: *Domain Names—Implementation and Specification*, www.ietf.org/rfc.

RFC 1349: *Type of Service in the Internet Protocol Suite*, www.ietf.org/rfc.

RFC 1631: *The IP Network Address Translator (NAT)*, www.ietf.org/rfc.

RFC 1918: *Address Allocation for Private Internets*, www.ietf.org/rfc.

RFC 2131: *Dynamic Host Configuration Protocol*, www.ietf.org/rfc.

RFC 2474: *Definition of the Differentiated Services Field (DS Field) in the IPv4 and IPv6 Headers*, www.ietf.org/rfc.

RFC 2597: *Assured Forwarding PHB Group*, www.ietf.org/rfc.

RFC 2598: *An Expedited Forwarding PHB*, www.ietf.org/rfc.

RFC 3022: *Traditional IP Network Address Translator (Traditional NAT)*, www.ietf.org/rfc.

RFC 3168: *The Addition of Explicit Congestion Notification (ECN) to IP*, www.ietf.org/rfc.

RFC 3246: *An Expedited Forwarding PHB (Per-Hop Behavior)*, https://tools.ietf.org/html/rfc3246.

RFC 3260: *New Terminology and Classifications for Diffserv*, https://tools.ietf.org/html/rfc3260.

RFC 4033: *DNS Security Introduction and Requirements*, www.ietf.org/rfc.

RFC 5798: *Virtual Router Redundancy Protocol (VRRP)*, www.ietf.org/rfc.

RFC 6014: *Cryptographic Algorithm Identifier Allocation for DNSSEC*, www.ietf.org/rfc.

RFC 6840: *Clarification and Implementation Notes for DNS Security (DNSSEC)*, www.ietf.org/rfc.

ARIN, "Request IPv4 Addresses," https://www.arin.net/resources/guide/ipv4/request/#reserved-ipv4-address-blocks.

IANA, "Number Resources," https://www.iana.org/numbers.

## Exam Preparation Tasks

As mentioned in the section "How to Use This Book" in the Introduction, you have a couple of choices for exam preparation: the exercises here, Chapter 13, "Final Preparation," and the exam simulation questions on the companion website.

## Review All Key Topics

Review the most important topics in the chapter, noted with the Key Topic icon in the outer margin of the page. Table 1-33 lists these key topics and the page number on which each is found.

**Table 1-33**   Key Topics

| Key Topic Element | Description | Page |
|---|---|---|
| Figure 1-1 | IP header | 5 |
| Table 1-2 | IP protocol numbers | 6 |
| Table 1-3 | IPv4 header fields | 6 |
| Paragraph | Type of Service field for specifying QoS parameters | 7 |
| Table 1-4 | IP precedence bit values | 8 |
| Table 1-8 | IP DSCP values | 9 |
| List | IPv4 address types | 13 |
| Table 1-11 | IPv4 address type | 14 |
| Table 1-12 | IPv4 private address space | 14 |
| Table 1-13 | NAT concepts | 14 |
| Paragraph | IPv4 address subnets | 16 |
| Table 1-15 | Subnet masks | 17 |
| Paragraph | VLSM | 24 |
| Table 1-27 | Public versus private IP addresses | 26 |
| List | Three address allocation mechanisms of DHCP | 31 |
| Paragraph | DNS | 32 |
| Table 1-31 | DNS resource records | 33 |

## Complete Tables and Lists from Memory

Print a copy of Appendix D, "Memory Tables," found on the companion website, or at least the section for this chapter, and complete the tables and lists from memory. Appendix E, "Memory Tables Answer Key," includes completed tables and lists to check your work.

## Define Key Terms

Define the following key terms from this chapter and check your answers in the glossary:

Differentiated Services Code Point (DSCP), Domain Name System (DNS), Dynamic Host Configuration Protocol (DHCP), Internet Protocol version 4 (IPv4), Network Address Translation (NAT), Port Address Translation (PAT), Type of Service (ToS), variable-length subnet masking (VLSM)

## Q&A

The answers to these questions appear in Appendix A. For more practice with exam format questions, use the exam engine on the companion website.

1. List the RFC 1918 private address ranges.

2. True or false: You can use DHCP to specify the TFTP host's IP address to a client PC.

3. True or false: 255.255.255.248 and /28 are two representations of the same IP mask.

4. True or false: Upper-layer protocols are identified in the IP header's Protocol field. TCP is protocol 6, and UDP is protocol 17.

5. Fill in the blank: Without any options, the IP header is _____ bytes in length.

6. The IP header's ToS field is redefined as the DS field. How many bits does DSCP use for packet classification, and how many levels of classification are possible?

7. True or false: NAT uses different IP addresses for translations. PAT uses different port numbers to identify translations.

8. True or false: The IP header's header Checksum field performs the checksum of the IP header and data.

9. Calculate the subnet, the address range within the subnet, and the subnet broadcast of the address 172.56.5.245/22.

10. When packets are fragmented at the network layer, where are the fragments reassembled?

11. Which protocol can you use to configure a default gateway setting on a host?

    a. ARP

    b. DHCP

    c. DNS

    d. RARP

**12.** How many host addresses are available with a Class B network with the default mask?

   **a.** 63,998

   **b.** 64,000

   **c.** 65,534

   **d.** 65,536

**13.** Which of the following is a dotted-decimal representation of a /26 prefix mask?

   **a.** 255.255.255.128

   **b.** 255.255.255.192

   **c.** 255.255.255.224

   **d.** 255.255.255.252

**14.** Which network and mask summarizes both the 192.170.20.16/30 and 192.170.20.20/30 networks?

   **a.** 192.170.20.0/24

   **b.** 192.170.20.20/28

   **c.** 192.170.20.16/29

   **d.** 192.170.20.0/30

**15.** Which AF class is backward compatible with flash traffic of the IP precedence bits?

   **a.** AF2

   **b.** AF3

   **c.** AF4

   **d.** EF

**16.** Which of the following is true about fragmentation?

   **a.** Routers between source and destination hosts can fragment IPv4 packets.

   **b.** Only the first router in the network can fragment IPv4 packets.

   **c.** IPv4 packets cannot be fragmented.

   **d.** IPv4 packets are fragmented and reassembled at each link through the network.

**17.** A packet sent to a multicast address reaches what destinations?

   **a.** The nearest destination in a set of hosts

   **b.** All destinations in a set of hosts

   **c.** All hosts

   **d.** Reserved global destinations

**18.** What are three types of IPv4 addresses? (Choose three.)

   **a.** Anycast

   **b.** Multicast

   **c.** Dynamic

   **d.** Broadcast

   **e.** Unicast

   **f.** Global

   **g.** Static

**19.** Which devices should be assigned an IP address dynamically? (Choose three.)

    **a.** Cisco IP phones

    **b.** LAN switches

    **c.** Workstations

    **d.** Mobile devices

    **e.** Routers

**20.** Which name resolution method reduces administrative overhead?

    **a.** Static name resolution

    **b.** Dynamic name resolution

    **c.** DHCP name resolution

    **d.** Host.txt name resolution

**21.** How many hosts can be addressed with the IPv4 subnet 172.30.192.240/28?

    **a.** 6

    **b.** 14

    **c.** 126

    **d.** 1024

**22.** What is the smallest subnet and mask that can be used in a DMZ network that needs to have only three hosts?

    **a.** 192.168.10.32/30

    **b.** 192.168.10.32/29

    **c.** 192.168.10.32/28

    **d.** 192.168.10.32/27

**23.** Which modules cannot use private IPv4 address space? (Choose all that apply.)

    **a.** Access

    **b.** Distribution

    **c.** Core

    **d.** E-commerce

    **e.** LAN

    **f.** WAN

    **g.** Internet connection

    **h.** Data center

    **i.** Remote access/VPN

**24.** Which technology allows a company to use a single public IP address when using private IPv4 addresses in the internal LAN?

    **a.** NAT

    **b.** Redistribution

    **c.** PAT

    **d.** Access list

**25.** Which of the following is the European RIR?

    **a.** IANA

    **b.** ARIN

    **c.** RIPE

    **d.** ERIR

**26.** Which technology allows you to divide address blocks into subnets of different sizes?

    **a.** NAT

    **b.** VLSM

    **c.** PAT

    **d.** Variable division subnet masking

**27.** Which regional registry allocates address blocks in North America?

    **a.** IANA

    **b.** RIPE

    **c.** ARIN

    **d.** APNIC

    **e.** LACNIC

    **d.** AfriNIC

**28.** Which regional registry allocates address blocks in China?

    **a.** IANA

    **b.** RIPE

    **c.** ARIN

    **d.** APNIC

    **e.** LACNIC

    **d.** AfriNIC

**29.** In what subnet does 172.16.45.227/27 reside?

    **a.** 172.16.45.128

    **b.** 172.16.45. 192

    **c.** 172.16.45.224

    **d.** 172.16.45.0

Answer the following questions based on the given scenario and Figure 1-12.

Company VWX has the network shown in Figure 1-12. The main site has three LANs, with 100, 29, and 60 hosts. The remote site has two LANs, each with 100 hosts. The network uses private addresses. The Internet service provider assigned the company the network 210.200.200.8/26.

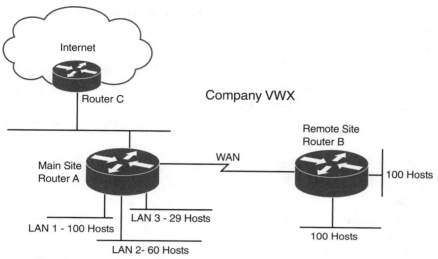

**Figure 1-12** *Scenario diagram*

**30.** The remote site uses the network prefix 192.168.10.0/24. What subnets and masks can you use for the LANs at the remote site to conserve address space?

   **a.** 192.168.10.64/26 and 192.168.10.192/26

   **b.** 192.168.10.0/25 and 192.168.10.128/25

   **c.** 192.168.10.32/28 and 192.168.10.64/28

   **d.** 192.168.10.0/30 and 192.168.10.128/30

**31.** The main site uses the network prefix 192.168.15.0/24. What subnets and masks can you use to provide sufficient addresses for LANs at the main site and conserve address space?

   **a.** 192.168.15.0/25 for LAN 1, 192.168.15.128/26 for LAN 2, and 172.15.192.0/27 for LAN 3

   **b.** 192.168.15.0/27 for LAN 1, 192.168.15.128/26 for LAN 2, and 172.15.192.0/25 for LAN 3

   **c.** 192.168.15.0/100 for LAN 1, 192.168.15.128/60 for LAN 2, and 172.15.192.0/29 for LAN 3

   **d.** 192.168.15.0/26 for LAN 1, 192.168.15.128/26 for LAN 2, and 172.15.192.0/29 for LAN 3

**32.** Which network and mask would you use for the WAN link to save the most address space?

   **a.** 192.168.11.240/27

   **b.** 192.168.11.240/28

   **c.** 192.168.11.240/29

   **d.** 192.168.11.240/30

**33.** What networks does Router C announce to the Internet service provider's Internet router?

   **a.** 210.200.200.8/26

   **b.** 192.168.10.0/24 and 192.168.11.0/24

   **c.** 192.168.10.0/25 summary address

   **d.** 201.200.200.8/29 and 192.168.10.0/25

**34.** What technology does Router C use to convert private addresses to public addresses?

   **a.** DNS

   **b.** NAT

   **c.** ARP

   **d.** VLSM

**35.** What mechanism supports the ability to divide a given subnet into smaller subnets based on need?

   **a.** DNS

   **b.** NAT

   **c.** ARP

   **d.** VLSM

# CHAPTER 2

# Internet Protocol Version 6 (IPv6) Design

## This chapter covers the following subjects:

**IPv6 Header:** This section describes the fields in the IPv6 header.

**IPv6 Address Representation:** This section describes the hexadecimal representation of the 128-bit IPv6 addresses.

**IPv6 Address Scope Types and Address Allocations:** This section covers unicast, multicast, and anycast scopes and the IPv6 prefix allocations.

**IPv6 Mechanisms:** This section covers ICMPv6, Neighbor Discovery, and IPv6 name resolution.

**IPv6 Routing Protocols:** This section covers routing protocols that support IPv6.

**IPv4-to-IPv6 Migration Strategies and Deployment Models:** This section covers tunneling, dual-stacking, and translation strategies and deployment models.

This chapter provides an overview of Internet Protocol Version 6 (IPv6) address structures, address assignments, representations, and mechanisms used to deploy IPv6. Expect plenty of questions about IPv6 on the ENSLD 300-420 exam. A CCNP Enterprise Design candidate must understand how to develop structured IPv6 addressing plans and determine different IPv6 migration strategies. This chapter also covers the benefits of IPv6 over IPv4, compares the protocols, and examines options for transitioning to IPv6.

As IPv6 matures, different deployment models will be used to implement the new protocol with existing IPv4 networks. This chapter covers these models at a high level. This chapter does not discuss the configuration of IPv6 because it is not a requirement for the ENSLD 300-420 exam.

This chapter covers the following objectives from the ENSLD 300-420 exam:

- Create structured addressing plans for IPv4 and IPv6
- Determine IPv6 migration strategies

## "Do I Know This Already?" Quiz

The "Do I Know This Already?" quiz helps you identify your strengths and deficiencies in this chapter's topics. This quiz, derived from the major sections in the "Foundation Topics" portion of the chapter, helps you determine how to spend your limited study time. Table 2-1 outlines the major topics discussed in this chapter and the "Do I Know This Already?" quiz questions that correspond to those topics. You can find the answers in Appendix A, "Answers to the 'Do I Know This Already?' Quiz Questions Q&A Questions."

**Table 2-1**   "Do I Know This Already?" Foundation Topics Section-to-Question Mapping

| Foundation Topics Section | Questions Covered in This Section |
|---|---|
| IPv6 Header | 1–2 |
| IPv6 Address Representation | 5, 8–9 |
| IPv6 Address Types and Address Allocations | 3–4, 7 |
| IPv6 Mechanisms | 10 |
| IPv4-to-IPv6 Migration Strategies and Deployment Models | 6, 11, 13–14 |
| IPv6 Routing Protocols | 12 |

**1.** How many more bits does IPv6 use for addresses than IPv4?

   **a.**  32

   **b.**  64

   **c.**  96

   **d.**  128

**2.** What is the length of the IPv6 header?

   **a.**  20 bytes

   **b.**  30 bytes

   **c.**  40 bytes

   **d.**  128 bytes

**3.** What address type is the IPv6 address FE80::300:34BC:123F:1010?

   **a.**  Aggregatable global

   **b.**  Unique-local

   **c.**  Link-local

   **d.**  Multicast

**4.** What are three scope types of IPv6 addresses?

   **a.**  Unicast, multicast, broadcast

   **b.**  Unicast, anycast, broadcast

   **c.**  Unicast, multicast, endcast

   **d.**  Unicast, anycast, multicast

**5.** What is a compact representation of the address 3f00:0000:0000:a7fb:0000:0000: b100:0023?

   **a.**  3f::a7fb::b100:0023

   **b.**  3f00::a7fb:0000:0000:b100:23

   **c.**  3f::a7fb::b1:23

   **d.**  3f00:0000:0000:a7fb::b1:23

**6.** What does DNS64 do?

   **a.** It translates IPv6 addresses to IPv4.

   **b.** It is a DNS mechanism that is integrated into NAT-PT.

   **c.** It is a DNS mechanism that synthesizes AAAA records from A records.

   **d.** It is a DNS mechanism that is integrated into NAT64.

**7.** What IPv6 address scope type replaces the IPv4 broadcast address?

   **a.** Unicast

   **b.** Multicast

   **c.** Broadcast

   **d.** Anycast

**8.** What is the IPv6 equivalent to 127.0.0.1?

   **a.** 0:0:0:0:0:0:0:0

   **b.** 0:0:0:0:0:0:0:1

   **c.** 127:0:0:0:0:0:0:1

   **d.** FF::1

**9.** Which of the following is an "IPv4-compatible" IPv6 address?

   **a.** ::180.10.1.1

   **b.** f000:0:0:0:0:0:180.10.1.1

   **c.** 180.10.1.1::

   **d.** 2010::180.10.1.1

**10.** Which protocol maps names to IPv6 addresses?

   **a.** Address Resolution Protocol (ARP)

   **b.** Neighbor Discovery (ND)

   **c.** Domain Name System (DNS)

   **d.** DNSv2

**11.** Which of the following are IPv6 enhancements over IPv4?

   **a.** Larger address space, globally private IP address, multicast

   **b.** Larger address space, globally unique IP addresses, no broadcasts

   **c.** Larger address space, globally private IP address, multicast

   **d.** Larger address space, address auto-configuration, enhanced broadcasts

**12.** Which of the following supports routing on IPv6 networks?

   **a.** RIPv3, OSPFv3, EIGRP for IPv6

   **b.** RIPng, OSPFv3, EIGRPv6

   **c.** RIPng, OSPFv3, EIGRP for IPv6

   **d.** RIPv2, OSPFv2, EIGRP

**13.** What changed from IPv4 to IPv6?

   **a.** Protocol Type became the Next Header field.

   **b.** ND is used rather than ARP.

   **c.** AAAA records are used rather than A records.

   **d.** All of these answers are correct.

**14.** Which is not an IPv6 migration strategy?

    **a.** Dual-Stack

    **b.** IP Migrate

    **c.** Tunneling

    **d.** Translation

# Foundation Topics

This chapter covers important topics for the CCNP Enterprise Designer. The section "IPv6 Header" covers each field of the IPv6 header, which helps you understand the protocol. The section "IPv6 Address Representation" covers the hexadecimal representation of IPv6 addresses and the compressed representation. The section "IPv6 Address Scope Types and Address Allocations" covers unicast, multicast, and anycast IPv6 addresses, special address types, and the current allocations of IPv6 addresses.

The section "IPv6 Mechanisms" covers Internet Control Message Protocol version 6 (ICMPv6), Neighbor Discovery, and address assignment and resolution, and it introduces IPv6 routing protocols. The section "IPv4-to-IPv6 Migration Strategies and Deployment Models" is especially important for the 300-420 exam. This section covers dual-stack back-bones, IPv6-over-IPv4 tunnels, dual-stack hosts, and Network Address Translation–Protocol Translation (NAT-PT).

# Introduction to IPv6

To prepare for the ENSLD 300-420 exam, you should become very familiar with IPv6 specifications, addressing, and design. The driving motivation for the adoption of a new version of IP is the limitation imposed by the 32-bit address field in IPv4. In the 1990s, there was concern that the IP address space would be depleted soon. Although classless interdomain routing (CIDR) and NAT have slowed down the deployment of IPv6, its standards and deployments are becoming mature. IPv6 is playing a significant role in the deployment of IP services for wireless phones. Some countries, such as Japan, directed IPv6 compatibility back in 2005. Other countries, such as China, France, and Korea, have been implementing IPv6. The 2008 Summer Olympics was accessible from the IPv6 Internet. The U.S. federal government mandated all agencies to support IPv6 by mid-2008.

Operating systems such as Windows 10, Windows 7, Linux, and macOS support IPv6. By default, Windows 10 and recent versions of macOS and iPhone's iOS favor IPv6 global unicast addresses over IPv4. Google, Microsoft, LinkedIn, and Facebook are also accessible on the IPv6 Internet. According to the Internet Society, as of 2018, in some countries, major mobile networks were driving IPv6 adoption. In Japan in 2018, NTT was at 7%, KDDI at 42%, and Softbank at 34% IPv6 adoption. In India in 2018, Reliance JIO was at 87%. And in the United States in 2018, Verizon Wireless was at 84%, Sprint at 70%, T-Mobile at 93%, and AT&T Wireless at 57% IPv6 adoption. Furthermore, broadband ISPs also have a large IPv6 deployments: As of 2018, Comcast had an IPv6 deployment measurement of over 66%, British Sky Broadcasting in excess of 86%, and Deutsche Telekom in Germany at 56%.

The IPv6 specification provides 128 bits for addressing, which is a significant increase from 32 bits. The overall specification of IPv6 is in RFC 2460. Other RFCs describing IPv6 include 8064, 7371, 7346, 7136, 6052, 5952, 4921, 3513, 3587, 3879, 2373, 2374, 2461, 1886, and 1981.

IPv6 includes the following enhancements over IPv4:

- **Larger address space:** IPv6 uses 128-bit addresses rather than the 32-bit addresses in IPv4. This means IPv6 supports more address hierarchy levels and uses simpler address autoconfiguration.

- **Globally unique IP addresses:** The additional address space allows each node to have a unique address and eliminates the need for NAT.

- **Header format efficiency:** The IPv6 header length is fixed, reducing header processing time and thus allowing vendors to improve packet switching efficiency.

- **Improved option mechanism:** IPv6 options are placed in separate extension headers that are located between the IPv6 header and the transport layer header. The option headers are not required.

- **Address autoconfiguration:** This capability provides for dynamic assignment of IPv6 addresses. IPv6 hosts can automatically configure themselves, with or without a Dynamic Host Configuration Protocol (DHCP) server. Stateful and stateless autoconfiguration are supported.

- **Flow labeling capability:** Instead of using a Type of Service field, as IPv4 does, IPv6 enables the labeling of packets belonging to a particular traffic class for which the sender requests special handling, such as quality of service (QoS) and real-time service. This support aids specialized traffic, such as real-time voice or video.

- **Security capabilities:** IPv6 includes features that support authentication and privacy. IP Security (IPsec) is a requirement.

- **Maximum transmission unit (MTU) path discovery:** IPv6 eliminates the need to fragment packets by implementing MTU path discovery before sending packets to a destination.

- **Site multihoming:** IPv6 allows multihoming by allowing hosts to have multiple IPv6 addresses and networks to have multiple IPv6 prefixes, which facilitates connection to multiple ISPs.

- **Support for mobility:** Mobile IPv6 allows for IPv6 nodes to change locations on a network yet maintain existing connections. The mobile node is always reachable via one permanent address.

- **Eliminate the use of broadcasts:** IPv6 reduces unnecessary bandwidth usage by eliminating the use of broadcasts and replacing them with multicasts.

# IPv6 Header

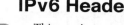

This section covers the field of the IPv6 header. The IPv6 header is simpler than the IPv4 header. Some IPv4 fields have been eliminated or changed to optional fields. The IPv6 header size is 40 bytes. The Fragment Offset fields and flags in IPv4 have been eliminated from the header. IPv6 adds a Flow Label field for QoS mechanisms to use.

The use of 128 bits for source and destination addresses provides a significant improvement over IPv4. With 128 bits, there are $3.4 \times 10^{38}$—or 340 billion billion billion billion—IPv6 addresses, compared to only 4.3 billion IPv4 addresses.

IPv6 improves over IPv4 by using a fixed-length header (see Figure 2-1). The following is a description of each field in the IP header:

- **Version:** This field, which is 4 bits long, indicates the format, based on the version number, of the IP header. These bits are set to 0110 for IPv6 packets.

- **Traffic Class:** This field, which is 8 bits in length, describes the class or priority of the IPv6 packet and provides functionality similar to that of the IPv4 Type of Service field.

- **Flow Label:** This field, which is 20 bits in length, indicates a specific sequence of packets between a source and destination that requires special handling, such as real-time data (voice and video).

```
0                       1                       2                       3
0 1 2 3 4 5 6 7 8 9 0 1 2 3 4 5 6 7 8 9 0 1 2 3 4 5 6 7 8 9 0 1
```

| Version | Traffic Class | Flow Label |
|---|---|---|

| Payload Length | Next Header | Hop Limit |

| 128-Bit Source Address |

| 128-Bit Destination Address |

**Figure 2-1**   *IPv6 Header Format*

- **Payload Length:** This field, which is 16 bits in length, indicates the payload's size, in bytes. Its length includes any extension headers.

- **Next Header:** This field, which is 8 bits in length, indicates the type of extension header, if present, that follows this IPv6 header. If no Next Header field is present, it identifies the upper-layer protocol (TCP or UDP). This field is called the Protocol field in the IPv4 header. It uses values defined by the Internet Assigned Numbers Authority (IANA). Table 2-2 shows some key protocol numbers. You can find a full list at https://www.iana.org/assignments/protocol-numbers/protocol-numbers.xhtml.

**Table 2-2**   IP Protocol Numbers

| Protocol Number | Protocol |
|---|---|
| 6 | Transmission Control Protocol (TCP) |
| 17 | User Datagram Protocol (UDP) |
| 50 | Encapsulating Security Payload (ESP) |
| 51 | Authentication Header (AH) |
| 85 | ICMP for IPv6 |
| 59 | No Next Header field for IPv6 |
| 60 | Destination options for IPv6 |
| 88 | Enhanced IGRP (EIGRP) |
| 89 | Open Shortest Path First (OSPF) |

- **Hop Limit:** This field, which is 8 bits in length, is decremented by 1 by each router that forwards the packets. If this field is 0, the packet is discarded.

- **Source Address:** This field, which is 128 bits in length, indicates the sender's IPv6 address.

- **Destination Address:** This field, which is 128 bits in length, indicates the destination host's IPv6 address.

Notice that although an IPv6 address is four times the length of an IPv4 address, the IPv6 header is only twice the length (40 bytes). Optional network layer information is not included in the IPv6 header; instead, it is included in separate extended headers. Some extended headers are the routing header, fragment header, and hop-by-hop options header. The routing header is used for source routing. The fragment header is included in fragmented datagrams to provide information to allow the fragments to be reassembled. The hop-by-hop extension header is used to support jumbo-grams.

Two important extended headers are the Authentication Header (AH) and the Encapsulating Security Payload (ESP) header. These headers are covered later in the chapter.

## IPv6 Address Representation

RFC 4291 (which obsoletes RFC 3513 and RFC 2373) specifies the IPv6 addressing architecture. IPv6 addresses are 128 bits in length. For display, the IPv6 addresses have eight 16-bit groups. Each 16-bit group is represented using hexadecimal numbers. (See Appendix C, "OSI Model, TCP/IP Architecture, and Numeric Conversion," for a quick review on hexadecimal numbers.) The hexadecimal value is $x:x:x:x:x:x:x:x$, where each $x$ represents four hexadecimal digits (16 bits).

An example of a full IPv6 address is 1111111000011010 0100001010111001 0000000000011011 0000000000000000 0000000000000000 0001001011010000 0000000001011011 0000011010110000.

The hexadecimal representation of the preceding IPv6 binary number is

FE1A:42B9:001B:0000:0000:12D0:005B:06B0

Groups with a value of 0000 can be represented with a single 0. For example, you can also represent the preceding number as

FE1A:42B9:01B:0:0:12D0:05B:06B0

You can represent multiple groups of 16-bit 0s with ::, which is allowed to appear only once in the number. Also, you do not need to represent leading 0s in a 16-bit group. Furthermore, RFC 5952 states that "leading zeros MUST be suppressed." Therefore, the preceding IPv6 address can be further shortened to

FE1A:42B9:1B::12D0:5B:6B0

**Tip** Remember that the fully expanded address has eight blocks and that the double colon represents only 0s. You can use the double colon only once in an IPv6 address.

RFC 5952 also states that when you have two options to suppress zeros, the longest run of 16-bit 0 fields must be shortened. If both options have the same length, then the first sequence of zero bits must be shortened. For example:

2001:4C:0000:0000:9EA:0000:0000:1

Is shortened to:

2001:4C::9EA:0:0:1, and not to 2001:4C:0:0:9EA::1.

To expand a compressed address, the process described earlier is reversed: Add leading 0s in groups where they have been omitted, then add 0s represented by ::. For example, the IPv6 address 2001:4C::50:0:0:741 expands as follows:

2001:004C::0050:0000:0000:0741

Because there should be eight blocks of addresses and you have six in this address, you can expand the double colon to two blocks as follows:

2001:004C:0000:0000:0050:0000:0000:0741

## IPv4-Mapped IPv6 Addresses

As described in RFCs 4921 and 4038, IPv6 allows for IPv4-mapped IPv6 addresses. In a mixed IPv6/IPv4 environment, the IPv4 portion of the address requires the last two 16-bit blocks, or 32 bits of the address, which is represented in IPv4 dotted-decimal notation. The portion of the IPv6 address preceding the IPv4 information is 80 0s and then 16 1s. Six hexadecimal 16-bit blocks are concatenated with the dotted-decimal format. This form is *0:0:0:0:0:FFFF:d.d.d.d*, where each *block* represents the hexadecimal digits, and *d.d.d.d* is the dotted-decimal representation.

An example of a mixed full address is 0000:0000:0000:0000:0000:FFFF:100.1.1.1; this example can be shortened to 0:0:0:0:0:FFFF:100.1.1.1 or ::FFFF:100.1.1.1.

## IPv6 Prefix Representation

IPv6 prefixes are represented much as in IPv4, with the following format:

*IPv6-address/prefix*

The *IPv6-address* portion is a valid IPv6 address. The *prefix* portion is the number of leftmost contiguous bits that represent the *prefix*. You use the double colon only once in the representation. An example of an IPv6 prefix is 200C:001b:1100:0:0:0:0/40, and this address could be condensed to 200C:1b:1100::/40.

For another example, look at these representations of the 60-bit prefix 2001000000000ab0:

2001:0000:0000:0ab0:0000:0000:0000:0000/60

2001:0000:0000:0ab0:0:0:0:0/60

2001:0000:0000:ab0::/60

2001:0:0:ab0::/60

The rules for address representation are still valid when using a prefix. The following is not a valid representation of the preceding prefix:

2001:0:0:ab0/60

The preceding representation is missing the trailing double colon:

2001::ab0/60

The preceding representation expands to 2001:0:0:0:0:0:0:0ab0, which is not the prefix 2001:0000:0000:0ab0::/60.

When representing an IPv6 host address with its subnet prefix, you combine the two. For example, the IPv6 address 2001:0000:0000:0ab0:001c:1bc0:08ba:1c9a in subnet prefix 2001:0000:0000:0ab0::/60 is represented as follows:

2001:0000:0000:0ab0:001c:1bc0:08ba:1c9a/60

# IPv6 Address Scope Types and Address Allocations

This section covers the major types of IPv6 addresses. IPv4 addresses are unicast, multicast, or broadcast. IPv6 maintains each of these address functions, except that the IPv6 address types are defined a little differently. A special "all-nodes" IPv6 multicast address handles the broadcast function. IPv6 also introduces the anycast address type.

Also important to understand are the IPv6 address allocations. Sections of the IPv6 address space are reserved for particular functions, which are covered in this section. To provide you with a full understanding of address types, the following sections describe each one.

## IPv6 Address Allocations

The leading bits of an IPv6 address can define the IPv6 address type or other reservations. These leading bits are of variable lengths and are called the format prefix (FP). Table 2-3 shows the allocation of address prefixes. The IPv6 address space was delegated to IANA. You can find current IPv6 allocations at https://www.iana.org/assignments/ipv6-address-space/ipv6-address-space.xhtml. Many prefixes are still unassigned.

**Table 2-3**   IPv6 Prefix Allocation

| Binary Prefix | Hexadecimal/Prefix | Allocation |
|---|---|---|
| 0000 0000 | 0000::/8 | Unspecified, loopback, IPv4-compatible |
| 0000 0001 | 0100::/8 | Reserved, 0100::/64 reserved for discard-only address block |
| 0000 001 | 0200:/7 | Reserved by IETF |
| 0000 010 | 0400::/6 | Reserved, deprecated use for Internetwork Packet Exchange (IPX) allocation |
| 0000 1 | 0800::/5 | Reserved by IETF |
| 0001 | 1000::/4 | Reserved by IETF |
| 001 | 2000::/3 | Global unicast address; IANA unicast address assignments are limited within this range |
| 010 | 4000::/3 | Reserved by IETF |
| 011 | 6000::/3 | Reserved by IETF |
| 100 | 8000::/3 | Reserved for geographic-based unicast addresses |
| 101 | A000::/3 | Reserved by IETF |
| 110 | C000::/3 | Reserved by IETF |
| 1110 | E000::/3 | Reserved by IETF |
| 1111 0 | F000::/5 | Reserved by IETF |
| 1111 10 | F800::/6 | Reserved by IETF |
| 1111 110 | FC00::/7 | Unique local unicast |
| 1111 1110 0 | FE00::/9 | Reserved by IETF |
| 1111 1110 10 | FE80:/10 | Link-local unicast addresses |
| 1111 1110 11 | FEC0::/10 | Unassigned; was site-local unicast addresses (deprecated) |
| 1111 1111 | FF00::/8 | Multicast addresses |

An unspecified address is all 0s: 0:0:0:0:0:0:0:0. It signifies that an IPv6 address is not specified for the interface. Unspecified addresses are not forwarded by an IPv6 router.

The IPv6 loopback address is 0:0:0:0:0:0:0:1. This address is similar to the IPv4 loopback address 127.0.0.1.

## IPv6 Unicast Addresses

The IPv6 *unicast* (one-to-one) address is a logical identifier of a single-host interface. With a unicast address, a single source sends to a single destination. It is similar to IPv4 unicast addresses. There are three types of unicast addresses:

- Global unicast addresses
- Link-local addresses
- Unique local addresses

## Global Unicast Addresses

IPv6 global addresses connect to the public network. These unicast addresses are globally unique and routable. This address format was initially defined in RFC 2374. RFC 3587 provides updates to the format.

The original specification defined the address format with a three-layer hierarchy: public topology, site topology, and interface identifier. The *public topology* consisted of service providers that provided transit services and exchanges of routing information. It used a top-level aggregator (TLA) identifier and a next-level identifier (NLA). A site-level aggregator (SLA) was used for site topology. The *site topology* is local to the company or site and does not provide transit services. The TLA, NLA, and SLA identifiers are deprecated by RFC 3587. RFC 3587 simplifies these identifiers with a global routing prefix and subnet identifier for the network portion of the address.

Figure 2-2 shows the format of the standard IPv6 global unicast address. The Global Routing Prefix field is generally 48 bits in length, and the Subnet ID field is 16 bits. The Interface ID field is 64 bits in length and uniquely identifies the interface on the link.

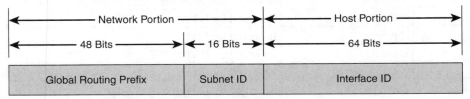

**Figure 2-2**   *IPv6 Global Unicast Address Format*

The Interface ID field is obtained from the 48-bit MAC address of the host. The MAC address is converted to the EUI-64 identifier format by inserting the FFFE hexadecimal value in between the 24-bit leftmost and rightmost values.

For example, with the MAC address 01:00:0C:A4:BC:D0, the leftmost 24 bits are 01:00:0C, and the rightmost bits are A4:BC:D0. By inserting FFFE, the IPv6 64-bit identifier becomes

   01:00:0C:FF:FE:A4:BC:D0

## Link-Local Addresses

IPv6 link-local addresses are significant to nodes on only a single link. Routers do not forward packets with link-local source or destination addresses beyond the local link. Link-local addresses are identified by leading FE8 hexadecimal numbers. Link-local addresses are configured automatically or manually.

As shown in Figure 2-3, the format of the link-local address is an FP of 1111111010, followed by 54 0s and a 64-bit Interface ID field. The Interface ID field is obtained from the device MAC address and verified automatically through communication with other nodes in the link. The interface ID is then concatenated with the link-local address prefix FE80::/64 to obtain the interface link-local address.

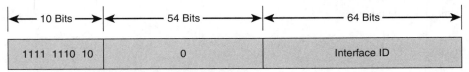

**Figure 2-3**   *IPv6 Link-Local Address Format*

## Unique Local IPv6 Address

RFC 4193 defines the unique local address. Unique local addresses (ULAs) are designed for use in local networks and are not routable on the Internet. They substitute the deprecated site-local addresses. Unique local IPv6 addresses have a globally unique prefix. This global unique prefix is well known to allow for easy filtering at site boundaries.

As shown in Figure 2-4, the format of the unique local address is an FP of 1111 110 (FC00::/7) followed by the Global ID field, followed by the Subnet ID field and then the 64-bit Interface Identifier (ID) field. The bit labeled L is set to 1 if the prefix is locally assigned and a setting of 0 has not been defined.

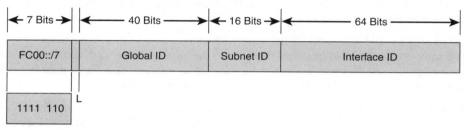

**Figure 2-4**  *IPv6 Unique Local Address*

## Global Aggregatable IPv6 Address

Global aggregatable unicast addresses are a type of global unicast address that allows the aggregation of routing prefixes. This aggregation makes it possible to reduce the number of routes in the global routing table. These addresses are used in links to aggregate (summarize) routes upward to the core in large organizations or to ISPs. Global aggregatable addresses are identified by a fixed prefix of 2000:/3. As shown in Figure 2-5, the format of the global aggregatable IPv6 address is a Global Routing Prefix field starting with binary 001, followed by the Subnet ID field and then the 64-bit Interface ID field. The device MAC address is normally used as the interface ID.

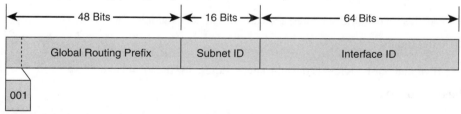

**Figure 2-5**  *IPv6 Link-Local Address Format*

## IPv4-Compatible IPv6 Addresses

IPv4-compatible IPv6 addresses were defined to assist in the transition to IPv6 but have been deprecated. Such an address begins with 96 binary 0s (six 16-bit groups) followed by the 32-bit IPv4 address, as in 0:0:0:0:0:0:130.100.50.1, or just ::130.100.50.1. IPv4-compatible IPv6 addresses have been deprecated because updated transition mechanisms no longer require this format.

### IPv4-Mapped IPv6 Addresses

RFC 4038 defines a second type of IPv6 address that holds an embedded IPv4 address. This format contains 80 bits of 0s, 16 bits of 1s, and then the 32-bit IPv4 address. This type of address is used for IPv4 clients to reach IPv6 applications. Here is an example:

::FFFF:0:0/96

### IPv6 Anycast Addresses

An IPv6 *anycast* (one-to-nearest) address identifies a set of devices. There is no allocated prefix to identify anycast addresses. An anycast address is allocated from a set of global unicast addresses. These destination devices should share common characteristics and are explicitly configured for anycast.

You can use the anycast address to identify a set of routers or servers in an area. When a packet is sent to the anycast address, it is delivered to the nearest device, as determined by the routing protocol. Network nodes to which the anycast address is assigned must be explicitly configured to recognize that the address is an anycast address.

An example of the use of anycast addresses is to assign an anycast address to a set of servers, such as one in North America and another in Europe. Users in North America would be routed to the North American server, and those in Europe would be routed to the European server.

You cannot use an anycast address as a source address. Also, you must explicitly configure nodes to which the anycast address is assigned to recognize the anycast address.

### IPv6 Multicast Addresses

An IPv6 *multicast* (one-to-many) address identifies a set of hosts. A packet with this type of address is delivered to all the hosts identified by that address. This type is similar to IPv4 multicast (Class D) addresses. IPv6 multicast addresses also supersede the broadcast function of IPv4 broadcasts; you use an "all-nodes" multicast address instead. One additional function of IPv6 multicast is to provide the IPv4 broadcast equivalent with the all-nodes multicast group.

For example, this IPv6 multicast address indicates the all-nodes address for interface-local scope:

FF01:0:0:0:0:0:0:1

And this IPv6 multicast address is the all-routers address for the local link:

FF02:0:0:0:0:0:0:2

RFC 4291 specifies the format of IPv6 multicast addresses. As shown in Figure 2-6, the fields of the IPv6 multicast address are the FP, a value of 0xFF, followed by a 4-bit flags field, a 4-bit scope field, and 112 bits for the Group ID field. A quick way to recognize an IPv6 multicast address is that it begins with FF::/8.

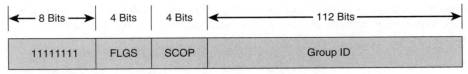

**Figure 2-6**  *Multicast Address Format*

The FLGS (flags) field consists of 0RPT.

The R flag R = 1 indicates a multicast address that embeds the address on the RP. R = 0 indicates a multicast address that does not embed the address of the RP.

If the P flag is 0, it indicates that a multicast address is not assigned based on the network prefix. If P=1, the multicast address is assigned based on the network prefix.

If T = 0, the address is a well-known multicast address assigned by IANA. If T = 1, the address is not a permanently assigned address.

The SCOP (scope) field limits the scope of the multicast group. Table 2-4 shows the assigned scope values.

**Table 2-4**    Multicast Scope Assignments

| SCOP (Binary) | SCOP (Hexadecimal) | Assignment |
|---|---|---|
| 0000 | 0 | Reserved |
| 0001 | 1 | Interface-local scope |
| 0010 | 2 | Link-local scope |
| 0011 | 3 | Reserved |
| 0100 | 4 | Admin-local scope |
| 0101 | 5 | Site-local scope |
| 0110 | 6 | Unassigned |
| 0111 | 7 | Unassigned |
| 1000 | 8 | Organization-local scope |
| 1001 | 9 | Unassigned |
| 1010 | A | Unassigned |
| 1011 | B | Unassigned |
| 1100 | C | Unassigned |
| 1101 | D | Unassigned |
| 1110 | E | Global scope |
| 1111 | F | Reserved |

The Group ID field identifies the multicast group within the given scope. The group ID is independent of the scope. A group ID of 0:0:0:0:0:0:1 identifies nodes, whereas a group ID of 0:0:0:0:0:0:2 identifies routers. Some well-known multicast addresses are listed in Table 2-5; they are associated with a variety of scope values.

**Table 2-5**    Well-Known IPv6 Multicast Addresses

| Multicast Address | Multicast Group |
|---|---|
| FF01::1 | All nodes (interface-local) |
| FF02::1 | All nodes (link-local) |
| FF01::2 | All routers (interface-local) |
| FF02::2 | All routers (link-local) |
| FF02::5 | Open Shortest Path First version 3 (OSPFv3) |
| FF02::6 | OSPFv3 designated routers |

| Multicast Address | Multicast Group |
|---|---|
| FF02::9 | Routing Information Protocol (RIPng) |
| FF02::A | EIGRP routers |
| FF02::B | Mobile agents |
| FF02::C | DHCP servers/relay agents |
| FF02::D | All Protocol Independent Multicast (PIM) routers |
| FF05::1 | All nodes in the local network site |
| FF0x::FB | Multicast DNS |
| FF02::1:2 | All DHCP and relay agents on the local network site (RFC 3313) |
| FF05::1:3 | All DHCP servers on the local network site (RFC 3313) |

Table 2-6 summarizes the IPv6 address types.

**Table 2-6**   IPv6 Address Types

| IPv6 Address Type | Description |
|---|---|
| Unicast | The IP address of an interface on a single host. It can be a source or destination address. |
| Anycast | An IP address that identifies a set of devices within an area. It can be only a destination address. |
| Multicast | An IP address that reaches a group of hosts identified by the address. It can be only a destination address. |

A CCNP enterprise designer should know how to identify address types based on the prefix. Table 2-7 summarizes the address types and their prefixes.

**Table 2-7**   IPv6 Address Prefixes

| IPv6 Address Type | Prefix |
|---|---|
| Loopback address | 0000::0001 |
| Unspecified address | 0000::0000 |
| Global unicast address | 2000::/3 |
| Unique local unicast | FC00::/7 |
| Link-local unicast address | FE80:/10 |
| Multicast address | FF00::/8 |
| OSPFv3 | FF02::5 |
| EIGRP routers | FF02::A |
| DHCP | FF02::C |

# IPv6 Mechanisms

The changes to the 128-bit address length and IPv6 header format modified the underlying protocols that support IP. This section covers ICMPv6, IPv6 Neighbor Discovery (ND), address resolution, address assignment, and IPv6 routing protocols. These protocols must now support 128-bit addresses. For example, DNS adds a new record locator for resolving fully qualified domain names (FQDNs) to IPv6 addresses. IPv6 also replaces ARP with the IPv6 ND protocol. IPv6 ND uses ICMPv6.

# ICMPv6

ICMP needed some modifications to support IPv6. RFC 2463 describes the use of ICMPv6 for IPv6 networks. All IPv6 nodes must implement ICMPv6 to perform network layer functions. ICMPv6 performs diagnostics (ping), reports errors, and provides reachability information. Although IPv4 ICMP uses IP protocol 1, IPv6 uses a Next Header field number of 58.

Informational messages are

- Echo request
- Echo reply

Some error messages are

- Destination unreachable
- Packet too big
- Time exceeded
- Parameter problem

The destination-unreachable messages also provide further details:

- No route to destination
- Destination administratively prohibited
- Address unreachable
- Port unreachable

Other IPv6 mechanisms use ICMPv6 to determine neighbor availability, path MTU, destination link-layer address, or port reachability.

## IPv6 Neighbor Discovery Protocol

IPv6 does not implement ARP, which is used in IPv4. Instead, IPv6 implements the Neighbor Discovery (ND) protocol described in RFC 2461. Hosts use ND to implement plug-and-play functions that discover all other nodes in the same link, check for duplicate addresses, and find routers in the link. The protocol also searches for alternative routers if the primary router fails.

The IPv6 ND protocol performs the following functions:

- **Stateless address autoconfiguration:** The host can determine its full IPv6 address without the use of DHCP.
- **Duplicate address detection:** The host can determine whether the address it will use is already in use on the network.
- **Prefix discovery:** The host can determine the link's IPv6 prefix.
- **Parameter discovery:** The host can determine the link's MTU and hop count.
- **Address resolution:** The host can determine the MAC addresses of other nodes without the use of ARP.

- **Router discovery:** The host can find local routers without the use of DHCP.

- **Next-hop determination:** The host can determine a destination's next hop.

- **Neighbor unreachability detection:** The host can determine whether a neighbor is no longer reachable.

- **Redirect:** The host can tell another host if a preferred next hop exists to reach a particular destination.

IPv6 ND uses ICMPv6 to implement some of its functions. The ICMPv6 messages are as follows:

- **Router Advertisement (RA):** Sent by routers to advertise their presence and link-specific parameters

- **Router Solicitation (RS):** Sent by hosts to request RA messages from local routers

- **Neighbor Solicitation (NS):** Sent by hosts to request link layer addresses of other hosts (also used for duplicate address detection)

- **Neighbor Advertisement (NA):** Sent by hosts in response to NS messages

- **Redirect:** Sent to a host to notify it of a better next hop to a destination

The link address resolution process uses NS messages to obtain a neighbor's link layer address. Nodes respond with an NA message that contains the link layer address.

## IPv6 Name Resolution

Name resolution for IPv6 addresses can be static or dynamic. Just as with IPv4, resolution of static names to IPv6 addresses can be manually configured in the host configuration file. Dynamic name resolution relies on the Domain Name System (DNS).

IPv4 uses A records to provide FQDN-to-IPv4 address resolution. DNS adds a resource record (RR) to support name-to-IPv6 address resolution. RFC 3596 describes the addition of a new DNS resource record type to support the transition to IPv6 name resolution. The new record type is AAAA, commonly known as "quad-A." Given a domain name, the AAAA record returns an IPv6 address to the requesting host.

RFC 2874 specifies another DNS record for IPv6: the A6 resource record. The A6 record provides additional features and was intended to be a replacement for the AAAA RR. But RFC 3363 has changed the status of the A6 RR to deprecated.

Current DNS implementations need to be able to support A (for IPv4) and AAAA resource records, with type A having the highest priority and AAAA the lowest.

For hosts that support dual-stack (IPv4 and IPv6), the application decides which stack to use and accordingly requests an AAAA or A record. As shown in Figure 2-7, the client device requests the AAAA record of the destination IPv6 server. The DNS server returns the IPv6 address. Note that this is the same DNS server that supports IPv4 addresses; no separate DNS servers are needed for IPv6 networks.

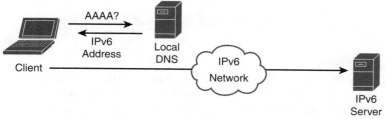

**Figure 2-7** *IPv6 DNS AAAA Request*

## Path MTU Discovery

IPv6 does not allow packet fragmentation throughout the internetwork. Only sending hosts are allowed to fragment. Routers are not allowed to fragment packets. RFC 2460 specifies that the MTU of every link in an IPv6 address must be 1280 bytes or greater. RFC 1981 recommends that nodes should implement IPv6 path MTU discovery to determine whether any paths are greater than 1280 bytes. ICMPv6 packet-too-big error messages determine the path MTU. Nodes along the path send the ICMPv6 packet-too-big message to the sending host if the packet is larger than the outgoing interface MTU.

Figure 2-8 shows a host sending a 2000-byte packet. Because the outgoing interface MTU is 1500 bytes, Router A sends an ICMPv6 packet-too-big error message back to Host A. The sending host then sends a 1500-byte packet. The outgoing interface MTU at Router B is 1300 bytes. Router B sends an ICMPv6 packet-too-big error message to Host A. Host A then sends the packet with 1300 bytes.

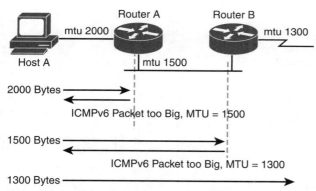

**Figure 2-8** *ICMPv6 Packet-Too-Big Message*

## IPv6 Address-Assignment Strategies

Assignment of IPv6 addresses to a host can occur statically or dynamically. Static IPv6 address assignment involves manual configuration on the host's configuration files. Dynamic IPv6 address assignment can be done via stateless or stateful methods. Stateless address assignment may result in a link-local or globally unique address. The following sections explain these three methods to assign IPv6 addresses:

- Manual configuration

- Stateless address autoconfiguration (SLAAC)

- Stateful configuration with DHCPv6

### Manual Configuration

As with IPv4, devices such as routers, switches, servers, and firewalls should have IPv6 addresses configured manually.

### SLAAC of Link-Local Address

The dynamic configuration of link-local IPv6 addresses is a stateless autoconfiguration method—that is, without DHCP. Hosts obtain their link-local addresses automatically as an interface is initialized. First, the host performs a duplicate address-detection process. The host joins the all-nodes multicast group to receive neighbor advertisements from other nodes. The neighbor advertisements include the subnet or prefix associated with the link. The host then sends a neighbor-solicitation message with the tentative IP address (interface identifier) as the target. If a host is already using the tentative IP address, that host replies with a neighbor advertisement. If the host receives no neighbor advertisement, the target IP address becomes the link-local address of the originating host. It uses the link-local prefix FE80::/10 (binary: 1111 1110 10). An alternative is to manually configure the link-local address.

### SLAAC of Globally Unique IPv6 Address

RFC 4862 describes IPv6 stateless address autoconfiguration. With autoconfiguration of globally unique IP addresses, IPv6 hosts can use SLAAC—without DHCP—to acquire their own IP address information. This is done on a per-interface basis. As shown in Figure 2-9, after a host has autoconfigured a link-local address, it listens for router advertisement (RA) messages. These router messages contain the prefix address to be used for the network. The IPv6 address is then formed from the prefix plus the interface ID (which derives from the MAC address).

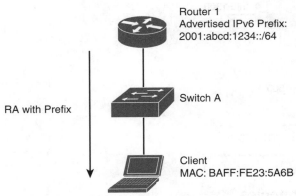

**Figure 2-9**   *Stateless Autoconfiguration*

Creating the globally unique IPv6 address using SLAAC involves the following steps:

**Step 1.**   Router Advertisement (RA) messages are sent by Router 1.

**Step 2.**   The client learns the prefix from the RA message. In the case of Figure 2-9, the prefix is 2001:abcd:1234/64.

**Step 3.**   The client identifier is created by splitting the local MAC address and adding FF:FE in the middle. Hence, in our example, the MAC address 0200:FE23:5A6B becomes 0200:FEFF:FE23:5A6B.

**Step 4.**   The seventh bit is flipped (binary 00000010 becomes binary 0000000); thus, the identifier becomes 0000:FEFF:FE23:5A6B.

**Step 5.**   The merging of the prefix and identifier becomes 2001:abcd:1234:0000:0000:FEFF:FE23:5A6B.

**Step 6.**   The address is shortened to 2001:abcd:1234:: FEFF:FE23:5A6B.

Table 2-8 summarizes IPv6 address configuration schemes.

**Table 2-8**   IPv6 Address Autoconfiguration Scheme

| IPv6 Address Configuration Scheme | Description |
| --- | --- |
| Manual configuration | Used for routers, switches, servers, and firewalls. |
| SLAAC link-local | Host sends a Neighbor Solicitation message that includes the target IPv6 address that begins with FE80::. |
| SLAAC global unique | Combines the router prefix with the local MAC address. |
| DHCPv6 | Provides stateful address allocation. |

## DHCPv6

DHCPv6 is an updated version of DHCP that provides dynamic IP address assignment for IPv6 hosts. DHCPv6, described in RFC 3315, provides the same functions as DHCP, with more control than stateless autoconfiguration, and it supports renumbering without routers. DHCPv6 assignment is stateful, whereas IPv6 link-local and globally unique autoconfiguration are not.

## DHCPv6 Lite

SLAAC is simpler than DHCPv6, although it offers less control and fewer capabilities. For example, SLAAC is not able to send DNS parameters. To overcome this limitation, there is another (special case) option for clients to receive both their IPv6 address and other information statelessly. This is accomplished using SLAAC initially and then using stateless DHCPv6 service, also known as DHCPv6 Lite. With DHCPv6 Lite, DNS server, domain name, SIP server, and other information can be sent to the client. With DHCPv6 Lite, the client performs the SLAAC to obtain its IPv6 address and then sends a DHCP information request to the router. The router then responds with a reply message in the requested information.

## IPv6 Security

IPv6 has two integrated mechanisms to provide security for communications. It natively supports IP Security (IPsec), which is mandated at the operating system level for all IPsec hosts. RFC 2401 describes IPsec. Extension headers carry the IPsec AH and ESP headers. The AH provides authentication and integrity. The ESP header provides confidentiality by encrypting the payload. For IPv6, the AH defaults to Message Digest Algorithm 5 (MD5), and the ESP encryption defaults to Data Encryption Standard–Cipher Block Chaining (DES-CBC).

A description of the IPsec mechanisms appears in Chapter 8, "WAN for Enterprise." More information also appears in RFC 2402: *IP Authentication Header* and in RFC 2406: *IP Encapsulating Security Payload (ESP)*.

Table 2-9 summarizes IPv6 mechanisms.

**Table 2-9**    IPv6 Mechanisms

| IPv6 Mechanism | Description |
|---|---|
| ICMPv6 | Performs diagnostics and reachability information. Has a Next Header number of 58. |
| IPv6 Neighbor Discovery | Discovers all nodes in the same link and checks for duplicate addresses. |
| AAAA | DNS resource record for IPv6. |
| SLAAC | Performs stateless IPv6 address assignment. |
| DHCPv6 | Provides stateful IPv6 address assignment. |
| RIPng | Routing protocol that uses UDP port 521. |
| EIGRP for IPv6 | Cisco routing protocol for IPv6. |
| OSPFv3 | Link-state routing protocol for IPv6. |

# IPv6 Routing Protocols

New routing protocols have been developed to support IPv6, such as RIPng, Intermediate System-to-Intermediate System (IS-IS), Enhanced Interior Gateway Routing Protocol (EIGRP) for IPv6, and Open Shortest Path First Version 3 (OSPFv3). Border Gateway Protocol (BGP) also includes changes that support IPv6. These routing protocols are only briefly mentioned here because they are covered in detail in Chapter 3, "Routing Protocol Characteristics, EIGRP, and IS-IS," and Chapter 4, "OSPF, BGP, and Route Manipulation."

## RIPng

RFC 2080 describes changes to RIP to support IPv6 networks, called RIP next generation (RIPng). RIP mechanisms remain the same. RIPng still has a 15-hop limit, counting to infinity, and split horizon with poison reverse. Instead of using User Datagram Protocol (UDP) port 520, as RIPv2 does, RIPng uses UDP port 521. RIPng supports IPv6 addresses and prefixes. Cisco IOS software currently supports RIPng. RIPng uses multicast group FF02::9 for RIP updates to all RIP routers.

## EIGRP for IPv6

Cisco has developed EIGRP support for IPv6 networks to route IPv6 prefixes. EIGRP for IPv6 is configured and managed separately from EIGRP for IPv4; no network statements are used. EIGRP for IPv6 retains all the characteristics (network discovery, DUAL, modules) and functions of EIGRP for IPv4. EIGRP uses multicast group FF02::A for EIGRP updates.

## OSPFv3

RFC 5340 describes OSPFv3 to support IPv6 networks. OSPF algorithms and mechanisms (flooding, designated router [DR] election, areas, and shortest path first [SPF] calculations) remain the same. Changes are made for OSPF to support IPv6 addresses, address hierarchy, and IPv6 for transport. Cisco IOS software currently supports OSPFv3.

OSPFv3 uses multicast group FF02::5 for all OSPF routers and FF02::6 for all DRs.

## IS-IS for IPv6

Specifications for routing IPv6 with integrated IS-IS are described in RFC 5308: *Routing IPv6 with IS-IS*. The draft specifies new type, length, and value (TLV) objects, reachability TLVs, and an interface address TLV to forward IPv6 information in the network. IOS supports IS-IS for IPv6, as currently described in the draft standard.

## BGP4 Multiprotocol Extensions (MP-BGP) for IPv6

RFC 2545 specifies the use of BGP attributes for passing on IPv6 route information. MP-BGP is also referred to as BGP4+. The MP_REACH_NLRI (multiprotocol-reachable) attribute describes reachable destinations. It includes the next-hop address and a list of Network Layer Reachability Information (NLRI) prefixes of reachable networks. The MP_UNREACH_NLRI (multiprotocol-unreachable) attribute conveys unreachable networks. IOS currently supports these BGP4 multiprotocol attributes to communicate reachability information for IPv6 networks.

## IPv6 Addressing Design

This section covers IPv6 design topics that a CCNP enterprise designer should be aware of: planning for IPv6 addressing, IPv6 route summarization, IPv6 address allocation, and IPv6 private addressing. Some IPv6 design concepts are similar to those in IPv4 (such as the goal to do summarization), and some concepts are unique to IPv6. As with IPv4, each company will have a unique set of requirements that will drive the allocation and subnetting of the IPv6 address space.

## Planning for Addressing with IPv6

When designing LAN subnets with IPv6, it is recommended that you use a /64 subnet. This is similar to the /24 subnet in IPv4. It provides more than enough addresses for devices contained in the subnet, allows for future growth, and prevents renumbering in the future. It also allows for easier aggregation of subnets.

If you are allocated IPv6 addresses from an Internet service provider (ISP), you most likely will have to renumber your IPv6 addresses if you move to a different ISP. The best way to avoid this is to obtain an IPv6 address block from a Regional Internet Registry (RIR). This way, your IPv6 addresses are independent of which ISP you use. Address allocations are from the 2000::/3 global unicast block. The five RIRs are

- **AfriNIC:** Africa

- **APNIC:** Asia Pacific

- **ARIN:** Canada, the United States, and part of the Caribbean islands

- **LACNIC:** Latin America and part of the Caribbean islands

- **RIPE NCC:** Europe, the Middle East, and Central Asia

## Route Summarization with IPv6

As a designer, you will want to allocate IPv6 address space to allow for route summarization. Large networks can grow quickly from 500 routes to 1000 and higher. Route summarization reduces the amount of route traffic on the network and unnecessary route computation, regardless of whether IPv4 or IPv6 addressing is used. Route summarization enables the network address space to scale as the company grows.

As an example, say a company has assigned the following IPv6 subnets to a site:

- 2001:db8:2a3e:8180::/64 for data networks

- 2001:db8:2a3e:8184::/64 for VoIP networks

- 2001:db8:2a3e:8188:/64 for wireless networks

- 2001:db8:2a3e:818F::/64 for small server farm and other systems

Instead of announcing each and every subnet of this network to the WAN, the recommendation is to summarize the site with a 2001:db8:2a3e:8180::/60 route. This summary encompasses 16 subnets from 2001:db8:2a3e:8180::/64 to 2001:db8:2a3e:818F::/64, so this address block would be assigned to this site.

## IPv6 Private Addressing

IPv6 private addressing should be very limited compared to its use in IPv4. IPv6 private IP addresses are referred to as unique local addresses (ULAs) and use the prefix FC00::/7. In both small and large companies, you should not expect to use ULAs in IPv6 networks. Furthermore, the Internet Engineering Task Force (IETF) does not recommend the use of NAT for IPv6. In the remote event that ULAs are needed, you will also use NAT66 for the IPv6-to-IPv6 private-to-public translation.

## IPv6 for the Enterprise

IPv6 addresses are assigned in a hierarchical manner. IANA allocates IPv6 addresses to the RIRs. The RIRs, in turn, allocate address blocks to Local Internet Registries (LIRs), and most LIRs are ISPs. In some regions (for example, APNIC), RIRs allocate addresses to National Internet Registries (NIRs), which in turn allocate addresses to ISPs. Normally, ISPs are allocated /32 blocks of addresses. Companies are allocated address blocks from /40 to /64. Large companies are allocated a /40 block of IPv6 addresses. Small companies might receive a /56 block, but a normal allocation is a /48 block of IPv6 addresses. Private consumers, such as residential user, are allocated a /64 address block.

A /48 address block is equal to $2^{16}$ (that is, 65,536) /64 subnets. As an example, if a company is allocated 2001:DB8:0ABC::/48, this allows the company to assign subnets from 2001:DB8:0ABC:0000::/64, 2001:DB8:0ABC:0001::/64, 2001:DB8:0ABC:0002::/64, all the way to 2001:DB8:0ABC:FFFF::/64. That is $2^{16}$ = 65,536 subnets!

## IPv6 Address Allocation

There are several schemas to allocate IPv6 addresses within an organization. Because IPv6 addresses are usually allocated to a network that already has IPv4 addresses, you can attempt to use the IPv4 address or subnet as part of the IPv6 address. You can also allocate IPv6 address space to show a location and type.

### Partly Linked IPv4 Address into IPv6

IPv6 deployments are not expected to be greenfield; there will be IPv4 subnets on the network. One method to allocate IPv6 addresses is to match the IPv6 /64 subnet with the IPv4 /24 subnet. In addition, the IP subnet can match the VLAN number used. Table 2-10 shows an example. The third octet of the IPv4 subnet is used as the subnet for the IPv6 /64 subnet; furthermore, it matches the VLAN number. Note that this works very well with IPv4 /24 subnets, but it does not work optimally with /30 and other smaller links.

**Table 2-10**    IPv6 Address Allocation Partly Linked to IPv4

| VLAN Number | IPv4 Subnet | IPv6 Subnet |
| --- | --- | --- |
| VLAN 11 | 172.16.11.0/24 | 2001:DB8:ABC:11::/64 |
| VLAN 12 | 172.16.12.0/24 | 2001:DB8:ABC:12::/64 |
| VLAN 13 | 172.16.13.0/24 | 2001:DB8:ABC:13::/64 |
| VLAN 111 | 172.16.111.0/24 | 2001:DB8:ABC:111::/64 |
| VLAN 112 | 172.16.112.0/24 | 2001:DB8:ABC:112::/64 |
| VLAN 113 | 172.16.113.0/24 | 2001:DB8:ABC:113::/64 |

### Whole IPv4 Address Linked to IPv6

Another method of IPv6 address allocation is to link a whole IPv4 address to the lowest significant bits of the IPv6 address. Table 2-11 shows an example using the same subnets as in Table 2-10. Converting the numbers, 172 decimal is 0xAC, and 16 is 0x10. The drawback with this schema is that it is not obvious that the IPv6 and IPv4 subnets are linked. At first sight, can you tell that 0xAC10 is 172.16?

**Table 2-11**    IPv6 Address Allocation Completely Linked to IPv4

| VLAN Number | IPv4 Subnet | IPv6 Subnet |
| --- | --- | --- |
| VLAN 11 | 172.16.11.0/24 | 2001:DB8:ABC::AC10:0B:00/120 |
| VLAN 12 | 172.16.12.0/24 | 2001:DB8:ABC::AC10:0C00/120 |
| VLAN 13 | 172.16.13.0/24 | 2001:DB8:ABC::AC10:0D00/120 |
| VLAN 111 | 172.16.111.0/24 | 2001:DB8:ABC:AC10:6F00/120 |
| VLAN 112 | 172.16.112.0/24 | 2001:DB8:ABC:AC10:7000/120 |
| VLAN 113 | 172.16.113.0/24 | 2001:DB8:ABC:AC10:7100/120 |

### IPv6 Addresses Allocated per Location and/or Type

Another schema for allocating IPv6 addresses is to assign bits to identify a location (such as a data center, core, edge, or branch) and/or other bits to identify a site type (such as a server, an end client, a router, or a switch). As shown in Figure 2-10, 4 bits can be used for location codes, and 4 additional bits used for type codes. The remaining bits of the /64 subnet can be used within the sites for specific VLANs.

| 2001:DB8:ABC: | L | L | L | L | T | T | T | T | 0000 | 0000 | ::/64 |
| --- | --- | --- | --- | --- | --- | --- | --- | --- | --- | --- | --- |

L = Location

T = Type

**Figure 2-10**    *IPv6 Address Allocated per Location/Type*

# IPv4-to-IPv6 Migration Strategies and Deployment Models

This section describes transition mechanisms and deployment models to migrate from IPv4 to IPv6. During a transition time, both protocols can coexist in the network. The three major migration strategies are

- **Dual-stack:** IPv4 and IPv6 coexist in hosts and networks.

- **Tunneling:** IPv6 packets are encapsulated into IPv4 packets.

■ **Translation:** IPv6 packets are translated to IPv4 packets.

IPv6 deployment models are also divided into three major categories:

■ **Dual-stack model:** IPv4 and IPv6 coexist on hosts and the network.

■ **Hybrid model:** Combination of Intra-Site Automatic Tunneling Addressing Protocol (ISATAP) or manually configured tunnels and dual-stack mechanisms.

■ **Service block model:** Combination of ISATAP and manually configured tunnels and dual-stack mechanisms.

Each model provides several advantages and disadvantages, and you should familiarize yourself with them. Of all these models, the dual-stack model is recommended because it requires no tunneling and is easiest to manage.

## Dual-Stack Migration Strategy

Dual-stack is also referred to as native mode. Devices running dual-stack can communicate with both IPv4 and IPv6 devices. The IPv4 protocol stack is used between IPv4 hosts, and the IPv6 protocol stack is used between IPv6 hosts. An application decides which stack to use to communicate with destination hosts. As shown in Figure 2-11, when a frame is received, the Ethernet type code identifies whether the packet needs to be forwarded to IPv4 (0x0800) or IPv6 (ox86DD).

When using dual-stack, a host also uses DNS to determine which stack to use to reach a destination. If DNS returns an IPv6 (AAAA record) address to the host, the host uses the IPv6 stack. If DNS returns an IPv4 (A record) address to the host, the host uses the IPv4 stack. As mentioned before, current operating systems, such as Windows 10, macOS, and iOS, are configured to prefer IPv6 by default.

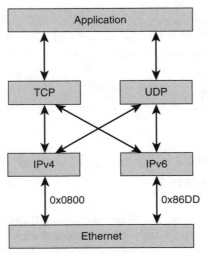

**Figure 2-11**  *Dual-Stack Mechanism*

## IPv6 over IPv4 Tunneling Strategy

In the IPv6 over IPv4 tunneling migration strategy, isolated IPv6-only networks are connected using IPv4 tunnels. With overlay tunnels, IPv6 packets are encapsulated within IPv4 packets so that they are sent over the IPv4 WAN. Overlay tunnels can be configured between border devices or between a border device and a host; however, both tunnel endpoints must support the IPv4 and IPv6 protocol stacks. The advantage of this method is that you do not need separate circuits to connect the IPv6 isolated networks.

A disadvantage of this method is the increased protocol overhead of the encapsulated IPv6 headers. Furthermore, overlay tunnels reduce the maximum transmission unit (MTU) by 20 octets.

### Manual Configured Tunnels and GRE Tunnels

As defined in RFC 4213, manually configured (static configuration) tunnels are configured with IPv4 and IPv6 addresses for tunnel source and destination. Tunnels can be built between border routers or between routers and hosts. A tunnel is equivalent to a permanent link between two IPv6 domains over an IPv4 backbone. The border routers at each end of the tunnel must support both IPv6 and IPv4 protocol stacks.

IPv6 packets can also be carried over IPv4 generic routing encapsulation (GRE) tunnels for stable connectivity between two IPv6 domains. A GRE tunnel is not tied to a specific passenger or transport protocol and can support other Layer 3 protocols (such as IS-IS) over the same tunnel. Because GRE has a protocol field, it can identify the passenger protocol (such as IPv6 or IS-IS); therefore, it is advantageous to tunnel IS-IS and IPv6 inside GRE.

## Automatic Tunnel Mechanisms

Automatic tunnel mechanisms include the following:

- 6to4

- 6RD

- ISATAP

### 6to4 Tunnels

RFC 3056 specifies the 6to4 method for transition by assigning an interim unique IPv6 prefix. 2002::/16 is the assigned range for 6to4. Each 6to4 site uses a /48 prefix that is concatenated with 2002. An automatic 6to4 tunnel may be configured on a border router of an isolated IPv6 network to create a tunnel over an IPv4 infrastructure to a border router in another IPv6 network. The border router extracts the IPv4 address that is embedded in the IPv6 destination address and encapsulates the IPv6 packet in an IPv4 packet with the extracted destination IPv4 address. The destination router extracts the IPv6 packet and forwards it to the IPv6 destination.

Figure 2-12 shows a network using IPv4 tunnels. Site A and Site B both have IPv4 and IPv6 networks. The IPv6 networks are connected using an IPv4 tunnel in the WAN.

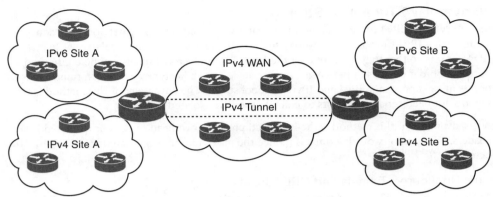

**Figure 2-12**  *IPv6 over IPv4 Tunnels*

### 6RD Tunnels

IPv6 Rapid Deployment (6RD) tunnels are an extension of 6to4 and allow a service provider to provide unicast IPv6 service to customers over its IPv4 network by using encapsulation of IPv6 in IPv4. It is defined in RFC 5969.

With 6RD, service providers do not have to use a 2002::/16 prefix; instead, they use a prefix from their own SP address block. The IPv6 operational domain is within the SP's networks. Furthermore, with 6RD, the 32 bits of the IPv4 destination do not need to be carried within the IPv6 payload. The IPv4 destination is obtained from a combination of bits in the payload header and information on the router.

A 6RD Border Relay (BR) is a 6RD-enabled router managed by the SP. A BR has an interface in the IPv6 network, another interface in the IPv4 network, and a virtual interface that is the endpoint for the 6RD IPv6-in-IPv4 tunnel.

### IPv6 ISATAP Tunnels

Another method to tunnel IPv6 over IPv4 is to use Intra-Site Automatic Tunnel Addressing Protocol (ISATAP). With ISATAP, a tunnel is automatically created between dual-stack hosts or routers to transmit IPv6 packets over an IPv4 network within a site. ISATAP does not require IPv4 to be multicast enabled.

ISATAP uses a well-defined IPv6 address format composed of any unicast prefix of 64 bits, which can be a link-local or global IPv6 unicast prefix. It then uses the 32 bits 0000:5EFE that define the ISATAP address ending with the 32-bit IPv4 address of the ISATAP link.

As an example, the link-local address is generated by concatenating FE80:0000:0000:0000: to 0000:5EFE: with the IPv4 address expressed in hexadecimal. For example, with IPv4 192.168.10.10, the link-local address is FE80:0000:0000:0000:0000:5EFE:C0A8:0A0A. ISATAP also requires the use of a routable address (for example, a global unicast IPv6 address that uses the same 0000:5EFE IANA reserved value for the interface ID along with the 32-bit IPv4 embedded address).

## IPv6/IPv4 Translation Strategy

One of the mechanisms for an IPv6-only host to communicate with an IPv4-only host without using dual stacks is protocol translation. Translation is basically an extension to IPv4 NAT techniques. RFC 6144 provides a framework for IPv4/IPv6 translation. It replaces the deprecated Network Address Translation–Protocol Translation (NAT-PT), which was not considered a viable strategy for transitioning to IPv6. NAT-PT was deprecated because of its tight coupling with DNS.

## DNS64

With DNS64, as defined in RFC 6147, when an IPv6 AAAA resource record (RR) is not available, DNS64 enables the DNS server to synthesize an AAAA record from an IPv4 A record. It allows an IPv6-only client to initiate communications by name to an IPv4-only server. The IPv6 address is generated based on the IPv4 address returned from the A record, an IPv6 prefix, and other parameters.

There are two options for the IPv6 prefix:

- A well-known prefix (WKP) of 64:FF9B::/96 is reserved for representing IPv4 addresses in IPv6 space.

- A network-specific prefix (NSP) is assigned by an organization for representing IPv4 addresses in IPv6 space.

DNS64 is used with NAT64 to provide network translation.

## NAT64

NAT64 is specified by RFC 7915 for stateless operation and by RFC 6146 for stateful operation. Unlike NAT-PT, NAT64 separates DNS functions from its mechanism.

### Stateless NAT64

In NAT64 stateless translation, an IPv4 address is directly embedded into an IPv6 address. A limitation of stateless NAT64 translation is that it directly translates only the IPv4 options that have direct IPv6 counterparts, and it does not translate any IPv6 extension headers beyond the fragmentation extension header; however, these limitations are not significant in practice.

With stateless NAT64, a specific IPv6 address range represents IPv4 systems in the IPv6 domain. This range needs to be manually configured on the translation device. The IPv6 hosts are assigned specific IPv6 addresses using manual configuration or DHCPv6. Similar to dual-stack deployments, stateless NAT64 consumes an IPv4 address for each IPv6-only device that desires translation.

### Stateful NAT64

Stateful NAT64 multiplexes many IPv6 addresses into a single IPv4 address. The state is created in the NAT64 device for every flow, and only IPv6-initiated flows are supported. There is no binding between an IPv6 address and an IPv4 address, as there is in stateless NAT64.

If an IPv4-only device wants to speak to an IPv6-only server, manual configuration of the translation is required, making this mechanism less attractive for providing IPv6 services toward the IPv4 Internet.

DNS64 is usually also necessary with stateful NAT64, and it works the same with both stateless and stateful NAT64.

Figure 2-13 shows an example of communications between an IPv6 client and an IPv4 server using DNS64 and stateful NAT64. This process involves the following steps:

**Step 1.**  The IPv6 client performs an AAAA record DNS lookup for www.ENSLD.com.

**Step 2.**  The DNS64 server receives the DNS AAAA query.

**Step 3.** DNS64 sends the AAAA query to the DNS AAAA authoritative server for the domain. Because this server only has an A record, an empty AAAA response is returned.

**Step 4.** On receiving an empty answer, the DNS64 server sends an A query to the IPv4 DNS A authoritative server.

**Step 5.** DNS64 receives a DNA A record for www.ENSLD.com.

**Step 6.** DNS64 synthesizes the AAAA record with the predetermined well-known prefix or the network-specific prefix and returns the AAAA record to the IPv6 client.

**Step 7.** The IPv6 client connects to www.ENSLD.com using the AAAA DNS response.

**Step 8.** The NAT64 router receives the IPv6 packet. If the destination address matches the stateful NAT64 prefix, the IPv6 packet undergoes translation:

    **a.** The IPv6 header is translated to an IPv4 header.

    **b.** The IPv6 destination address is translated into an IPv4 address by removing the NAT64 prefix.

    **c.** The IPv6 source address is translated into an IPv4 address from an address pool.

    **d.** Stateful NAT64 IP address translation states are created for both source and destination addresses.

**Step 9.** The translated IPv4 packet is forwarded to the server.

**Step 10.** The www.ENSLD.com server replies to the NAT64 router.

**Step 11.** The NAT64 router receives the IPv4 packet and performs the following steps:

    **a.** The router checks that NAT64 translation states exist.

    **b.** If a translation state does not exist, the router discards the IPv4 packet.

    **c.** If the translation state exists, then the IPv4 header is translated into an IPv6 header, the IPv4 sources address is translated into an IPv6 source address by adding the IPv6 stateful NAT prefix, and the IPv4 destination address is translated into an IPv6 address by using the NAT64 translation state.

**Step 12.** IPv6 packets are forwarded back to the IPv6 client.

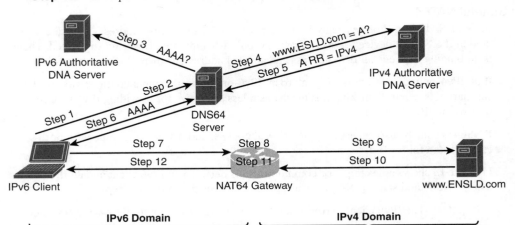

**Figure 2-13** *DNS64 and Stateful NAT64 Operation*

Table 2-12 provides a comparison of stateless and stateful NAT64.

**Table 2-12**   NAT64 Stateless and Stateful NAT64 Comparison

| Factor | Stateless | Stateful |
|---|---|---|
| Translation | 1:1 translation, which is limited in the number of endpoints | 1:many translation |
| Address conservation | No conservation of IPv4 addresses | Conserves IPv4 addresses |
| Address transparency | Helps ensure end-to-end transparency | Uses address overloading; lacks end-to-end address transparency |
| IPv6 address type | Requires IPv4-translatable IPv6 addresses | No requirement for the characteristics of IPv6 addresses |
| Address assignment | Requires manual or DHCPv6 address assignment | Can use manual address assignment, DHCPv6, or SLAAC |

## IPv6 Deployment Models

Deployment of IPv6 can be done in one of the following models:

- **Dual-stack model:** IPv4 and IPv6 coexist on hosts and on the network.

- **Hybrid model:** This model uses a combination of ISATAP or manually configured tunnels and dual-stack mechanisms.

- **Service block model:** This model uses a combination of ISATAP and manually configured tunnels and dual-stack mechanisms.

### Dual-Stack Model

In the dual-stack model, devices and the network routers and switches all run both IPv4 and IPv6 protocol stacks. The applications on the devices decide which stack to use to communicate with destination hosts. Alternatively, DNS is used to decide which stack to use. A DNS AAAA RR return uses IPv6, and a DNS A RR return uses IPv4. Because most mature operating systems now support IPv6, this is the preferred technique for transition to IPv6. Figure 2-14 shows a dual-stack network where both protocols reside. Older IPv4 sites that have not migrated to the dual-stack model can communicate throughout the network with other IPv4 devices.

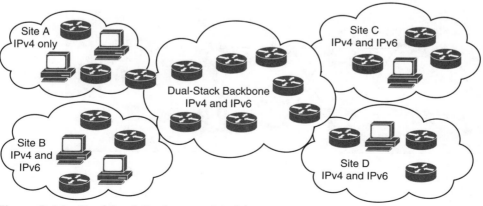

**Figure 2-14**   *Dual-Stack Deployment Model*

## Hybrid Model

The hybrid model uses a combination of transition mechanisms, depending on multiple network criteria, such as number of hosts, IPv6-capable hardware, and location of IPv6 services. The hybrid model can use these transition mechanisms:

- Dual-stack mechanism

- ISATAP

- Manually configured tunnels

The hybrid model can be used to tunnel a dual-stack host on an IPv4 access layer to an IPv6 core. As shown in Figure 2-15, the dual-stack computer establishes an ISATAP tunnel to the core layer to access services from the dual-stack server on the right.

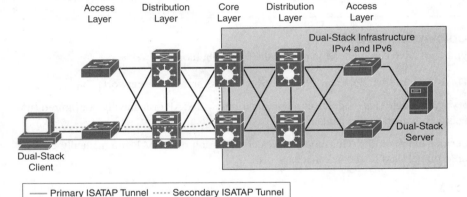

**Figure 2-15** *IPv6 Hybrid Model with ISATAP Tunnel*

Another scenario is to tunnel dual-stack distribution layers over an IPv4-only core. As shown in Figure 2-16, the dual-stack computer on the left can access the dual-stack server on the right via the manually configured tunnels. Multiple tunnels are configured to provide redundancy and load balancing.

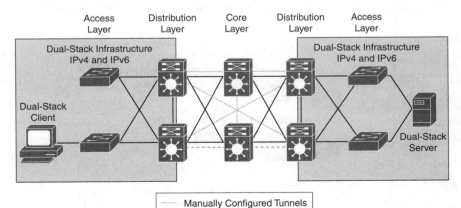

**Figure 2-16** *IPv6 Hybrid Model with Manually Configured Tunnels*

## Service Block Model

In the service block model, a centralized layer that services dual-stack devices is created with tunnels manually configured between the distribution layer and the service block. Dual-stack hosts also connect via ISATAP tunnels. In Figure 2-17, the dual-stack client on the left connects to the service block to establish connectivity with the dual-stack server on the right.

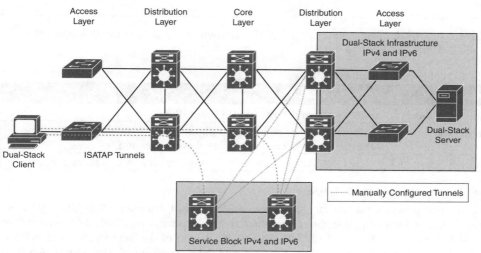

**Figure 2-17**   *Service Block Deployment Model*

## IPv6 Deployment Model Comparison

Table 2-13 summarizes the advantages and disadvantages of the IPv6 deployment models.

**Table 2-13**   IPv6 Deployment Model Comparison

| IPv6 Deployment Model | Advantages | Disadvantages |
|---|---|---|
| Dual-stack model | Tunneling not required. | Network equipment upgrades. |
| | Better processing performance. | |
| | IPv4 and IPv6 independent routing, QoS, security, and multicast policies. | |
| Hybrid model with ISATAP tunnel | Existing network can be leveraged with no upgrades. | IPv6 multicast not supported within ISATAP tunnels. |
| | | Terminating ISATAP tunnels in the core makes the core appear to be in IPv6 access layer. |
| Hybrid model with manually configured tunnels | IPv4 and IPv6 have independent routing, QoS, security, and multicast policies. | Many static tunnels, which makes it difficult to manage. |

| IPv6 Deployment Model | Advantages | Disadvantages |
|---|---|---|
| Server block model | Lesser impact on existing network. | Large amounts of tunneling. |
| | Flexible when controlling access to IPv6-enabled applications. | Cost of additional equipment. |

Table 2-14 provides simple descriptions of the deployment models. Study this table for the ENSLD 300-420 exam.

**Table 2-14** IPv6 Deployment Models

| Model | Description |
|---|---|
| Dual-stack model | All routers and hosts run IPv6 and IPv4. |
| Hybrid model | Uses ISATAP or manually configured tunnels to allow dual-stack clients to connect to dual-stack servers over an IPv4 core. |
| Service block model | Uses ISATAP and manually configured tunnels to a service module. |

## IPv6 Comparison with IPv4

This section provides a summary comparison of IPv6 to IPv4. For the ENSLD 300-420 exam, you should be knowledgeable about the characteristics summarized in Table 2-15. Some of the main differences are the use of 128 bits over 32 bits; the use of the Next Header field in IPv6 instead of the Protocol Type field used in IPv4; and the replacement of ARP with IPv6 ND.

**Table 2-15** IPv6 and IPv4 Characteristics

| Characteristic | IPv6 | IPv4 |
|---|---|---|
| Address length | 128 bits | 32 bits |
| Address representation | Hexadecimal | Dotted decimal |
| Header length | Fixed (40 bytes) | Variable |
| Upper-layer protocols | Next Header field | Protocol Type field |
| Link address resolution | ND | ARP |
| Address configuration | SLAAC or stateful DHCP | Stateful DHCP |
| DNS (name-to-address resolution) | AAAA records | A records |
| Interior routing protocols | EIGRPv6, OSPFv3, RIPng, IS-IS for IPv6 | EIGRP, OSPFv2, RIPv2, IS-IS |
| Classification and marking | Traffic Class and Flow Label fields, Differentiated Services Codepoint (DSCP) | IP Precedence bits, Type of Service field, DSCP |
| Private addresses | Unique local addresses | RFC 1918 private address space |
| Fragmentation | Sending host only | Sending host and intermediate routers |
| Loopback address | 0:0:0:0:0:0:0:1 | 127.0.0.1 |
| Address scope types | Unicast, anycast, multicast | Unicast, multicast, broadcast |

# References and Recommended Readings

RFC 363: *Representing Internet Protocol Version 6 (IPv6) Addresses in the Domain Name System (DNS)*, www.ietf.org/rfc.

RFC 1886: *DNS Extensions to Support IP Version 6*, www.ietf.org/rfc.

RFC 1981: *Path MTU Discovery for IP Version 6*, www.ietf.org/rfc.

RFC 2080: *RIPng for IPv6*, www.ietf.org/rfc.

RFC 2373: *IP Version 6 Addressing Architecture*, www.ietf.org/rfc.

RFC 2374: *An IPv6 Aggregatable Global Unicast Address Format*, www.ietf.org/rfc.

RFC 2401: *Security Architecture for the Internet Protocol*, www.ietf.org/rfc.

RFC 2402: *IP Authentication Header*, www.ietf.org/rfc.

RFC 2406: *IP Encapsulating Security Payload (ESP)*, www.ietf.org/rfc.

RFC 2460: *Internet Protocol, Version 6 (IPv6) Specification*, www.ietf.org/rfc.

RFC 2461: *Neighbor Discovery for IP Version 6 (IPv6)*, www.ietf.org/rfc.

RFC 2463: *Internet Control Message Protocol (ICMPv6) for the Internet Protocol Version 6 (IPv6) Specification*, www.ietf.org/rfc.

RFC 2545: *Use of BGP-4 Multiprotocol Extensions for IPv6 Inter-Domain Routing*, www.ietf.org/rfc.

RFC 2740: *OSPF for IPv6*, www.ietf.org/rfc.

RFC 2766: *Network Address Translation–Protocol Translation (NAT-PT)*, www.ietf.org/rfc.

RFC 2874: *DNS Extensions to Support IPv6 Address Aggregation and Renumbering*, www.ietf.org/rfc.

RFC 3014: *Privacy Extensions for Stateless Address Autoconfiguration in IPv6*, www.ietf.org/rfc.

RFC 3056: *Connection of IPv6 Domains via IPv4 Clouds*, www.ietf.org/rfc.

RFC 3315: *Dynamic Host Configuration Protocol for IPv6 (DHCPv6)*, www.ietf.org/rfc.

RFC 3513: *Internet Protocol Version 6 (IPv6) Addressing Architecture*, www.ietf.org/rfc.

RFC 3587: *IPv6 Global Unicast Address Format*, www.ietf.org/rfc.

RFC 3736: *Stateless Dynamic Host Configuration Protocol (DHCP) for IPv6*, www.ietf.org/rfc.

RFC 3849: *IPv6 Address Prefix Reserved for Documentation*, www.ietf.org/rfc.

RFC 3879: *Deprecating Site Local Addresses*, www.ietf.org/rfc.

RFC 4213: *Basic Transition Mechanisms for IPv6 Hosts and Routers*, https://tools.ietf.org/html/rfc4213.

RFC 4291: *IP Version 6 Addressing Architecture*, www.ietf.org/rfc.

RFC 4862: *IPv6 Stateless Address Autoconfiguration*, www.ietf.org/rfc.

RFC 5214: *Intra-Site Automatic Tunnel Addressing Protocol (ISATAP)*, www.ietf.org/rfc.

RFC 5308: *Routing IPv6 with IS-IS*, www.ietf.org/rfc.

RFC 5340: *OSFP for IPv6*, www.ietf.org/rfc.

RFC 5952: *A Recommendation for IPv6 Address Text Representation*, https://tools.ietf.org/html/rfc5952.

RFC 6052: *IPv6 Addressing of IPv4/IPv6 Translators*, https://tools.ietf.org/html/rfc6052.

RFC 6146: *Stateful NAT64: Network Address and Protocol Translation from IPv6 Clients to IPv4 Servers*, https://tools.ietf.org/html/rfc6146.

RFC 6147: *DNS64: DNS Extensions for Network Address Translation from IPv6 Clients to IPv4 Servers*, https://tools.ietf.org/html/rfc6147.

RFC 6296: *IPv6-to-IPv6 Network Prefix Translation*, www.ietf.org/rfc.

RFC 6845: *OSFP Hybrid Broadcast and Point-to-Multipoint Interface Type*, www.ietf.org/rfc.

RFC 6860: *Hiding Transit-Only Networks in OSPF*, www.ietf.org/rfc.

RFC 7136: *Significance of IPv6 Interface Identifiers*, https://tools.ietf.org/html/rfc7136.

RFC 7346: *IPv6 Multicast Address Scopes*, https://tools.ietf.org/html/rfc7346.

RFC 7371: *Updates to the IPv6 Multicast Addressing Architecture*, https://tools.ietf.org/html/rfc7371.

RFC 7381: *Enterprise IPv6 Deployment Guidelines*, https://tools.ietf.org/html/rfc7381.

RFC 7503: *OSPFv3 Autoconfiguration*, www.ietf.org/rfc.

RFC 7527: *Enhanced Duplicate Address Detection*, www.ietf.org/rfc.

RFC 7915: *IP/ICMP Translation Algorithm*, https://tools.ietf.org/html/rfc7915.

RFC 8064: *Recommendation on Stable IPv6 Interface Identifiers*, https://tools.ietf.org/html/rfc8064.

Doyle, J., and J. Carroll. *Routing TCP/IP, Volume I, 2nd edition*. Indianapolis: Cisco Press, 2005.

Doyle, J., and J. Carroll. *Routing TCP/IP, Volume II*. Indianapolis: Cisco Press, 2001.

Hopps, C. *Routing IPv6 for IS-IS (draft)*, www.simpleweb.org/ietf/internetdrafts/complete/draft-ietf-isis-ipv6-03.txt.

APNIC guidelines for IPv6 allocation and assignment requests, https://www.apnic.net/about-apnic/corporate-documents/documents/resource-guidelines/ipv6-guidelines/

ARIN, "IPv6 Information," https://www.arin.net/resources/guide/ipv6/.

Cisco, "Cisco IOS IPv6 Provider Edge Router (6PE) over MPLS," www.cisco.com/en/US/products/sw/iosswrel/ps1835/products_data_sheet09186a008052edd3.html.

2

Cisco, "IPv6 Integration in Federal Government: Adopt a Phased Approach for Minimal Disruption and Earlier Benefits," www.cisco.com/web/strategy/docs/gov/IPv6FedGov_wp.pdf.

Cisco, "IPv6 Extension Headers Review and Considerations," www.cisco.com/en/US/technologies/tk648/tk872/technologies_white_paper0900aecd8054d37d.html.

Cisco, "NAT64 Technology: Connecting IPv6 and IPv4 Networks," https://www.cisco.com/c/en/us/products/collateral/ios-nx-os-software/enterprise-ipv6-solution/white_paper_c11-676278.html.

Cisco, "Understanding IPv6 Link Local Address," http://www.cisco.com/c/en/us/support/docs/ip/ip-version-6-ipv6/113328-ipv6-lla.html.

IANA, "Protocol Numbers," https://www.iana.org/assignments/protocol-numbers/protocol-numbers.xhtml.

IANA, "Internet Protocol Version 6 Address Space," https://www.iana.org/assignments/ipv6-address-space/ipv6-address-space.xhtml.

Internet Society, "State of IPv6 Deployment 2018," https://www.internetsociety.org/resources/2018/state-of-ipv6-deployment-2018/.

IPv6 Forum, "Preparing an IPv6 Address Plan," http://www.ipv6forum.com/dl/presentations/IPv6-addressing-plan-howto.pdf.

ISATAP, "Intra-Site Automatic Tunnel Addressing Protocol (ISATAP)," www.isatap.org.

Microsoft, "Guidance for Configuring IPv6 in Windows for Advanced Users," https://support.microsoft.com/en-us/help/929852/guidance-for-configuring-ipv6-in-windows-for-advanced-users.

# Exam Preparation Tasks

As mentioned in the section "How to Use This Book" in the Introduction, you have a couple of choices for exam preparation: the exercises here, Chapter 13, "Final Preparation," and the exam simulation questions on the companion website.

## Review All Key Topics

Review the most important topics in the chapter, noted with the Key Topic icon in the outer margin of the page. Table 2-16 lists these key topics and the page number on which each is found.

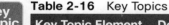

**Table 2-16**   Key Topics

| Key Topic Element | Description | Page |
|---|---|---|
| List | Enhancements of IPv6 over IPv4 | 48 |
| Paragraph | The fields of the IPv6 header | 49 |
| Table 2-2 | IP protocol numbers | 50 |
| Paragraph | IPv6 addresses | 50 |
| Table 2-3 | IPv6 prefix allocation | 53 |
| Paragraph | Unicast address types | 53 |

| Key Topic Element | Description | Page |
|---|---|---|
| Paragraph | Anycast address types | 56 |
| Paragraph | Multicast address types | 56 |
| Table 2-4 | Multicast scope assignments | 57 |
| Table 2-5 | Well-known IPv6 multicast addresses | 57 |
| Table 2-7 | IPv6 address prefixes | 58 |
| Paragraph | ICMPv6, IPv6 ND, and address resolution | 58 |
| List | Stateless autoconfiguration and stateful DHCP address assignment | 61 |
| Table 2-8 | IPv6 address autoconfiguration scheme | 63 |
| Table 2-9 | IPv6 mechanisms | 64 |
| List | Dual-stack, tunneling, and translation-transition mechanisms | 67 |
| Table 2-12 | NAT64 stateless and stateful NAT64 comparison | 73 |
| List | Dual-stack, hybrid, and service block deployment models | 73 |
| Table 2-13 | IPv6 deployment model comparison | 75 |
| Table 2-14 | IPv6 deployment models | 76 |
| Table 2-15 | IPv6 and IPv4 characteristics | 76 |

## Complete Tables and Lists from Memory

Print a copy of Appendix D, "Memory Tables," found on the companion website, or at least the section for this chapter, and complete the tables and lists from memory. Appendix E, "Memory Tables Answer Key," includes completed tables and lists to check your work.

## Define Key Terms

Define the following key terms from this chapter and check your answers in the glossary:

DNS64, Dynamic Host Configuration Protocol version 6 (DHCPv6), fully qualified domain name (FQDN), identifier (ID), Internet Assigned Numbers Authority (IANA), Internet Control Message Protocol version 6 (ICMPv6), Internet Protocol Security (IPsec), Intra-Site Automatic Tunnel Addressing Protocol (ISATAP), IPv6 Rapid Deployment (6RD), maximum transmission unit (MTU), Multiprotocol BGP (MP-BGP), NAT64, Neighbor Discovery (ND), Open Short Path First version 3 (OSPFv3), Routing Information Protocol next generation (RIPng)

## Q&A

The answers to these questions appear in Appendix A. For more practice with exam format questions, use the exam engine on the companion website.

**1.** True or false: OSPFv2 supports IPv6.

**2.** True or false: DNS AAAA records are used in IPv6 networks for name-to-IPv6 address resolution.

**3.** Fill in the blank: IPv6 ND is similar to _____ for IPv4 networks.

4. How many bits are there between the colons in an IPv6 address?

5. The first field of the IPv6 header is 4 bits in length. What binary number is it always set to?

6. True or false: DHCP is required for dynamic allocation of IPv6 addresses.

7. IPv6 multicast addresses begin with what hexadecimal prefix?

8. IPv6 link-local addresses begin with what hexadecimal prefix?

9. True or false: ISATAP allows tunneling of IPv6 through IPv4 networks.

10. List the eight fields of the IPv6 header.

11. Which of the following is not an IPv6 address type?

   a. Unicast

   b. Broadcast

   c. Anycast

   d. Multicast

12. True or false: The IPv6 address 2001:0:0:1234:0:0:0:abcd can be represented as 2001::1234:0:0:0:abcd and 2001:0:0:1234::abcd.

13. What is the subnet prefix of 2001:1:0:ab0:34:ab1:0:1/64?

14. An IPv6 address has 128 bits. How many hexadecimal numbers does an IPv6 address have?

15. What type of IPv6 address is FF01:0:0:0:0:0:0:2?

16. What is the compact format of the address 2102:0010:0000:0000:0000:fc23:0100:00ab?

   a. 2102:10::fc23:01:ab

   b. 2102:001::fc23:01:ab

   c. 2102:10::fc23:100:ab

   d. 2102:0010::fc23:01:ab

17. When using the dual-stack backbone, which of the following statements is correct?

   a. The backbone routers have IPv4/IPv6 dual stacks, and end hosts do not.

   b. The end hosts have IPv4/IPv6 dual stacks, and backbone routers do not.

   c. Both the backbone routers and the end hosts have IPv4/IPv6 dual stacks.

   d. Neither the backbone routers nor the end hosts have IPv4/IPv6 dual stacks.

18. How does a dual-stack host know which stack to use to reach a destination?

   a. It performs an ND, which returns the destination host type.

   b. It performs a DNS request to return the IP address. If the returned address is IPv4, the host uses the IPv4 stack. If the returned address is IPv6, the host uses the IPv6 stack.

   c. The IPv6 stack makes a determination. If the destination is IPv4, the packet is sent to the IPv4 stack.

   d. The IPv4 stack makes a determination. If the destination is IPv6, the packet is sent to the IPv6 stack.

**19.**   What protocol numbers are used by Ethernet to identify IPv4 versus IPv6?

    **a.**   Protocol 6 for IPv4 and protocol 17 for IPv6.

    **b.**   0x86DD for IPv6 and 0x0800 for IPv4.

    **c.**   0x8000 for IPv4 and 0x86DD for IPv6.

    **d.**   0x0800 for both IPv4 and IPv6; they are identified in the packet layer.

**20.**   Which of the following is true of the IPv6 header? (Choose two.)

    **a.**   It is 40 bytes in length.

    **b.**   It is of variable length.

    **c.**   The Protocol Number field describes the upper-layer protocol.

    **d.**   The Next Header field describes the upper-layer protocol.

**21.**   Which of the following is true about fragmentation?

    **a.**   Routers between source and destination hosts can fragment IPv4 and IPv6 packets.

    **b.**   Routers between source and destination hosts cannot fragment IPv4 and IPv6 packets.

    **c.**   Routers between source and destination hosts can fragment IPv6 packets only. IPv4 packets cannot be fragmented.

    **d.**   Routers between source and destination hosts can fragment IPv4 packets only. IPv6 packets cannot be fragmented.

**22.**   A packet sent to an anycast address reaches what?

    **a.**   The nearest destination in a set of hosts

    **b.**   All destinations in a set of hosts

    **c.**   All hosts

    **d.**   Global unicast destinations

**23.**   Which of the following is/are true about IPv6 and IPv4 headers?

    **a.**   The IPv6 header is of fixed length, and the Next Header field describes the upper-layer protocol.

    **b.**   The IPv4 header is of variable length, and the Protocol field describes the upper-layer protocol.

    **c.**   The IPv6 header is of fixed length, and the Protocol field describes the upper-layer protocol.

    **d.**   A and B

    **e.**   B and C

**24.**   An organization uses an IPv6 address range that it received from its ISP. The IPv6 addresses will be used internally, and employees will access the Internet by using Port Address Translation. What is required for DNS?

    **a.**   DNS servers need to support only IPv4 addresses.

    **b.**   DNS servers need to support only IPv6 addresses.

    **c.**   No changes are needed to the DNS servers.

    **d.**   DNS servers need to support both IPv4 and IPv6 addresses.

    **e.**   Additional DNS servers for IPv6 addresses are needed.

    **f.**   DNS servers are not needed for PAT.

**25.** Which statements about IPv6 addresses are true? (Choose two.)

    **a.**   Leading 0s are required.

    **b.**   Two colons (::) are used to separate fields.

    **c.**   Two colons (::) are used to represent successive hexadecimal fields of 0s.

    **d.**   A single interface will have multiple IPv6 addresses of different types.

**26.** You have duplicate file servers at multiple locations. Which IPv6 address type allows each end station to send a request to the nearest file server using the same destination address, regardless of the location of that end station?

    **a.**   Anycast

    **b.**   Broadcast

    **c.**   Unicast

    **d.**   Global unicast

    **e.**   Multicast

**27.** Which strategy allows both IPv4 and IPv6 addressing/stacks to coexist on a host and over time facilitate a transition to an IPv6-only network?

    **a.**   Deploy NAT64 between the networks.

    **b.**   Have hosts run IPv4 and routers run native IPv6.

    **c.**   Enable anycast in the routing protocol.

    **d.**   Deploy both IPv4 and IPv6 address stacks.

    **e.**   Redistribute between the IPv4 and IPv6 networks.

**28.** Which strategy would be most flexible for a corporation with the following characteristics?

    ■  2,400,000 hosts

    ■  11,000 routers

    ■  Internet connectivity

    ■  High volume of traffic with customers and business partners

    **a.**   Deploy NAT64 between the business and Internet networks.

    **b.**   Have hosts run IPv4 and routers run native IPv6.

    **c.**   Have both hosts and routers run dual-stack.

    **d.**   Enable anycast in the routing protocol.

    **e.**   Redistribute between the IPv4 and IPv6 networks.

**29.** What is the hierarchy for IPv6 aggregatable addresses?

    **a.**   Global, site, loop

    **b.**   Public, site, interface

    **c.**   Internet, site, interface

    **d.**   Multicast, anycast, unicast

**30.** NAT-PT translates between what address types?

    **a.** RFC 1918 private addresses and public IPv4 addresses

    **b.** IPv4 and IPv6 addresses

    **c.** Network addresses and IPv6 ports

    **d.** Private IPv6 addresses and public IPv6 addresses

**31.** In a network where IPv6 exists within an IPv4 network, which two strategies allow the two schemes to coexist? (Choose two.)

    **a.** Translate between the protocols.

    **b.** Have hosts run IPv4 and routers run native IPv6.

    **c.** Encapsulate IPv6 packets into IPv4 packets.

    **d.** Enable anycast in the routing protocol.

    **e.** Redistribute between the IPv4 and IPv6 networks.

**32.** Which IPv6 feature enables routing to distribute connection requests to the nearest content server?

    **a.** Anycast

    **b.** Link-local

    **c.** Aggregatable

    **d.** Multicast

    **e.** Site-local

**33.** Which statement best describes the efficiency of the IPv6 header?

    **a.** It is less efficient than the IPv4 header.

    **b.** It has the same efficiency as the IPv4 header; the larger IPv6 address makes it faster.

    **c.** It is more efficient than the IPv4 header.

    **d.** It is larger than the IPv4 header.

**34.** What of the following provides one-to-nearest communication for IPv6?

    **a.** Anycast

    **b.** Broadcast

    **c.** Multicast

    **d.** Unicast

**35.** Which tunneling protocol allows dual-stack hosts to tunnel over an IPv4 network that is not multicast enabled?

    **a.** 6to4

    **b.** 6over4

    **c.** IPsec

    **d.** ISATAP

**36.** How would you summarize the following networks?

2001:0db8:2a3e:4490::/64

2001:0db8: 2a3e:4a1b::/64

2001:0db8: 2a3e:4ff2::/64

2001:0db8: 2a3e:4c5b::/64

   **a.** 2001:0db8:2a3e:4000::/52

   **b.** 2001:0db8: 2a3e:4000::/56

   **c.** 2001:0db8: 2a3e:4000::/60

   **d.** 2001:0db8: 2a3e:4000::/64

**37.** Which statement is true of IPv6 address assignment?

   **a.** You should configure devices manually using IPv6 address assignment.

   **b.** You should configure servers using SLAAC.

   **c.** You should use SLAAC to assign IPv6 addresses and then DHCPv6 to assign additional information to hosts.

   **d.** You cannot use DHCPv6 after a host is assigned an IPv6 address via SLAAC.

**38.** Which IPv6 feature allows a single node to send packets that are routed to the nearest receiver from a group of potential receivers?

   **a.** Link-local

   **b.** Site-local

   **c.** Anycast

   **d.** Multicast

**39.** Which statement is correct?

   **a.** IPv6 does not use multicast addresses.

   **b.** IPv6 routers do not forward a packet that has a link-local source address.

   **c.** DHCPv6 is the only method for dynamic address assignment.

   **d.** IPv6 routers forward a packet that has a link-local destination address.

**40.** Which two link-state routing protocols support IPv6 routing? (Choose two.)

   **a.** RIPng

   **b.** OSPF

   **c.** EIGRP

   **d.** IS-IS

   **e.** BGP4+

**41.** Which are transition strategies to IPv6 for an enterprise network? (Choose three.)

   **a.** Dual-stack

   **b.** Top-down

   **c.** Tunneled

   **d.** Merge

   **e.** Translation

   **f.** Fork-lift

   **g.** Hybrid

**42.** How can an ISATAP packet be identified?

   **a.** The FF05/64 prefix is used.

   **b.** The fifth and sixth 16-bit words are 0000:5EFE.

   **c.** The 2002::/16 prefix is used.

   **d.** The FE80:/10 prefix is used.

**43.** If an application uses broadcast traffic for IPv4, how will it communicate using IPv6?

   **a.** Anycast

   **b.** Broadcast

   **c.** Multicast

   **d.** Unicast

**44.** What type of address begins with the prefix FC00::/?

   **a.** Local-link

   **b.** Broadcast

   **c.** Multicast

   **d.** Unique local unicast

**45.** Which IPv6 migration strategy is recommended if only a few IPv6 clients need to access network servers that support only IPv4?

   **a.** IPv4-mapped IPv6 addresses

   **b.** IPv6 over IPv4 GRE tunnels

   **c.** NAT64

   **d.** 6PE

**46.** Which is the correct representation of 2001:004C:0000:0000:9A:0000:0000:0001?

   **a.** 2001:4C::9A::1

   **b.** 2001:4C:0:0:9A::1

   **c.** 2001:4C:0:0:9A::1

   **d.** 2001:4C::9A:0:0:1

**47.** Which type of IPv6 address is ::FFFF:AA11/96?

   **a.** Global unicast address

   **b.** Link local address

   **c.** IPv4-compatible IPv6 address

   **d.** IPv4-mapped IPv6 address

**48.** Which translation mechanism is recommended to support flow-based translations for multiple IPv6 devices to a single IPv4 address?

   **a.** NAT4to6

   **b.** Stateful NAT46

   **c.** Stateful NAT64

   **d.** Stateless NAT64

**49.** Which tunnel solution allows an SP to provide IPv6 unicast service to its customers?

    **a.** GRE tunnels

    **b.** 6RD tunnels

    **c.** 6to4 tunnels

    **d.** ISATAP tunnels

**50.** What does a DNS64 server do if an IPv6 AAAA record is returned empty?

    **a.** Query the IPv4 DNS authoritative server.

    **b.** Query the IPv6 DNS authoritative server.

    **c.** Query the NAT64 server.

    **d.** Drop the packet since there is an IPv6 address.

**51.** An enterprise network designer wants to use the WKP 64:ff9b::/96 for NAT64 to reach servers outside the organization. Is this a viable solution?

    **a.** Yes, the NAT64 WKP 64:ff9b::/96 provides a globally unique solution.

    **b.** No, the NAT64 WKP 64:ff9b::/96 is not a globally routable prefix.

    **c.** Yes, define a NAT64 NSP.

    **d.** No, use the NAT WKP 2001:FF9b::/96 instead.

    **e.** Answers B and C are correct.

    **d.** Answers C and D are correct.

Questions 52 through 55 are based on the following scenario and Figure 2-18.

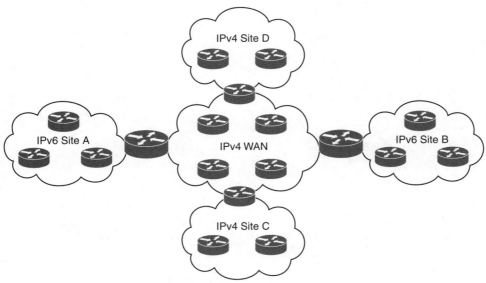

**Figure 2-18** *Company Adds Sites A and B*

A company has an existing WAN that uses IPv4. Sites C and D use IPv4. As shown in Figure 2-18, the company plans to add two new locations (Sites A and B). The new sites will implement IPv6. The company does not want to lease more WAN circuits.

**52.**   What options does the company have to connect Site A to Site B?

**53.**   What mechanism needs to be implemented so that IPv6 hosts can communicate with IPv4 hosts and vice versa?

**54.**   If a dual-stack backbone is implemented, do all WAN routers and all hosts need an IPv6/IPv4 dual stack?

**55.**   If an IPv4 tunnel is implemented between Sites A and B, do all WAN routers require an IPv6/IPv4 dual stack?

## CHAPTER 3

# Routing Protocol Characteristics, EIGRP, and IS-IS

## This chapter covers the following subjects:

**Routing Protocol Characteristics:** This section covers different characteristic of routing protocols, such as metrics, path calculation, and administrative distance.

**Routing Protocol Metrics and Loop Prevention:** This section focuses on the different metrics used by routing protocols.

**EIGRP:** This section covers characteristics and design considerations when using EIGRP.

**IS-IS:** This section covers characteristics and design considerations when using IS-IS.

This chapter provides an overview of the metrics used and other characteristics of routing protocols. This chapter also covers the Enhanced Interior Gateway Routing Protocol (EIGRP) and Intermediate System-to-Intermediate System (IS-IS) routing protocols in more detail. A CCNP enterprise designer must be knowledgeable about routing protocols, including EIGRP and ISIS.

This chapter covers the following objectives from the ENSLD 300-420 exam:

- Create stable, secure, and scalable routing designs for IS-IS
- Create stable, secure, and scalable routing designs for EIGRP

## "Do I Know This Already?" Quiz

The "Do I Know This Already?" quiz helps you identify your strengths and deficiencies in this chapter's topics. This quiz, derived from the major sections in the "Foundation Topics" portion of the chapter, helps you determine how to spend your limited study time. Table 3-1 outlines the major topics discussed in this chapter and the "Do I Know This Already?" quiz questions that correspond to those topics. You can find the answers in Appendix A, "Answers to the 'Do I Know This Already?' Quiz Questions Q&A Questions."

**Table 3-1** "Do I Know This Already?" Foundation Topics Section-to-Question Mapping

| Foundation Topics Section | Questions Covered in This Section |
|---|---|
| Routing Protocol Characteristics | 4, 7 |
| Routing Protocol Metrics and Loop Prevention | 6, 9 |
| EIGRP | 3, 7–10 |
| IS-IS | 1, 2, 5 |

1. What is the default metric for any interface for the IS-IS routing protocol?
    a. 5
    b. 10
    c. 70
    d. 100
2. Which type of routers are used to interconnect areas in IS-IS?
    a. Level 1 routers
    b. Level 2 routers
    c. Level 1/2 routers
    d. Level 2 routers and Level 1/2 routers
3. Which routing protocol is a distance-vector and classless protocol?
    a. RIPv2
    b. EIGRP
    c. OSPF
    d. IS-IS
4. Which type of routing protocol sends periodic routing updates?
    a. Static
    b. Distance-vector
    c. Link-state
    d. Hierarchical
5. Which routing protocol has a default metric of 10?
    a. OSPFv2
    b. IS-IS
    c. EIGRP
    d. BGPv4
6. Which of the following is true regarding routing metrics?
    a. If the metric is bandwidth, the path with the lowest bandwidth is selected.
    b. If the metric is bandwidth, the path with the highest bandwidth is selected.
    c. If the metric is bandwidth, the highest sum of the bandwidth is used to calculate the highest cost.
    d. If the metric is cost, the path with the highest cost is selected.
7. Both OSPF and EIGRP are enabled on a router with default values. Both protocols have a route to a destination network in their databases. Which route is entered into the routing table?
    a. The OSPF route is entered.
    b. The EIGRP route is entered.
    c. Both routes are entered with load balancing.
    d. Neither route is entered; an error has occurred.

**8.** Which is a route that satisfies the feasibility condition and is installed as a backup route?

**a.** The successor

**b.** The feasible successor

**c.** The reported successor

**d.** The backup successor

**9.** Which parameters are included in the computation of the EIGRP composite metric that is used by default?

**a.** Bandwidth and load

**b.** Bandwidth and delay

**c.** Bandwidth and reliability

**d.** Bandwidth and maximum transmission unit (MTU)

**10.** Which routing protocol implements the Diffusing Update Algorithm (DUAL)?

**a.** IS-IS

**b.** IGRP

**c.** EIGRP

**d.** OSPF

## Foundation Topics

This chapter covers the high-level characteristics of routing protocols and their metrics. You should be familiar with the different categories of routing protocols and their characteristics for the ENSLD 300-420 exam. Furthermore, this chapter covers the characteristics and design of the EIGRP and IS-IS routing protocols.

## Routing Protocol Characteristics

This section discusses the different types and characteristics of routing protocols.

Routing protocols have the following characteristics:

- **Distance-vector, link-state, or hybrid:** These types have to do with how routes are learned.

- **Interior or exterior:** Some protocols are used in private networks and others on the public Internet.

- **Classless (classless interdomain routing [CIDR] support) or classful:** CIDR enables aggregation of network advertisements (supernetting) between routers.

- **Fixed-length masks or variable-length subnet masking (VLSM):** Masking can be used to conserve addresses in a network.

- **Flat or hierarchical:** These factors are related to scalability in large internetworks.

- **IPv4 or IPv6:** Newer routing protocols are used for IPv6 networks.

This section covers the default administrative distances assigned to routes learned from each routing protocol and from static assignment. Routes are categorized as statically (manually) configured or dynamically learned from a routing protocol. The following sections cover all these characteristics.

## Static Versus Dynamic Route Assignment

Static routes are manually configured on a router. When configured manually and not learned from a neighbor, static routes do not react to network outages. The one exception is when a static route specifies the outbound interface or the IP address of the next hop is not resolved in the routing table. In this situation, if the interface goes down or the next hop IP address is not resolved in the routing table, the static route is removed from the routing table. Because static routes are unidirectional, they must be configured for each outgoing interface the router will use. The size of today's networks makes it impossible to manually configure and maintain all the routes in all the routers in a timely manner. Human configuration can involve many mistakes. Dynamic routing protocols were created to address these shortcomings. They use algorithms to advertise, learn about, and react to changes in the network topology.

The main benefit of static routing is that a router generates no routing protocol overhead. Because no routing protocol is enabled, no bandwidth is consumed by route advertisements between network devices. Another benefit of static routing is that static routing protocols are easier to configure and troubleshoot than dynamic routing protocols. Static routing is recommended for hub-and-spoke topologies with low-speed remote connections and where only a single path to the network exists. A default static route is configured at each remote site because the hub is the only route used to reach all other sites. Static routes are also used at network boundaries (the Internet or partners) where routing information is not exchanged. These static routes are then redistributed into the internal dynamic routing protocol used.

Figure 3-1 shows a hub-and-spoke WAN with static routes defined in the remote WAN routers because no routing protocols are configured. This setup eliminates routing protocol traffic on the low-bandwidth WAN circuits.

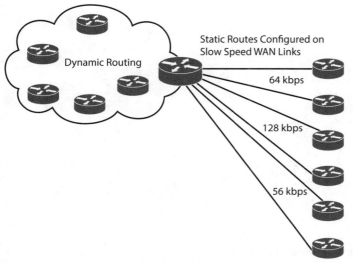

**Figure 3-1**   *Static Routes in a Bub-and-Spoke Network*

Routing protocols dynamically determine the best route to a destination. When the network topology changes, the routing protocol adjusts the routes without administrative intervention. Routing protocols use a metric to determine the best path toward a destination network. Some use a single measured value such as hop count. Others compute a metric value using one or more parameters. Routing metrics are discussed later in this chapter. The following is a list of dynamic routing protocols:

- RIPv1

- RIPv2

- EIGRP

- OSPF

- IS-IS

- RIPng

- OSPFv3

- EIGRP for IPv6

- Border Gateway Protocol (BGP)

## Interior Versus Exterior Routing Protocols

Routing protocols can be categorized as interior gateway protocols (IGPs) or exterior gateway protocols (EGPs). IGPs are meant for routing within an organization's administrative domain (in other words, the organization's internal network). EGPs are routing protocols used to communicate with exterior domains, where routing information is exchanged between administrative domains. Figure 3-2 shows where an internetwork uses IGPs and EGPs with multiple autonomous administrative domains. BGP exchanges routing information between the internal network and an ISP. IGPs appear in the internal private network.

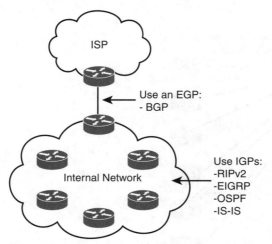

**Figure 3-2**   *Interior and Exterior Routing Protocols*

One of the first EGPs was called exactly that: Exterior Gateway Protocol. Today, BGP is the de facto (and the only available) EGP.

Potential IGPs for an IPv4 network are

- RIPv2

- OSPFv2

- IS-IS

- EIGRP

Potential IGPs for an IPv6 network are

- RIPng

- OSPFv3

- EIGRP for IPv6

- IS-IS

RIPv1 is no longer recommended because of its limitations. RIPv2 addresses many of the limitations of RIPv1 and is the most recent version of RIP. IGRP is an earlier version of EIGRP. RIPv1, RIPv2, and IGRP are not included on the ENSLD 300-420 exam blueprint. Table 3-2 provides a quick high-level summary of routing protocol uses.

**Table 3-2**  Routing Protocol Uses

| Routing Protocol | Description |
| --- | --- |
| BGP | Used to connect to an ISP. |
| OSPF | IGP used in enterprise networks. Supports large networks and is multivendor. |
| EIGRP | IGP used in large enterprise networks with Cisco routers. |
| IS-IS | Used in large enterprise networks and by service providers. |

## Distance-Vector Routing Protocols

The first IGP routing protocols introduced were distance-vector routing protocols. They used the Bellman-Ford algorithm to build routing tables. With distance-vector routing protocols, routes are advertised as vectors of distance and direction. The distance metric is usually router hop count. The direction is the next-hop router (IP address) toward which to forward the packet. For RIP, the maximum number of hops is 15, which can be a serious limitation, especially in large nonhierarchical internetworks.

Distance-vector algorithms call for each router to send its entire routing table to only its immediate neighbors. The table is sent periodically (every 30 seconds for RIP). In the period between advertisements, each router builds a new table to send to its neighbors at the end of the period. Because each router relies on its neighbors for route information, it is commonly said that distance-vector protocols "route by rumor." A 30 second wait for a new routing table with new routes is too long for today's networks. This is why distance-vector routing protocols have slow convergence.

RIPv2 and RIPng can send triggered updates—that is, full routing table updates sent before the update timer has expired. A router can receive a routing table with 500 routes with only one route change, which creates serious overhead on the network (another drawback). Furthermore, RFC 2091 updates RIP with triggered extensions to allow triggered updates with only route changes. Cisco routers support this on fixed point-to-point interfaces.

The following is a list of IP distance-vector routing protocols:

- RIPv1 and RIPv2

- EIGRP (which could be considered a hybrid)

- RIPng

### EIGRP

EIGRP is a hybrid routing protocol. It is a distance-vector protocol that implements some link-state routing protocol characteristics. Although EIGRP uses distance-vector metrics, it sends partial updates and maintains neighbor state information just as link-state protocols do. EIGRP does not send periodic updates as other distance-vector routing protocols do. The important thing to consider for the ENSLD 300-420 exam is that EIGRP could be presented as a hybrid protocol. EIGRP metrics and mechanisms are discussed in detail later in this chapter.

## Link-State Routing Protocols

Link-state routing protocols address some of the limitations of distance-vector protocols. When running a link-state routing protocol, routers originate information about themselves (IP addresses), their connected links (the number and types of links), and the state of those links (up or down). The information is flooded to all routers in the network as changes in the link state occur. Each router makes a copy of the information received and forwards it without change. Each router independently calculates the best path to each destination network by using Dijkstra's shortest path algorithm, creating a shortest path tree with itself as the root, and maintaining a map of the network.

After the initial exchange of information, link-state updates are not sent unless a change in the topology occurs. Routers do send small hello messages between neighbors to maintain neighbor relationships. If no updates have been sent, the link-state route database is refreshed after 30 minutes.

The following is a list of link-state routing protocols:

- OSPFv2

- IS-IS

- OSPFv3

OSPFv2 and OSPFv3 are covered in Chapter 4, "OSPF, BGP, and Route Manipulation."

## Distance-Vector Routing Protocols Versus Link-State Protocols

When choosing a routing protocol, consider that distance-vector routing protocols use more network bandwidth than link-state protocols. Distance-vector protocols generate more bandwidth overhead because of the large periodic routing updates. Link-state routing protocols do not generate significant routing update overhead but do use more router CPU and memory resources than distance-vector protocols. This occurs because with link-state routing protocols (generally speaking), WAN bandwidth is a more expensive resource than router CPU and memory in modern devices.

Table 3-3 compares distance-vector and link-state routing protocols.

**Table 3-3**   Distance-Vector Versus Link-State Routing Protocols

| Characteristic | Distance Vector | Link State |
|---|---|---|
| Scalability | Limited | Good |
| Convergence | Slow | Fast |
| Routing overhead | More traffic | Less traffic |
| Implementation | Easy | More complex |
| Protocols | RIPv1, RIPv2, EIGRP, RIPng | OSPF, IS-IS, OSPFv3 |

EIGRP is a distance-vector protocol with link-state characteristics (hybrid) that give it high scalability, fast convergence, less routing overhead, and relatively easy configuration. If "distance-vector" is not an answer to a question on the ENSLD 300-420 exam, then "hybrid" would be a valid option.

## Hierarchical Versus Flat Routing Protocols

Some routing protocols require a network topology that must have a backbone network defined. This network contains some or all of the routers in the internetwork. When the internetwork is defined hierarchically, the backbone consists of only some devices. Backbone routers service and coordinate the routes and traffic to or from routers not in the local internetwork. The supported hierarchy is relatively shallow. Two levels of hierarchy are generally sufficient to provide scalability. Selected routers forward routes into the backbone. OSPF and IS-IS are hierarchical routing protocols. By default, EIGRP is a flat routing protocol, but it can be configured with manual summarization to support hierarchical designs.

Flat routing protocols do not allow a hierarchical network organization. They propagate all routing information throughout the network without dividing or summarizing large networks into smaller areas. Carefully designing network addressing to naturally support aggregation within routing-protocol advertisements can provide many of the benefits offered by hierarchical routing protocols. Every router is a peer of every other router in flat routing protocols; no router has a special role in the internetwork. EIGRP, RIPv1, and RIPv2 are flat routing protocols.

## Classless Versus Classful Routing Protocols

Routing protocols can be classified based on their support of VLSM and CIDR. Classful routing protocols do not advertise subnet masks in their routing updates; therefore, the configured subnet mask for the IP network must be the same throughout the entire internetwork. Furthermore, the subnets must, for all practical purposes, be contiguous within the larger internetwork. For example, if you use a classful routing protocol for network 200.170.0.0, you must use the chosen mask (such as 255.255.255.0) on all router interfaces using the 200.170.0.0 network. You must configure serial links with only two hosts and LANs with tens or hundreds of devices with the same mask, 255.255.255.0. The big disadvantage of classful routing protocols is that the network designer cannot take advantage of address summarization across networks (CIDR) or allocation of smaller or larger subnets within an IP network (VLSM). For example, with a classful routing protocol that uses a default mask of /25 for the entire network, you cannot assign a /30 subnet to a serial point-to-point circuit. The following protocols are classful routing protocols:

- RIPv1

- IGRP (this protocol is not covered on the ENSLD 300-420 exam)

Classless routing protocols advertise the subnet mask with each route. You can configure subnetworks of a given IP network number with different subnet masks (using VLSM). You can configure large LANs with a smaller subnet mask and configure serial links with a larger subnet mask, thereby conserving IP address space. Classless routing protocols also allow flexible route summarization and supernetting (using CIDR). You can create supernets by aggregating classful IP networks. For example, 200.100.100.0/23 is a supernet of 200.100.100.0/24 and 200.100.101.0/24. The following protocols are classless routing protocols:

- RIPv2

- OSPF

- EIGRP

- IS-IS

- RIPng

- OSPFv3

- EIGRP for IPv6

- BGP

## IPv4 Versus IPv6 Routing Protocols

With the increasing use of the IPv6 protocol, a CCNP enterprise designer must be prepared to design networks using IPv6 routing protocols. As IPv6 was defined, routing protocols needed to be updated to support the new IP address structure. None of the IPv4 routing protocols support IPv6 networks, and none of the IPv6 routing protocols are backward compatible with IPv4 networks. But both protocols can coexist on the same network, each with its own routing protocol. Devices with dual stacks recognize which protocol is being used by the IP Version field in the IP header.

RIPng is the IPv6-compatible RIP routing protocol. EIGRP for IPv6 is the new version of EIGRP that supports IPv6 networks. OSPFv3 was developed for IPv6 networks, and OSPFv2 remains for IPv4 networks. Internet drafts were written to provide IPv6 routing using IS-IS. Multiprotocol extensions for BGP provide IPv6 support for BGP. Table 3-4 lists IPv4 and IPv6 routing protocols.

**Table 3-4**   IPv4 and IPv6 Routing Protocols

| IPv4 Routing Protocols | IPv6 Routing Protocols |
|---|---|
| RIPv2 | RIPng |
| EIGRP | EIGRP for IPv6 |
| OSPFv2 | OSPFv3 |
| IS-IS | IS-IS for IPv6 |
| BGP | Multiprotocol BGP |

## Administrative Distance

On Cisco routers running more than one routing protocol, it is possible for two different routing protocols to have a route to the same destination. Cisco routers assign each routing protocol an administrative distance. When multiple routes exist for a destination, the router selects the longest match. For example, to reach the destination 170.20.10.1, if OSPF has a route prefix of 170.20.10.0/24, and EIGRP has a route prefix of 170.20.0.0/16, the OSPF route is preferred because the /24 prefix is longer than the /16 prefix. This means it is more specific.

If two or more routing protocols offer the same route (with the same prefix length) for inclusion in the routing table, the Cisco IOS router selects the route with the lowest administrative distance.

The administrative distance is a rating of the trustworthiness of a routing information source. Table 3-5 shows the default administrative distances for configured (static) or learned routes. In the table, you can see that static routes are trusted over dynamically learned routes. With IGP routing protocols, EIGRP internal routes are trusted over OSPF, IS-IS, and RIP routes.

**Table 3-5**   Default Administrative Distances for IP Routes

| IP Route | Administrative Distance |
|---|---|
| Connected interface | 0 |
| Static route directed to a connected interface | 1 |
| Static route directed to an IP address | 1 |
| EIGRP summary route | 5 |
| External BGP route | 20 |
| Internal EIGRP route | 90 |
| IGRP route | 100 |
| OSPF route | 110 |
| IS-IS route | 115 |
| RIP route | 120 |
| EGP route | 140 |
| External EIGRP route | 170 |
| Internal BGP route | 200 |
| Route of unknown origin | 255 |

The administrative distance establishes the precedence used among routing algorithms. Suppose a router has an internal EIGRP route to network 172.20.10.0/24 with the best path out Ethernet 0 and an OSPF route for the same network out Ethernet 1. Because EIGRP has an administrative distance of 90 and OSPF has an administrative distance of 110, the router enters the EIGRP route in the routing table and sends packets with destinations of 172.20.10.0/24 out Ethernet 0.

Static routes have a default administrative distance of 1. You can configure static routes with a different distance by appending the distance value to the end of the command.

Table 3-6 provides a summary of routing protocol characteristics.

**Table 3-6**   Routing Protocol Characteristics

| Routing Protocol | Distance Vector or Link State | Interior or Exterior | Classful or Classless | Administrative Distance |
|---|---|---|---|---|
| RIPv2 | Distance vector | Interior | Classless | 120 |
| EIGRP | Distance vector (hybrid) | Interior | Classless | 90 (170 if external) |
| OSPF | Link state | Interior | Classless | 110 |
| IS-IS | Link state | Interior | Classless | 115 |
| BGP | Path vector | Both | Classless | 20 (200 if internal) |

# Routing Protocol Metrics and Loop Prevention

Routing protocols use metrics to determine best routes to a destination. Some routing protocols use a combination of metrics to build a composite metric for best path selection. This section describes metrics and covers routing loop-prevention techniques. You must understand each metric for the ENSLD 300-420 exam.

The following are some common routing metric parameters:

- Hop count

- Bandwidth

- Cost

- Load

- Delay

- Reliability

- Maximum transmission unit (MTU)

## Hop Count

The hop count parameter counts the number of links between routers that a packet must traverse to reach a destination. The RIP routing protocol uses hop count as the metric for route selection. If all links were the same bandwidth, this metric would work well. The problem with routing protocols that use only this metric is that the shortest hop count is not always the most appropriate path. For example, between two paths to a destination network—one with two 56 kbps links and another with four T1 links—the router chooses the first path because of the lower number of hops (see Figure 3-3). However, this is not necessarily the best path. You would prefer to transfer a 20 MB file via the T1 links rather than the 56 kbps links.

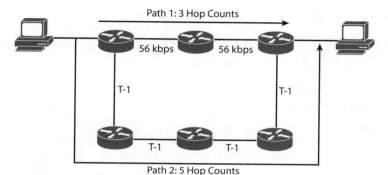

**Figure 3-3**  *Hop Count Metric*

## Bandwidth

The bandwidth parameter uses the interface bandwidth to determine the best path to a destination network. When bandwidth is the metric, the router prefers the path with the highest bandwidth to a destination. For example, a Fast Ethernet (100 Mbps) link is preferred over a DS-3 (45 Mbps) link. As shown in Figure 3-3, a router using bandwidth to determine a path would select Path 2 because of the greater bandwidth (1.5 Mbps over 56 kbps).

If a routing protocol uses only bandwidth as the metric and the path has several different speeds, the protocol can use the lowest speed in the path to determine the bandwidth for the path. EIGRP and IGRP use the minimum path bandwidth, inverted and scaled, as one part of the metric calculation. In Figure 3-4, Path 1 has two segments, with 256 kbps and 512 kbps of bandwidth. Because the smaller speed is 256 kbps, this speed is used as Path 1's bandwidth. The smallest bandwidth in Path 2 is 384 kbps. When the router has to choose between Path 1 and Path 2, it selects Path 2 because 384 kbps is larger than 256 kbps.

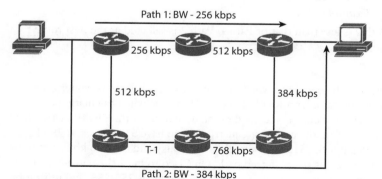

**Figure 3-4**  *Bandwidth Metric Example*

## Cost

Cost is the metric used by OSPF and IS-IS. In OSPF on a Cisco router, a link's default cost is derived from the interface's bandwidth. Cisco's implementation of IS-IS assigns a default cost of 10 to all interfaces.

The formula to calculate cost in OSPF is

$$10^8/BW$$

where BW is the interface's default or configured bandwidth.

For 10 Mbps Ethernet, cost is calculated as follows:

BW = 10 Mbps = $10 \times 10^6$ = 10,000,000 = $10^7$

cost (Ethernet) = $10^8/10^7$ = 10

The sum of all the costs to reach a destination is the metric for that route. The lowest cost is the preferred path.

The path cost is the sum of all costs in the path. Figure 3-5 shows an example of how the path costs are calculated. The cost for Path 1 is 350 + 180 = 530. The cost for Path 2 is 15 + 50 + 100 + 50 = 215.

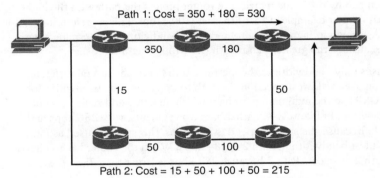

**Figure 3-5** *Cost Metric Example*

Because the cost of Path 2 is less than that of Path 1, Path 2 is selected as the best route to the destination.

## Load

The load parameter refers to the degree to which the interface link is busy. A router keeps track of interface utilization; routing protocols can use this metric when calculating the best route. Load is one of the five parameters included in the definition of the EIGRP metric. By default, it is not used to calculate the composite metric. If you have 512 kbps and 256 kbps links to reach a destination, but the 512 kbps circuit is 99% busy and the 256 kbps circuit is only 5% busy, the 256 kbps link is the preferred path. On Cisco routers, the percentage of load is shown as a fraction over 255. Utilization at 100% is shown as 255/255, and utilization at 0% is shown as 0/255. Example 3-1 shows the load of a serial interface at 5/255 (1.9%).

**Example 3-1**  *Interface Load*

```
router3>show interface serial 1
Serial1 is up, line protocol is up
  Hardware is PQUICC Serial
  Internet address is 10.100.1.1/24
  MTU 1500 bytes, BW 1544 Kbit, DLY 20000 usec, rely 255/255, load 5/255
```

## Delay

The delay parameter refers to how long it takes to move a packet to the destination. Delay depends on many factors, such as link bandwidth, utilization, port queues, and physical distance traveled. Total delay is one of the five parameters included in the definition of the EIGRP composite metric. By default, it is used to calculate the composite metric. You can configure an interface's delay with the **delay** *tens-of-microseconds* command, where *tens-of-microseconds* specifies the delay, in tens of microseconds, for an interface or network segment. The interface delay can be checked with the **show interface** command. In Example 3-2, the interface's delay is 20,000 microseconds.

**Example 3-2**  *Interface Delay*

```
router3>show interface serial 1
Serial1 is up, line protocol is up
  Hardware is PQUICC Serial
  Internet address is 10.100.1.1/24
  MTU 1500 bytes, BW 1544 Kbit, DLY 20000 usec, rely 255/255, load 1/255
```

## Reliability

The reliability parameter is the dependability of a network link. Some WAN links tend to go up and down throughout the day. These links get a small reliability rating. Reliability is measured by factors such as a link's expected received keepalives and the number of packet drops and interface resets. If the ratio is high, the line is reliable. The best rating is 255/255, which is 100% reliability. Reliability is one of the five parameters included in the definition of the EIGRP metric. By default, it is not used to calculate the composite metric. As shown in Example 3-3, you can verify an interface's reliability by using the **show interface** command.

**Example 3-3**  *Interface Reliability*

```
router4#show interface serial 0
Serial0 is up, line protocol is up
  Hardware is PQUICC Serial
  MTU 1500 bytes, BW 1544 Kbit, DLY 20000 usec, rely 255/255, load 1/255
```

## Maximum Transmission Unit

The MTU parameter is simply the maximum size of bytes a unit can have on an interface. If the outgoing packet is larger than the MTU, the IP protocol might need to fragment it. If a packet larger than the MTU has the Do Not Fragment flag set, the packet is dropped. As shown in Example 3-4, you can verify an interface's MTU by using the **show interface** command.

**Example 3-4** *Interface MTU*

```
router4#show interface serial 0
Serial0 is up, line protocol is up
  Hardware is PQUICC Serial
  MTU 1500 bytes, BW 1544 Kbit, DLY 20000 usec, rely 255/255, load 1/255
```

## Routing Loop-Prevention Schemes

Some routing protocols employ schemes to prevent the creation of routing loops in the network. The following are the commonly used loop-prevention schemes:

- Split horizon

- Poison reverse

- Counting to infinity

### Split Horizon

Split horizon is a technique used by distance-vector routing protocols to prevent routing loops. Routes that are learned from a neighboring router are not sent back to that neighboring router, thus suppressing the route. If the neighbor is already closer to the destination, it already has a better path.

In Figure 3-6, Routers 1, 2, and 3 learn about Networks A, B, C, and D. Router 2 learns about Network A from Router 1 and also has Networks B and C in its routing table. Router 3 advertises Network D to Router 2. Now, Router 2 knows about all networks. Router 2 sends its routing table to Router 3 without the route for Network D because it learned that route from Router 3.

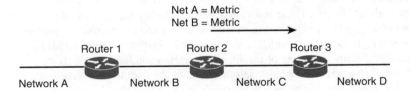

**Figure 3-6** *Simple Split-Borizon Example*

### Poison Reverse

Poison reverse is a route update sent out an interface with an infinite metric for routes learned (received) from the same interface. Poison reverse simply indicates that the learned route is unreachable. It is more reliable than split horizon alone. Examine Figure 3-7. Instead of suppressing the route for Network D, Router 2 sends that route in the routing table marked as unreachable. In RIP, the poison-reverse route is marked with a metric of 16 (infinite) to prevent that path from being used.

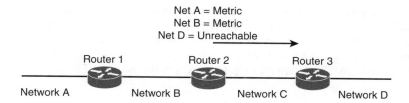

With Poison Reverse, Router 2 sends Net A
and Net B routes to Router 3; also, a
route for Net D is sent with an infinite metric.

**Figure 3-7**  *Poison Reverse*

## Counting to Infinity

Some routing protocols keep track of router hops as a packet travels through the network. In large networks where a routing loop might be present because of a network outage, routers might forward a packet without it reaching its destination.

Counting to infinity is a loop-prevention technique in which the router discards a packet when it reaches a maximum limit. It assumes that the network diameter is smaller than the maximum allowed hops. RIP has a maximum of 16 hops, and EIGRP has a maximum of 100 hops by default. Maximum values are considered infinity.

## Triggered Updates

Another loop-prevention and fast-convergence technique used by routing protocols is triggered updates. When a router interface changes state (up or down), the router is required to send an update message, even if it is not time for the periodic update message. Immediate notification about a network outage is key to maintaining valid routing entries in all routers in the network by allowing faster convergence. Some distance-vector protocols, including RIP, specify a small delay to avoid having triggered updates generate excessive network traffic. The time delay is variable for each router.

## Summarization

Another characteristic of routing protocols is the ability to summarize routes. Protocols that support VLSM can perform summarization outside IP class boundaries. By summarizing, a routing protocol can reduce the size of the routing table, and fewer routing updates occur on the network.

# EIGRP

Cisco Systems released EIGRP in the early 1990s as an evolution of IGRP toward a more scalable routing protocol for large internetworks. EIGRP is a classless protocol that permits the use of VLSM and that supports CIDR for the scalable allocation of IP addresses. EIGRP does not send routing updates periodically, as does IGRP. EIGRP allows for authentication with MD5. EIGRP autosummarizes networks at network borders and can load share over unequal-cost paths. Packets using EIGRP use IP number 88. Only Cisco routers use EIGRP. However, Cisco has released EIGRP as an IETF draft, so it might be possible that other vendors will implement EIGRP in their network devices.

EIGRP is an advanced distance-vector protocol that implements some characteristics similar to those of link-state protocols. Some Cisco documentation refers to EIGRP as a hybrid protocol. EIGRP advertises its routing table to its neighbors as distance-vector protocols do, but it uses hellos and forms neighbor relationships as link-state protocols do. EIGRP sends partial updates when a metric or the topology changes on the network. It does not send full routing table updates in periodic fashion as do distance-vector protocols. EIGRP uses Diffusing Update Algorithm (DUAL) to determine loop-free paths to destinations. This section discusses DUAL.

By default, EIGRP load balances traffic if several paths have an equal cost to the destination. EIGRP performs unequal-cost load sharing if you configure it with the **variance** *n* command. EIGRP includes routes that are equal to or less than *n* times the minimum metric route to a destination. Like RIP and IGRP, EIGRP also summarizes IP networks at network boundaries.

EIGRP internal routes have an administrative distance of 90. EIGRP summary routes have an administrative distance of 5, and EIGRP external routes (from redistribution) have an administrative distance of 170.

## EIGRP Components

EIGRP is characterized by four components:

- Protocol-dependent modules
- Neighbor discovery and recovery
- Reliable Transport Protocol (RTP)
- Diffusing Update Algorithm (DUAL)

You should know the role of the EIGRP components, which are described in the following sections.

### Protocol-Dependent Modules

EIGRP uses different modules that independently support IP—and even the older Internetwork Packet Exchange (IPX) and AppleTalk routing protocols. These modules are the logical interface between DUAL and routing protocols such as IPX RIP and AppleTalk Routing Table Maintenance Protocol (RTMP). The EIGRP module sends and receives packets but passes received information to DUAL, which makes routing decisions.

When configured to support IPX, EIGRP communicates with the IPX RIP and forwards the route information to DUAL to select the best paths. AppleTalk EIGRP automatically redistributes routes with AppleTalk RTMP to support AppleTalk networks. IPX and AppleTalk are not covered on the ENSLD 300-420 exam and are therefore not covered in this book.

### Neighbor Discovery and Recovery

EIGRP discovers and maintains information about its neighbors. EIGRP neighbors exchange the entire routing table when forming an adjacency. Incremental updates are advertised only when topology changes occur. EIGRP multicasts hello packets (224.0.0.10) every 5 seconds on most interfaces. The router builds a table with EIGRP neighbor information. The holdtime to maintain a neighbor is three times the hello time: 15 seconds. If the router does not receive a hello in 15 seconds, it removes the neighbor from the table. EIGRP multicasts hellos every 60 seconds on multipoint WAN interfaces (that is, X.25, Frame Relay, ATM) with speeds less than a T1 (1.544 Mbps), inclusive. The neighbor holdtime is 180 seconds on these types of interfaces. To summarize, hello/holdtime timers are 5/15 seconds for high-speed links and 60/180 seconds for low-speed links.

Example 3-5 shows an EIGRP neighbor database. The table in this example lists the neighbor's IP address, the interface to reach it, the neighbor holdtime timer, and the uptime.

**Example 3-5**   *EIGRP Neighbor Database*

```
Router# show ip eigrp neighbor
IP-EIGRP neighbors for process 100
H  Address           Interface    Hold Uptime  SRTT RTO Q    Seq Type
                     c            (sec)        (ms)     Cnt  Num
1 172.17.1.1         Se0          11 00:11:27  16   200 0    2
0 172.17.2.1         Et0          12 00:16:11  22   200 0    3
```

## RTP

EIGRP uses RTP to manage EIGRP packets. RTP ensures the reliable delivery of route updates and uses sequence numbers to ensure ordered delivery. It sends update packets using multicast address 224.0.0.10. It acknowledges updates using unicast hello packets with no data.

## DUAL

EIGRP implements DUAL to select paths and guarantee freedom from routing loops. J.J. Garcia Luna-Aceves developed DUAL, which is mathematically proven to result in a loop-free topology, providing no need for periodic updates or route holddown mechanisms that make convergence slower.

DUAL selects a best path and a second-best path to reach a destination. The successor route is the route with the lowest path metric to reach a destination. The successor is the first next-hop router for the successor route. The best path selected by DUAL is the successor, and the second-best path (if available) is the feasible successor. The feasible successor is a route that satisfies the feasibility condition and is maintained as a backup route.

The reported distance (RD) is the distance reported by a route to reach a prefix. The feasible distance (FD) is the lowest calculated metric of a path to reach the destination. A feasibility condition exists for a route to be considered a backup route where the RD received for that route must be less than the FD calculated on the local router.

Table 3-7 summarizes EIGRP terminology.

**Table 3-7**   Default EIGRP Values for Bandwidth and Delay

| EIGRP Term | Definition |
|---|---|
| Successor route | The route with the lowest metric to reach a destination. |
| Successor | The first next-hop router for the successor route. |
| Feasible distance (FD) | The best metric along a path to a destination network, including the metric to the neighbor advertising that path. |
| Reported distance (RD) | The total metric along a path to a destination network, as advertised by an upstream neighbor. |
| Feasibility condition | A condition in which the reported distance received for a route is less than the feasible distance calculated locally, thus making it a backup route. |
| Feasible successor | A route that satisfies the feasibility condition and is maintained as a backup route. |

The topology table in Example 3-6 shows the feasible distance. The example also shows two paths (Ethernet 0 and Ethernet 1) to reach 172.16.4.0/30. Because the paths have different metrics, DUAL chooses only one successor.

**Example 3-6**   *Feasible Distance, as Shown in the EIGRP Topology Table*

```
Router8# show ip eigrp topology
IP-EIGRP Topology Table for AS(100)/ID(172.16.3.1)


Codes: P - Passive, A - Active, U - Update, Q - Query, R - Reply,
       r - reply Status, s - sia Status


P 172.16.4.0/30, 1 successors, FD is 2195456
          via 172.16.1.1 (2195456/2169856), Ethernet0
          via 172.16.5.1 (2376193/2348271), Ethernet1
P 172.16.1.0/24, 1 successors, FD is 281600
          via Connected, Ethernet0
```

The route entries in Example 3-6 are marked with a P for the passive state. A destination is in passive state when the router is not performing recomputations for the entry. If the successor goes down and the route entry has feasible successors, the router does not need to perform recomputations and does not go into active state.

DUAL places the route entry for a destination into active state if the successor goes down and there are no feasible successors. EIGRP routers send query packets to neighboring routers to find a feasible successor to the destination. A neighboring router can send a reply packet that indicates it has a feasible successor or a query packet. The query packet indicates that the neighboring router does not have a feasible successor and will participate in the recomputation. A route does not return to passive state until it has received a reply packet from each neighboring router. If the router does not receive all the replies before the "active-time" timer expires, DUAL declares the route as stuck in active (SIA). The default active timer is 3 minutes.

Table 3-8 summarizes EIGRP route states.

**Table 3-8**   EIGRP Route States

| EIGRP Route State | Definition |
| --- | --- |
| Active | The current successor no longer satisfies the feasibility condition, and there are no feasible successors identified for that destination. The router is in the query process to find a loop-free alternative route. |
| Passive | The router has identified successors to a destination. The router is not performing a recomputation. |
| Stuck-in-active | The router that issued the query gives up and clears its connection to the router that is not answering, effectively restarting the neighbor session. |

## EIGRP Timers

EIGRP sends updates only when necessary and sends them only to neighboring routers. There is no periodic update timer.

EIGRP uses hello packets to learn of neighboring routers. On high-speed networks, the default hello packet interval is 5 seconds. On multipoint networks with link speeds of T1 and slower, hello packets are unicast every 60 seconds.

The holdtime to maintain a neighbor adjacency is three times the hello time: 15 seconds. If a router does not receive a hello within the holdtime, it removes the neighbor from the table. Hellos are multicast every 60 seconds on multipoint WAN interfaces with speeds less than 1.544 Mbps, inclusive. The neighbor holdtime is 180 seconds on these types of interfaces. To summarize, hello/holdtime timers are 5/15 seconds for high-speed links and 60/180 seconds for multipoint WAN links less than 1.544 Mbps, inclusive.

> **Note**   EIGRP does not send updates using a broadcast address; instead, it sends them to the multicast address 224.0.0.10 (all EIGRP routers). It also can send any updates using unicast packets if the **neighbor** command is used.

## EIGRP Metrics

EIGRP uses the same composite metric as IGRP, but the bandwidth (BW) term is multiplied by 256 for finer granularity. The composite metric is based on bandwidth, delay, load, and reliability. MTU is not an attribute for calculating the composite metric.

EIGRP calculates the composite metric with the following formula:

$$\text{EIGRP}_{metric} = \{k1 \times BW + [(k2 \times BW)/(256 - load)] + k3 \times delay\} \times \{k5/(reliability + k4)\}$$

In this formula, BW is the lowest interface bandwidth in the path, and delay is the sum of all outbound interface delays in the path. The router dynamically measures reliability and load. It expresses 100% reliability as 255/255. It expresses load as a fraction of 255. An interface with no load is represented as 1/255.

Bandwidth is the inverse minimum bandwidth (in kbps) of the path, in bits per second, scaled by a factor of $256 \times 10^7$. The formula for bandwidth is

$$(256 \times 10^7)/BW_{min}$$

The delay is the sum of the outgoing interface delays (in tens of microseconds) to the destination. A delay of all 1s (that is, a delay of hexadecimal FFFFFFFF) indicates that the network is unreachable. The formula for delay is

$$\text{sum\_of\_delays} \times 256$$

Reliability is a value between 1 and 255. Cisco IOS routers display reliability as a fraction of 255. That is, 255/255 is 100% reliability, or a perfectly stable link; a value of 229/255 represents a 90% reliable link.

Load is a value between 1 and 255. A load of 255/255 indicates a completely saturated link. A load of 127/255 represents a 50% saturated link.

By default, k1 = k3 = 1 and k2 = k4 = k5 = 0. EIGRP's default composite metric, adjusted for scaling factors, is

$$\text{EIGRP}_\text{metric} = 256 \times \{\, [10^7/\text{BW}_\text{min}] + [\text{sum\_of\_delays}] \,\}$$

$\text{BW}_\text{min}$ is in kbps, and sum_of_delays is in tens of microseconds. The bandwidth and delay for an Ethernet interface are 10 Mbps and 1 ms, respectively.

The calculated EIGRP BW metric is

$256 \times 10^7/\text{BW} = 256 \times 10^7/10,000$

$= 256 \times 1000$

$= 256,000$

The calculated EIGRP delay metric is

$256 \times \text{sum of delay} = 256 \times 1 \text{ ms}$

$= 256 \times 1000 \times 1 \text{ microseconds}$

$= 256,000 \text{ microseconds}$

Table 3-9 shows some default values for bandwidth and delay.

**Table 3-9**   Default EIGRP Classic Metric Values

| Media Type | Delay | Bandwidth | Metric |
| --- | --- | --- | --- |
| 10 Gigabit Ethernet | 10 μs | 10,000 Mbps | 512 |
| Gigabit Ethernet | 10 μs | 1,000 Mbps | 2816 |
| Fast Ethernet | 100 μs | 100 Mbps | 28,160 |
| Ethernet | 1000 μs | 10 Mbps | 281,600 |
| T1 (1.544 Mbps) | 20,000 μs | 1544 kbps | 2,170,031 |
| 64 kbps | 512,000 μs | 64 kbps | 53,107,200 |

The **metric weights** subcommand is used to change EIGRP metric computation. You can change the k values in the EIGRP composite metric formula to select which EIGRP metrics to use. The command to change the k values is the **metric weights tos** *k1 k2 k3 k4 k5* subcommand under **router eigrp** *n*. The **tos** value is always 0. You set the other arguments to 1 or 0 to alter the composite metric. For example, if you want the EIGRP composite metric to use all the parameters, the command is as follows:

```
router eigrp n
 metric weights 0 1 1 1 1 1
```

## EIGRP Packet Types

EIGRP uses five packet types:

- **Hello:** EIGRP uses hello packets in the discovery of neighbors. They are multicast to 224.0.0.10. By default, EIGRP sends hello packets every 5 seconds (60 seconds on WAN links with 1.544 Mbps speeds or less).

- **Acknowledgment:** An acknowledgment packet acknowledges the receipt of an update packet. It is a hello packet with no data. EIGRP sends acknowledgment packets to the unicast address of the sender of the update packet.

- **Update:** Update packets contain routing information for destinations. EIGRP unicasts update packets to newly discovered neighbors; otherwise, it multicasts update packets to 224.0.0.10 when a link or metric changes. Update packets are acknowledged to ensure reliable transmission.

- **Query:** EIGRP sends query packets to find feasible successors to a destination. Query packets are always multicast unless they are sent as a response; then they are unicast back to the originator.

- **Reply:** EIGRP sends reply packets to respond to query packets. Reply packets provide a feasible successor to the sender of the query. Reply packets are unicast to the sender of the query packet.

## EIGRP Design

When designing a network with EIGRP, remember that it supports VLSM and network summarization. EIGRP allows for the summarization of routes in a hierarchical network. EIGRP is not limited to 16 hops as RIP is; therefore, the network diameter can exceed this limit. In fact, the EIGRP diameter can be 225 hops. The default diameter is 100. EIGRP can be used in site-to-site WANs and IPsec virtual private networks (VPNs). In the enterprise campus, EIGRP can be used in data centers, server distribution, building distribution, and the network core.

EIGRP does not broadcast its routing table periodically, so there is no large network overhead. You can use EIGRP for large networks; it is a potential routing protocol for the core of a large network. EIGRP further provides for route authentication.

As shown in Figure 3-8, when you use EIGRP, all segments can have different subnet masks.

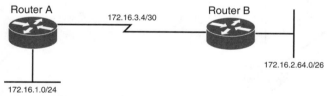

**Figure 3-8**    *EIGRP Design*

EIGRP is suited for almost all enterprise environments, including LANs and WANs, and is simple to design. The only caveat is that it is a Cisco-proprietary routing protocol that cannot be used with routers from other vendors. The use of EIGRP is preferred over RIP in all environments.

## EIGRP Stub Routers

EIGRP allows for the configuration of stub routers for remote branches. It is used to reduce EIGRP query traffic between hub routers and remote branch routers that are connected over WAN links. EIGRP stub routing conserves memory and CPU resources and improves network stability. When the stub routing feature is enabled on the spoke router, the router only advertises specified routes to the hub router. The router does not advertise routes received from other EIGRP neighbors to the hub router. The only disadvantage is that the stub router cannot be used as a backup path between two hub sites.

Figure 3-9 shows an example of EIGRP stub router operation. If the LAN 10.10.10.0/24 goes down, the Hub1 router sends query packets everywhere; however, there is no need to send query packets to stub branches because there are no alternate routes there. Once you configure the branch routers as EIGRP stub routers, the query is sent only to the Hub2 router.

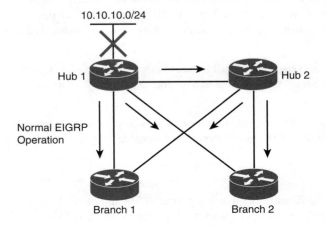

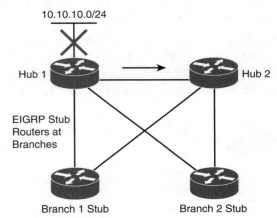

**Figure 3-9**   *EIGRP Stub Routers*

There are a few options when configuring the EIGRP stub routers:

- **Receive-only:** The stub router does not advertise network.

- **Connected:** The stub router can advertise directly connected networks.

- **Static:** The stub router can advertise static routes.

- **Summary:** The stub router can advertise summary routes.

- **Redistribute:** The stub router can advertise redistributed routes.

### EIGRP Variance Command

EIGRP allows unequal-cost routing with the use of the **variance #** command. If you have an active route with a metric of 10 and have feasible successors of 15, 25, and 55, you can adjust the variance number to make those routes active. If you use **variance 2**, then the active metric of 10 gets multiplied by 2, which equals 20. Any feasible successor less than 20 gets added as an active route. The route with a metric of 15 is added, so you have two active routes.

If you use **variance 3**, the routes with metrics of 10, 15, and 25 become active (3 × 10 = 30). Note that for this example, using a variance of 4 or 5 does not add the route with a metric of 55. You need to use a variance of 6 to add the route with a metric of 55 (6 × 10 = 60).

## EIGRP for IPv4 Summary

The characteristics of EIGRP for IPv4 are as follows:

- EIGRP for IPv4 is a hybrid routing protocol (a distance-vector protocol that has link-state protocol characteristics).

- EIGRP for IPv4 uses IP protocol number 88.

- EIGRP for IPv4 is a classless protocol; it supports VLSM.

- The default composite metric uses bandwidth and delay.

- You can factor load and reliability into the metric.

- EIGRP for IPv4 sends partial route updates only when there are changes.

- EIGRP for IPv4 supports MD5 authentication.

- EIGRP for IPv4 uses DUAL for loop prevention.

- EIGRP for IPv4 provides fast convergence.

- By default, EIGRP for IPv4 uses equal-cost load balancing with equal metrics. Unequal-cost load sharing is possible with the **variance** command.

- The administrative distances are 90 for EIGRP internal routes, 170 for EIGRP external routes, and 5 for EIGRP summary routes.

- EIGRP for IPv4 allows for good scalability and is used in large networks.

- EIGRP for IPv4 multicasts updates to 224.0.0.10.

- EIGRP for IPv4 does not require a hierarchical physical topology.

## EIGRP for IPv6 (EIGRPv6) Networks

EIGRP was originally an IPv4 routing protocol, although Cisco has developed IPv6 support into EIGRP to route IPv6 prefixes. EIGRP for IPv6 is configured and managed separately from EIGRP for IPv4; no network statements are used. EIGRP for IPv6 retains all the same characteristics (network discovery, DUAL, modules) and functions as EIGRP for IPv4. The major themes with EIGRP for IPv6 are as follows:

- EIGRP for IPv6 implements protocol-independent modules.

- EIGRP for IPv6 allows for neighbor discovery and recovery.

- EIGRP for IPv6 provides reliable transport.

- It implements the DUAL algorithm for a loop-free topology.

- EIGRP for IPv6 uses the same metrics as EIGRP for IPv4 networks.

- EIGRP for IPv6 uses the same timers as EIGRP for IPv4.

- EIGRP for IPv6 uses the same concepts of feasible successors and feasible distance as EIGRP for IPv4.

- EIGRP for IPv6 uses the same packet types as EIGRP for IPv4.

- EIGRP for IPv6 is managed and configured separately from EIGRP for IPv4.

- EIGRP for IPv6 requires a router ID before it can start running.

- EIGRP for IPv6 is configured on interfaces. No network statements are used.

One difference between EIGRP for IPv4 and EIGRP for IPv6 is the use of IPv6 prefixes and the use of IPv6 multicast group FF02::A for EIGRP updates, which are sourced from the link-local IPv6 address. This means that neighbors do not need to share the same global prefix, except for those neighbors that are explicitly specified for unicast updates.

Another difference is that EIGRP for IPv6 defaults to a shutdown state for the routing protocols and must be manually or explicitly enabled on an interface to become operational. Because EIGRP for IPv6 uses the same characteristics and functions as EIGRP for IPv4, as covered in the previous section, they are not repeated here.

### EIGRP for IPv6 Design

Use EIGRP for IPv6 in large geographic IPv6 networks. EIGRP's diameter can scale up to 255 hops, but this network diameter is not recommended. EIGRP authentication can be used instead of IPv6 authentication.

EIGRP for IPv6 can be used in site-to-site WANs and IPsec VPNs. In the enterprise campus, EIGRP can be used in data centers, server distribution, building distribution, and the network core.

EIGRP's DUAL algorithm provides for fast convergence and routing loop prevention. EIGRP does not broadcast its routing table periodically, so there is no large network overhead. The only constraint is that EIGRP for IPv6 is restricted to Cisco routers.

### EIGRP in the Data Center

When EIGRP is used in the data center (DC), several design considerations are important. Because DCs will have many different services, networks, and applications, you should design for summarizing data center subnets, just as you would do in wide-area networking. Furthermore, it is a good idea to advertise a default route into the DC from the aggregation layer. This way, you do not have to advertise all global network routes into the DC.

### EIGRP for IPv6 Summary

The characteristics of EIGRP for IPv6 are as follows:

- EIGRP for IPv6 uses the same characteristics and functions as EIGRP for IPv4.

- EIGRP for IPv6 is a hybrid routing protocol (a distance-vector protocol that has link-state protocol characteristics).

- EIGRP for IPv6 uses Next Header protocol 88.

- EIGRP for IPv6 routes IPv6 prefixes.

- The default composite metric uses bandwidth and delay.

- You can factor load and reliability into the metric.

- EIGRP for IPv6 sends partial route updates only when there are changes.

- EIGRP for IPv6 supports MD5 authentication.

- EIGRP for IPv6 uses DUAL for loop prevention and fast convergence.

- By default, EIGRP for IPv6 uses equal-cost load balancing. Unequal-cost load balancing is possible with the **variance** command.

- The administrative distances are 90 for EIGRP internal routes, 170 for EIGRP external routes, and 5 for EIGRP summary routes.

- EIGRP for IPv6 uses IPv6 multicast FF02::A for EIGRP updates.

- EIGRP for IPv6 enables high scalability and can be used in large networks.

A CCNP should understand EIGRP-specific characteristics and benefits. Table 3-10 provides a summary for reference.

**Table 3-10**    EIGRP Protocol Characteristics

| Characteristic | EIGRP Support |
| --- | --- |
| Distance vector or link state | Hybrid: distance-vector routing protocol with link-state characteristics |
| Convergence | Fastest convergence with DUAL for a loop-free topology |
| Classless or classful | Classless routing protocol, supports VLSM |
| Scalability | Highly scalable, supports large networks |
| Multiprotocol support | Supports IPv4, IPv6, and legacy protocols such as IPX and AppleTalk |
| Multicast address for updates | 224.0.0.10 for IPv4; FF02::A for IPv6 |

# IS-IS

Intermediate System-to-Intermediate System (IS-IS) is an International Organization for Standardization (ISO) dynamic routing specification. IS-IS is described in ISO/IEC 10589, reprinted by the Internet Engineering Task Force (IETF) as RFC 1195. IS-IS is a link-state routing protocol that floods link-state information throughout the network to build a picture of network topology. IS-IS was primarily intended for routing OSI Connectionless Network Protocol (CNLP) packets, but it has the capability to route IP packets. IP packet routing uses Integrated IS-IS, which provides the capability to route protocols such as IP.

IS-IS is a common alternative to other powerful routing protocols such as OSPF and EIGRP in large networks. Although not seen much in enterprise networks, IS-IS is commonly used for internal routing in large ISP networks. IS-IS is also getting more use in data center technologies such as Overlay Transport Virtualization (OTV) and fabric path. As with OSPF,

IS-IS uses the Dijkstra algorithm to calculate the shortest path tree (SPF); it also uses link-state packets (LSPs) instead of OSPF link-state advertisements (LSAs). Also, neither OSPF nor IS-IS are proprietary protocols.

IS-IS creates two levels of hierarchy, with Level 1 for intra-area routing and Level 2 for inter-area routing. IS-IS distinguishes between Level 1 and Level 2 intermediate systems (ISs). Level 1 ISs communicate with other Level 1 ISs in the same area. Level 2 ISs route between Level 1 areas and form an interarea routing backbone. Hierarchical routing simplifies backbone design because Level 1 ISs only need to know how to get to the nearest Level 2 IS.

> **Note**    In IS-IS, a router is usually the IS, and personal computers, workstations, and servers are end systems (ESs). ES-to-IS links are Level 0.

## IS-IS Metrics

IS-IS, as originally defined, uses a composite metric with a maximum path value of 1024. The required default metric is arbitrary and is typically assigned by a network administrator. By convention, it is intended to measure the capacity of the circuit for handling traffic, such as its throughput in bits per second. Higher values indicate lower capacity. Any single link can have a maximum value of 64. IS-IS calculates path values by summing link values. The standard sets the maximum metric values to provide the granularity to support various link types, while ensuring that the shortest path algorithm used for route computation is reasonably efficient.

In Cisco routers, all active interfaces have a default metric of 10. If an interface is passive, the default value is 0. The administrator must configure the interface metric to get a different value. This small metric value range has proved insufficient for large networks and provides too little granularity for new features such as traffic engineering and other applications, especially with high-bandwidth links. Cisco IOS software addresses this issue with the support of a 24-bit metric field, the "wide metric." Wide metrics are also required for route leaking. Using the new metric style, link metrics now have a maximum value of 16,777,215 ($2^{24} - 1$) with a total path metric of 4,261,412,864 ($254 \times 2^{24} = 2^{32}$). Deploying IS-IS in the IP network with wide metrics is recommended for enabling finer granularity and supporting future applications such as traffic engineering.

IS-IS also defines three optional metrics (costs): delay, expense, and error. Cisco routers do not support the three optional metrics. The wide metric noted earlier uses the octets reserved for these metrics.

## IS-IS Operation and Design

This section discusses IS-IS areas, designated routers, authentication, and the Network Entity Title (NET). IS-IS defines areas differently from OSPF; area boundaries are links and not routers. IS-IS has no BDRs. Because IS-IS is an OSI protocol, it uses a NET to identify each router.

### IS-IS NET Addressing

Although you can configure IS-IS to route IP, the communication between routers uses OSI PDUs. The NET is the OSI address used for each router to communicate with OSI PDUs. A NET address ranges from 8 to 20 bytes in length and is hexadecimal. It consists of an authority and format identifier (AFI), area ID, system ID, and selector (SEL), as shown in Figure 3-10.

The system ID must be unique within the network. An example of an IS-IS NET is 49.0001.1290.6600.1001.00, which consists of the following parts:

- **AFI:** 49

- **Area ID:** 0001

- **System ID:** 1290.6600.1001

- **SEL:** 00

| AFI<br>2 Bytes | Area ID<br>4 Bytes | System ID<br>6 Bytes | SEL<br>2 Bytes |
|---|---|---|---|

**Figure 3-10**  *IS-IS NET*

Level 2 routers use the area ID. The system ID must be the same length for all routers in an area. For Cisco routers, it must be 6 bytes in length. Usually, a router MAC address identifies each unique router. The SEL is configured as 00. You configure the NET with the **router isis** command. In this example, the domain authority and format identifier (AFI) is 49, the area is 0001, the system ID is 00aa.0101.0001, and the SEL is 00:

```
router isis

net 49.0001.00aa.0101.0001.00
```

## IS-IS DRs

As with OSPF, IS-IS selects DRs on multiaccess networks. It does not choose a backup DR, as OSPF does. By default, the priority value is 64. You can change the priority value to a value from 0 to 127. If you set the priority to 0, the router is not eligible to become a DR for that network. IS-IS uses the highest system ID to select the DR if there is a tie with the priorities. On point-to-point networks, the priority is 0 because no DR is elected. In IS-IS, all routers in a multiaccess network establish adjacencies with all others in the subnetwork, and IS-IS neighbors become adjacent upon the discovery of one another. Both of these characteristics are different from OSPF behavior.

## IS-IS Interface Types

IS-IS only has two network types (or interface types): point-to-point and broadcast. Unlike OSPF, IS-IS does not have nonbroadcast and point-to-multipoint interface types.

## IS-IS Area Design

IS-IS uses a two-level hierarchy. Routers are configured to route Level 1 (L1), Level 2 (L2), or both Level 1 and Level 2 (L1/L2). Level 1 routers are like OSPF internal routers in a Cisco totally stubby area. (OSPF is covered in Chapter 4.) An L2 router is similar to an OSPF backbone router. A router that has both Level 1 and 2 routes is similar to an OSPF area border router (ABR). IS-IS does not define a backbone area like OSPF's area 0, but you can consider the IS-IS backbone a continuous path of adjacencies among Level 2 ISs. When creating a backbone, there should never be Level 1 routers between L2-only or L1/L2 routers.

L1/L2 routers maintain separate link-state databases for the L1 routes and for the L2 routes. Also, the L1/L2 routers do not advertise L2 routes to the L1 area. L1 routers do not have information about destinations outside the area and use L1 routes to the L1/L2 routers to reach outside destinations.

As shown in Figure 3-11, IS-IS areas are not bounded by the L1/L2 routers but by the links between L1/L2 routers and L2 backbone routers.

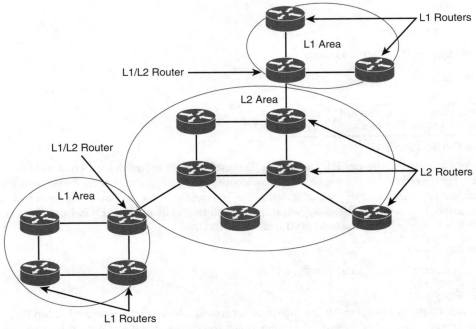

**Figure 3-11**  *IS-IS Areas and Router Types*

With IS-IS, you can create three types of topologies:

- Flat
- Hierarchical
- Hybrid

The IS-IS flat design consists of a single area. As shown in Figure 3-12, all routers are on the same level. There is no summarization with this design. This design is recommended for a small network.

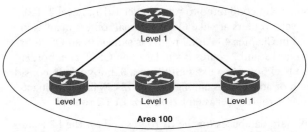

**Figure 3-12**  *IS-IS flat Topology Design*

An IS-IS hierarchical topology is recommended for large networks. A backbone area can be created, much as with OSPF, and can have other areas connected via L1/L2 routers, as shown in Figure 3-13. This design allows for network summarization.

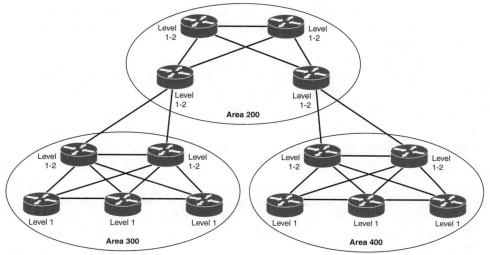

**Figure 3-13**   *IS-IS Hierarchical Topology Design*

A hybrid IS-IS design is recommended for networks that might not be large enough for a backbone area. As shown in Figure 3-14, the IS-IS areas are connected using L1/L2 routers. This design allows for summarization between areas.

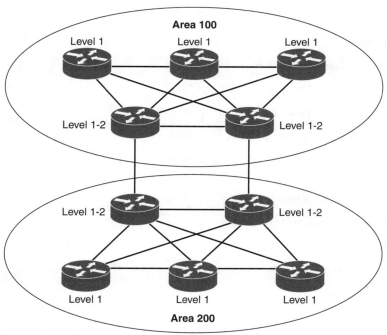

**Figure 3-14**   *IS-IS Hybrid Topology Design*

### IS-IS Authentication

IS-IS supports three types of plaintext authentication: link authentication, area authentication, and domain authentication. All these types support only plaintext password authentication. An RFC draft has added support for IS-IS MD5. The design recommendation is to not use any plaintext authentication and to use MD5 hashing for authentication. With MD5, a cryptographic hash is used instead of plaintext, and the password is never included in the PDU, thus making it more secure.

Routers in a common subnetwork (such as Ethernet or a private line) use link authentication. The plaintext password must be common only between the routers in the link. Level 1 and Level 2 routes use separate passwords. With area authentication, all routers in the area must use authentication and must have the same password.

Only L2 and L1/L2 routers use domain authentication. All L2 and L1/L2 routers must be configured for authentication and must use the same password.

### IS-IS for IPv6

IS-IS in IPv6 functions the same as IS-IS in IPv4 and offers many of the same benefits. IPv6 enhancements to IS-IS allow IS-IS to advertise IPv6 prefixes in addition to IPv4 and OSI routes. Extensions to the IS-IS command-line interface (CLI) allow configuration of IPv6-specific parameters. IPv6 IS-IS extends the address families supported by IS-IS to include IPv6, in addition to OSI and IPv4.

IS-IS supports IPv6 as a separate protocol, as described in RFC 5308. The network layer protocol ID (NLPID) 142 (0x8E) identifies it as IPv6. Its operation and design retain the same characteristics as with IS-IS support for IPv4.

## IS-IS Summary

The characteristics of IS-IS are as follows:

- It is a link-state protocol.

- It uses OSI CNLP to communicate with routers.

- It is a classless protocol (and supports VLSM and CIDR).

- The default metric is set to 10 for all active interfaces.

- IS-IS has two interface types: point-to-point and broadcast.

- It uses a single path metric, with a single link maximum of 64 and a path maximum of 1024.

- It sends partial route updates only when there are changes.

- IS-IS authentication uses plaintext passwords.

- The administrative distance is 115.

- It is used in large networks and is sometimes attractive as compared to OSPF and EIGRP.

- It is described in ISO/IEC 10589, reprinted by the IETF as RFC 1142.

- IS-IS provides support for IPv4 and IPv6 as separate topologies.

# References and Recommended Readings

RFC 1058: *Routing Information Protocol*, www.ietf.org/rfc.

RFC 1142: *OSI IS-IS Intra-domain Routing Protocol*, www.ietf.org/rfc.

RFC 1195: *Use of OSI IS-IS for Routing in TCP/IP and Dual Environments*, www.ietf.org/rfc.

RFC 1321: *The MD5 Message-Digest Algorithm*, www.ietf.org/rfc.

RFC 1723: *RIP Version 2–Carrying Additional Information*, www.ietf.org/rfc.

RFC 2080: *RIPng for IPv6*, www.ietf.org/rfc.

RFC 2328: *OSPF Version 2*, www.ietf.org/rfc.

RFC 2453: *RIP Version 2*, www.ietf.org/rfc.

RFC 5302: *Domain-Wide Prefix Distribution with Two-Level IS-IS*, www.ietf.org/rfc.

RFC 5308: *Routing IPv6 with ISIS*, https://tools.ietf.org/html/rfc5308.

RFC 7142: *Reclassification of RFC 1142 to Historic*, www.ietf.org/rfc.

Cisco, "EIGRP Stub Router Functionality," https://www.cisco.com/en/US/technologies/tk648/tk365/technologies_white_paper0900aecd8023df6f.html.

Cisco, "Enhanced Interior Gateway Routing Protocol," https://www.cisco.com/c/en/us/products/ios-nx-os-software/enhanced-interior-gateway-routing-protocol-eigrp/index.html.

Cisco, "Enterprise IPv6 Deployment," https://www.cisco.com/c/dam/en/us/products/collateral/ios-nx-os-software/enterprise-ipv6-solution/ent_ipv6_dep.pdf.

Cisco, "Implementing EIGRP for IPv6," www.cisco.com/en/US/partner/products/sw/iosswrel/ps5187/products_configuration_guide_chapter09186a00805fc867.html#wp1049317.

Cisco, "IP Routing: RIP Configuration Guide," https://www.cisco.com/c/en/us/td/docs/ios-xml/ios/iproute_rip/configuration/xe-3se/3850/irr-xe-3se-3850-book/irr-rip.html.

Cisco, "Tech Notes: How Does Unequal Cost Path Load Balancing (Variance) Work in IGRP and EIGRP?" http://www.cisco.com/c/en/us/support/docs/ip/enhanced-interior-gateway-routing-protocol-eigrp/13677-19.html.

Doyle, J. *Routing TCP/IP*, Volume I. Indianapolis: Cisco Press, 1998.

# Exam Preparation Tasks

As mentioned in the section "How to Use This Book" in the Introduction, you have a couple of choices for exam preparation: the exercises here, Chapter 13, "Final Preparation," and the exam simulation questions on the companion website.

## Review All Key Topics

Review the most important topics in the chapter, noted with the Key Topic icon in the outer margin of the page. Table 3-11 lists these key topics and the page number on which each is found.

**Table 3-11**　Key Topics

| Key Topic Element | Description | Page |
|---|---|---|
| List | Routing protocol characteristics | 92 |
| Table 3-2 | Routing protocol uses | 95 |
| Table 3-3 | Distance-vector versus link-state routing protocols | 97 |
| Table 3-4 | IPv4 and IPv6 routing protocols | 99 |
| Table 3-5 | Default administrative distances for IP routes | 99 |
| Table 3-6 | Routing protocol characteristics | 100 |
| List | EIGRP components | 106 |
| List | EIGRP for IPv4 summary | 113 |
| List | EIGRP for IPv6 summary | 114 |
| List | IS-IS summary | 120 |

## Complete Tables and Lists from Memory

Print a copy of Appendix D, "Memory Tables," found on the companion website, or at least the section for this chapter, and complete the tables and lists from memory. Appendix E, "Memory Tables Answer Key," includes completed tables and lists to check your work.

## Define Key Terms

Define the following key terms from this chapter and check your answers in the glossary:

administrative distance, bandwidth (BW), delay, distance-vector routing protocol, Enhanced Interior Gateway Routing Protocol (EIGRP), exterior gateway protocol (EGP), hop count, interior gateway protocol (IGP), Intermediate System-to-Intermediate System (IS-IS), link-state routing protocol, load, Network Entity Title (NET), variable-length subnet masking (VLSM)

## Q&A

The answers to these questions appear in Appendix A. For more practice with exam format questions, use the exam engine on the companion website.

1. True or false: Link-state routing protocols send periodic routing updates.

2. True or false: The path with the lowest cost is preferred.

3. True or false: A link with a reliability of 200/255 is preferred over a link with a reliability of 10/255.

4. True or false: A link with a load of 200/255 is preferred over a link with a load of 10/255.

5. On a router, both EIGRP and OSPF have internal routes to 198.168.10.0/24. Which route is injected into the routing table?

6. On a router, both RIPv2 and IS-IS have a route to 198.168.10.0/24. Which route is injected into the routing table?

7. On a router, EIGRP has a route to the destination with a prefix of /28, and OSPF has a route to the destination with a prefix of /30. Which is used to reach the destination?

8. Which of the following is the best measurement of an interface's reliability and load?

    a. Reliability 255/255, load 1/255

    b. Reliability 255/255, load 255/255

    c. Reliability 1/255, load 1/255

    d. Reliability 1/255, load 255/255

9. Which routing protocols permit an explicit hierarchical topology? (Choose two.)

    a. BGP

    b. EIGRP

    c. IS-IS

    d. RIP

    e. OSPF

10. What routing protocol parameter is concerned with how long a packet takes to travel from one end to another in an internetwork?

11. Match each loop-prevention technique (numerals) with its description (letters).

    i. Split horizon

    ii. Poison reverse

    iii. Triggered updates

    iv. Counting to infinity

    a. Sends an infinite metric from which the route was learned

    b. Drops a packet when the hop count limit is reached

    c. Suppresses a route announcement from which the route was learned

    d. Sends a route update when a route changes

12. Which standards-based protocol would you select in a large IPv6 network?

    a. RIPng

    b. OSPFv3

    c. EIGRP for IPv6

    d. RIPv2

**13.** Which of the following routing protocols are fast in converging when a change in the network occurs? (Choose three.)

    **a.** RIPv1

    **b.** RIPv2

    **c.** EIGRP

    **d.** OSPF

    **e.** IS-IS

    **f.** BGP

**14.** If you were designing a large corporate network that cannot be designed in a hierarchy, which routing protocol would you recommend?

    **a.** RIPv1

    **b.** RIPv2

    **c.** EIGRP

    **d.** OSPF

    **e.** IS-IS

    **f.** BGP

**15.** You are connecting your network to an ISP. Which routing protocol should you use to exchange routes?

    **a.** RIPv1

    **b.** RIPv2

    **c.** EIGRP

    **d.** OSPF

    **e.** IS-IS

    **f.** BGP

    **g.** All of the above

**16.** Which routing protocol would be supported on an IPv6 network with multiple vendor routers?

    **a.** RIPv2

    **b.** EIGRP for IPv6

    **c.** BGPv6

    **d.** OSPFv3

    **e.** RIPv3

**17.** Which statements are true for IGPs and EGPs? (Choose two.)

    **a.** IGPs can be substituted with static routing.

    **b.** IGPs are better at finding the fastest paths across the network.

    **c.** IGPs must converge quickly, but EGPs do not have to.

    **d.** IGPs are for inter-autonomous system connections, and EGPs are used for intra-autonomous system connections.

**18.** How is convergence related to routing information?

   **a.** The speed of convergence affects the frequency of routing updates.

   **b.** The faster the convergence, the less consistent routing information is produced.

   **c.** The faster the convergence, the more consistent routing information is produced.

   **d.** There is no relationship between convergence and routing information consistency.

**19.** Which EIGRP features make it appropriate for a company's network? (Choose two.)

   **a.** Slow convergence

   **b.** VLSM support

   **c.** DUAL

   **d.** Automatic summarization

   **e.** Multivendor support

**20.** Match each protocol with its characteristic.

   **i.** EIGRP for IPv6

   **ii.** RIPv2

   **iii.** RIPng

   **iv.** EIGRP

   **a.** Uses multicast FF02::9

   **b.** Uses multicast 224.0.0.9

   **c.** Uses multicast 224.0.0.10

   **d.** Uses multicast FF02::A

**21.** Match each EIGRP component with its description.

   **i.** RTP

   **ii.** DUAL

   **iii.** Protocol-dependent modules

   **iv.** Neighbor discovery

   **a.** Provides an interface between DUAL and IPX RIP, IGRP, and AppleTalk

   **b.** Used to deliver EIGRP messages reliably

   **c.** Builds an adjacency table

   **d.** Guarantees a loop-free network

**22.** Match each EIGRP parameter with its description.

   **i.** Feasible distance

   **ii.** Successor

   **iii.** Feasible successor

   **iv.** Active state

   **a.** The best path selected by DUAL

   **b.** Successor down

   **c.** The lowest calculated metric of a path to reach the destination

   **d.** The second-best path

**23.** On an IPv6 network, you have RIPng and EIGRP running. Both protocols have a route to destination 10.1.1.0/24. Which route gets injected into the routing table?

   **a.** The RIPng route

   **b.** The EIGRP route

   **c.** Both routes

   **d.** Neither route because of a route conflict

**24.** Which IGP protocol is a common alternative to EIGRP and OSPF as a routing protocol for large service provider networks?

   **a.** OSPFv3

   **b.** RIPv2

   **c.** BGP4

   **d.** IS-IS

**25.** What is the default IS-IS metric for a T1 interface?

   **a.** 5

   **b.** 10

   **c.** 64

   **d.** 200

**26.** In IS-IS networks, the backup designated router (BDR) forms adjacencies to what router or routers?

   **a.** It forms an adjacency only with the DR.

   **b.** It forms adjacencies with all routers.

   **c.** The BDR only becomes adjacent when the DR is down.

   **d.** There is no BDR in IS-IS.

**27.** Which routing protocol converges most quickly?

   **a.** BGP

   **b.** OSPF

   **c.** EIGRP

   **d.** RIPv2

   **e.** IS-IS

**28.** Which routing protocol allows for unequal-cost multipath routing?

   **a.** IS-IS

   **b.** OSPF

   **c.** EIGRP

   **d.** RIPv2

**29.** Which two link-state routing protocols support IPv6?

   **a.** BGP4

   **b.** EIGRP

   **c.** OSPF

    **d.**   RIPng

    **e.**   IS-IS

**30.** Which of the following are characteristics of EIGRP? (Choose four.)

    **a.**   ASN and K values must match to form neighbors.

    **b.**   It can use multiple unequal paths.

    **c.**   Summary routes have an AD of 150.

    **d.**   External routes have an AD of 170.

    **e.**   It exchanges the full routing table every 60 seconds.

    **f.**   It uses multicast address 224.0.0.10 for updates.

    **g.**   It does not support MD5 authentication

**31.** What does a hierarchical EIGRP design help with? (Choose two.)

    **a.**   Redistribution

    **b.**   Route summarization

    **c.**   Faster convergence

    **d.**   Load balancing

**32.** Which are design considerations with EIGRP? (Choose two.)

    **a.**   The **neighbor** command is used to enable unicast communication.

    **b.**   The **neighbor** command can be used to establish adjacency with non-Cisco routers.

    **c.**   The ASN and K values must match to establish neighbors.

    **d.**   Virtual links can be used to establish neighbors over an area.

**33.** Which are the two fastest converging routing protocols? (Choose two.)

    **a.**   IS-IS

    **b.**   OSPF

    **c.**   EIGRP

    **d.**   RIPv2

    **e.**   BGP4

**34.** Which routing protocol uses multicast FF02::A and Next Header protocol 88?

    **a.**   IS-IS for IPv6

    **b.**   OSPFv3

    **c.**   EIGRP for IPv6

    **d.**   RIPng

**35.** What is the system ID of the NET49.0001.1900.6500.0001.00?

    **a.**   49.0001

    **b.**   0001.1900.6500

    **c.**   1900.6500.0001

    **d.**   0001.00

**36.** EIGRP has a route with a metric of 20. There are two feasible successors with metrics of 35 and 45. If the **variance 2** command is invoked, how many active routes are there for this route?

  **a.**  1

  **b.**  2

  **c.**  3

  **d.**  0

**37.** Which routing protocol has the highest administrative distance?

  **a.**  RIP

  **b.**  EIGRP

  **c.**  OSPF

  **d.**  IS-IS

  **c.**  BGP

**38.** Which routing protocol has the lowest administrative distance?

  **a.**  RIP

  **b.**  EIGRP

  **c.**  OSPF

  **d.**  IS-IS

  **c.**  iBGP

**39.** For each column in Table 3-12, fill in the correct routing protocol.

**Table 3-12**  Routing Protocol Characteristics

| Characteristic | A | B | C | D | E |
|---|---|---|---|---|---|
| Supports VLSM | Yes | Yes | Yes | Yes | Yes |
| Convergence | Fast | Fast | Slow | Fast | Fast |
| Scalability | High | High | Low | High | High |
| Supports IPv6 | Yes | No | No | No | Yes |
| Proprietary | Yes | No | No | Yes | No |

Use Figure 3-15 to answer questions 40 to 43.

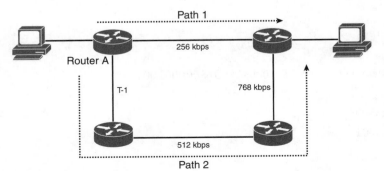

**Figure 3-15**  *Path Selection*

**40.** By default, if EIGRP is enabled on all routers, what path is taken?

    **a.** Path 1

    **b.** Path 2

    **c.** Unequal-cost load balancing with Path 1 and Path 2

    **d.** Equal-cost load balancing with Path 1 and Path 2

**41.** EIGRP is configured on the routers. If it is configured with the **variance** command, what path is taken?

    **a.** Path 1

    **b.** Path 2

    **c.** Unequal-cost load sharing Path 1 and Path 2

    **d.** Equal-cost load balancing with Path 1 and Path 2

**42.** By default, if EIGRP for IPv6 is enabled on all routers and this is an IPv6 network, what path is taken?

    **a.** Path 1

    **b.** Path 2

    **c.** Unequal-cost load balancing with Path 1 and Path 2

    **d.** Equal-cost load balancing with Path 1 and Path 2

**43.** By default, if IS-IS is enabled on all routers, and this is an IPv6 network, what path is taken?

    **a.** Path 1

    **b.** Path 2

    **c.** Unequal-cost load balancing with Path 1 and Path 2

    **d.** Equal-cost load balancing with Path 1 and Path 2

**44.** Which describes an EIGRP successor?

    **a.** The path with the lowest metric to a destination

    **b.** The route that satisfies the feasibility condition where the reported distance is less than the feasible distance

    **c.** The path with the highest path metric to a destination

    **d.** The path with the lowest path metric to a destination

**45.** Which route is used in the event that the successor route goes down?

    **a.** The backup successor route

    **b.** The feasible distance route

    **c.** The feasible successor route

    **d.** The reported distance route

**46.** Which metric can be modified in EIGRP that does not affect the OSPF metric?

    **a.** Bandwidth

    **b.** Delay

    **c.** Cost

    **d.** Administrative distance

**47.** An EIGRP route is stable. What is its EIGRP state?

  **a.** Active

  **b.** Passive

  **c.** Stuck in active

  **d.** Disabled

**48.** Which statement is true regarding IS-IS?

  **a.** IS-IS supports only OSI and IPv4 routing.

  **b.** IS-IS supports only IPv4 and IPv6 routing.

  **c.** IS-IS supports only OSI and IPv6 routing.

  **d.** IS-IS supports OSI, IPv4, and IPv6 routing.

## CHAPTER 4

# OSPF, BGP, and Route Manipulation

**This chapter covers the following subjects:**

**OSPFv2:** This section covers metrics and design for OSPFv2 in IPv4 networks.

**OSPFv3:** This section covers metrics and design for OSPFv3 in IPv6 networks.

**BGP:** This section covers metrics, characteristics, and design for BGP.

**Route Manipulation:** This section covers route redistribution and summarization.

This chapter reviews the characteristics of and design issues related to the Open Shortest Path First version 2 (OSPFv2) routing protocol. It also covers version 3 of this protocol, OSPFv3, for IPv6 networks. OSPFv2 and OSPFv3 are link-state routing protocols. They do not broadcast their route tables, as distance vector routing protocols do. Routers using link-state routing protocols send information about the status of their interfaces to all other routers in the area. Then they perform database computations to determine the shortest paths to each destination. This chapter also covers Border Gateway Protocol (BGP), which is used to exchange routes between autonomous systems. It is most frequently used between enterprises and service providers. The "Route Manipulation" section covers route summarization, route filtering, and redistribution of route information between routing protocols.

This chapter covers the following objectives from the ENSLD 300-420 exam:

- Create stable, secure, and scalable routing designs for OSPF
- Create stable, secure, and scalable routing designs for BGP

## "Do I Know This Already?" Quiz

The "Do I Know This Already?" quiz helps you identify your strengths and deficiencies in this chapter's topics. This quiz, derived from the major sections in the "Foundation Topics" portion of the chapter, helps you determine how to spend your limited study time. Table 4-1 outlines the major topics discussed in this chapter and the "Do I Know This Already?" quiz questions that correspond to those topics. You can find the answers in Appendix A, "Answers to the 'Do I Know This Already?' Quiz Questions Q&A Questions."

**Table 4-1** "Do I Know This Already?" Foundation Topics Section-to-Question Mapping

| Foundation Topics Section | Questions Covered in This Section |
| --- | --- |
| OSPFv2 | 1, 3–6 |
| OSPFv3 | 7 |
| BGP | 2, 8, 10 |
| Route Manipulation | 9 |

1. In OSPF, where does summarization of internal routes occur?
   a. Backbone router
   b. Designated router
   c. ABR
   d. ASBR
2. Which BGP metric is used to influence the path of outbound traffic?
   a. AS_Path
   b. Origin
   c. MED
   d. Weight
3. What is an ASBR?
   a. Area border router
   b. Autonomous system boundary router
   c. Auxiliary system border router
   d. Area system border router
4. What is the OSPFv2 link-state advertisement (LSA) type for autonomous system external LSAs?
   a. Type 1
   b. Type 2
   c. Type 3
   d. Type 4
   e. Type 5
5. What address do you use to multicast to the OSPFv2 designated router (DR)?
   a. 224.0.0.1
   b. 224.0.0.5
   c. 224.0.0.6
   d. 224.0.0.10
6. OSPF Type 1 LSAs are flooded _____.
   a. to the OSPF area
   b. to the OSPF domain
   c. from the area to the OSPF backbone
   d. through the virtual link
7. What OSPFv3 LSA carries address prefixes?
   a. Network LSA
   b. Summary LSA
   c. Interarea-router LSA
   d. Intra-area-prefix LSA

**8.** What protocol do you use to exchange IP routes between autonomous systems?

   **a.** IGMP

   **b.** eBGP

   **c.** EIGRP

   **d.** OSPF

**9.** Where should routes be summarized?

   **a.** On the core routers

   **b.** On the distribution routers

   **c.** On the access routers

   **d.** None of the above

**10.** What is the administrative distance of External BGP routes?

   **a.** 20

   **b.** 100

   **c.** 110

   **d.** 200

## Foundation Topics

This chapter covers the link-state routing protocol OSPF. OSPF is an Interior Gateway Protocol (IGP) used within an autonomous system. It is the most widely used IGP in enterprise networks. OSPFv2 is used for IPv4 networks, and OSPFv3 is used for IPv6 networks. Another link-state routing protocol, IS-IS, is covered in Chapter 3, "Routing Protocol Characteristics, EIGRP, and IS-IS."

The "BGP" section of this chapter covers the characteristics and design of BGP. eBGP, which exchanges routes between autonomous systems, is commonly used between enterprises and their service providers.

The section "Route Manipulation" covers how to use policy-based routing (PBR) to change packets' destination addresses based on policies. This section also covers route summarization, filtering, and redistribution of route information between routing protocols.

## OSPFv2

RFC 2328 defines Open Shortest Path First version 2 (OSPFv2), a link-state routing protocol that uses Dijkstra's shortest path first (SPF) algorithm to calculate paths to destinations. OSPFv2 is used in IPv4 networks. OSPF was created for use in large networks where RIP failed. OSPF improved the speed of convergence, provided for the use of variable-length subnet masking (VLSM), and improved the path calculation.

In OSPF, each router sends link-state advertisements (LSAs) about itself and its links to all other routers in the area. Note that it does not send routing tables but rather sends link-state information about its interfaces. Then, each router individually calculates the best routes to the destination by running the SPF algorithm. Each OSPF router in an area maintains an identical database describing the area's topology. The routing table at each router is individually constructed using the local copy of this database to construct a shortest-path tree.

OSPFv2 is a classless routing protocol that permits the use of VLSM. With Cisco routers, OSPF also supports equal-cost multipath load balancing and neighbor authentication. OSPF uses multicast addresses to communicate between routers. OSPF uses IP protocol 89.

This section covers OSPF theory and design concepts. It discusses OSPF LSAs, area types, and router types. OSPF uses a two-layer hierarchy with a backbone area at the top and all other areas below. Routers send LSAs informing other routers of the status of their interfaces. The use of LSAs and the characteristics of OSPF areas are important concepts to understand for the ENSLD 300-420 exam.

## OSPFv2 Metric

The metric that OSPFv2 uses is cost. It is an unsigned 16-bit integer in the range 1 to 65,535. The default cost for interfaces is calculated based on the bandwidth, using the formula $10^8$ / BW, where BW is the bandwidth of the interface expressed as a full integer of bits per second (bps). If the result is smaller than 1, the cost is set to 1. A 10BASE-T (10 Mbps = $10^7$ bps) interface has a cost of $10^8$ / $10^7$ = 10. OSPF performs a summation of the costs to reach a destination; the lowest cost is the preferred path. Table 4-2 shows some sample interface metrics.

**Table 4-2**   OSPF Default Interface Costs

| Interface Type | OSPF Cost |
|---|---|
| 10 Gigabit Ethernet | $10^8/10^{10}$ = .01 → 1 |
| Gigabit Ethernet | $10^8/10^9$ = .1 → 1 |
| OC-3 (155 Mbps) | .64516 → 1 |
| Fast Ethernet | $10^8/10^8$ = 1 |
| DS-3 (45 Mbps) | 2 |
| Ethernet | $10^8/10^7$ = 10 |
| T1 | 64 |
| 512 kbps | 195 |
| 256 kbps | 390 |

The default reference bandwidth used to calculate OSPF costs is $10^8$ (cost = $10^8$ / BW). Notice that for technologies that support speeds greater than 100 Mbps, the default metric gets set to 1 without regard for the network's different speeds.

Because OSPF was developed prior to high-speed WAN and LAN technologies, the default metric for 100 Mbps was 1. Cisco provides a method to modify the default reference bandwidth. The cost metric can be modified on every interface. It is highly recommended that you change the default reference bandwidth to a higher number on all routers in the OSPF network if OSPF links have a speed higher than 100 Mbps.

## OSPFv2 Adjacencies and Hello Timers

OSPF uses Hello packets for neighbor discovery. The default Hello interval is 10 seconds (30 seconds for nonbroadcast multiaccess [NBMA] networks). For point-to-point networks, the Hello interval is 10 seconds. Hellos are multicast to 224.0.0.5 (ALLSPFRouters). Hello packets include information such as the router ID, area ID, authentication, and router priority.

After two routers exchange Hello packets and set two-way communication, they establish adjacencies.

## OSPF Message Types

OSPF uses five different message types to exchange information between routers:

- **Type 1: Hello packets:** This message type is used to discover and maintain neighbor relationships.

- **Type 2: Database Description (DBD) packets:** This message type is used to summarize database information and ensure that the databases are in sync.

- **Type 3: Link-State Request (LSR) packets:** This message type is used for database downloads. It is sent to OSPF neighbors to request the most recent version of missing LSRs.

- **Type 4: Link-State Update (LSU) packets:** This message type is used to update the database. LSU packets are used for the flooding of LSAs and for sending LSA responses to LSR packets.

- **Type 5: Link-State Acknowledgement (LSAck) packets:** This message type is used to acknowledge the flooding of LSAs. Multiple LSAs can be acknowledged in a single LSAck packet.

DBD and LSR packets are used for database synchronization after adjacencies are formed between OSPF routers.

Figure 4-1 shows a point-to-point network and an NBMA network. For point-to-point networks, valid neighbors always become adjacent and communicate using multicast address 224.0.0.5. For broadcast (Ethernet) and NBMA networks (Frame Relay), all routers become adjacent to the designated router (DR) and backup designated router (BDR) but not to each other. All routers reply to the DR and BDR using the multicast address 224.0.0.6. The section "OSPF DRs," later in this chapter, covers the DR concept.

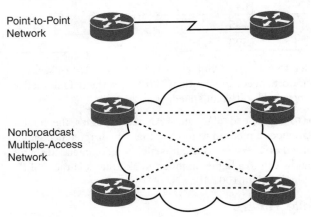

Point-to-Point
Network

Nonbroadcast
Multiple-Access
Network

**Figure 4-1**   *OSPF Networks*

On OSPF point-to-multipoint nonbroadcast networks, it is necessary to configure the set of neighbors that are directly reachable over the point-to-multipoint network. Each neighbor is identified by its IP address on the point-to-multipoint network. Nonbroadcast point-to-multipoint networks do not elect DRs, so the DR eligibility of configured neighbors is undefined. OSPF communication in point-to-point networks uses unicast or multicast addresses for neighbor communication.

OSPF virtual links send unicast OSPF packets. Later in this chapter, the section "Virtual Links" discusses virtual links.

## OSPFv2 Areas

As a network grows, the initial flooding and database maintenance of LSAs can burden a router's CPU. OSPF uses areas to reduce these effects. An area is a logical grouping of routers and links that divides the network. Routers share link-state information with only the routers in their areas. This setup reduces the size of the database and the cost of computing the SPF tree at each router.

Using a topology with multiple areas provides the following benefits:

- The segmentation of the network reduces the number of SFP tree calculations.

- The segmentation of the network reduces the amount of LSA flooding.

- Multi-area design allows for summarization at the area border routers (ABRs).

- One OSPF area hides the topology from another area.

Each area is assigned a 32-bit integer number. Area 0 (or 0.0.0.0) is reserved for the backbone area. Every OSPF network should have a backbone area. The backbone area must exist in any internetwork using OSPF as a routing protocol over multiple areas. As you can see in Figure 4-2, communication between Area 1 and Area 2 must flow through Area 0. This communication can be internal to a single router that has interfaces directly connected to Areas 0, 1, and 2.

Intra-area traffic is packets passed between routers in a single area.

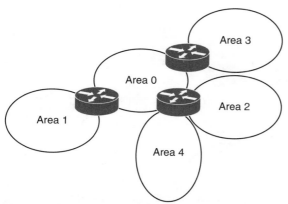

**Figure 4-2**  *OSPF Areas*

### OSPF Area Design Considerations

A CCNP enterprise designer should be aware of a few considerations in the design of OSPF areas. First, in a hub-and-spoke design, you have a remote branch keep the OSPF boundary at the hub side, as shown in Figure 4-3. This allows the branch router to calculate SPF only within its own area and limits the LSA flooding. If the OSPF Area 0 boundary were extended to the branch, the branch router would have to do OSPF calculations for Area 0 and its own area, and LSAs would flood over the WAN link.

The second design consideration is to avoid grouping remote branches into a single area. Having all remote branches in the same area is not scalable. Instead, place each remote branch in its own area to limit LSA flooding and SPF recalculations.

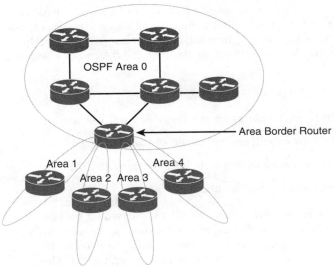

**Figure 4-3** *OSPF Area Design*

## OSPF Router Types

OSPF classifies participating routers based on their place and function in the area architecture. Figure 4-4 shows OSPF router types.

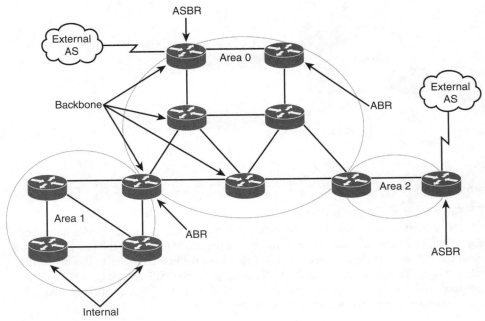

**Figure 4-4** *OSPF Router Types*

Table 4-3 explains the router types shown in Figure 4-4.

**Table 4-3**   OSPF Router Types

| Type | Description |
|---|---|
| Internal router | Any router whose interfaces all belong to the same OSPF area. Such a router keeps only one link-state database. |
| Area border router (ABR) | A router that is connected to more than one area. Such a router maintains a link-state database for each area it belongs to. These routers generate summary LSAs. |
| Autonomous system boundary router (ASBR) | A router that injects external LSAs into the OSPF database (redistribution). These external routes are learned via either other routing protocols or static routes. |
| Backbone router | A router with at least one interface attached to Area 0. |

**Tip**   An OSPF router can be an ABR, an ASBR, and a backbone router at the same time. A router is an ABR if it has an interface on Area 0 and another interface in another area. A router is a backbone router if it has one or more interfaces in Area 0. A router is an ASBR if it redistributes external routes into the OSPF network.

## OSPF DRs

On multiaccess networks (such as Ethernet), some routers get selected as DRs. The purpose of a DR is to collect LSAs for the multiaccess network and to forward the LSAs to all non-DR routers; this arrangement reduces the amount of LSA traffic generated. A router can be the DR for one multiaccess network and not the DR in another attached multiaccess network.

The DR also floods the network LSAs to the rest of the area. OSPF also selects a BDR; it takes over the function of the DR if the DR fails. Both the DR and the BDR become adjacent to all routers in the multiaccess network. All routers that are not a DR or a BDR are sometimes called DROTHERs. These routers are only adjacent to the DR and BDR. The DR generates a Type 2 (network) LSA, which advertises all other routers on the multiaccess segment. This allows the DROTHERs to get the Type 1 LSAs. OSPF routers multicast LSAs only to adjacent routers. DROTHERs multicast packets to the DR and BDR using the multicast address 224.0.0.6 (ALLDRouters). The DR floods updates using ALLSPFRouters (224.0.0.5).

DR and BDR selection is based on an OSPF DR interface priority. The default value is 1, and the highest priority determines the DR. In a tie, OSPF uses the numerically highest router ID. The router ID is the IP address of the configured loopback interface. The router ID is the highest configured loopback address, or if the loopback is not configured, it's the highest physical address. Routers with a priority of 0 are not considered for DR/BDR selection. The dotted lines in Figure 4-5 show the adjacencies in the network.

In Figure 4-5, Router A is configured with a priority of 10, and Router B is configured with a priority of 5. Assuming that these routers are turned on simultaneously, Router A becomes the DR for the Ethernet network. Router C has a lower priority and becomes adjacent to Router A and Router B but not to Router D. Router D has a priority of 0 and therefore is not a candidate to become a DR or BDR.

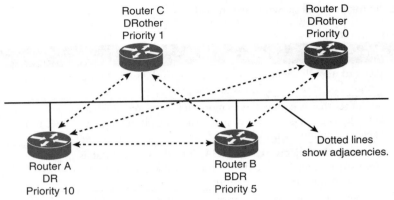

**Figure 4-5**  *DRs*

If you introduce to a network a new router that has a higher priority than that of the current DR and BDR, it does not become the selected DR unless both the DR and the BDR fail. If the DR fails, the current BDR becomes the DR.

## LSA Types

OSPF routers generate LSAs that are flooded within an area, between areas, and throughout the entire autonomous system. OSPF defines different LSA types for participating routers, DRs, ABRs, and ASBRs. Understanding the LSA types can help you with other OSPF concepts. Table 4-4 describes the major LSA types. For the ENSLD 300-420 exam, you need to know OSPF LSAs by type code (number) and by type name. Note that there are other LSA types that are not covered in this book.

Type 1 and Type 2 LSAs are intra-area LSAs that have an area-flooding scope. Type 3 LSAs provide summaries of destinations outside the local area but within the OSPF domain. Type 4 LSAs provide reachability about the ASBR. Type 3 and Type 4 LSAs are interarea LSAs that have an area-flooding scope. ABRs exchange Type 3 and Type 4 LSAs. Type 5 LSAs advertise external destinations. Type 5 LSAs have a domain-flooding scope, which means they are flooded throughout all areas. Type 7 LSAs are originated by ASBRs in an NSSA and are similar to the Type 5 LSA and only flooded within the NSSA.

**Table 4-4**   Major LSA Types

| Type Code | Type | Description |
|-----------|------|-------------|
| 1 | Router LSA | Produced by every router. Includes all the router's links, interfaces, link states, and costs. This LSA type is flooded within a single area and does not travel into other areas. |
| 2 | Network LSA | Produced by every DR on every broadcast or NBMA network. It lists all the routers in the multiaccess network. This LSA type is contained within an area. |
| 3 | Summary LSA for ABRs | Produced by ABRs. It is sent into an area to advertise destinations outside the area. |

| Type Code | Type | Description |
|-----------|------|-------------|
| 4 | Summary LSA for ASBRs | Originated by ABRs. Sent into an area by the ABR to advertise the IP addresses of the ASBRs. It does not advertise networks outside the OSPF network; only the ASBR does that. |
| 5 | Autonomous system external LSA | Originated by ASBRs. Advertises destinations external to the OSPF autonomous system, flooded throughout the whole OSPF autonomous system. |
| 7 | Not-so-stubby area (NSSA) external LSA | Originated by ASBRs in an NSSA. It is not flooded throughout the OSPF autonomous system but only to the NSSA. Similar to the Type 5 LSA. |

### Autonomous System External Path Types

The two types of autonomous system external paths are Type 1 (E1) and Type 2 (E2), and they are associated with Type 5 LSAs. ASBRs advertise external destinations whose cost can be just a redistribution metric (E2) or a redistribution metric plus the costs of each segment (E1) used to reach the ASBR.

By default, external routes are Type 2, which is the metric (cost) used in the redistribution. Type 1 external routes have a metric that is the sum of the redistribution cost plus the cost of the path to reach the ASBR.

## OSPF Stub Area Types

OSPF provides support for stub areas. The concept is to reduce the number of interarea or external LSAs that get flooded into a stub area. RFC 2328 defines OSPF stub areas. RFC 1587 defines support for NSSAs. Cisco routers use totally stubby areas, such as Area 2, as shown in Figure 4-6.

### Stub Areas

Consider Area 1 in Figure 4-6. Its only path to the external networks is via the ABR through Area 0. All external routes are flooded to all areas in the OSPF autonomous system. You can configure an area as a stub area to prevent OSPF external LSAs (Type 5) from being flooded into that area. A single default route is injected into the stub area instead. If multiple ABRs exist in a stub area, all of them inject the default route. Traffic originating within the stub area routes to the closest ABR.

Note that network summary LSAs (Type 3) from other areas are still flooded into the stub area's Area 1.

### Totally Stubby Areas

Let's take Area 1 in Figure 4-6 one step further. The only path to get from Area 1 to Area 0 and other areas is through the ABR. A totally stubby area does not flood network summary LSAs (Type 3). It stifles Type 4 LSAs, as well. Like regular stub areas, totally stubby areas do not flood Type 5 LSAs. A totally stubby area sends just a single LSA for the default route. If multiple ABRs exist in a totally stubby area, all ABRs inject the default route. Traffic originating within the totally stubby area routes to the closest ABR.

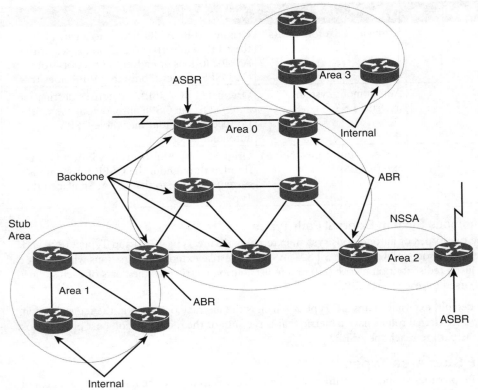

**Figure 4-6**   *OSPF Stub Networks*

## NSSAs

Notice that Area 2 in Figure 4-6 has an ASBR. If this area is configured as an NSSA, it generates the external LSAs (Type 7) into the OSPF system while retaining the characteristics of a stub area to the rest of the autonomous system. There are two options for the ABR. First, the ABR for Area 2 can translate the NSSA external LSAs (Type 7) to autonomous system external LSAs (Type 5) and flood the rest of the internetwork. Second, the ABR is not configured to convert the NSSA external LSAs to Type 5 external LSAs; therefore, the NSSA external LSAs remain within the NSSA.

There is also an NSSA totally stub area. The difference is that the default NSSA has no default route unless the ABR is explicitly configured to advertise one. The NSSA totally stub area does receive a default route.

## Virtual Links

OSPF requires that all areas be connected to a backbone router. Sometimes, WAN link provisioning or failures can prevent an OSPF area from being directly connected to a backbone router. You can use virtual links to temporarily connect (virtually) an area to the backbone.

In Figure 4-7, Area 4 is not directly connected to the backbone. A virtual link is configured between Router A and Router B. The flow of the virtual link is unidirectional and must be configured in each router of the link. Area 2 becomes the transit area through which the virtual link is configured. Traffic between Areas 2 and 4 does not flow directly to Router B. Instead, the traffic must flow to Router A to reach Area 0 and then pass through the virtual link.

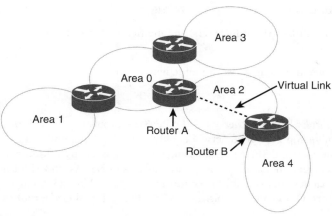

**Figure 4-7**  *OSPF Virtual Link*

## OSPFv2 Router Authentication

OSPFv2 supports the authentication of routes using 64-bit plaintext, cryptographic Message Digest 5 (MD5), and Secure Hash (SHA) Standard authentication. Authentication can be performed on a per-area or per-interface basis. Plaintext authentication passwords do not need to be the same for the routers throughout the area, but they must be the same between neighbors.

MD5 authentication provides higher security than plaintext authentication. As with plaintext authentication, passwords do not have to be the same throughout an area, but they do need to be the same between neighbors. SHA-1 authentication is recommended because it is the most secure.

OSPF supports the National Institute of Standards and Technology (NIST) Secure Hash Standard family of algorithms for authentication.

## OSPFv2 Summary

OSPFv2 is used in large enterprise IPv4 networks. The network topology must be hierarchical. OSPF is used in the enterprise campus building access, distribution, and core layers. OSPF is also used in the enterprise data center, WAN/MAN, and branch offices.

The characteristics of OSPFv2 follow:

- Link-state routing protocol

- Uses IP protocol 89

- Classless protocol (supports VLSM and CIDR)

- Uses cost as the metric (based on interface bandwidth, by default)

- Fast convergence, using link-state updates and SPF calculation

- Reduced bandwidth use thanks to sending LSA updates only when changes occur

- Labels routes as intra-area, interarea, external Type 1, or external Type 2

- Supports authentication

- Uses the Dijkstra algorithm to calculate the SPF tree

- Default administrative distance of 110

- Uses multicast address 224.0.0.5 (ALLSPFRouters) and multicast address 224.0.0.6 (ALLDRouters)

- Provides good scalability and recommended for large networks

# OSPFv3

RFC 5340 describes Open Shortest Path First version 3 (OSPFv3) as a routing protocol for IPv6 networks. OSPFv3 initially supported IPv6 networks only, but it has been updated to support both IPv6 and IPv4 networks. OSPF algorithms and mechanisms, such as flooding, router types, designated router election, backbone areas, stub areas and NSSAs, and SPF calculations, remain the same. Changes are made for OSPF to support IPv6 addresses, address hierarchy, and IPv6 for transport. OSPFv3 uses multicast group FF02::5 for all OSPF routers and FF02::6 for all designated routers.

## OSPFv3 Changes from OSPFv2

The following are the major changes from OSPFv2 to OSPFv3:

- **IPv6 only:** This newer version of OSPF runs over IPv6 only.

- **Support for IPv6 addressing:** New LSAs have been created to carry IPv6 addresses and prefixes.

- **Per-link processing:** OSPFv2 uses per-subnet processing. With link processing, routers in the same link can belong to multiple subnets.

- **Address semantics removed:** Addresses are removed from the router and network LSAs. These LSAs now provide topology information.

- **No authentication in OSPFv3:** OSPFv3 uses IPsec, the IPv6 authentication scheme.

- **New LSA:** There is a new LSA for local-link flooding scope.

- **New intra-area-prefix LSA:** This LSA, which carries all the IPv6 prefix information, is similar to an OSPFv2 router and network LSAs.

- **Identifying neighbors by router ID:** Neighbors are always identified by the router ID. This does not occur in OSPFv2 point-to-point and broadcast networks.

- **Options field changes:** Two Options bits, the R bit and the V6 bit, have been added to the Options field for processing router LSAs during the SPF calculation.

> **Note**    In OSPFv3, the router IDs, area IDs, and LSA link-state IDs remain 32 bits. Larger IPv6 addresses cannot be used.

## OSPFv3 Areas and Router Types

OSPFv3 retains the same structure and concepts as OSPFv2. The area topology, interfaces, neighbors, link-state database, and routing table remain the same. RFC 2740 does not define new area types or router types.

The OSPF areas shown in Figure 4-2 and the router types shown in Figure 4-4 remain the same. These are the router types in relationship to the OSPF areas:

- **Internal router:** An internal router is any router whose interfaces all belong to the same OSPF area. Such a router keeps only one link-state database.

- **ABR:** An ABR is connected to more than one area, where one area is Area 0. Such a router maintains a link-state database for each area it belongs to. ABRs generate summary LSAs.

- **ASBR:** This type of router injects external LSAs into the OSPF database (redistribution). These external routes are learned via either other routing protocols or static routes.

- **Backbone router:** A backbone router has at least one interface attached to Area 0.

## OSPFv3 LSAs

OSPFv3 retains the LSA types used by OSPFv2 with some modifications and introduces two new LSAs: link LSA and intra-area-prefix.

All LSAs use a common 20-byte header that indicates the LS type, the advertising router, and the sequence number. Figure 4-8 shows the format of the LSA header.

The LS Age field indicates the time in seconds since the LSA was generated.

The LS Type field indicates the function performed by this LSA. This field includes a U bit and S2 and S1 bits. When the U bit is set to 0, the LSA is flooded only locally. When the U bit is set to 1, the LSA is stored and flooded. The S1 and S2 bits have the functions indicated in Table 4-5.

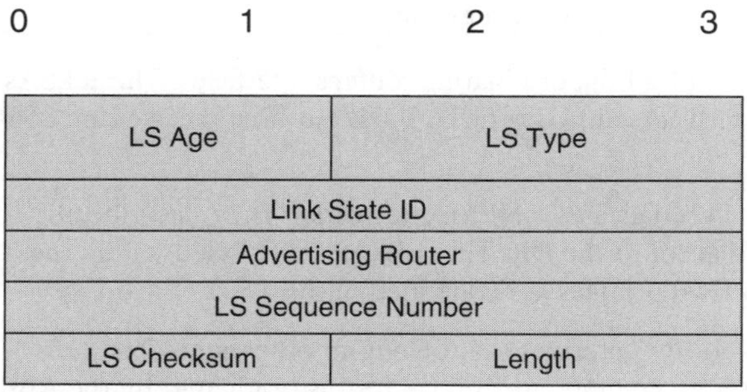

| 0 | 1 | 2 | 3 |
|---|---|---|---|

| LS Age | LS Type |
|---|---|
| Link State ID | |
| Advertising Router | |
| LS Sequence Number | |
| LS Checksum | Length |

**Figure 4-8**  *LSA Header*

**Table 4-5**   LSA Header S2 and S1 Bits

| S2 S1 Value | Flooding Scope |
|---|---|
| 00 | Link-local scope |
| 01 | Flood to all routers within the area |
| 10 | Flood to all routers within the autonomous system |
| 11 | Reserved |

The Link State ID field is used with the LS type and advertising router to identify the link-state database. The Advertising Router field contains the 32-bit router ID of the router that generated the LSA. The LS Sequence Number field is used to detect old or duplicate LSAs. The LS Checksum field is for error checking. The Length field indicates the length of the LSA, including the header.

Table 4-6 summarizes the nine LSAs that can be used in OSPF. Most LSAs retain the same function used in OSPFv2 for IPv4. The OSPFv3 LSAs are described in more detail following the table.

**Table 4-6**   OSPFv3 LSA Types

| LSA Name | LS Type | Description |
|---|---|---|
| Router LSA | 0x2001 | Specifies the state of a router interface |
| Network LSA | 0x2002 | Generated by DR routers in broadcast or NBMA networks |
| Interarea-prefix LSA | 0x2003 | Routes to prefixes in other areas |
| Interarea-router LSA | 0x2004 | Routes to routers in other areas |
| Autonomous system external LSA | 0x4005 | Routes to networks external to the autonomous system |
| Group-membership LSA | 0x2006 | Routes to networks that contain multicast groups |
| NSSA Type 7 LSA | 0x2007 | Routes to networks external to the autonomous system, injected into the NSSA |
| Link LSA | 0x0008 | Tells neighbors about link-local addresses and list IPv6 prefixes associated with the link |
| Intra-area-prefix LSA | 0x2009 | Specifies IPv6 prefixes connected to a router, a stub network, or an associated transit network segment |

Router LSAs describe the cost and state of all the originating router's interfaces. These LSAs are flooded within the area only. Router LSAs are LS type 0x2001. No IPv6 prefixes are contained in router LSAs.

Network LSAs are originated by DRs in broadcast or NBMA networks. They describe all routers attached to the link that are adjacent to the DR. These LSAs are flooded within the area only. The LS type is 0x2002. No IPv6 prefixes are contained in this LSA.

Interarea-prefix LSAs describe routes to IPv6 prefixes that belong to other areas. They are similar to OSPFv2 Type 3 summary LSAs. The interarea-prefix LSA is originated by the ABR and has LS type 0x2003. It is also used to send the default route in stub areas. These LSAs are flooded within the area only.

Each interarea-router LSA describes a route to a router in another area. It is similar to OSPF Type 4 summary LSAs. It is originated by the ABR and has LS type 0x2004. These LSAs are flooded within the area only.

Autonomous system external LSAs describe networks that are external to the autonomous system. These LSAs are originated by ASBRs, have LS type 0x4005, and are flooded to all routers in the autonomous system.

The group-membership LSA describes the directly attached networks that contain members of a multicast group. This LSA is limited to the area and has LS type 0x2006. This LSA is described further in RFC 1584. This LSA is not supported in Cisco IOS software.

Type 7 LSAs describe networks that are external to the autonomous system, but they are flooded to the NSSA only. NSSAs are covered in RFC 1587. This LSA is generated by the NSSA ASBR and has type 0x2007.

Link LSAs describe the router's link-local address and a list of IPv6 prefixes associated with the link. This LSA is flooded to the local link only and has type 0x0008.

The intra-area-prefix LSA is a new LSA type that is used to advertise IPv6 prefixes associated with a router, a stub network, or an associated transit network segment. This LSA contains information that used to be part of the router LSAs and network LSAs.

## OSPFv3 Summary

OSPFv3 is used in large enterprise IPv6 networks. The network topology must be hierarchical. OSPF is used in the enterprise campus building access, distribution, and core layers. OSPF is also used in the enterprise data center, WAN/MAN, and branch offices.

The characteristics of OSPFv3 follow:

- Is the link-state routing protocol for IPv6

- Uses IPv6 Next Header 89

- Uses cost as the metric (based on interface bandwidth by default)

- Sends partial route updates only when changes occur

- Labels routes as intra-area, interarea, external Type 1, or external Type 2

- Uses IPv6 for authentication

- Uses the Dijkstra algorithm to calculate the SPF tree

- Uses a default administrative distance of 110

- Uses multicast address FF02::5 (ALLSPFRouters) and multicast address FF02::6 (ALLDRouters)

- Provides fast convergence, scalability, and reduced bandwidth

- Recommended for large IPv6 networks

# BGP

This section covers Border Gateway Protocol (BGP) theory and design concepts. The current version of BGP, version 4, is defined in RFC 4271. BGP is an interdomain routing protocol, which means it is used to exchange routing information between autonomous systems. (It is used for inter-autonomous system routing.) The primary function of BGP is to provide and exchange network-reachability information between domains or autonomous systems. BGP is a path vector protocol. BGP is best suited for setting routing policies between autonomous systems. In the enterprise campus architecture, BGP is used for Internet connectivity.

BGP is the de facto standard for routing between service providers on the Internet because of its rich features. You can also use it to exchange routes in large internal networks. The Internet Assigned Numbers Authority (IANA) reserved TCP port 179 to identify BGP.

BGPv4 was created to provide CIDR, a feature that was not present in the earlier versions of BGP. BGP is a path vector routing protocol; it is neither a distance vector nor link-state routing protocol.

> **Note** RFC 1519 describes CIDR, which provides the capability to forward packets based on IP prefixes only, with no concern for IP address class boundaries. CIDR was created as a means to constrain the growth of the routing tables in the Internet core through the summarization of IP addresses across network class boundaries. The early 1990s saw an increase in the growth of Internet routing tables and a reduction in Class B address space. CIDR provides a way for service providers to assign address blocks smaller than a Class B network but larger than a Class C network.

## BGP Neighbors

BGP is usually configured between two directly connected routers that belong to different autonomous systems. Each autonomous system is under different technical administration. BGP is frequently used to connect the enterprise to service providers and to interconnect service providers, as shown in Figure 4-9. The routing protocol within the enterprise could be any Interior Gateway Protocol (IGP). Common IGP choices include RIPv2, EIGRP, OSPF, and IS-IS. BGPv4 is the only deployed Exterior Gateway Protocol (EGP).

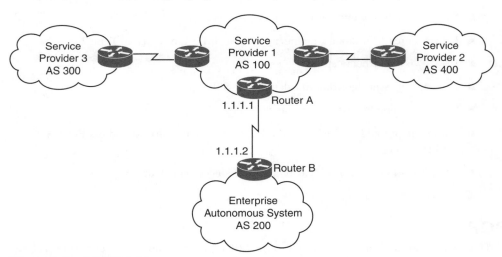

**Figure 4-9** *BGP Neighbors*

BGP is an interdomain routing protocol that allows BGP speakers residing in different autonomous systems to exchange routing network layer reachability information. An autonomous system is a collection of devices under common administration. BGP autonomous systems range from 1 through 65,535. Autonomous system numbers (ASNs) 1 through 64,511 are considered public ASNs. These are allocated by IANA to Regional Internet Registries (RIR). Entities wanting to receive an ASN must complete the application process with the local RIR and be approved before being assigned an ASN. ASNs 64,512 through 65,535 are considered private ASNs. These ASNs can be used by any organization, but, like RFC 1918 addresses, they cannot be used on the Internet.

Before two BGP routers can exchange routing updates, they must become established neighbors. After BGP routers establish a TCP connection, exchange information, and accept the information, they become established neighbors and start exchanging routing updates. If the neighbors do not reach an established state, they do not exchange BGP updates. The information exchanged before the neighbors are established includes the BGP version number, ASN, BGP router ID, and BGP capabilities.

## eBGP

*External Border Gateway Protocol* (*eBGP*) is the term used to describe BGP peering between neighbors in different autonomous systems. As required by RFC 1771, the eBGP peers share a common subnet (although Cisco does allow some flexibility to avoid doing so). In Figure 4-10, all routers speak eBGP with routers in other autonomous systems. Within AS 500, the routers communicate using iBGP, which is covered next.

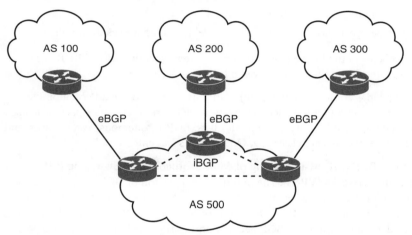

**Figure 4-10**  *eBGP Used Between Autonomous Systems*

## iBGP

*Internal Border Gateway Protocol* (*iBGP*) is the term used to describe the peering between BGP neighbors in the same autonomous system. iBGP is used primarily in transit autonomous systems. Transit autonomous systems forward traffic from one external autonomous system to another external autonomous system. If transit autonomous systems did not use iBGP, the eBGP-learned routes would have to be redistributed into an IGP and then redistributed into the BGP process in another eBGP router. Normally, the number of eBGP routes is too large for an IGP to handle.

iBGP provides a better way to control the routes within the transit autonomous system. With iBGP, the external route information (such as attributes) is forwarded. The various IGPs that might be used do not understand or forward BGP attributes, including autonomous system paths, between eBGP routers.

Another use of iBGP is in large corporations, where the IGP networks are in smaller independent routing domains along organizational or geographic boundaries. In Figure 4-11, a company has decided to use three independent IGPs: one for the Americas; another for Asia and Australia; and another for Europe, the Middle East, and Africa. Routes are redistributed into an iBGP core.

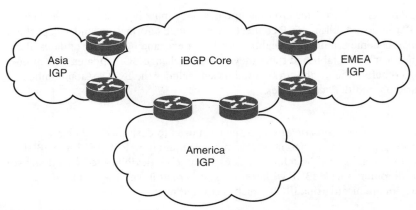

**Figure 4-11**  *iBGP in a Large Corporation*

A CCNP enterprise designer should know at a high level these other uses for iBGP:

- **Applying policies in the internal autonomous system with the help of BGP path attributes:** BGP path attributes are covered later in this chapter.

- **QoS policy propagation on BGP (QPPB):** QPPB uses iBGP to spread common QoS parameters from one router to other routers in the network. It classifies packets using IP precedence bits based on BGP community lists, BGP autonomous system paths, and access lists. After packets are classified, QoS features can enforce policies.

- **Multiprotocol BGP (MP-BGP) peering of Multiprotocol Label Switching (MPLS) virtual private networks (VPNs):** The multiprotocol version of BGP is used to carry MPLS VPN information between all provider edge (PE) routers within a VPN community. MP-BGP is defined in RFC 2858. It introduces a new BGP capabilities advertisement to determine whether a BGP peer supports MP-BGP. It introduces optional nontransitive attributes used to advertise feasible routes to a peer, network layer reachability information, and other characteristics. It defines an address family identifier (AFI) of 2 to identify IPv6, which is used to convey an IPv4 address as the BGP next hop for the advertised IPv6 prefixes.

## Route Reflectors

iBGP requires that all routers be configured to establish a logical connection with all other iBGP routers. The logical connection is a TCP link between all iBGP-speaking routers. The routers in each TCP link become BGP peers. In large networks, the number of iBGP-meshed peers can become very large. Network administrators can use route reflectors to reduce the number of required mesh links between iBGP peers. Some routers are selected to become the route reflectors to serve several other routers that act as route-reflector clients. Route reflectors allow a router to advertise or reflect routes to clients. The route reflector and its clients form a cluster. All client routers in the cluster peer with the route reflectors within the cluster. The route reflectors also peer with all other route reflectors in the internetwork. A cluster can have more than one route reflector.

In Figure 4-12, without route reflectors, all iBGP routers are configured in an iBGP mesh, as required by the protocol. When Routers A and G become route reflectors, they peer with Routers C and D; Router B becomes a route reflector for Routers E and F. Routers A, B, and G peer among each other.

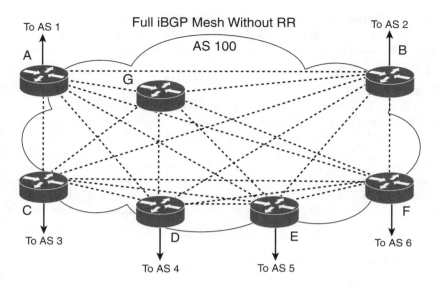

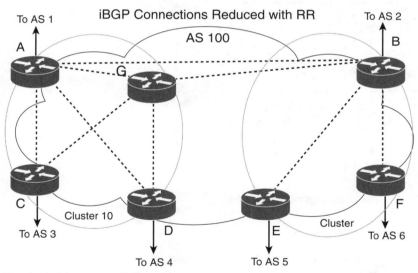

**Figure 4-12**  *Route Reflectors*

**Note**   The combination of the route reflector and its clients is called a *cluster*. In Figure 4-12, Routers A, G, C, and D form a cluster. Routers B, E, and F form another cluster.

Routers A and G are configured to peer with each other and with Routers B, C, and D. The configuration of Routers C and D is different from the configuration of the rest of the routers; they are configured to peer with Routers A and G only. All route reflectors in the same cluster must have the same cluster ID number.

Router B is the route reflector for the second cluster. Router B peers with Routers A and G and with Routers E and F in its cluster. Routers E and F are route-reflector clients and peer only with Router B. If Router B goes down, the cluster on the right goes down because no second route reflector is configured.

## Confederations

Another method to reduce the iBGP mesh within an autonomous system is to use BGP confederations. With confederations, the autonomous system is divided into smaller, sub-autonomous systems, and the whole group is assigned a confederation ID. The sub-ASNs or identifiers are not advertised to the Internet but are contained within the iBGP networks. The routers within each private autonomous system are configured with the full iBGP mesh. Each sub-autonomous system is configured with eBGP to communicate with other sub-autonomous systems in the confederation. External autonomous systems see only the ASN of the confederation, and this number is configured with the BGP confederation identifier.

In Figure 4-13, a confederation divides the autonomous system into two.

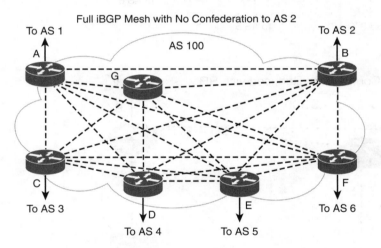

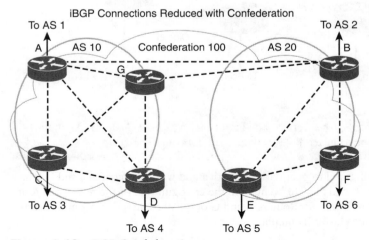

**Figure 4-13**  *BGP Confederations*

Routers A, B, and G are configured for eBGP between the sub-autonomous systems. This involves using the **bgp** *confederation identifier* command on all routers, where *confederation identifier* is the same for all routers in the network. You use the **bgp** *confederation peers* command to identify the ASN of other sub-autonomous systems in the confederation. Because Routers A and G are in AS 10, the peer confederation to Router B is AS 20. Router B is in AS 20, and its peer confederation to Routers A and G is AS 10. Routers C and D are part of AS 10 and peer with each other and with Routers A and G. Routers E and F are part of AS 20 and peer with each other and with Router B.

## BGP Administrative Distance

Cisco IOS software assigns an administrative distance to eBGP and iBGP routes, as it does with other routing protocols. For the same prefix, the route with the lowest administrative distance is selected for inclusion in the IP forwarding table. For BGP, the administrative distances are

- **eBGP routes:** 20
- **iBGP routes:** 200

## BGP Attributes, Weight, and the BGP Decision Process

BGP uses path attributes to select the best path to a destination. This section describes BGP attributes, the use of weight to influence path selection, and the BGP decision process.

### BGP Path Attributes

BGP uses several attributes, or metrics, for the path-selection process. BGP uses path attributes to communicate routing policies. BGP path attributes include next hop, local preference, autonomous system path, origin, multi-exit discriminator (MED), community, atomic aggregate, and aggregator. Of these, the autonomous system path is one of the most important attributes: It lists the number of autonomous system paths to reach a destination network.

BGP attributes can be categorized as *well known* or *optional*. Well-known attributes are recognized by all BGP implementations. Optional attributes do not have to be supported by the BGP process.

Well-known attributes can be further subcategorized as *mandatory* or *discretionary*. Mandatory attributes are always included in BGP update messages. Discretionary attributes might or might not be included in BGP update messages.

Optional attributes can be further subcategorized as *transitive* or *nontransitive*. Routers must advertise a route with transitive attributes to their peers even if they does not support the attribute locally. If the path attribute is nontransitive, the router does not have to advertise the route to its peers.

The following sections cover each attribute category.

### Next-Hop Attribute

The next-hop attribute is the IP address of the next IP hop that will be used to reach the destination. The next-hop attribute is a well-known mandatory attribute.

## Local Preference Attribute

The local preference attribute indicates which path to use to exit the autonomous system. It is a well-known discretionary attribute used between iBGP peers and is not passed on to external BGP peers. In Cisco IOS software, the default local preference is 100. The higher local preference is preferred.

The default local preference is configured on the BGP router with an external path; it then advertises its local preference to internal iBGP peers. Figure 4-14 shows an example of the local preference attribute where Routers B and C are configured with different local preference values. Router A and other iBGP routers then receive routes from both Router B and Router C. Between the two possible paths (shown with arrows), Router A prefers using Router C to route Internet packets because it has a higher local preference (400) than Router B (300).

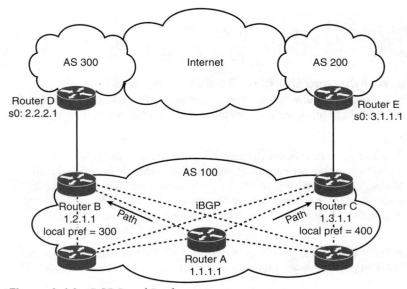

**Figure 4-14**   *BGP Local Preference*

## Origin Attribute

Origin is a well-known mandatory attribute that defines the source of the path information. Do not confuse the origin with comparing whether a route is external (eBGP) or internal (iBGP). The origin attribute is received from the source BGP router. There are three types:

- **IGP:** Indicated by an *i* in the BGP table. Present when the route is learned by way of the network statement.

- **EGP:** Indicated by an *e* in the BGP table. Learned from an EGP peer.

- **Incomplete:** Indicated by a question mark (**?**) in the BGP table. Learned from redistribution of the route.

In terms of choosing a route based on origin, BGP prefers routes that have been verified by an IGP over routes that have been learned from EGP peers, and BGP prefers routes learned from eBGP peers over incomplete paths.

## Autonomous System Path (AS_Path) Attribute

The autonomous system path is a well-known mandatory attribute that contains a list of ASNs in the path to the destination. Each autonomous system prepends its own ASN to the autonomous system path. The autonomous system path describes all the autonomous systems a packet would have to travel to reach the destination IP network. It is used to ensure that the path is loop free. When the AS_Path attribute is used to select a path, the route with the fewest autonomous system hops is preferred. In the case of a tie, other attributes, such as MED, break the tie. Example 4-1 shows the autonomous system path for network 200.50.32.0/19. To reach the destination, a packet must pass autonomous systems 3561, 7004, and 7418. The command **show ip bgp 200.50.32.0** displays the autonomous system path information.

**Example 4-1**   *Autonomous System Path Attribute*

```
Router# show ip bgp 200.50.32.0
BGP routing table entry for 200.50.32.0/19, version 93313535
Paths: (1 available, best #1)
  Not advertised to any peer
  3561 7004 7418
    206.24.241.181 (metric 490201) from 165.117.1.219 (165.117.1.219)
      Origin IGP, metric 4294967294, localpref 100, valid, internal, best
      Community: 2548:182 2548:337 2548:666 3706:153
```

## MED Attribute

The multi-exit discriminator (MED) attribute tells an external BGP peer the preferred path into the autonomous system when multiple paths into the same autonomous system exist. In other words, MED influences which one of many paths a neighboring autonomous system uses to reach destinations within the autonomous system. It is an optional nontransitive attribute carried in eBGP updates. The MED attribute is not used with iBGP peers. The lowest MED value is preferred, and the default value is 0. Paths received with no MED are assigned a MED of 0. The MED is carried into an autonomous system but does not leave the autonomous system.

Consider the diagram shown in Figure 4-15. With all attributes considered equal, say that Router C selects Router A as its best path into AS 100, based on Router A's lower router ID (RID). If Router A is configured with a MED of 200, Router C will select Router B as the best path to AS 100. No additional configuration is required on Router B because the default MED is 0.

## Community Attribute

Although it is not an attribute used in the routing-decision process, the community attribute groups routes and applies policies or decisions (accept, prefer) to those routes. It is a group of destinations that share some common property. The community attribute is an optional transitive attribute of variable length.

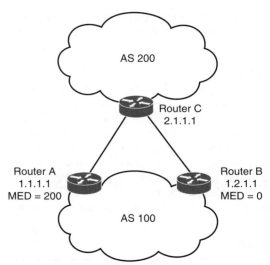

**Figure 4-15**   *MED Attribute*

## Atomic Aggregate and Aggregator Attributes

The atomic aggregate attribute informs BGP peers that the local router used a less specific (aggregated) route to a destination instead of using a more specific route.

The purpose of the attribute is to alert BGP speakers along the path that some information has been lost due to the route aggregation process, and the aggregate path might not be the best path to the destination. When some routes are aggregated by an aggregator, the aggregator does attach its RID to the aggregated route in the AGGREGATOR_ID attribute, and it sets the ATOMIC_AGGREGATE attribute (or not) based on whether the AS_Path information of the aggregated routes was preserved. The atomic aggregate attribute lets the BGP peers know that the BGP router used an aggregated route. A more specific route must be in the advertising router's BGP table before it propagates an aggregate route.

When the atomic aggregate attribute is used, the BGP speaker has the option to send the aggregator attribute. The aggregator attribute includes the ASN and the IP address of the router that originated the aggregated route. In Cisco routers, the IP address used is the RID of the router that performs the route aggregation. Atomic aggregate is a well-known discretionary attribute, and aggregator is an optional transitive attribute.

## Weight Attribute

Weight is assigned locally on a router to specify a preferred path if multiple paths exist out of a router for a destination. Weights can be applied to individual routes or to all routes received from a peer. Weight is specific to Cisco routers and is not propagated to other routers. The weight value ranges from 0 to 65,535. Routes with a higher weight are preferred when multiple routes to a destination exist. Routes that are originated by the local router have a default weight of 32,768. The default weight for learned routes is 0.

You can use weight rather than local preference to influence the selected path to external BGP peers. The difference is that weight is configured locally and is not exchanged in BGP updates. On the other hand, the local preference attribute is exchanged between iBGP peers and is configured at the gateway router.

When the same destinations are advertised from both Router B and Router C, as shown in Figure 4-16, Router A prefers the routes from Router C over those from Router B because the routes received from Router C have a larger weight (600) locally assigned.

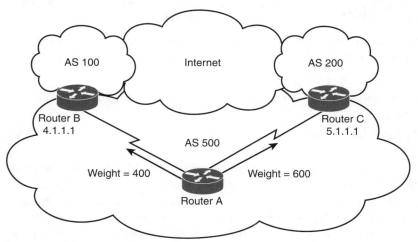

**Figure 4-16**  *BGP Weight*

Table 4-7 lists and describes the BGP attributes and their categories.

**Table 4-7**   BGP Attributes

| BGP Attribute | Description | Category |
|---|---|---|
| Origin | Indicates the source of the path information: IGP, EGP, or incomplete. | Well-known mandatory |
| AS_Path | Lists the ASNs in the path to the destination. | Well-known mandatory |
| Next hop | Specifies the IP address of the router as the next hop to the destination. | Well-known mandatory |
| Local preference | Specifies the path to use to exit the AS. | Well-known discretionary |
| MED | Tells an external BGP peer the preferred path into the AS. | Optional non-transitive |
| Community | Groups routes and applies policies or decisions (accept, prefer) to those routes. (Not an attribute used in the routing-decision process.) | Optional transitive |
| Atomic aggregate | Informs BGP peers that the local router used a less specific (aggregated) route to a destination instead of using a more specific route. | Well-known discretionary |
| Weight | Specifies a preferred path if multiple paths exist out of a router for a destination. Assigned locally on a router. | Optional (Cisco specific) |

## BGP Decision Process

By default, BGP selects only a single path to reach a specific destination (unless you specify maximum paths). The Cisco implementation of BGP uses a simple decision process. When the path is selected, BGP puts the selected path in its routing table and propagates the path to its neighbors.

To select the best path to a destination, Cisco routers running BGP use the following algorithm in the following order:

1. If the specified next hop is inaccessible, drop the path.

2. If the path is internal, and synchronization is enabled, and the path is not in the IGP, drop the path.

3. Prefer the path with the highest weight. (This step is Cisco specific, and weight is localized to the router.)

4. Prefer the path with the highest local preference. iBGP uses this path only to reach the preferred external BGP router.

5. Prefer the path that was locally originated via a **network** or **aggregate** BGP subcommand or through redistribution from an IGP. Local paths sourced by **network** or **redistribute** commands are preferred over local aggregates sourced by the **aggregate-address** command. (This step is Cisco specific.)

6. If no route was originated, prefer the route that has the shortest AS_Path.

7. If all paths have the same autonomous system path length, prefer the path with the lowest origin type. Paths with an origin type of IGP (lower) are preferred over paths originated from an EGP such as BGP, and EGP origin is preferred over a route with an incomplete origin. (IGP < EGP < incomplete.)

8. If the origin codes are the same, prefer the path with the lowest MED attribute. An eBGP peer uses this attribute to select a best path to the autonomous system. This attribute is exchanged between autonomous systems. (This step is a tiebreaker, as described in RFC 4271xxx.)

9. If the paths have the same MED, prefer the external (eBGP) path over the internal (iBGP) path.

10. If the paths are still the same, prefer the path through the closest IGP neighbor (best IGP metric). (This step is a tiebreaker, as described in RFC 4271xxx.)

11. Prefer the oldest known path.

12. Prefer the path with the BGP neighbor with the lowest BGP router ID. (The RFC that defines the BGP describes the router ID.)

13. Prefer the path with the minimum cluster list length.

14. Prefer the path with the lowest neighbor IP address.

After BGP decides on a best path, it marks it with a > sign in the output of the **show ip bgp** command and adds it to the IP routing table.

**Note**    Options for influencing outbound routing decisions include weight, local preference, and AS path length. Options for influencing inbound routing decisions include AS path length, BGP communities, and MED.

Table 4-8 shows a summary of the BGP best path order.

**Table 4-8**    BGP Best Path Order

| BGP Best Path Order |
| --- |
| Highest weight |
| Highest local preference |
| Prefer local originated route |
| Shortest AS_Path |
| Lowest origin type |
| Lowest MED |
| Prefer eBGP over iBGP |
| Lowest IGP metric to the BGP next hop |
| Oldest path |
| Lowest BGP router ID source |
| Minimum cluster list length |
| Lowest neighbor address |

## BGP Route Manipulation and Load Balancing

By default, BGP chooses a single path to a destination. With thousands of routes, this can cause uneven traffic patterns. When working with BGP, there are different methods to control traffic paths and handle load balancing of traffic. Furthermore, outbound and inbound traffic flows are independent of each other.

For incoming traffic, the following methods can be used to manipulate traffic:

- You can advertise a subset of the network via ISP 1 and another via ISP 2. For example, if you have a /22 network, you can advertise subnet /23 on your side and the second /23 on the other side and the /22 on both sides.

- With AS_Path prepending, you can add one or more AS numbers to the left of the AS_Path to make it longer.

- You can use the BGP multi-exit discriminator (MED) attribute. When there are multiple entry points, MED tells the other AS how to route traffic into the AS.

- You can use BGP communities with local preference to set up flags in order to mark a set of routes. Then the service provider can use those flags to apply local preference within the network.

- You can use the BGP **allow-as** and **as-override** subcommands to allow eBGP routers to accept routes from the same AS.

For outbound traffic, the following methods can be used to manipulate traffic:

- You can use default routes to provide outbound traffic load balancing.

- You can use provider-advertised partial routes from each provider or request full Internet tables and perform AS_Path filtering.

- You can use the local preference attribute to indicate which path to use to exit the autonomous system. The higher local preference is used.

### eBGP Multihop

eBGP Multihop can be used to connect to a BGP neighbor across multiple equal-cost links, as shown in Figure 4-17. The BGP peering is established between the loopback addresses and not the point-to-point links. This means the BGP peers do not have to be directly connected.

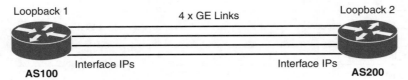

**Figure 4-17**  *eBGP Multihop and Multipath*

### BGP Multipath

BGP Multipath Load Sharing for eBGP and iBGP allows you to configure multipath load balancing with both eBGP and iBGP paths in BGP networks that are configured to use MPLS. This is accomplished using the **maximum-paths** command. For example, in Figure 4-17, the eBGP peering can be established by using the interface address of each link and not the loopback address. As a result, the routers receive multiple paths—one for each link—and install all paths up to the **maximum-paths** value that was configured.

## BGP Summary

The characteristics of BGP follow:

- BGP is an EGP used in routing on the Internet. It is an interdomain routing protocol.

- BGP is a path vector routing protocol suited for strategic routing policies.

- It uses TCP port 179 to establish connections with neighbors.

- BGPv4 implements CIDR.

- eBGP is used for external neighbors. It is used between different autonomous systems.

- iBGP is used for internal neighbors. It is used within an autonomous system.

- BGP uses several attributes in the routing-decision algorithm.

- It uses confederations and route reflectors to reduce BGP peering overhead.

- The MED attribute is used between autonomous systems to influence inbound traffic.

- Weight is used to influence the path of outbound traffic from a single router, configured locally.

- eBGP routes have an administrative distance of 20, and iBGP routes have an administrative distance of 200.

# Route Manipulation

This section covers policy-based routing (PBR), route summarization, route filtering, and route redistribution. You can use PBR to modify the next hop for packets from what is selected by the routing protocol. PBR is useful when path traffic engineering is required. Routes are summarized at network boundaries to reduce the size of routing tables. Redistribution between routing protocols is required to inject route information from one routing protocol to another. Route filtering is used to control network addresses that get redistributed or to control access to certain parts of the network. A CCNP enterprise designer must understand the issues with the redistribution of routes.

## PBR

You can use PBR to modify the next-hop addresses of packets or to mark packets to receive differential service. Routing is based on destination addresses; routers look at the routing table to determine the next-hop IP address based on a destination lookup. PBR is commonly used to modify the next-hop IP address based on the source address. You can also use PBR to mark the IP precedence bits in outbound IP packets so that you can apply QoS policies. In Figure 4-18, Router A exchanges routing updates with routers in the WAN. The routing protocol might select Serial 0 as the preferred path for all traffic because of the higher bandwidth. The company might have business-critical systems that use the T1 but may not want systems on Ethernet 1 to affect WAN performance. The company could configure PBR on Router A to force traffic from Ethernet 1 out on Serial 1.

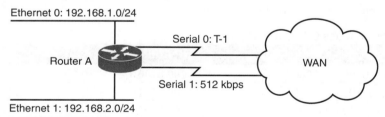

Ethernet 0: 192.168.1.0/24

Serial 0: T-1

Router A

WAN

Serial 1: 512 kbps

Ethernet 1: 192.168.2.0/24

**Figure 4-18**  *Policy-Based Routing*

## Route Summarization

Large networks can grow quickly, from 500 routes to 1000, to 2000, and higher. Network IP addresses should be allocated to allow for route summarization. Route summarization reduces the amount of route traffic on the network, unnecessary route computation, and the perceived complexity of the network. Route summarization also allows the network to scale as a company grows.

The recommendation for route summarization is to summarize at the distribution layer of the network topology. Figure 4-19 shows a hierarchical network. It has a network core, regional distribution routers, and access routes for sites. All routes in Brazil are summarized with a single 10.1.0.0/16 route. The North American and European routes are also summarized with 10.2.0.0/16 and 10.3.0.0/16, respectively. Routers in Europe need to know only the summarized route to get to Brazil and North America and vice versa. Again, a design best practice is to summarize at the distribution toward the core. The core needs to know only the summarized route of the regional areas.

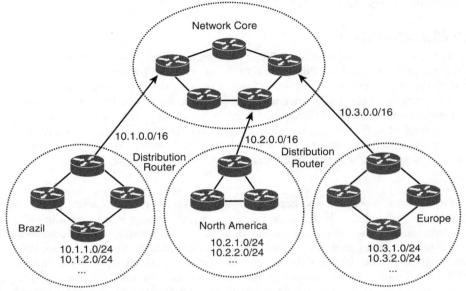

**Figure 4-19**   *Route Summarization to the Network Core*

In this case, you can also use summarization to aggregate four contiguous Class C networks at the /22 bit level. For example, networks 200.1.100.0, 200.1.101.0, 200.1.102.0, and 200.1.103.0 share common bits, as shown in Table 4-9. The resulting network is 200.1.100.0/22, which you can use for a 1000-node network.

**Table 4-9**   Common Bits in Class C Networks

| Binary Address | IP Address |
|---|---|
| 11001000 00000001 01100100 00000000 | 200.1.100.0 |
| 11001000 00000001 01100101 00000000 | 200.1.101.0 |
| 11001000 00000001 01100110 00000000 | 200.1.102.0 |
| 11001000 00000001 01100111 00000000 | 200.1.103.0 |

It is important for an Internet network designer to assign IP networks in a manner that permits summarization. It is preferred that a neighboring router receive 1 summarized route rather than 8, 16, 32, or more routes, depending on the level of summarization. Summarization reduces the size of the routing tables in the network.

For route summarization to work, the multiple IP addresses must share the same leftmost bits, and routers must base their routing decisions on the IP address and prefix length. Figure 4-20 shows another example of route summarization. All the edge routers send network information to their upstream routers. Router E summarizes its two LAN networks by sending 192.168.16.0/23 to Router A. Router F summarizes its two LAN networks by sending 192.168.18.0/23. Router B summarizes the networks it receives from Routers C and D. Routers B, E, and F send their routes to Router A. Router A sends a single route (192.168.16.0/21) to its upstream router instead of sending eight routes. This process reduces the number of networks that upstream routers need to include in routing updates.

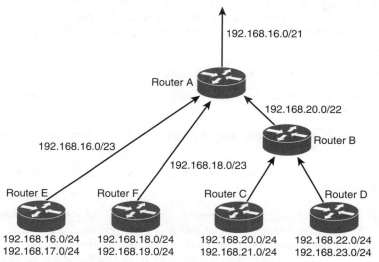

192.168.16.0/21

Router A

192.168.20.0/22

Router B

192.168.16.0/23

192.168.18.0/23

Router E          Router F          Router C          Router D

192.168.16.0/24    192.168.18.0/24    192.168.20.0/24    192.168.22.0/24
192.168.17.0/24    192.168.19.0/24    192.168.21.0/24    192.168.23.0/24

**Figure 4-20**  *Route Summarization of Networks*

Notice in Table 4-10 that all the Class C networks share a bit boundary with 21 common bits. The networks are different on the 22nd bit and thus cannot be summarized beyond the 21st bit. All these networks are summarized with 192.168.16.0/21.

**Table 4-10**  Summarization of Networks

| Binary Address | IP Address |
|---|---|
| 11000000 10101000 00010000 00000000 | 192.168.16.0 |
| 11000000 10101000 00010001 00000000 | 192.168.17.0 |
| 11000000 10101000 00010010 00000000 | 192.168.18.0 |
| 11000000 10101000 00010011 00000000 | 192.168.19.0 |
| 11000000 10101000 00010100 00000000 | 192.168.20.0 |
| 11000000 10101000 00010101 00000000 | 192.168.21.0 |
| 11000000 10101000 00010110 00000000 | 192.168.22.0 |
| 11000000 10101000 00010111 00000000 | 192.168.23.0 |

To summarize, the recommended practices regarding summarization include the following:

- Implement summarization at WAN connectivity and remote-access points toward the network core to reduce the size of the routing table.

- Summarize at the distribution layer for all network interfaces that point to the network core.

- Implement passive interfaces on access layer interfaces so that neighbor adjacencies are not established through the access layer. A more specific route might be created, which would be taken over by a summarized route.

## Route Redistribution

Route redistribution is an exchange of routes between routing protocols (for example, between EIGRP and OSPF). You configure the redistribution of routing protocols on routers that reside at the service provider edge of the network or an autonomous system boundary within the internal network. These routers exchange routes with other autonomous systems. Redistribution is also done on routers that run more than one routing protocol. Here are some reasons to do redistribution:

- Migration from an older routing protocol to a new routing protocol

- Mixed-vendor environment in which Cisco routers might be using EIGRP and other vendor routers might be using OSPF

- Different administrative domain between company departments using different routing protocols

- Mergers and acquisitions in which the networks initially need to communicate, when two different EIGRP processes might exist

Routes can be learned from different sources. One source is a static route that is configured when not peering with the AS external router. Another source is a different routing protocol where you might be running EIGRP and the other network uses OSPF. Another common example is when peering with an ISP, the enterprise is commonly using OSPF, and the Internet routers peer with the ISP router using BGP.

Figure 4-21 shows an example of the exchange of routes between two autonomous systems. Routes from AS 100 are redistributed into BGP on Router A. Routes from AS 200 are redistributed into BGP on Router B. Then Routers A and B exchange BGP routes. Router A and Router B also implement filters to redistribute only the desired networks.

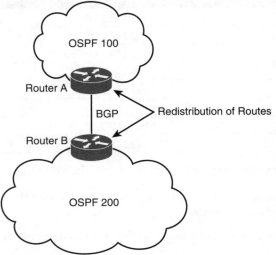

**Figure 4-21**  *IDS and IPS Operational Differences*

Say that a company acquires another company that is running another routing protocol. Figure 4-22 shows a network using both OSPF and EIGRP routing protocols. Routers A and B perform redistribution between OSPF and EIGRP. Both routers must filter routes from OSPF before redistributing them into EIGRP and must filter routes from EIGRP before redistributing them into OSPF. This setup prevents route feedback.

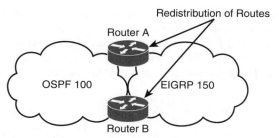

**Figure 4-22**    *Redistribution Between IGPs*

Route feedback occurs when a routing protocol learns routes from another routing protocol and then announces the routes to the other routing protocol. In Figure 4-21, OSPF should not advertise the routes it learned from EIGRP on Router A back to EIGRP on Router B. And EIGRP should not announce the routes it learned from OSPF on Router B back to OSPF on Router A.

You can use access lists, distribution lists, and route maps when redistributing routes. You can use these methods to specify (select) routes for redistribution, to set metrics, or to set other policies for the routes. These methods are used to prevent loops in the redistribution. They are also used to control routes' redistribution direction. Redistribution can be accomplished by two methods:

- **Two-way redistribution:** In two-way redistribution, routing information is exchanged between the two routing protocols. No static routes are used in this exchange. Route filters are used to prevent routing loops. Routing loops can be caused by one route protocol redistributing routes that were learned from a second route protocol back to that second routing protocol.

- **One-way redistribution:** One-way redistribution only allows redistribution from one routing protocol to another. Normally, it is used in conjunction with a default or static route at the edge of a network. Figure 4-23 shows an example of one-way redistribution. The routing information from the WAN routes is redistributed into the campus, but campus routes are not redistributed out to the WAN. The WAN routers use a default route to get back to the campus.

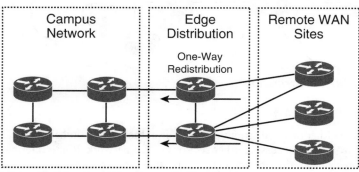

**Figure 4-23**    *One-Way Route Redistribution*

Other locations for one-way redistribution are from building access networks, from BGP routes or static routes into the IGP, and from VPN static routes into the IGP.

### Default Metric

You should configure the metric of the redistributed routes to a metric other than 0. You can configure the metric in the **redistribution** command or configure a default seed metric. You can also use the command **default-metric** with OSPF. IS-IS does not use the **default-metric** command. The **default-metric** command is used to specify the seed metric that is used if a metric is not specified during redistribution. The **default-metric** command has the following syntax for EIGRP:

**default-metric** *bandwidth delay reliability load mtu*

### OSPF Redistribution

This section reviews a few things you need to remember when designing a network that will redistribute with OSPF.

When redistributing routes into OSPF, use the **subnets** keyword to permit subnetted routes to be received. If you do not use it, only the major network route is redistributed, without subnetworks. In other words, OSPF performs automatic summarization to IP classful network values. Also, unlike EIGRP and RIPv2, OSPF does not need a metric to be specified during redistribution; it also does not need a seed metric to be specified because it uses a default metric for redistributed routes.

By default, redistributed routes are classified as external Type 2 (E2) in OSPF. You can use the **metric-type** keyword to change the external route to an external Type 1 (E1). The network design can take into account the after-redistribution cost (Type 2) or the after-redistribution cost plus the path's cost (Type 1).

In Figure 4-24, Router B is configured to perform mutual redistribution between EIGRP 100 and OSPF process ID 50. In this example, you can use route maps and access lists to prevent routing loops. The route maps permit or deny the networks that are listed in the access lists. The **subnets** keyword redistributes every subnet in EIGRP into OSPF. (This book does not cover exact configurations.)

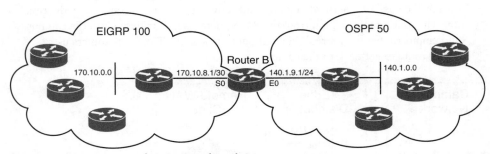

**Figure 4-24**   *OSPF and EIGRP Redistribution*

### Route Filtering

Filtering of routes can occur either on a redistribution point or in the routing domain to prevent some parts of the network from accessing other sections of the network. Route filtering could be used to filter routes when redistributing between routing protocols.

Filtering at a redistribution point provides the following benefits:

- Avoids routing loops

- Avoids suboptimal routing

- Prevents certain routes from entering the domain

### Transit Traffic

With BGP, you should be sure not to configure a network as a transit network between autonomous systems. A transit network can occur when connecting your enterprise network to two ISPs in a multihomed BGP configuration. When BGP routes get exchanged with multiple Internet service providers (ISPs), route filtering is used to prevent advertisement of private addresses and addresses that are out of the scope of the domain. The recommendation is to filter routes so that only the enterprise prefixes are advertised to the ISPs, as illustrated in Figure 4-25.

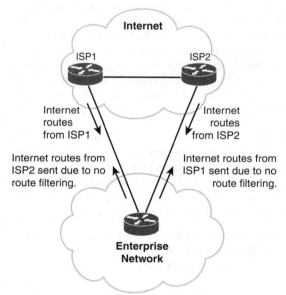

**Figure 4-25**  *Avoiding BGP Transit Traffic*

## Bidirectional Forwarding Detection (BFD)

BFD is a detection protocol designed to provide fast forwarding path failure detection times for all media types, encapsulations, topologies, and routing protocols. In addition to fast forwarding path failure detection, BFD provides a consistent failure detection method for network administrators. BFD provides fast BFD peer failure detection times independently of all media types, encapsulations, topologies, and routing protocols, including BGP, EIGRP, IS-IS, and OSPF. By sending rapid failure detection notices to the routing protocols in the local router to initiate the routing table recalculation process, BFD contributes to greatly reduced overall network convergence time.

There are several benefits to using BFD over reducing timer mechanisms for routing protocols:

- Although reducing the EIGRP, IS-IS, and OSPF timers can result in a minimum detection timer of one to two seconds, BFD can provide failure detection in less than one second.

- Because BFD is not tied to any particular routing protocol, it can be used as a generic and consistent failure detection mechanism for EIGRP, IS-IS, and OSPF.

- Because some parts of BFD can be distributed to the data plane, it can be less CPU-intensive than the reduced EIGRP, IS-IS, and OSPF timers, which exist wholly at the control plane.

### Graceful Restart and Non-Stop Routing

Graceful Restart (GR), also known as Non-Stop Forwarding (NSF), and Non-Stop Routing (NSR) are two different mechanisms to prevent routing protocol reconvergence during a processor switchover. Graceful Restart and Non-Stop Routing suppress routing changes on peers to Stateful Switch Over (SSO)–enabled devices during processor switchover events of SSO, reducing network instability and downtime. Graceful Restart and NSR both allow for the forwarding of data packets to continue along known routes while the routing protocol information is being restored (in the case of GR) or refreshed (in the case of NSR) following a processor switchover. GR is available for OSPF, ISIS, EIGRP, LDP, and BGP. NSR is available in Cisco IOS for ISIS and BGP. Compared to GR, NSR uses more system resources due to the information transfer to the standby processor.

### Virtual Routing and Forwarding (VRF)

Virtual routing and forwarding (VRF) is a technology that supports multiple routing instances inside a single router or Layer 3 switch. With VRF, a single router can have multiple separate routing tables, all completely isolated from each other. One or more logical or physical interfaces may have a VRF instance, and these VRF instances do not share routes; therefore, the packets are only forwarded between interfaces on the same VRF instance.

VRF instances are the TCP/IP Layer 3 equivalent of VLANs. Because the routing instances are independent, the same or overlapping IP addresses can be used without conflicting with each other. Network functionality is improved because network paths can be segmented without requiring multiple routers.

VRF instances are used to provide network segmentation, such as to separate business traffic from process control traffic in plants. Because VRF allows for true routing and forwarding separation, dedicated data and control planes are defined to handle traffic belonging to groups with various requirements or policies. This provides an additional level of segregation and security because no communication between devices belonging to different VRF instances is allowed unless explicitly configured.

## References and Recommended Readings

RFC 1075: *Distance Vector Multicast Routing Protocol*, https://tools.ietf.org/html/rfc1075.

RFC 1584: *Multicast Extensions to OSPF*, https://tools.ietf.org/html/rfc1584.

RFC 1587: *The OSPF NSSA Opti*on, https://tools.ietf.org/html/rfc1587.

RFC 1997: *BGP Communities Attribute*, https://tools.ietf.org/html/rfc1997.

RFC 2328: *OSPF Version 2*, https://tools.ietf.org/html/rfc2328.

RFC 2740: *OSPF for IPv6*, https://tools.ietf.org/html/rfc2740.

RFC 2858: *Multiprotocol Extensions for BGP-4*, https://tools.ietf.org/html/rfc2858.

RFC 4271: *A Border Gateway Protocol 4 (BGP-4)*, https://tools.ietf.org/html/rfc4271.

RFC 5340: *OSPF for IPv6*, https://tools.ietf.org/html/rfc5340.

RFC 5709: *OSPFv2 HMAC-SHA Cryptographic Authentication*, https://tools.ietf.org/html/rfc5709.

RFC 5838: *Support of Address Families in OSPFv3*, https://tools.ietf.org/html/rfc5838.

RFC 6969: *OSPFv3 Instance ID Registry Update*, https://tools.ietf.org/html/rfc6969.

Cisco, "Border Gateway Protocol," https://www.cisco.com/c/en/us/products/ios-nx-os-software/border-gateway-protocol-bgp/index.html.

Cisco, "IP Multicast Technology Overview" (white paper), http://www.cisco.com/c/en/us/td/docs/ios/solutions_docs/ip_multicast/White_papers/mcst_ovr.html.

Doyle, J., and J. Carroll. *Routing TCP/IP, Volume I, 2nd ed*. Indianapolis: Cisco Press, 2005.

Doyle, J., and J. Carroll. *Routing TCP/IP, Volume II*. Indianapolis: Cisco Press, 2001.

Halabi, S. *Internet Routing Architectures*. Indianapolis: Cisco Press, 2000.

Martey, A. *IS-IS Network Design Solutions. Indianapolis*: Cisco Press, 2002.

Networkers-Online, "BGP Attributes: Atomic Aggregate Attribute," http://www.networkers-online.com/blog/2010/12/bgp-attributes-atomic-aggregate-atribute/.

## Exam Preparation Tasks

As mentioned in the section "How to Use This Book" in the Introduction, you have a couple of choices for exam preparation: the exercises here, Chapter 13, "Final Preparation," and the exam simulation questions on the companion website.

## Review All Key Topics

Review the most important topics in the chapter, noted with the Key Topic icon in the outer margin of the page. Table 4-11 lists these key topics and the page number on which each is found.

**Table 4-11**  Key Topics

| Key Topic Element | Description | Page |
|---|---|---|
| Paragraph | OSPFv2 areas | 137 |
| Paragraph | OSPF router types | 138 |
| Paragraph | OSPF LSA types | 140 |
| Table 4-4 | Major LSA types | 140 |
| List | Major changes to OSPFv3 | 144 |
| Paragraph | OSPFv3 LSAs | 145 |

| Key Topic Element | Description | Page |
|---|---|---|
| Table 4-6 | OSPFv3 LSA types | 146 |
| Paragraph | eBGP | 149 |
| Paragraph | iBGP | 149 |
| List | BGP administrative distances | 153 |
| Paragraph | BGP path attributes | 153 |
| Paragraph | Route summarization | 161 |
| Paragraph | Route redistribution | 164 |
| Paragraph | Route filtering | 166 |

## Complete Tables and Lists from Memory

Print a copy of Appendix D, "Memory Tables," found on the companion website, or at least the section for this chapter, and complete the tables and lists from memory. Appendix E, "Memory Tables Answer Key," includes completed tables and lists to check your work.

## Define Key Terms

Define the following key terms from this chapter and check your answers in the glossary:

area border router (ABR), autonomous system boundary router (ASBR), Border Gateway Protocol (BGP), designated router (DR),, link-state advertisement (LSA), Multiprotocol Border Gateway Protocol (MP-BGP), not-so-stubby area (NSSA), Open Shortest Path First version 2 (OSPFv2), Open Shortest Path First version 3 (OSPFv3), policy-based routing (PBR)

## Q&A

The answers to these questions appear in Appendix A. For more practice with exam format questions, use the exam engine on the companion website.

1. True or false: A router needs to have all its interfaces in Area 0 to be considered an OSPF backbone router.

2. True or false: OSPF and IS-IS use a designated router in multiaccess networks.

3. Which multicast addresses do OSPFv2 routers use?

4. Which multicast addresses do OSPFv3 routers use?

5. What is the Cisco administrative distance of OSPF?

6. Which OSPFv2 router type generates the OSPF Type 3 LSA?

7. Which OSPFv2 router type generates the OSPF Type 2 LSA?

8. What is included in an OSPFv2 router LSA?

9. True or false: The router with the lowest priority is selected as the OSPF DR.

10. True or false: You use iBGP to exchange routes between different autonomous systems.

11. True or false: eBGP and iBGP redistribute automatically on a router if the BGP peers are configured with the same autonomous system number.

12. eBGP routes have an administrative distance of ____, and iBGP routes have an administrative distance of ____.

**13.** Match each routing protocol with its description.

    **i.** EIGRP

    **ii.** OSPFv2

    **iii.** RIPv2

    **iv.** BGP

    **a.** Distance vector protocol used at the edge of the network

    **b.** IETF link-state protocol used in the network core

    **c.** Hybrid protocol used in the network core

    **d.** Path vector protocol

**14.** Which routing protocol do you use in the core of a large enterprise network that supports VLSM for a network with a mix of Cisco and non-Cisco routers?

**15.** What is the benefit of designing for stub areas?

**16.** What constraint does the OSPF network design have for traffic traveling between areas?

**17.** How is OSPFv3 identified as the upper-layer protocol in IPv6?

**18.** Which routing protocol or protocols are recommended for large enterprise networks?

    **a.** RIPv2

    **b.** OSPFv2

    **c.** EIGRP

    **d.** IS-IS

    **e.** A and B

    **f.** B and C

    **g.** B and D

    **h.** A, B, C, and D

**19.** What OSPFv3 LSA has LS type 0x0008?

    **a.** Router LSA

    **b.** Interarea-router LSA

    **c.** Link LSA

    **d.** Intra-area-prefix LSA

**20.** Which routing protocol or protocols have fast convergence for IPv4 networks?

    **a.** BGP

    **b.** OSPFv2

    **c.** EIGRP

    **d.** RIPv2

    **e.** B and C

    **f.** B, C, and D

    **g.** A, B, and C

**21.** Which routing protocol or protocols have fast convergence for IPv6 networks?

   **a.** RIPng

   **b.** OSPFv3

   **c.** EIGRP for IPv6

   **d.** RIPv2

   **e.** MP-BGP

   **f.** B and C

   **g.** B, C, and D

   **h.** B, C, and E

**22.** A retail chain has about 800 stores that connect to the headquarters and a backup location. The company wants to limit the amount of routing traffic on the WAN links. What routing protocol or protocols are recommended?

   **a.** RIPv1

   **b.** RIPv2

   **c.** OSPFv2

   **d.** EIGRP

   **e.** IS-IS

   **f.** BGP

   **g.** B, C, and D

   **h.** C and D

   **i.** C, D, and E

**23.** If OSPF is enabled on all routers in Figure 4-26 with the default metrics unchanged, what path is taken?

   **a.** Path 1

   **b.** Path 2

   **c.** Unequal-cost load balancing with Path 1 and Path 2

   **d.** Equal-cost load balancing with Path 1 and Path 2

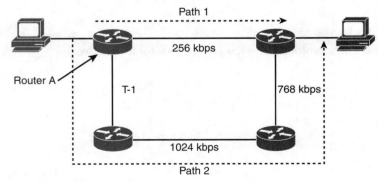

**Figure 4-26**   *Path Selection*

**24.** Identify the OSPF router types shown in Figure 4-27.

Router A = _____

Router B = _____

Router C = _____

Router D = _____

Router E = _____

Router F = _____

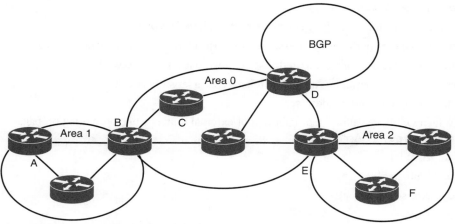

**Figure 4-27**  *OSPF Router Types*

**25.** Match each BGP attribute with its description.

**i.**   Local preference

**ii.**   MED

**iii.**   Autonomous system path

**iv.**   Next hop

**a.**   IP address

**b.**   Indicates the path used to exit the autonomous system

**c.**   Tells external BGP peers the preferred path into the autonomous system

**d.**   List of ASNs

**26.** Which Cisco feature can you use instead of local preference to influence the selected path to external BGP routers?

**27.** What is the purpose of route reflectors?

**28.** When BGP confederations are used, which number do external peers see?

**29.** With _____, all routers peer with each other within the private autonomous system. With _____, client routers peer only with the reflector.

**30.** Which of the following is the order of attributes that BGP uses to select a best path?

**a.**   Origin, lowest IP, autonomous system path, weight, local preference, MED

**b.**   Weight, local preference, autonomous system path, origin, MED, lowest IP

      **c.**   Lowest IP, autonomous system path, origin, weight, MED, local preference

      **d.**   Weight, origin, local preference, autonomous system path, MED, lowest IP

**31.**  What of the following should be used to summarize the networks 10.150.80.0/23, 10.150.82.0/24, 10.150.83.0/24, and 10.150.84.0/22?

      **a.**   10.150.80.0/23, 10.150.82.0/23, and 10.150.84.0/22

      **b.**   10.150.80.0/22 and 10.150.84/22

      **c.**   10.150.80.0/21

      **d.**   10.150.80.0/20

**32.**  Which of the following best describes route summarization?

      **a.**   Grouping contiguous addresses to advertise a large Class A network

      **b.**   Grouping noncontiguous addresses to advertise a larger network

      **c.**   Grouping contiguous addresses to advertise a larger network

      **d.**   Grouping Internet addresses

**33.**  Which OSPF area allows redistribution of external routers while preventing propagation of Type 5 LSAs?

      **a.**   Area 0

      **b.**   Stub area

      **c.**   Not-so-stubby area

      **d.**   ABR

      **e.**   Area 1 over a virtual link

**34.**  Which protocol is commonly used to connect to an ISP?

      **a.**   RIPv2

      **b.**   OSPF

      **c.**   EIGRP

      **d.**   BGP

**35.**  Which of the following statements are true regarding OSPF? (Choose two.)

      **a.**   ABRs require manual configuration for summarization.

      **b.**   ABRs automatically summarize.

      **c.**   External routes are injected into the autonomous system via the ABR.

      **d.**   External routes are injected into the autonomous system via the ASBR.

**36.**  Which routing protocol is recommended for large IPv6 multivendor networks?

      **a.**   RIPng

      **b.**   OSPFv3

      **c.**   EIGRP for IPv6

      **d.**   BGP

**37.** As a network designer, you need to influence the outbound routing with your ISP. Which of the following are BGP options to do this?

    **a.** AS_Path, local preference, weight

    **b.** MED, local preference, weight

    **c.** AS_Path, BGP communities, MED

    **d.** BGP communities, local preference, MED

**38.** As a network designer, you need to influence the inbound routing with your ISP. Which of the following are BGP options to do this?

    **a.** AS_Path, local preference, weight

    **b.** MED, local preference, weight

    **c.** AS_Path, BGP communities, MED

    **d.** BGP communities, local preference, MED

**39.** Which statements are correct? (Choose two.)

    **a.** The Dijkstra algorithm is used by both OSPF and IS-IS to calculate the shortest best path.

    **b.** IS-IS is a proprietary protocol. OSPF is a standards-based protocol.

    **c.** OSPF is used only on enterprise networks, and IS-IS is used only by service providers.

    **d.** ISIS boundaries are links; OSPF area boundaries are within the routers.

**40.** In Figure 4-28, where should route redistribution occur?

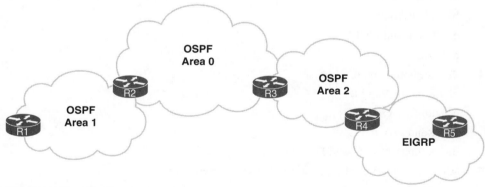

**Figure 4-28** *Redistribution Question*

    **a.** R1

    **b.** R2

    **c.** R3

    **d.** R4

    **e.** R5

Refer to Figure 4-29 to answer questions 40 to 44.

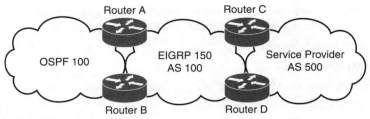

**Figure 4-29** *Network Scenario*

**41.** Where should you configure BGP?

    **a.** Routers A and B

    **b.** Routers C and D

    **c.** Routers A, B, C, and D

    **d.** Routers A and C

**42.** On which router should you configure redistribution for OSPF and EIGRP?

    **a.** Router A only

    **b.** Router B only

    **c.** Routers A and B

    **d.** None; redistribution occurs automatically

**43.** To announce the networks from AS 100 to AS 500, which routing protocols should you redistribute into BGP?

    **a.** OSPF only

    **b.** EIGRP only

    **c.** OSPF and EIGRP

    **d.** iBGP

**44.** Where should you use filters?

    **a.** Routers A and B

    **b.** Routers C and D

    **c.** Routers A and C

    **d.** Routers A, B, C, and D

**45.** Which two BGP attributes are well-known discretionary?

    **a.** AS_Path and next hop

    **b.** MED and origin

    **c.** Aggregator and community

    **d.** Atomic aggregate and local preference

**46.** Which two BGP attributes are well-known mandatory?

    **a.** AS_Path and next hop

    **b.** MED and origin

    **c.**   Aggregator and community

    **d.**   Atomic aggregate and local preference

**47.**   Which two BGP attributes are optional transitive?

    **a.**   AS_Path and next hop

    **b.**   MED and origin

    **c.**   Aggregator and community

    **d.**   Atomic aggregate and local preference

**48.**   The IP address of the eBGP peer of a router is reached via OSPF. Which condition should be avoided that might cause the BGP peers to flap?

    **a.**   The OSPF Area 0 is not transverse network to reach the eBGP peer.

    **b.**   The BGP peer address is also sent via the BGP peer.

    **c.**   BGP multipath is not configured.

    **d.**   eBGP peers cannot be configured over OSPF.

**49.**   Which of the following is true about iBGP?

    **a.**   iBGP is preferred over eBGP when connecting to an ISP.

    **b.**   iBGP carries eBGP attributes that otherwise would be lost in IGP.

    **c.**   iBGP's administrative distance is 20.

    **d.**   iBGP peers need to be directly connected.

**50.**   What is the default metric used when redistributing OSPF into EIGRP?

    **a.**   0

    **b.**   1

    **c.**   Cost

    **d.**   Infinity

**4**

## CHAPTER 5

# IP Multicast and Network Management

**This chapter covers the following subjects:**

**IP Multicast Review:** This section covers IP multicast concepts and services, including multicast source and shared trees, Protocol Independent Multicast (PIM), and MSDP.

**Network Management Design:** This section discusses network management protocols and components, including Simple Network Management Protocol (SNMP), Management Information Base (MIB), Remote Monitoring (RMON) protocol, Cisco Discovery Protocol (CDP), and NetFlow and system logging (syslog).

This chapter covers IP multicast concepts and services, including multicast source and shared trees, Protocol Independent Multicast (PIM), and MSDP. It reviews network management design considerations such as out-of-band network management. It also introduces network management protocols and components, including Simple Network Management Protocol (SNMP), Management Information Base (MIB), Remote Monitoring (RMON) protocol, Cisco Discovery Protocol (CDP), and NetFlow and system logging (syslog).

This chapter covers the following objectives from the ENSLD 300-420 exam:

■ Describe multicast routing concepts (source trees, shared trees, RPF, rendezvous points)

■ Design multicast services (SSM, Bidirectional PIM, MSDP)

■ Design network management techniques (in-band versus out-of-band, segmented management networks, prioritizing network management traffic)

## "Do I Know This Already?" Quiz

The "Do I Know This Already?" quiz helps you identify your strengths and deficiencies in this chapter's topics. This quiz, derived from the major sections in the "Foundation Topics" portion of the chapter, helps you determine how to spend your limited study time. Table 5-1 outlines the major topics discussed in this chapter and the "Do I Know This Already?" quiz questions that correspond to those topics. You can find the answers in Appendix A, "Answers to the 'Do I Know This Already?' Quiz Questions Q&A Questions."

**Table 5-1** "Do I Know This Already?" Foundation Topics Section-to-Question Mapping

| Foundation Topics Section | Questions Covered in This Section |
| --- | --- |
| IP Multicast Review | 1, 5, 6, 10 |
| Network Management Design | 2–4, 7–9 |

1. What does IGMP stand for?
   a. Interior Group Management Protocol
   b. Internet Group Management Protocol
   c. Interior Gateway Routing Protocol
   d. Interior Gateway Media Protocol
2. How many bits are mapped from the Layer 3 IPv4 multicast address to a Layer 2 MAC address?
   a. 16 bits
   b. 23 bits
   c. 24 bits
   d. 32 bits
3. Which version of SNMP introduces security extensions for authentication and encryption?
   a. SNMPv1
   b. SNMPv2
   c. SNMPv3
   d. SNMPv4
4. Which SNMP component contains an agent?
   a. Managed device
   b. Agent
   c. NMS manager
   d. MIB
5. Which of the following is correct regarding an OOB management network?
   a. It can be used as a backup network.
   b. It uses the same infrastructure as the primary network.
   c. It uses a separate physical network.
   d. It provides no segmentation.
6. Which multicast protocol eliminates the RP and shared trees?
   a. PIM-SM
   b. BIDIR-PIM
   c. SSM
   d. MSDP
7. Which SNMP operation obtains full table information from an agent?
   a. Get
   b. GetNext
   c. GetBulk
   d. Inform

**8.** RMON1 provides information at what levels of the OSI model?

   **a.** Data link and physical

   **b.** Network, data link, and physical

   **c.** Transport and network

   **d.** Application to network

**9.** Which of the following is not an SNMP operation?

   **a.** Get

   **b.** Community

   **c.** Set

   **d.** Trap

**10.** Which are called shortest-path trees (SPTs)?

   **a.** Ssource trees

   **b.** Shared trees

   **c.** Spanning trees

   **d.** Routing trees

## Foundation Topics

This chapter covers multicast protocols such as IGMP, CGMP, and PIM. It also covers BIDIR-PIM, SSM, and MSDP.

In addition, this chapter reviews SNMP characteristics and network management design considerations, such as RMON, NetFlow, LLDP, and syslog.

## IP Multicast Review

With multicast, packets are sent to a multicast group, which is identified with an IP multicast address. Multicast supports the transmission of IP packets from one source to multiple hosts. Packets with unicast addresses are sent to one device, and broadcast addresses are sent to all hosts; packets with multicast addresses are sent to a group of hosts.

### Multicast Addresses

Multicast addressing uses Class D addresses from the IPv4 protocol. Class D addresses range from 224.0.0.0 to 239.255.255.255. IANA manages multicast addresses.

Routing protocols (such as RIPv2, EIGRP, and OSPF) use multicast addresses to speak to their neighbors. For example, OSPF routers use 224.0.0.6 to speak to the designated router (DR) in a multiaccess network. Class D multicast addresses range from 224.0.0.0 to 239.255.255.255. Multicast addresses in the range 224.0.0.1 to 224.255.255.255 are reserved for special addresses or network protocols on a multiaccess link. RFC 2365 reserves multicast addresses in the range 239.192.000.000 to 239.251.255.255 for organization-local scope. Similarly, 239.252.000.000 to 239.252.255.255, 239.254.000.000 to 239.254.255.255, and 239.255.000.000 to 239.255.255.255 are reserved for site-local scope.

Table 5-2 lists some well-known and multicast address blocks.

**Table 5-2**   Multicast Addresses

| Multicast Address | Description |
|---|---|
| 224.0.0.0/24 | Local network control block |
| 224.0.0.1 | All hosts or all systems on the subnet |
| 224.0.0.2 | All multicast routers |
| 224.0.0.4 | Distance Vector Multicast Routing Protocol (DVMRP) routers |
| 224.0.0.5 | All OSPF routers |
| 224.0.0.6 | All OSPF DR routers |
| 224.0.0.9 | RIPv2 routers |
| 224.0.0.10 | EIGRP routers |
| 224.0.0.13 | All PIM routers |
| 224.0.1.0/24 | Internetwork control block |
| 224.0.1.39 | Rendezvous point (RP) announcement |
| 224.0.1.40 | RP discovery |
| 224.0.2.0 to 224.0.255.0 | Ad hoc block |
| 239.000.000.000 to 239.255.255.255 | Administratively scoped |
| 239.192.000.000 to 239.251.255.255 | Organization-local scope |
| 239.252.000.000 to 239.254.255.255 | Site-local scope |

## Layer 3 to Layer 2 Mapping

Multicast-aware Ethernet, Token Ring, and Fiber Distributed Data Interface (FDDI) network interface cards use the reserved IEEE 802 address 0100.5e00 for multicast addresses at the MAC layer. This includes Fast Ethernet and Gigabit Ethernet. Notice that for the address, the high-order byte 0x01 has the low-order bit set to 1. This bit is the Individual/Group (I/G) bit, and it signifies whether the address is an individual address (0) or a group address (1). Hence, for multicast addresses, this bit is set to 1.

Ethernet interfaces map the lower 23 bits of the IP multicast address to the lower 23 bits of the MAC address 0100.5e00.0000. As an example, the IP multicast address 224.0.0.2 is mapped to the MAC layer as 0100.5e00.0002. Figure 5-1 shows another example, looking at the bits of multicast IP address 239.192.44.56, which in hexadecimal is EF:C0:2C:38. The lower 23 bits get mapped to the lower 23 bits of the base multicast MAC to produce the multicast MAC address 01:00:5E:40:2C:38.

## IGMP

Internet Group Management Protocol (IGMP) is the protocol used in multicast implementations between the end hosts and the local router. RFC 1112 describes the first version of IGMP, RFC 2236 describes IGMP version 2 (IGMPv2), and RFC 3376 describes IGMP version 3 (IGMPv3).

IP hosts use IGMP to report their multicast group memberships to routers. IGMP messages use IP protocol number 2. IGMP messages are limited to the local interface and are not routed.

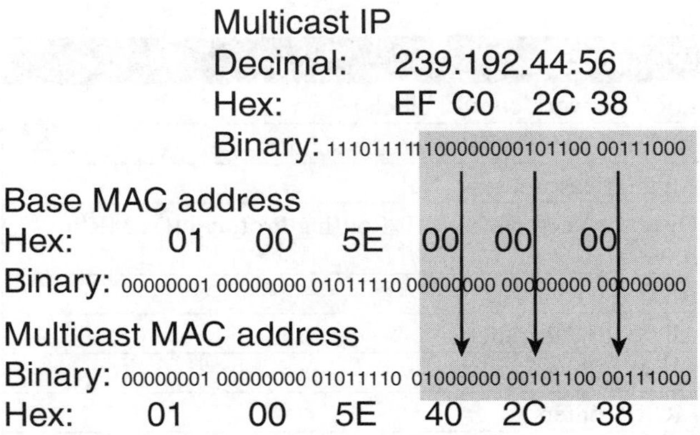

Multicast IP
Decimal:    239.192.44.56
Hex:          EF C0    2C 38
Binary: 1110111111100000000101100 00111000

Base MAC address
Hex:        01     00     5E    00    00    00
Binary: 00000001 00000000 01011110 00000000 00000000 00000000

Multicast MAC address
Binary: 00000001 00000000 01011110 01000000 00101100 00111000
Hex:     01     00     5E    40    2C    38

**Figure 5-1** *Mapping of Multicast IP Addressing to MAC Addresses*

## IGMPv1

The first RFC describing IGMP (RFC 1112), written in 1989, describes the host extensions for IP multicasting. IGMPv1 provides simple message types for communication between hosts and routers. These messages are:

- **Membership query:** Sent by the router to check whether a host wants to join a multicast group

- **Membership report:** Sent by the host to join a multicast group in the segment

The problem with IGMPv1 is the latency involved for a host to leave a group. With IGMPv1, the router sends membership queries periodically; a host must wait for the membership query message to leave a group. The query interval is 60 seconds, and it takes three query intervals (3 minutes) for a host to leave the group.

## IGMPv2

IGMPv2 improves on IGMPv1 by allowing faster termination or leaving of multicast groups.

IGMPv2 has three message types, plus one for backward compatibility:

- **Membership query:** Sent by the router to check whether a host wants to join a group.

- **Version 2 membership report:** Sent to the group address with the multicast group members (IP addresses). It is sent by hosts to join and remain in multicast groups on the segment.

- **Version 2 leave group:** Sent by the hosts to indicate that a host will leave a group; it is sent to destination 224.0.0.2. After the host sends the leave group message, the router responds with a group-specific query.

- **Version 1 membership report:** For backward compatibility with IGMPv1 hosts.

You enable IGMP on an interface when you configure a multicast routing protocol, such as PIM. You can configure the interface for IGMPv1, IGMPv2, or IGMPv3.

## IGMPv3

IGMPv3 provides the extensions required to support Source-Specific Multicast (SSM). It is designed to be backward compatible with the two earlier versions of IGMP.

IGMPv3 has two message types, plus three for backward compatibility:

- **Membership query:** Sent by the router to check that a host wants to join a group.

- **Version 3 membership report:** Sent to the group address with the multicast group members (IP addresses). It is sent by hosts to request and remain in multicast groups on the segment. It is always sent to multicast 224.0.0.22.

- **Version 2 membership report:** Sent to the group address with the multicast group members (IP addresses). It is sent by hosts to request and remain in multicast groups on the segment. It is sent to the multicast group address. This message is used for backward compatibility with IGMPv2 hosts.

- **Version 2 leave group:** Sent by the hosts to indicate that a host will leave a group, to destination 224.0.0.2. The message is sent without having to wait for the IGMPv2 membership report message. This message is used for backward compatibility with IGMPv2 hosts.

- **Version 1 membership report:** Used for backward compatibility with IGMPv1 hosts.

You enable IGMP on an interface when you enable a multicast routing protocol, such as PIM. You can configure the interface for IGMPv1, IGMPv2, or IGMPv3.

## CGMP

Cisco Group Management Protocol (CGMP) is a Cisco-proprietary protocol implemented to control multicast traffic at Layer 2 (see Figure 5-2). Because a Layer 2 switch is unaware of Layer 3 IGMP messages, it cannot keep multicast packets from being sent to all ports.

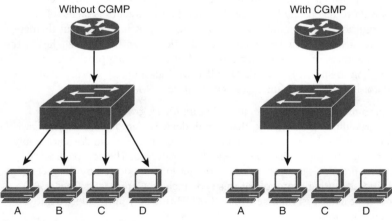

**Figure 5-2**  *CGMP*

When a router receives an IGMP report, it processes the report and then sends a CGMP message to the switch. The switch can then forward the multicast messages to the port with the host receiving multicast traffic. CGMP fast-leave processing allows the switch to detect IGMP version 2 leave messages sent by hosts on any of the switch ports. When a host sends an IGMPv2 leave message, the switch can then disable multicasting for the port.

CGMP is no longer used and is not covered on the ENSLD 300-420 exam. IGMP snooping is the standards-based method used in today's networks.

### IGMP Snooping

IGMP snooping is a standards-based method for switches to control multicast traffic at Layer 2. It has replaced CGMP. It listens to IGMP messages between the hosts and routers. If a router or an IGMP querier host sends an IGMP query message, the switch adds the host to the multicast group and permits that port to receive multicast traffic. The port is removed from multicast traffic if the host sends an IGMP leave message to the router. The disadvantage of IGMP snooping is that it has to process every IGMP control message, which can impact the CPU utilization of the switch.

## Sparse Versus Dense Multicast

IP multicast traffic for a particular (source, destination group) multicast pair is transmitted from the source to the receivers using a spanning tree from the source that connects all the hosts in the group. Multicast destinations are represented in the following form:

- **(\*,G):** This means any source is sending to group G.

- **(S,G):** This means source S is sending to group G.

Any multicast transmission has a Class D multicast group address, G. A multicast group can have more than one source, and each such source will also have a "regular" (Class A, B, or C or CIDR) Internet address, S.

Each destination host registers itself as a member of interesting multicast groups through the use of IGMP. Routers keep track of these groups dynamically and build distribution trees that chart paths from each sender to all receivers. IP multicast routing protocols follow two approaches.

The first approach assumes that the multicast group members are densely distributed throughout the network (with many of the subnets containing at least one group member), that all devices want to receive multicast traffic, and that bandwidth is plentiful. The approach with dense multicast routing protocols is to flood the traffic throughout the network and then, at the request of receiving routers, stop the flow of traffic on branches of the network that have no members of the multicast group. Multicast routing protocols that use this technique of flooding the network include DVMRP, Multicast Open Shortest Path First (MOSPF), and Protocol-Independent Multicast–Dense Mode (PIM-DM).

The second approach to multicast routing assumes that multicast group members are sparsely distributed throughout the network, that not all devices want to receive multicast traffic, and that bandwidth is not necessarily widely available. Sparse mode does not imply that the group has few members, just that they are widely dispersed. The approach with sparse multicast routing protocols is to not send traffic until it is requested by the receiving routers or hosts. Multicast routing protocols of this type include Core-Based Trees (CBT) and Protocol-Independent Multicast–Sparse Mode (PIM-SM). CBT is not widely deployed and is not discussed in this book.

## Multicast Source and Shared Trees

Multicast distribution trees control the path that multicast packets take to the destination hosts. The two types of distribution trees are source and shared. With *source* trees, the tree roots from the source of the multicast group and then expands throughout the network in spanning-tree fashion to the destination hosts. Source trees are also called shortest-path trees (SPTs) because they create paths without having to go through a rendezvous point (RP). The drawback is that all routers through the path must use memory resources to maintain a list of all multicast groups. PIM-DM uses a source-based tree.

*Shared* trees create the distribution tree's root somewhere between the network's source and receivers. The root is called the RP. The tree is created from the RP in spanning-tree fashion with no loops. Sources initially send their multicast packets to the RP, which, in turn, forwards data to the member of the group in the shared tree.

The advantage of shared trees is that they reduce the memory requirements of routers in the multicast network. The drawback is that initially the multicast packets might not take the best paths to the receivers because they need to pass through the RP. After the data stream begins to flow from sender to RP to receiver, the routers in the path optimize the path automatically to remove any unnecessary hops. The RP function consumes significant memory on the assigned router. PIM-SM uses an RP.

# PIM

PIM comes in two flavors: Protocol Independent Multicast–Sparse Mode (PIM-SM) and Protocol Independent Multicast–Dense Mode (PIM-DM). PIM-SM uses shared trees and RPs to reach widely dispersed group members with reasonable protocol bandwidth efficiency. PIM-DM uses source trees and reverse path forwarding (RPF) to reach relatively close group members with reasonable processor and memory efficiency in the network devices of the distribution trees.

With RPF, received multicast packets are forwarded out all other interfaces, allowing the data stream to reach all segments. If no hosts are members of a multicast group on any of the router's attached or downstream subnets, the router sends a prune message up the distribution tree (the reverse path) to tell the upstream router not to send packets for the multicast group. So, the analogy for PIM-DM is the push method for sending junk mail, and the intermediate router must tell upstream devices to stop sending it.

## PIM-SM

PIM-SM, which is defined in RFC 7761, assumes that no hosts want to receive multicast traffic unless it is specifically requested. The RP gathers the information from senders and makes the information available to receivers. Routers with receivers have to register with the RP. The end-host receivers request multicast group membership using IGMP with their local last-hop routers. The routers serving the end systems then register as traffic receivers with the RPs for the specified group in the multicast network. Senders register with the RP via the first-hop router.

The shared tree for each multicast group is rooted at the RP multicast router. Different multicast groups can use separate RPs within a PIM domain.

## PIM DR

A designated router is selected in multiaccess segments running PIM. The PIM DR is responsible for sending join, prune, and register messages to the RP. The PIM router with the highest IP address is selected as the DR.

### Joining PIM-SM

With PIM-SM, DRs on end segments receive IGMP query messages from hosts wanting to join a multicast group. The router checks whether it is already receiving the group for another interface. If it is receiving the group, the router adds the new interface to the table and queries periodically on the new interface.

If the multicast group is not in the multicast table, the router adds the interface to the multicast table and sends a join message to the RP with multicast address 224.0.0.13 (all PIM routers) requesting the multicast group.

### Pruning PIM-SM

When a PIM-SM does not have any more multicast receiving hosts or receiving routers out any of its interfaces, it sends a prune message to the RP. The prune message includes the group to be pruned or removed.

### Auto-RP

Another way to configure the RP for a network is to have the RP announce its services to the PIM network. This process is called auto-RP. Candidate RPs send their announcements to RP mapping agents with multicast address 224.0.1.39 (using the command **cisco-rp-announce**). RP mapping agents are also configured. In a small network, the RP can be the mapping agent. The 224.0.1.40 address used in auto-RP discovery is the destination address for messages from the RP mapping agent to discover candidates. Configured RP mapping agents listen to the announcements. The RP mapping agent selects the RP for a group based on the highest IP address of all the candidate RPs. The RP mapping agents then send RP discovery messages to the rest of the PIM-SM routers in the internetwork with the selected RP-to-group mappings.

### BIDIR-PIM

Bidirectional PIM (BIDIR-PIM), which is defined in RFC 5015, is a variant of PIM-SM that builds bidirectional shared trees connecting multicast sources and receivers. It never builds a shortest path tree, so it scales well because it does not need a source-specific state.

BIDIR-PIM eliminates the need for a first-hop route to encapsulate data packets being sent to the RP. BIDIR-PIM dispenses with both encapsulation and source state by allowing packets to be natively forwarded from a source to the RP using shared tree state.

### SSM

Source-Specific Multicast (SSM) is a variant of PIM-SM that builds trees that are rooted in just one source. SSM, defined in RFC 3569, eliminates the RPs and shared trees of sparse mode and only builds an SPT. SSM trees are built directly based on the receipt of group membership reports that request a given source. SSM is suitable for when well-known sources exist within the local PIM domain and for broadcast applications.

### MSDP

Multicast Source Discovery Protocol (MSDP), described in RFC 3618, is used to interconnect multiple PIM-SM domains. MSDP reduces the complexity of interconnecting multiple PIM-SM domains by allowing the PIM-SM domains to use an interdomain source tree.

With MSDP, the RPs exchange source information with RPs in other domains. Each PIM-SM domain uses its own RP and does not depend on the RPs in other domains.

When an RP in a PIM-SM domain first learns of a new sender, it constructs a Source-Active (SA) message and sends it to its MSDP peers. All RPs that intend to originate or receive SA messages must establish MSDP peering with other RPs, either directly or via an intermediate MSDP peer.

The SA message contains the following information:

- The source address of the data source

- The multicast group address

- The IP address of the RP

Sources cause PIM to register with the RP, and MSDP can tell RPs in other domains of their sources. Each MSDP peer receives and forwards the message away from the RP address in a "peer-RPF flooding" fashion (with respect to forwarding SA messages). The Multicast RPF Routing Information Base (MRIB) is examined to determine which peer toward the originating RP of the SA message is selected.

## Summary of Multicast Protocols

Table 5-3 summarizes IP Multicast protocols.

**Table 5-3**    IP Multicast Protocols

| IP Multicast Protocol | Description |
|---|---|
| IGMP | A host sends an IGMP query message to the router, and the switch adds the host to the multicast group and permits that port to receive multicast traffic. |
| PIM-SM | This protocol assumes that no hosts want to receive multicast traffic unless specifically requested. |
| BIDIR-PIM | This protocol never builds a shortest path tree. |
| SSM | This protocol eliminates the RPs and shared trees and only builds an SPT. |
| MSDP | This protocol is used to interconnect multiple PIM-SM domains. |

## IPv6 Multicast Addresses

IPv6 retains the use and function of multicast addresses as a major address class. IPv6 prefix FF00::/8 is allocated for all IPv6 multicast addresses. IPv6 multicast addresses are described in RFC 2373. The EIGRP for IPv6, OSPFv3, and RIPng routing protocols use multicast addresses to communicate between router neighbors.

The format of the IPv6 multicast address is described in Chapter 2, "Internet Protocol Version 6 (IPv6) Design." Table 5-4 lists the common multicast addresses.

**Table 5-4**    Well-Known Multicast Addresses

| Multicast Address | Multicast Group |
|---|---|
| FF01::1 | All nodes (node-local) |
| FF02::1 | All nodes (link-local) |
| FF01::2 | All routers (node-local) |
| FF02::2 | All routers (link-local) |
| FF02::5 | OSPFv3 routers |
| FF02::6 | OSPFv3 DRs |

| Multicast Address | Multicast Group |
|---|---|
| FF02::9 | Routing Information Protocol (RIPng) |
| FF02::A | EIGRP routers |
| FF02::B | Mobile agents |
| FF02::C | DHCP servers/relay agents |
| FF02::D | All PIM routers |

# Network Management Design

After a new network is designed, installed, and configured, it must be managed by the operations team. Network management tools are used to gather operating statistics and to manage devices. These network management devices use protocols such as SNMP and RMON to obtain information on network performance.

Statistics are gathered on WAN bandwidth utilization, router CPU and memory utilization, and interface counters. Configuration changes are also made through network management tools such as Cisco Prime. The ISO defines five types of network management processes that are commonly known as FCAPS:

- **Fault management:** Refers to detecting and correcting network fault problems

- **Configuration management:** Refers to baselining, modifying, and tracking configuration changes

- **Accounting management:** Refers to keeping track of circuits for billing of services

- **Performance management:** Measures the network's effectiveness at delivering packets

- **Security management:** Tracks the authentication and authorization information

Network management is supported by the elements listed in Table 5-5.

**Table 5-5**   Network Management Elements

| Network Management Element | Description |
|---|---|
| Network management system (NMS) | Runs the applications that manage and monitor managed devices. |
| Network management protocols and standards | Used to exchange management information between the NMS and the managed devices. The key protocols and standards are SNMP, MIB, and RMON. |
| Managed devices | Managed by the NMS. |
| Management agents | Reside in the managed devices and include SNMP agents and RMON agents. |

The protocols and tools described in this chapter perform some of these functions. SNMP is the underlying protocol used for network management. Agents are configured in managed devices (routers) that allow the NMS to manage the devices. RMON is used for advanced monitoring of routers and switches. CDP is a Cisco proprietary protocol that enables the discovery of Cisco devices. NetFlow is a network monitoring solution that allows for greater scalability than RMON. Syslog allows system messages and error events to be gathered for review.

## Simple Network Management Protocol

Simple Network Management Protocol (SNMP) is an IP application layer protocol that has become the standard for the exchange of management information between network devices. SNMP, which was initially described in RFC 1157, is a simple solution that requires little code to implement and allows vendors to build SNMP agents on their products.

SNMP runs over User Datagram Protocol (UDP) and therefore does not inherently provide for sequencing and acknowledgment of packets, but it still reduces the amount of overhead used for management information.

### SNMP Components

SNMP has three network-managed components:

- **The managed devices:** A managed device is a router or LAN switch or any other device that contains an SNMP agent. Managed devices collect and store management information and make this information available to the NMS. SNMP community strings (passwords) are configured on routers and switches to allow for SNMP management.

- **The agent:** The agent is the network management software that resides in the managed device. The agent gathers the information and puts it in SNMP format. It responds to the manager's request for information and generates traps.

- **The NMS:** The NMS has applications that are used to monitor and configure managed devices. It is also known as the manager. The NMS provides the bulk of the processing resources used for network management. It polls agents on the network and correlates and displays the management information.

Figure 5-3 shows the relationship between these components.

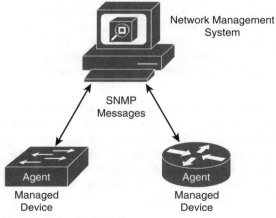

**Figure 5-3**   *SNMP Components*

## Network Management Design Considerations

Network routers and switches need to be monitored and managed remotely. Network architects must keep in mind several design considerations for NMS systems and solutions.

### In-Band Versus Out-of-Band Network Management

A network architect should define VLANs and reserve IP address subnets for network management. These addresses are used to allocate network management IPs for routers, switches, and firewalls. For in-band network management, the IP subnet used is part of the internal routing domain and is trunked like any other VLAN in the network. One common solution is to use a loopback address for network management, separate from the loopback address used for routing. An in-band solution is not segmented from the primary traffic and address bandwidth usage.

For an out-of-band (OOB) management solution, a separate network is built for access devices via the OOB or auxiliary ports of devices. Note that OOB network management should have separate credentials (for logging in to devices) and should not be used as a backup to the primary network that is being managed. The OOB management network does not use bandwidth of the primary network; a separate infrastructure has to be built.

### Network Management Traffic Prioritization

Although network management traffic may not be considered as critical as voice and video traffic, it does merit some prioritization. In Cisco QoS classification and marking recommendations, network management traffic is given a Layer 3 classification of CS1 PHB (DSCP 16) or Layer 2 CoS of 2.

## MIB

A Management Information Base (MIB) is a collection of information that is stored on the local agent of a managed device. MIBs are organized hierarchically and are accessed by the NMS. MIBs are databases of objects organized in a tree-like structure, with each branch containing similar objects. Each object has an object identifier (number) that uniquely identifies the managed object of the MIB hierarchy. Read and write community strings are used to control access to MIB information.

The top-level MIB object IDs belong to different standards organizations, and lower-level object IDs are allocated to associated organizations. Standard MIBs are defined by RFCs. Vendors define private branches that include managed objects for their products. Figure 5-4 shows a portion of the MIB tree structure. RFC 1213 describes the MIBs for TCP/IP. Cisco defines the MIBs under the Cisco head object. For example, a Cisco MIB can be uniquely identified by either the object name iso.org.dod.internet.private.enterprise.cisco or the equivalent object descriptor 1.3.6.1.4.1.9.

Each manageable feature in the MIB is called an *MIB variable*. The MIB module is a document that describes each manageable feature that is contained in an agent. The MIB module is written in Abstract Syntax Notation 1 (ASN.1). Three ASN.1 data types are required: name, syntax, and encoding. The name serves as the object identifier. The syntax defines the object's data type (integer or string). The encoding data describes how information associated with a managed object is formatted as a series of data items for transmission on the network. The following are examples of standard managed objects that can be obtained from the MIB tree:

- Interfaces

- Buffers

- Memory

- Standard protocols

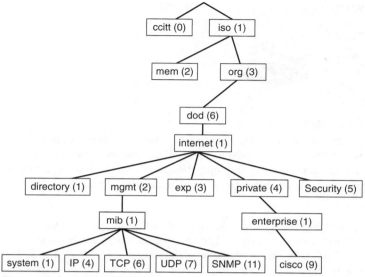

**Figure 5-4**   *MIB Tree Structure*

From the Cisco private tree, you can obtain the following additional information:

- Small, medium, and large buffers

- Primary and secondary memory

- Proprietary protocols (such as Enhanced Interior Gateway Routing Protocol [EIGRP])

## SNMP Versions

SNMP was initially defined in RFC 1157. Since then, SNMP has evolved, and each new version has added new message types.

### SNMPv1

SNMPv1, defined in RFC 1157, is a simple request-and-response protocol. The NMS manager issues a request, and managed devices return responses. The data types are limited to 32-bit values. SNMPv1 uses four protocol operations with five message types to carry out the communication:

- **Get Request:** Retrieves the value of a specific MIB variable.

- **GetNext Request:** Retrieves the next instance of the MIB variable.

- **Get Response:** Contains the values of the requested variable.

- **Set Request:** Specifies a request from the manager to the agent to set a MIB variable. It can be used to modify the agent's configuration.

- **Trap:** Transmits an unsolicited alarm condition.

Figure 5-5 shows the SNMPv1 message types.

The NMS manager uses the Get operation to retrieve the value-specific MIB variable from an agent. The GetNext operation is used to retrieve the next object instance in a table or list within an agent. The Get Response contains the value of the requested variable.

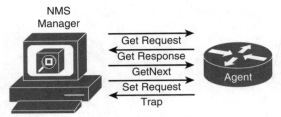

**Figure 5-5** *SNMPv1 Message Types*

The NMS manager uses the Set operation to set values of the object instance within an agent. For example, the Set operation can be used to set an IP address on an interface or to bring an interface up or down. Agents use the Trap operation to inform the NMS manager of a significant alarm event. For example, a trap is generated when a WAN circuit goes down.

## SNMPv2

SNMPv2, defined in RFCs 1901 and 1902, is an evolution of the initial SNMPv1. SNMPv2 offers improvements to SNMPv1, including additional protocol operations. The Get, GetNext, and Set operations used in SNMPv1 are exactly the same as those used in SNMPv2. The SNMP Trap operation serves the same function as in SNMPv1, but it uses a different message format.

SNMPv2 defines two new protocol operations:

- **GetBulk:** Reduces repetitive requests for MIB variables.

- **Inform Request:** Alerts an SNMP manager about specific conditions with confirmation.

The NMS manager uses the GetBulk operation to retrieve large blocks of data, such as multiple rows in a table. This is more efficient than repeating GetNext commands. If the agent responding to the GetBulk operation cannot provide values for all the variables in a list, it provides partial results. The Inform operation allows one NMS manager to send trap information to other NMS managers and to receive information. The difference between Inform Request and Trap is that Inform Request requires an acknowledgement. Another improvement is that data type values can be 64 bits.

Table 5-6 summarizes SNMP message types.

**Table 5-6** SNMP Message Types

| SNMP Message | Description |
| --- | --- |
| Get Request | Retrieves the value of a specific MIB variable. |
| GetNext Request | Retrieves the next issuance of the MIB variable. |
| Get Response | Contains the values of the requested variable. |
| Set Request | Modifies the value of a MIB variable. |
| Trap | Transmits an unsolicited alarm condition. |
| GetBulk | Reduces repetitive requests for MIB variables. |
| Inform Request | Alerts an SNMP manager about specific conditions with a confirmation. |

## SNMPv3

SNMPv3 was developed to correct several deficiencies in the earlier versions of SNMP, especially related to security. SNMPv3, defined in RFCs 3410 through 3415, provides authentication and privacy via usernames and access control through key management. SNMPv3 also verifies each message to ensure that it has not been modified during transmission. SNMPv3 removes the use of community-based authentication strings sent in plaintext over the network. It is recommended that SNMPv1 and SNMPv2 be used only for read-only access and that SNMPv3 be used with read/write access.

SNMPv3 introduces three levels of security:

- **noAuthNoPriv:** No authentication and no encryption

- **authNoPriv:** Authentication and no encryption

- **authPriv:** Authentication and encryption

Authentication for SNMPv3 is based on the Hash-Based Message Authentication Code–Message Digest 5 (HMAC-MD5) and HMAC–Secure Hash (HMAC-SHA) algorithms. The Cipher Block Chaining–Data Encryption Standard (CBC-DES) standard is used for encryption.

Table 5-7 summarizes SNMP security levels.

**Table 5-7    SNMP Security Levels**

| Version | Level | Authentication | Encryption |
|---------|-------|----------------|------------|
| SNMPv1 | NoAuthNoPriv | Community string | None |
| SNMPv2 | NoAuthNoPriv | Community string | None |
| SNMPv3 | NoAuthNoPriv | Username | None |
| SNMPv3 | AuthNoPriv | MD5 or SHA | None |
| SNMPv3 | AuthPriv | MD5 or SHA | DES, 3DES, AES |

## Other Network Management Technologies

This section covers technologies used to gather network information, such as RMON, NetFlow, CDP, LLDP, and syslog.

## RMON

Remote Monitoring (RMON) is a standard monitoring specification that enables network monitoring devices and console systems to exchange network monitoring data. RMON provides more information than SNMP, but it also requires more sophisticated data collection devices (network probes). RMON looks at MAC-layer data and provides aggregate information on the statistics and LAN traffic.

Enterprise networks deploy network probes on several network segments; these probes report back to the RMON console. RMON allows network statistics to be collected even if a failure occurs between a probe and the RMON console. RMON1 is defined in RFCs 1757 and 2819, and additions for RMON2 are defined in RFC 2021.

The RMON MIB is located at iso.org.dod.internet.mgt.mib.rmon or the equivalent object descriptor 1.3.6.1.2.1.16. RMON1 defines nine monitoring groups, each of which provides specific sets of data. An additional group beyond these nine is defined for Token Ring. Each group is optional, so vendors do not need to support all the groups in the MIB. Table 5-8 shows the RMON1 groups.

**Table 5-8** RMON1 Groups

| Group ID | Group Name | Description |
|---|---|---|
| 1 | Statistics | Contains real-time statistics for interfaces, including packets sent, bytes, cyclic redundancy check (CRC) errors, and fragments. |
| 2 | History | Stores periodic statistical samples for later retrieval. |
| 3 | Alarm | Generates an alarm event if a statistical sample crosses a threshold. |
| 4 | Host | Provides host-specific statistics. |
| 5 | HostTopN | Lists the most active hosts. |
| 6 | Matrix | Stores statistics for conversations between two hosts. |
| 7 | Filters | Allows packets to be filtered. |
| 8 | Packet Capture | Allows packets to be captured for subsequent analysis. |
| 9 | Events | Generates event notifications. |

## RMON2

RMON1 is focused on the data link and physical layers of the OSI model. As shown in Figure 5-6, RMON2 provides an extension for monitoring upper-layer protocols.

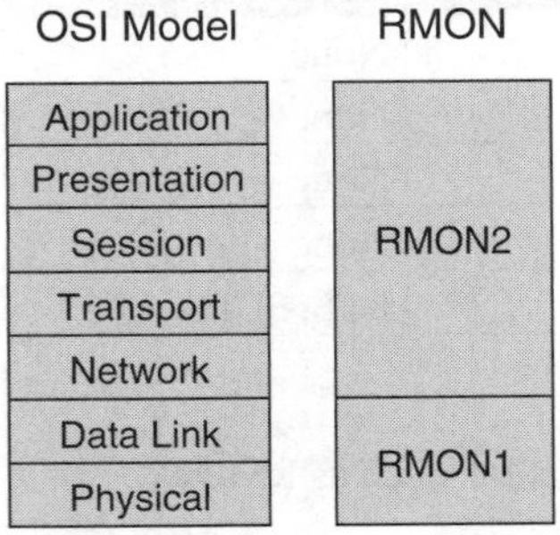

**Figure 5-6** *RMON1 and RMON2 Compared to the OSI Model*

RMON2, defined in RFC 2021, extends the RMON group with the MIB groups listed in Table 5-9.

**Table 5-9** RMON2 Groups

| Group ID | Group Name | Description |
|---|---|---|
| 11 | Protocol Directory | Lists the protocols the device supports. |
| 12 | Protocol Distribution | Provides traffic statistics for each protocol. |
| 13 | Address Mapping | Contains network-to-MAC-layer address mapping (IP address to MAC address). |
| 14 | Network Layer Host | Contains statistics for traffic sent to or from network layer hosts. |
| 15 | Network Layer Matrix | Contains statistics for conversations between two network layer hosts. |

| Group ID | Group Name | Description |
|----------|------------|-------------|
| 16 | Application Layer Host | Contains application layer statistics for traffic sent to or from hosts. |
| 17 | Application Layer Matrix | Contains application layer statistics for conversations between pairs of hosts. |
| 18 | User History | Contains periodic samples of specified variables. |
| 19 | Probe Configuration | Probes parameter configuration. |

## NetFlow

Cisco NetFlow enables tracking of IP flows as they are passed through routers and multilayer switches. An IP flow is a set of IP packets within a specific time slot that share a number of properties, such as the same source address, destination address, type of service, and protocol number. NetFlow information is forwarded to a network data analyzer, network planning tools, RMON applications, or accounting and billing applications. NetFlow allows for network planning, traffic engineering, usage-based network billing, accounting, denial-of-service monitoring capabilities, and application monitoring. One big benefit is that NetFlow provides the necessary data for billing of network usage. The most recent version of NetFlow is NetFlow version 9, which is defined in RFC 3954. The NetFlow protocol itself has been superseded by Internet Protocol Flow Information Export (IPFIX). Based on the NetFlow version 9 implementation, IPFIX is on the IETF standards track with RFCs 7011 and 7015.

As shown in Figure 5-7, NetFlow consists of three major components:

- **NetFlow accounting:** Collects IP data flows entering router or switch interfaces and prepares data for export. It enables the accumulation of data on flows with unique characteristics, such as IP addresses, applications, and classes of service.

- **Flow collector engines:** Captures exported data from multiple routers and filters and aggregates the data according to customer policies and then stores this summarized or aggregated data. Examples of collectors are Cisco NetFlow Collector, SolarWinds, and CA NetQoS.

- **Network data analyzers:** Displays a graphical user interface (GUI) and analyzes NetFlow data collected from flow collector files. This allows users to complete near-real-time visualization or trending analysis of recorded and aggregated flow data. Users can specify the router and aggregation scheme and the desired time interval.

**NetFlow Accounting:**
-Data Switching
-Data Export
-Data Aggregation

**NetFlow Flow Collector:**
-Data Collection
-Data Filtering
-Data Aggregation
-Data Storage
-File System Management

**Network Data Analyzer:**
-Data Presentation
-Network Planning
-Accounting and Billing

**Figure 5-7**  *NetFlow Components*

The benefits of using NetFlow include the following:

- Ability to obtain detailed information with minimal impact to the network devices

- Ability to customize the data captures for each interface

- Ability to include data timestamping across a large number of devices

- Ability to meter network traffic providing data for billing based on network usage

- Ability to detect and mitigate threats

Routers and switches are the network accounting devices that gather the statistics. These devices aggregate data and export the information. Each unidirectional network flow is identified by both source and destination IP addresses and transport layer port numbers. NetFlow can also identify flows based on IP protocol number, type of service, and input interface. NetFlow data records contain the following information:

- Source and destination IP addresses

- Source and destination TCP/UDP ports

- Type of service (ToS)

- Packet and byte counts

- Start and end timestamps

- Input and output interface numbers

- TCP flags and encapsulated protocol (TCP/UDP)

- Routing information (including next-hop address, source and destination autonomous system number, and destination prefix mask)

- Data analyzers

The NetFlow export or transport mechanism sends the NetFlow data to a collection engine or network management collector. Flow collector engines perform data collection and filtering. They aggregate data from several devices and store the information. Different NetFlow data analyzers can be used, depending on the intended purpose. NetFlow data can be analyzed for the following key applications:

- **Accounting and billing:** Service providers can use NetFlow data for charging based on bandwidth and application usage and quality of service (QoS).

- **Network planning and analysis:** NetFlow data can be used to determine link and router capacity.

- **Network and security monitoring:** NetFlow data can be used to visualize real-time traffic patterns.

- **Application monitoring and profiling:** NetFlow data can be used to get time-based views of application usage.

- **User monitoring and profiling:** NetFlow data can be used to identify customer and user network utilization and resource application.

- **NetFlow data warehousing and mining:** NetFlow data can be warehoused for later retrieval and analysis.

Looking ahead, Cisco has introduced Flexible NetFlow as the next generation in flow technology. Flexible NetFlow has many benefits beyond the Cisco traditional NetFlow functionality available for years in Cisco hardware and software.

The key advantages to using Flexible NetFlow are as follows:

- Flexibility and scalability of flow data beyond traditional NetFlow

- The ability to monitor a wider range of packet information to produce new information about network behavior that was not available previously

- Enhanced network anomaly and security detection

- User-configurable flow information to perform customized traffic identification and the ability to focus and monitor specific network behavior

- Convergence of multiple accounting technologies into one accounting mechanism

Flexible NetFlow is an integral part of Cisco IOS software that collects and measures data, allowing all routers or switches in the network to become sources of telemetry and monitoring devices. Flexible NetFlow allows extremely granular and accurate traffic measurements and high-level aggregated traffic collection. Because it is part of Cisco IOS software, Flexible Net-Flow enables Cisco product-based networks to perform traffic flow analysis without external probes being purchased, thus making traffic analysis economical for large IP networks.

Flexible NetFlow can track the following packet information for Layer 2, IPv4, and IPv6 flows:

- Source and destination MAC addresses

- Source and destination IPv4 or IPv6 addresses

- Source and destination TCP/User Datagram Protocol (UDP) ports

- Type of service (ToS)

- DSCP

- Packet and byte counts

- Flow timestamps

- Input and output interface numbers

- TCP flags and encapsulated protocol (TCP/UDP) and individual TCP flags

- Sections of packets for deep packet inspection

- All fields in the IPv4 header, including IP-ID and TTL

- All fields in the IPv6 header, including Flow Label and Option Header

- Routing information such as next-hop address, source autonomous system (AS) number, destination AS number, source prefix mask, destination prefix mask, BGP next hop, and BGP policy accounting traffic index

### NetFlow Compared to RMON and SNMP

NetFlow enables you to gather more statistical information than RMON with fewer resources. It provides greater detail on the collected data, with date- and timestamping. NetFlow has greater scalability and does not require network probes. NetFlow reports on traffic statistics and is push based, whereas SNMP reports primarily on device statistics and is pull based.

NetFlow can be configured on individual Layer 3 interfaces on routers and Layer 3 switches. NetFlow provides detailed information on the following:

- Source and destination IP addresses
- Source and destination interface identifiers
- TCP/UDP source and destination port numbers
- Number of bytes and packets per flow
- Source and destination autonomous system numbers
- IP type of service (ToS)

### CDP

Cisco Discovery Protocol (CDP) is a Cisco-proprietary protocol that can be used to discover only Cisco network devices. CDP is media and protocol independent, so it works over Ethernet, Frame Relay, ATM, and other media. The requirement is that the media support Subnetwork Access Protocol (SNAP) encapsulation. CDP runs at the data link layer of the OSI model. CDP uses Hello messages; packets are exchanged between neighbors, but CDP information is not forwarded. In addition to routers and switches, Cisco IP Phones and Cisco Unified Communication Manager (CUCM) servers advertise CDP information.

Being protocol and media independent is CDP's biggest advantage over other network management technologies. CDP provides key information about neighbors, including platforms, capabilities, and IP addresses, which is significant for network discovery. It is useful when SNMP community strings are unknown when performing network discovery.

When displaying CDP neighbors, you can obtain the following information:

- **Local interface:** The local interface that is connected to the discovered neighbor
- **Device ID:** The name of the neighbor device and its MAC address or serial number
- **Device IP address:** The IP address of the neighbor
- **Hold time:** How long (in seconds) to hold the neighbor information
- **Device capabilities:** The type of device discovered: router, switch, transparent bridge, host, IGMP, or repeater
- **Version:** The IOS or switch OS version
- **Platform:** The router or switch model number
- **Port ID:** The interface of the neighboring device

Network management devices can obtain CDP information for data gathering. CDP should be disabled on untrusted interfaces, such as those that face the Internet, third-party networks, and other secure networks. CDP works only on Cisco devices.

**Note**   Disable CDP on interfaces for which you do not want devices to be discovered, such as Internet connections.

## LLDP

Link Layer Discovery Protocol (LLDP), defined in the IEEE 802.1AB (LLDP) specification, is an option for discovering network devices in multivendor networks. LLDP performs functions similar to those of CDP. With LLDP, devices send information at a fixed interval from each of their interfaces in the form of an Ethernet frame with Ethertype 0x88CC. The information shared includes the following:

- System name and description
- Port name and description
- VLAN name
- IP management address
- System capabilities
- MAC/PHY layer information
- Link aggregation

## Syslog

Syslog, which is defined in RFC 3164, transmits event notification messages over the network. Network devices send the event messages to an event server for aggregation. Network devices include routers, servers, switches, firewalls, and network appliances. Syslog operates over UDP, so messages are not sequenced or acknowledged. The syslog messages are also stored on the device that generates the message and can be viewed locally.

Syslog messages are generated in many broad areas, called *facilities*. Cisco IOS has more than 500 facilities. Common facilities include the following:

- IP
- CDP
- OSPF
- TCP
- Interface
- IPsec
- SYS operating system
- Security/authorization
- Spanning Tree Protocol

Each syslog message has a level, and the syslog level determines the criticality of an event. Lower syslog levels are more important. Table 5-10 lists the syslog levels.

**Table 5-10**   Syslog Message Levels

| Syslog Level | Severity | Description |
|---|---|---|
| 0 | Emergency | System is unusable. |
| 1 | Alert | Take action immediately. |
| 2 | Critical | Critical conditions. |
| 3 | Error | Error messages. |
| 4 | Warning | Warning conditions. |
| 5 | Notice | Normal but significant events. |
| 6 | Informational | Informational messages. |
| 7 | Debug | Debug level messages. |

Common syslog messages are interface up and interface down events. Access lists can also be configured on routers and switches to generate syslog messages when a match occurs. Each syslog message includes a timestamp, a level, and a facility. Syslog messages have the following format:

```
mm/dd/yy:hh/mm/ss:FACILITY-LEVEL-mnemonic:description
```

Syslog messages can use considerable network bandwidth. It is important to enable only syslog facilities and levels that are of particular importance.

Table 5-11 summarizes some of the protocols covered in this section.

**Table 5-11**   NetFlow, CDP, Syslog, and RMON

| Technology | Description |
|---|---|
| NetFlow | Collects network flow data for network planning, performance, accounting, and billing applications. |
| CDP | Proprietary protocol for network discovery that provides information on neighboring devices. |
| Syslog | Reports state information based on facility and severity levels. |
| RMON | Provides aggregate information of network statistics and LAN traffic. |

# References and Recommended Readings

RFC 1075: *Distance Vector Multicast Routing Protocol*, https://tools.ietf.org/html/rfc1075.

RFC 1112: *Host Extensions for IP Multicasting*, https://tools.ietf.org/html/rfc1112.

RFC 1157: *A Simple Network Management Protocol (SNMP)*, https://tools.ietf.org/html/rfc1157

RFC 1441: *Introduction to Version 2 of the Internet-Standard Network Management Framework*, https://tools.ietf.org/html/rfc1441

RFC 1584: *Multicast Extensions to OSPF*, https://tools.ietf.org/html/rfc1584.

RFC 1757: *Remote Network Monitoring Management Information Base*, https://tools.ietf.org/html/rfc1757

RFC 1901: *Introduction to Community-Based SNMPv2*, https://tools.ietf.org/html/rfc1901.

RFC 1902: *Structure of Management Information for Version 2 of the Simple Network Management Protocol (SNMPv2)*, https://tools.ietf.org/html/rfc1902.

RFC 2021: *Remote Network Monitoring Management Information Base Version 2 Using SMIv2*, https://tools.ietf.org/html/rfc2021.

RFC 2236: *Internet Group Management Protocol, Version 2*, https://tools.ietf.org/html/rfc2236.

RFC 2365: *Administratively Scoped IP Multicast*, https://tools.ietf.org/html/rfc2365.

RFC 2576: *Coexistence Between Version 1, Version 2, and Version 3 of the Internet Standard Network Management Framewor*, https://tools.ietf.org/html/rfc2576.

RFC 3164: *The BSD Syslog Protocol*, https://tools.ietf.org/html/rfc3164.

RFC 3410: *Introduction and Applicability Statements for Internet Standard Management Framework*, https://tools.ietf.org/html/rfc3410.

RFC 3411: *An Architecture for Describing Simple Network Management Protocol (SNMP) Management Frameworks*, https://tools.ietf.org/html/rfc3411.

RFC 3412: *Message Processing and Dispatching for the Simple Network Management Protocol (SNMP)*, https://tools.ietf.org/html/rfc3412.

RFC 3414: *User-Based Security Model (USM) for Version 3 of the Simple Network Management Protocol (SNMPv3)*, https://tools.ietf.org/html/rfc3414.

RFC 3415: *View-Based Access Control Model (VACM) for the Simple Network Management Protocol (SNMP)*, https://tools.ietf.org/html/rfc3415.

RFC 3416: *Protocol Operations for SNMPv2*, https://tools.ietf.org/html/rfc3416.

RFC 3418: *Management Information Base for SNMPv2*, https://tools.ietf.org/html/rfc3418.

RFC 3569: *An Overview of Source-Specific Multicast (SSM)*, https://tools.ietf.org/html/rfc3569.

RFC 3618: *Multicast Source Discovery Protocol (MSDP)*, https://tools.ietf.org/html/rfc3618.

RFC 3954: *Cisco Systems NetFlow Services Export Version 9*, https://tools.ietf.org/html/rfc3954.

RFC 5103: *Bidirectional Flow Export Using IP Flow Information Export (IPFIX)*, https://tools.ietf.org/html/rfc5103.

RFC 7011: *Specification of the IP Flow Information Export (IPFIX) Protocol for the Exchange of Flow Information*, https://tools.ietf.org/html/rfc7011.

RFC 7015: *Flow Aggregation for the IP Flow Information Export (IPFIX) Protocol*, https://tools.ietf.org/html/rfc7015.

RFC 7761: *Protocol Independent Multicast-Sparse Mode (PIM-SM): Protocol Specification (Revised)*, https://tools.ietf.org/html/rfc7761.

Cisco, "Cisco IOS Flexible," http://www.cisco.com/c/en/us/products/collateral/ios-nx-os-software/flexible-netflow/product_data_sheet0900aecd804b590b.html.

5

Cisco, "Cisco IOS NetFlow Data Sheet," http://www.cisco.com/c/en/us/products/collateral/ios-nx-os-software/ios-netflow/product_data_sheet0900aecd80173f71.html.

Cisco, "Enterprise QoS Solution Reference Network Design Guide," https://www.cisco.com/c/en/us/td/docs/solutions/Enterprise/WAN_and_MAN/QoS_SRND/QoS-SRND-Book/QoSIntro.html.

Cisco, "IP Multicast Technology Overview" (white paper), http://www.cisco.com/c/en/us/td/docs/ios/solutions_docs/ip_multicast/White_papers/mcst_ovr.html.

Cisco, "MIBs Supported by Product," http://tools.cisco.com/ITDIT/MIBS/servlet/index.

Cisco, "NetFlow Performance Analysis," https://www.cisco.com/c/dam/en/us/solutions/collateral/service-provider/secure-infrastructure/net_implementation_white_paper0900aecd80308a66.pdf.

Cisco, "NetFlow Version 9," www.cisco.com/en/US/products/ps6645/products_ios_protocol_option_home.html.

Doyle, J., and J. Carroll. *Routing TCP/IP, Volume I, 2nd ed*. Indianapolis: Cisco Press, 2005.

Doyle, J., and J. Carroll. *Routing TCP/IP, Volume II*. Indianapolis: Cisco Press, 2001.

EE|Times, "Tutorial on Link Layer Discovery Protocol," http://www.eetimes.com/document.asp?doc_id=1272069.

Williamson, B. *Developing IP Multicast Networks*. Indianapolis: Cisco Press, 1999.

## Exam Preparation Tasks

As mentioned in the section "How to Use This Book" in the Introduction, you have a couple of choices for exam preparation: the exercises here, Chapter 13, "Final Preparation," and the exam simulation questions on the companion website.

## Review All Key Topics

Review the most important topics in the chapter, noted with the Key Topic icon in the outer margin of the page. Table 5-12 lists these key topics and the page number on which each is found.

**Table 5-12**   Key Topics

| Key Topic Element | Description | Page |
|---|---|---|
| Paragraph | Multicast | 180 |
| Table 5-1 | Multicast addresses | 181 |
| Table 5-3 | IP multicast protocols | 187 |
| Table 5-4 | Well-known multicast addresses | 187 |
| Table 5-5 | Network management elements | 188 |
| Paragraph | Simple Network Management Protocol | 189 |
| Table 5-6 | SNMP message types | 192 |
| Table 5-7 | SNMP security levels | 193 |
| Table 5-10 | Syslog message levels | 200 |
| Table 5-11 | NetFlow, CDP, Syslog, and RMON | 200 |

## Complete Tables and Lists from Memory

Print a copy of Appendix D, "Memory Tables," found on the companion website, or at least the section for this chapter, and complete the tables and lists from memory. Appendix E, "Memory Tables Answer Key," includes completed tables and lists to check your work.

## Define Key Terms

Define the following key terms from this chapter and check your answers in the glossary:

Bidirectional PIM (BIDIR-PIM), Internet Group Management Protocol (IGMP), Multicast Source Discovery Protocol (MSDP), network management system (NMS), out-of-band (OOB) management, Protocol Independent Multicast–Sparse Mode (PIM-SM), Remote Monitoring (RMON), Simple Network Management Protocol (SNMP), Source-Specific Multicast (PIM-SSM).

## Q&A

The answers to these questions appear in Appendix A. For more practice with exam format questions, use the exam engine on the companion website.

**1.** True or false: IGMP snooping and CGMP are methods to reduce the multicast traffic at Layer 2.

**2.** True or false: PIM has a hop count limit of 32.

**3.** True or false: PIM-SM routers use the multicast address 224.0.0.13 to request a multicast group from the RP.

**4.** Match each IP multicast address with its description.

   **i.**   224.0.0.1

   **ii.**   224.0.0.2

   **iii.**   224.0.0.5

   **iv.**   224.0.0.10

   **a.**   All OSPF routers

   **b.**   All routers

   **c.**   EIGRP routers

   **d.**   All hosts

**5.** Match each IPv6 multicast address with its description.

   **i.**   FF02::1

   **ii.**   FF02::2

   **iii.**   FF02::5

   **iv.**   FF02::9

   **v.**   FF02::A

   **a.**   OSPFv3 routers

   **b.**   RIPng routers

   **c.**   All routers

    **d.**  EIGRP routers

    **e.**  All nodes

**6.**  PIM-SM is configured on the network. Which protocol prevents media streams from being broadcast on the access switch?

    **a.**  PIM-SM RD

    **b.**  IGMPv3

    **c.**  Auto-RP

    **d.**  IGMP snooping

**7.**  CDP runs at what layer of the OSI model?

**8.**  What is the name of syslog level 5 severity?

**9.**  True or false: RMON provides more scalability than NetFlow.

**10.**  True or false: NetFlow provides detailed information on the number of bytes and packets per conversation.

**11.**  What information can be obtained from a neighbor by using CDP?

**12.**  What SNMP message is sent by an agent when an event occurs?

    **a.**  Get

    **b.**  Set

    **c.**  GetResponse

    **d.**  Trap

**13.**  What SNMP message is sent to an agent to obtain an instance of an object?

    **a.**  Get

    **b.**  Set

    **c.**  GetResponse

    **d.**  Trap

**14.**  What SNMP message is used to configure a managed device?

    **a.**  Get

    **b.**  Set

    **c.**  GetResponse

    **d.**  Trap

**15.**  About how many facilities are available for syslog in Cisco routers?

    **a.**  25

    **b.**  100

    **c.**  500

    **d.**  1000

**16.**  Which SNMPv3 provides authentication with no encryption?

    **a.**  authPriv

    **b.**  authNoPriv

    **c.** noAuthNoPriv

    **d.** noauthPriv

**17.** What encryption standard does SNMPv3 use?

    **a.** 3DES

    **b.** CBC-DES

    **c.** HMAC-MD5

    **d.** MD5

**18.** Which of the following are true about CDP? (Choose three.)

    **a.** It uses UDP.

    **b.** It is a data link protocol.

    **c.** It provides information on neighboring routers and switches.

    **d.** It is media and protocol independent.

    **e.** It uses syslog and RMON.

**19.** RMON2 provides information at what levels of the OSI model?

    **a.** Data link and physical

    **b.** Network, data link, and physical

    **c.** Transport and network only

    **d.** Network to application

**20.** Which SNMPv3 level provides authentication and privacy?

    **a.** authPriv

    **b.** authNoPriv

    **c.** noAuthNoPriv

    **d.** noauthPriv

**21.** Match each RMON group with its description.

    **i.** Statistics

    **ii.** Matrix

    **iii.** Application Layer Host

    **iv.** protocoldir

    **a.** Stores statistics for conversations between two hosts

    **b.** Lists the protocols that the device supports

    **c.** Contains real-time statistics for interfaces, including packets sent, bytes, CRC errors, and fragments

    **d.** Contains application layer statistics for traffic sent to or from each host

**22.** What is the most critical syslog priority level?

    **a.** 0

    **b.** 1

    **c.** 6

    **d.** 7

**23.** Which management protocol can help a company concentrate on Layer 4 monitoring and gain information to assist in long-term trending analysis?

   **a.** SNMPv3

   **b.** RMON2

   **c.** NetFlow

   **d.** CDP

   **e.** MIB

**24.** Which management protocol performs network traffic analysis?

   **a.** SNMPv3

   **b.** RMON2

   **c.** NetFlow

   **d.** CDP

   **e.** MIB

**25.** What virtual information store is used by SNMP?

   **a.** SNMPv3

   **b.** RMON2

   **c.** ASN.1

   **d.** CDP

   **e.** MIB

**26.** What standard language is used by SNMP?

   **a.** SNMPv3

   **b.** RMON2

   **c.** ASN.1

   **d.** CDP

   **e.** MIB

**27.** Which SNMPv3 method provides authentication but no encryption?

   **a.** noAuthNoPriv

   **b.** authPriv

   **c.** authNoPriv

   **d.** noauthPriv

**28.** Which is not an SNMP operation?

   **a.** GetNext

   **b.** Trap

   **c.** Inform Request

   **d.** Community

   **e.** GetBulk

**29.** Which protocol allows for vendor-specific information?

    **a.** SNMPv3

    **b.** RMON2

    **c.** ASN.1

    **d.** CDP

    **e.** MIB

**30.** Which protocol allows for ISPs to bill customers for network usage?

    **a.** SNMPv3

    **b.** RMON2

    **c.** NetFlow

    **d.** CDP

    **e.** MIB

**31.** Which solution can be customized in each interface to include data timestamping across a large number of interfaces?

    **a.** SNMPv3

    **b.** RMON2

    **c.** NetFlow

    **d.** CDP

    **e.** MIB

**32.** Which of the following are components of Cisco NetFlow? (Choose three.)

    **a.** NetFlow accounting

    **b.** FlowCollector

    **c.** NetFlow billing server

    **d.** Network data analyzer

    **e.** NetFlow traffic generator tool

**33.** What is multicast RPF information used for?

    **a.** To enable forwarding loops

    **b.** To prevent forwarding loops

    **c.** To reverse forwarding loops

    **d.** None of the above

**34.** In PIM-SM, which router knows about all sources in the network?

    **a.** The IGMP router

    **b.** The RP source hop router

    **c.** The RP

    **d.** The SSM router

**35.** What does (*,G) mean?

    **a.** From any source to the global group

    **b.** From source G to any group

    **c.** From any source to group G

    **d.** From *.* to group G

**36.** What are two benefits of BIDIR-PIM?

    **a.** No packets are encapsulated and there are no (S,G) states.

    **b.** The first packets from the source are not encapsulated and there are no (S,G) states.

    **c.** All packets are encapsulated and there are no (*,G) states.

    **d.** The last packets are not encapsulated and there are no (*,G) states.

**37.** When is SSM recommended?

    **a.** For broadcast applications

    **b.** For well-known sources

    **c.** For well-known receivers

    **d.** For nonbroadcast applications

    **e.** Answers A and B

    **f.** Answers B and D

**38.** What solution used to interconnect PIM-SM domains is recommended?

    **a.** BIDIR-PIM

    **b.** SSM

    **c.** MSDP

    **d.** Auto-RP

**39.** Which Layer 2 CoS classification should be assigned to network management traffic?

    **a.** 2

    **b.** 3

    **c.** 5

    **d.** 6

**40.** What solution eliminates the RPs and shared trees and only builds an SPT?

    **a.** BIDIR-PIM

    **b.** SSM

    **c.** MSDP

    **d.** Auto-RP

# CHAPTER 6

# Enterprise LAN Design and Technologies

This chapter covers the following subjects:

**Hierarchical Network Models:** This section reviews hierarchical network models.

**LAN Media:** This section covers different media types and their capacities.

**Spanning Tree Protocol Design Considerations:** This section covers design considerations for managing spanning tree protocol.

This chapter reviews hierarchical design models and architecture. It also covers LAN media and Spanning Tree Protocol design considerations.

## "Do I Know This Already?" Quiz

The "Do I Know This Already?" quiz helps you identify your strengths and deficiencies in this chapter's topics. This quiz, derived from the major sections in the "Foundation Topics" portion of the chapter, helps you determine how to spend your limited study time. Table 6-1 outlines the major topics discussed in this chapter and the "Do I Know This Already?" quiz questions that correspond to those topics. You can find the answers in Appendix A, "Answers to the 'Do I Know This Already?' Quiz Questions Q&A Questions."

**Table 6-1** "Do I Know This Already?" Foundation Topics Section-to-Question Mapping

| Foundation Topics Section | Questions Covered in This Section |
|---|---|
| Hierarchical Network Models | 1, 3, 8 |
| LAN Media | 2, 4, 6–7 |
| Spanning Tree Protocol Design Considerations | 5 |

1. In the Cisco hierarchical network model, which layer is responsible for fast transport?

   a. Network layer

   b. Core layer

   c. Distribution layer

   d. Access layer

2. What is the maximum segment distance for Fast Ethernet over UTP?

   a. 100 feet

   b. 500 feet

   c. 100 meters

   d. 285 feet

3. In the hierarchical network model, at which layer do security filtering, address aggregation, and media translation occur?

   a. Network layer

   b. Core layer

   c. Distribution layer

   d. Access layer

4. Which type of cable is the best solution in terms of cost for connecting an access switch to the distribution layer requiring 140 meters?

   a. UTP

   b. Copper

   c. Multimode fiber

   d. Single-mode fiber

5. Which mechanism transitions an access port directly to the forwarding state?

   a. UplinkFast

   b. Root Guard

   c. PortFast

   d. AccessPortFast

6. You have powered devices that require a maximum power of 60 watts per PSE port. Which PoE solution do you recommend?

   a. PoE

   b. PoE+

   c. Cisco UPOE

   d. Cisco UPOE+

7. Which solution remotely powers up a machine?

   a. PoE

   b. WoL

   c. OOB switch

   d. ON switch

8. High availability, port security, and rate limiting are functions of which hierarchical layer?

   a. Network layer

   b. Core layer

   c. Distribution layer

   d. Access layer

## Foundation Topics

Network design involves many complexities, and an enterprise designer should understand network models used to simplify the design process. The hierarchical network model, which was one of the first Cisco models, divides a network into core, distribution, and access layers.

This chapter provides an overview of design considerations for different LAN media and Power over Ethernet (PoE) capabilities. It also covers local VLANs and Spanning Tree Protocol design considerations.

This chapter covers the following objectives from the ENSLD 300-420 exam:

- Design campus networks for high availability

- Design campus Layer 2 infrastructures (Spanning Tree Protocol scalability, fast convergence, loop-free technologies, PoE, and WoL)

# Hierarchical Network Models

Hierarchical models enable you to design internetworks that use specialization of function combined with a hierarchical organization. Such a design simplifies the tasks required to build a network that meets current requirements and that can grow to meet future requirements. Hierarchical models use layers to simplify the tasks for internetworking. Each layer can focus on specific functions, allowing you to choose the right systems and features for each layer. Hierarchical models apply to both LAN and WAN design.

## Benefits of the Hierarchical Model

The benefits of using hierarchical models for your network design include the following:

- Cost savings

- Ease of understanding

- Modular network growth

- Improved fault isolation

After adopting hierarchical design models, many organizations report cost savings because they are no longer trying to do everything in one routing or switching platform. The modular nature of such a model enables appropriate use of bandwidth within each layer of the hierarchy, reducing the provisioning of bandwidth in advance of actual need.

Keeping each design element simple and functionally focused facilitates ease of understanding, which helps control training and staff costs. You can distribute network monitoring and management reporting systems to the different layers of modular network architectures, which also helps control management costs.

Hierarchical design facilitates changes and growth. In a network design, modularity lets you create design elements that you can replicate as the network grows—allowing maximum scalability. Because each element in the network design requires change, the cost and complexity of making the upgrade are contained to a small subset of the overall network. In large, flat network architectures, changes tend to impact a large number of systems. Limited mesh topologies within a layer or component, such as the campus core or backbone connecting central sites, retain value even in the hierarchical design models.

Structuring the network into small, easy-to-understand elements improves fault isolation. Network managers can easily understand the transition points in the network, which helps identify failure points. A network without hierarchical design is more difficult to troubleshoot because the network is not divided into segments.

Today's fast-converging protocols were designed for hierarchical topologies. To control the impact of routing-protocol processing and bandwidth consumption, you must use modular hierarchical topologies with protocols designed with these controls in mind, such as the Open Shortest Path First (OSPF) routing protocol.

Hierarchical network design facilitates route summarization. Enhanced Interior Gateway Routing Protocol (EIGRP) and all other routing protocols benefit greatly from route summarization. Route summarization reduces routing-protocol overhead on links in the network and reduces routing-protocol processing within the routers. It is less possible to provide route summarization if the network is not hierarchical.

## Hierarchical Network Design

As shown in Figure 6-1, a traditional hierarchical LAN design has three layers:

- **Core:** The core layer provides fast transport between distribution switches within the enterprise campus.

- **Distribution:** The distribution layer provides policy-based connectivity.

- **Access:** The access layer provides workgroup and user access to the network.

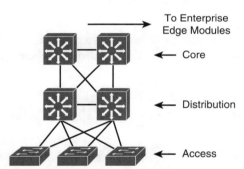

**Figure 6-1**  *Hierarchical Network Design Has Three Layers: Core, Distribution, and Access*

Each layer provides necessary functionality to the enterprise campus network. You do not need to implement the layers as distinct physical entities. You can implement each layer in one or more devices or as cooperating interface components sharing a common chassis. Smaller networks can "collapse" multiple layers to a single device with only an implied hierarchy. Maintaining an explicit awareness of hierarchy is useful as the network grows.

### Core Layer

The core layer is the network's high-speed switching backbone and is crucial to corporate communications. It is also referred to as the *backbone*. The core layer should have the following characteristics:

- Fast transport

- High reliability

- Redundancy

- Fault tolerance

- Low latency and good manageability

- Avoidance of CPU-intensive packet manipulation caused by security, inspection, quality of service (QoS) classification, or other processes

- Limited and consistent diameter

- QoS

When a network uses routers, the number of router hops from edge to edge is called the *diameter*. As noted, it is considered good practice to design for a consistent diameter within a hierarchical network. The trip from any end station to another end station across the backbone should have the same number of hops. The distance from any end station to a server on the backbone should also be consistent.

Limiting the internetwork's diameter provides predictable performance and ease of troubleshooting. You can add distribution layer routers and client LANs to the hierarchical model without increasing the core layer's diameter. Use of a block implementation isolates existing end stations from most effects of network growth.

## Distribution Layer

The network's distribution layer is the isolation point between the network's access and core layers. The distribution layer can have many roles, including implementing the following functions:

- Policy-based connectivity (for example, ensuring that traffic sent from a particular network is forwarded out one interface while all other traffic is forwarded out another interface)

- Redundancy and load balancing

- Aggregation of LAN wiring closets

- Aggregation of WAN connections

- QoS

- Security filtering

- Address or area aggregation or summarization

- Departmental or workgroup access

- Broadcast or multicast domain definition

- Routing between virtual local-area networks (VLANs)

- Media translations (for example, between Ethernet and Token Ring)

- Redistribution between routing domains (for example, between two different routing protocols)

- Demarcation between static and dynamic routing protocols

You can use several Cisco IOS software features to implement policy at the distribution layer:

- Filtering by source or destination address

- Filtering on input or output ports

■ Hiding internal network numbers through route filtering

■ Static routing

■ QoS mechanisms, such as priority-based queuing

The distribution layer performs aggregation of routes providing route summarization to the core. In the campus LANs, the distribution layer provides routing between VLANs that also apply security and QoS policies.

## Access Layer

The access layer provides user access to local segments on the network. The access layer is characterized by switched LAN segments in a campus environment. Microsegmentation using LAN switches provides high bandwidth to workgroups by reducing the number of devices on Ethernet segments. Functions of the access layer include the following:

■ Layer 2 switching

■ High availability

■ Port security

■ Broadcast suppression

■ QoS classification and marking and trust boundaries

■ Rate limiting/policing

■ Address Resolution Protocol (ARP) inspection

■ Virtual access control lists (VACLs)

■ Spanning tree

■ Trust classification

■ Power over Ethernet (PoE) and auxiliary VLANs for VoIP

■ Network access control (NAC)

■ Auxiliary VLANs

Table 6-2 summarizes the hierarchical layer functions.

**Table 6-2**   Cisco Hierarchical Layer Functions

| Hierarchical Layer | Layer Functions |
|---|---|
| Core | Fast transport |
|  | High reliability |
|  | Redundancy |
|  | Fault tolerance |
|  | Low latency and good manageability |
|  | Avoidance of slow packet manipulation caused by filters or other processes |
|  | Limited and consistent diameter |
|  | QoS |

| Hierarchical Layer | Layer Functions |
|---|---|
| Distribution | Policy-based connectivity |
| | Redundancy and load balancing |
| | Aggregation of LAN wiring closets |
| | Aggregation of WAN connections |
| | QoS |
| | Security filtering |
| | Address or area aggregation or summarization |
| | Departmental or workgroup access |
| | Broadcast or multicast domain definition |
| | Routing between VLANs |
| | Media translations (for example, between Ethernet and Token Ring) |
| | Redistribution between routing domains (for example, between two different routing protocols) |
| | Demarcation between static and dynamic routing protocols |
| Access | Layer 2 switching |
| | High availability |
| | Port security |
| | Broadcast suppression |
| | QoS |
| | Rate limiting |
| | ARP inspection |
| | VACLs |
| | Spanning tree |
| | Trust classification |
| | Network access control (NAC) |
| | PoE and auxiliary VLANs for VoIP |

## Hierarchical Model Examples

You can implement the hierarchical model by using a traditional switched campus design or routed campus network. Figure 6-2 is an example of a switched hierarchical design in the enterprise campus. In this design, the core provides high-speed transport between the distribution layers. The building distribution layer provides redundancy and allows policies to be applied to the building access layer. Layer 3 links between the core and distribution switches are recommended to allow the routing protocol to take care of load balancing and fast route redundancy in the event of a link failure.

The distribution layer is the boundary between the Layer 2 domains and the Layer 3 routed network. Inter-VLAN communications are routed in the distribution layer. Route summarization is configured under the routing protocol on interfaces toward the core layer. The drawback with this design is that Spanning Tree Protocol allows only one of the redundant links between the access switch and the distribution switch to be active. In the event of a failure, the second link becomes active, but at no point does load balancing occur.

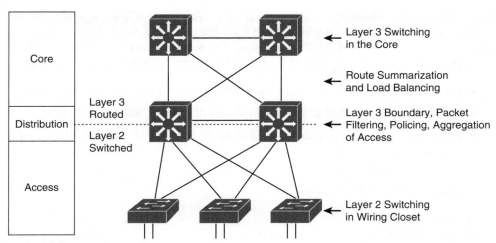

**Figure 6-2**   *Switched Hierarchical Design*

Figure 6-3 shows examples of a routed hierarchical design. In this design, the Layer 3 boundary is pushed toward the access layer. Layer 3 switching occurs in the access, distribution, and core layers. Route filtering is configured on interfaces toward the access layer. Route summarization is configured on interfaces toward the core layer. The benefit of this design is that load balancing occurs from the access layer because the links to the distribution switches are routed.

## VSS

One solution for providing redundancy between the access and distribution switching is Virtual Switching System (VSS). VSS solves the Spanning Tree Protocol looping problem by converting the distribution switching pair into a logical single switch. It removes Spanning Tree Protocol and eliminates the need for Hot Standby Router Protocol (HSRP), Virtual Router Redundancy Protocol (VRRP), or Gateway Load Balancing Protocol (GLBP).

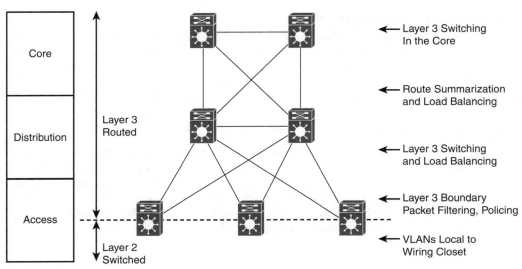

**Figure 6-3**   *Routed Hierarchical Design*

With VSS, the physical topology changes as each access switch has a single upstream distribution switch rather than two upstream distribution switches. As shown in Figure 6-4, the two switches are connected via 10 Gigabit Ethernet links called virtual switch links (VSLs), which makes them seem as a single switch. The key benefits of VSS include the following:

- Layer 3 switching used toward the access layer to enhance nonstop communication

- Simplified management of a single configuration of the VSS distribution switch

- Better return on investment (ROI) thanks to increased bandwidth between the access layer and the distribution layer

- Multichassis EtherChannel (MEC) creating loop-free technologies and eliminating the need for Spanning Tree Protocol

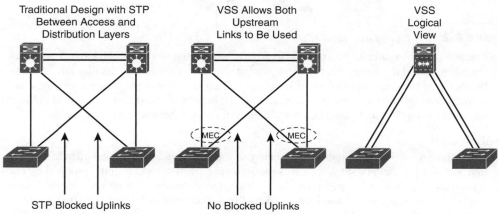

**Figure 6-4**   *VSS*

## Hub-and-Spoke Design

The hub-and-spoke network design (see Figure 6-5) provides better convergence times than ring topology. The hub-and-spoke design also scales better and is easier to manage than ring or mesh topologies. For example, implementing security policies in a full-mesh topology would become unmanageable because you would have to configure policies at each point location. Using the formula $n(n - 1)/2$, a mesh of 6 devices would generate 6 (6 − 1)/2 = 30/2 = 15 links.

## Collapsed Core Design

One alternative to the three-layer hierarchy is the collapsed core design, which is a two-layer hierarchy used with smaller networks. It is commonly used in sites with a single building with multiple floors. As shown in Figure 6-6, the core and distribution layers are merged, providing all the services needed for those layers. Design parameters to decide if you need to migrate to the three-layer hierarchy include not enough capacity and throughput at the distribution layer, network resiliency, and geographic dispersion.

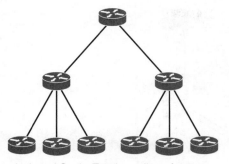

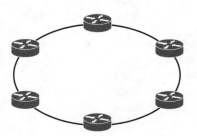

Hub-and-Spoke Topology allows for more scalability and easier management.

Ring Topology adds more delay as you add more nodes.

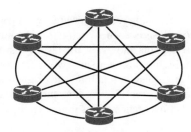

Mesh Topology requires a network connection to all other devices.

**Figure 6-5**   *Hub-and-Spoke Versus Ring and Mesh Designs*

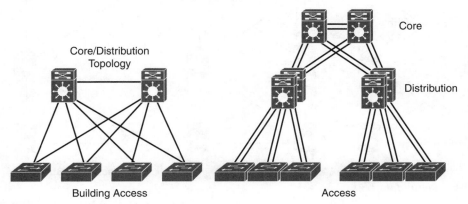

**Figure 6-6**   *Collapsed Core Design*

## Building Triangles and Redundant Links

A common thread that you will see in Cisco design is building redundant triangles rather than building squares. When you build in triangles, you take advantage of equal-cost redundant paths for best deterministic convergence. In the networks shown in Figure 6-7, when the link at location A goes down, the design with triangles does not require routing protocol convergence because each switch has two routes and two associated hardware Cisco Express Forwarding adjacency entries. In the design with squares, routing convergence is required.

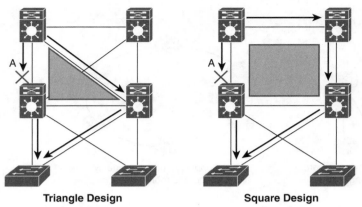

**Triangle Design**          **Square Design**

**Figure 6-7**  *Building Triangles*

When designing a hierarchical campus, using redundant links with triangles enables equal-cost path routing. In equal-path cost design, each switch has two routes and two Cisco Express Forwarding adjacency entries. This allows for the fastest restoration of voice, video, and data traffic flows. As shown in Figure 6-8, there are two Cisco Express Forwarding entries in the initial state. When there is a switch failure, the originating switch still has a remaining route and associated Cisco Express Forwarding entry; because of this, it does not trigger or wait for routing protocol convergence and is immediately able to continue forwarding all traffic.

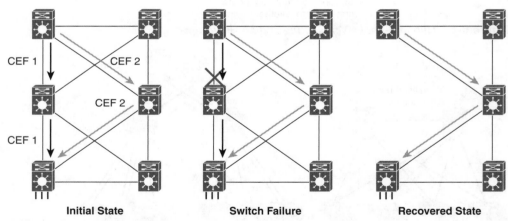

**Initial State**          **Switch Failure**          **Recovered State**

**Figure 6-8**  *Redundant Links*

## Local Versus End-to-End VLAN Design Models

In the enterprise campus, you could deploy VLANs across the campus or contain VLANs within the physical location. The term *end-to-end VLANs* refers to the design that allows VLANs to be widely dispersed throughout the enterprise network. The advantage of this design is that a user can move from one building to another and remain in the same VLAN. The problem is that this does not scale well for thousands of users, which makes it difficult to manage.

The recommended solution is to implement local VLANs where users are grouped into VLANs based on their physical locations. A Layer 2 to Layer 3 demarcation is created at the distribution layer, providing the ability to apply distribution layer summaries, QoS, segmentation, and other features. Furthermore, local VLANs decrease convergence times, and traffic flow is predictable, which makes troubleshooting easier. Figure 6-9 shows Local VLANs versus End-to-End VLANs.

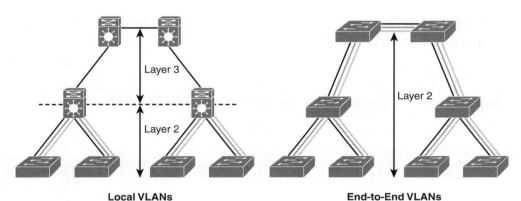

**Figure 6-9**  *Local VLANs Versus End-to-End VLANs*

# LAN Media

This section identifies some of the constraints you should consider when provisioning various LAN media types. It covers the physical specifications of Ethernet, Fast Ethernet, and Gigabit Ethernet.

## Ethernet Design Rules

Ethernet is the underlying basis for the technologies most widely used in LANs. In the 1980s and early 1990s, most networks used 10 Mbps Ethernet, defined initially by Digital, Intel, and Xerox (DIX Ethernet Version II) and later by the IEEE 802.3 working group. The IEEE 802.3-2002 standard contains physical specifications for Ethernet technologies through 10 Gbps.

### 100 Mbps Fast Ethernet Design Rules

The IEEE introduced the IEEE 802.3u-1995 standard to provide Ethernet speeds of 100 Mbps over UTP and fiber cabling. The 100BASE-T standard is similar to 10 Mbps Ethernet in that it uses Carrier Sense Multiple Access/Collision Detect (CSMA/CD); runs on Category (CAT) 3, 4, 5, and 6 UTP cable; and preserves the frame formats.

100 Mbps Ethernet (or Fast Ethernet) topologies present some distinct constraints on the network design because of their speed. The combined latency due to cable lengths and repeaters must conform to the specifications for the network to work properly. This section discusses these issues and provides sample calculations.

The overriding design rule for 100 Mbps Ethernet networks is that the round-trip collision delay must not exceed 512-bit times. However, the bit time on a 100 Mbps Ethernet network is 0.01 microseconds, as opposed to 0.1 microseconds on a 10 Mbps Ethernet network. Therefore, the maximum round-trip delay for a 100 Mbps Ethernet network is 5.12 microseconds, as opposed to the more lenient 51.2 microseconds in a 10 Mbps Ethernet network.

The following are specifications for Fast Ethernet, which are described in the following sections:

- 100BASE-TX
- 100BASE-T4
- 100BASE-FX

### 100BASE-TX Fast Ethernet

The 100BASE-TX specification uses CAT 5 or 6 UTP wiring. Fast Ethernet uses only two pairs of the four-pair UTP wiring. The specifications are as follows:

- Transmission occurs over CAT 5 or 6 UTP wire.
- RJ-45 connectors are used (the same as in 10BASE-T).
- Punchdown blocks in the wiring closet must be CAT 5 certified.
- 4B5B coding is used.

### 100BASE-T4 Fast Ethernet

The 100BASE-T4 specification was developed to support UTP wiring at the CAT 3 level. This specification takes advantage of higher-speed Ethernet without recabling to CAT 5 UTP. This implementation is not widely deployed. The specifications are as follows:

- Transmission occurs over CAT 3, 4, 5, or 6 UTP wiring.
- Three pairs are used for transmission, and the fourth pair is used for collision detection.
- No separate transmit and receive pairs are present, so full-duplex operation is not possible.
- 8B6T coding is used.

### 100BASE-FX Fast Ethernet

The 100BASE-FX specification for fiber is as follows:

- It operates over two strands of multimode or single-mode fiber cabling.
- It can transmit over greater distances than copper media.
- It uses media interface connector (MIC), stab and twist (ST), or stab and click (SC) fiber connectors defined for FDDI and 10BASE-FX networks.
- 4B5B coding is used.

## Gigabit Ethernet Design Rules

Gigabit Ethernet was first specified by two standards: IEEE 802.3z-1998 and 802.3ab-1999. The IEEE 802.3z standard specifies the operation of Gigabit Ethernet over fiber and coaxial cable and introduced the Gigabit Media-Independent Interface (GMII). These standards have been superseded by the latest revision of all the 802.3 standards included in IEEE 802.3-2002.

The IEEE 802.3ab standard specified the operation of Gigabit Ethernet over CAT 5 UTP. Gigabit Ethernet still retains the frame formats and frame sizes, and it still uses CSMA/CD. As with Ethernet and Fast Ethernet, full-duplex operation is possible. Differences appear in the encoding; Gigabit Ethernet uses 8B10B coding with simple nonreturn to zero (NRZ). Because of the 20% overhead, pulses run at 1250 MHz to achieve 1000 Mbps throughput.

Table 6-3 provides an overview of Gigabit Ethernet scalability constraints.

**Table 6-3**   Gigabit Ethernet Scalability Constraints

| Type | Speed | Maximum Segment Length | Encoding | Media |
|------|-------|------------------------|----------|-------|
| 1000BASE-T | 1000 Mbps | 100 m | Five-level | CAT 5 UTP |
| 1000BASE-LX (long wavelength) | 1000 Mbps | 550 m | 8B10B | Single-mode/multimode fiber |
| 1000BASE-SX (short wavelength) | 1000 Mbps | 62.5 micrometers: 220 m<br><br>50 micrometers: 500 m | 8B10B | Multimode fiber |
| 1000BASE-CX | 1000 Mbps | 25 m | 8B10B | Shielded balanced copper |

The following are the physical specifications for Gigabit Ethernet, which are described in the following sections:

- 1000BASE-LX

- 1000BASE-SX

- 1000BASE-CX

- 1000BASE-T

## 1000BASE-LX Long-Wavelength Gigabit Ethernet

IEEE 1000BASE-LX uses long-wavelength optics over a pair of fiber strands. The specifications are as follows:

- It uses long wavelengths (1300 nm [nanometers]).

- It can be used on multimode or single-mode fiber.

- Maximum lengths for multimode fiber are as follows:

  - 62.5-micrometer fiber: 440 meters

  - 50-micrometer fiber: 550 meters

- The maximum length for single-mode fiber (9 micrometers) is 5 km.

- It uses 8B10B encoding with simple NRZ.

### 1000BASE-SX Short-Wavelength Gigabit Ethernet

IEEE 1000BASE-SX uses short-wavelength optics over a pair of multimode fiber strands. The specifications are as follows:

- It uses short wavelengths (850 nm).

- It can be used on multimode fiber.

- Maximum lengths are as follows:

  - 62.5-micrometer fiber: 260 m

  - 50-micrometer fiber: 550 m

- It uses 8B10B encoding with simple NRZ.

### 1000BASE-CX Gigabit Ethernet over Coaxial Cable

The IEEE 1000BASE-CX standard is for short copper runs between servers. The specifications are as follows:

- It is used on short-run copper.

- It runs over a pair of 150-ohm balanced coaxial cables (twinax).

- The maximum length is 25 meters.

- It is mainly for server connections.

- It uses 8B10B encoding with simple NRZ.

### 1000BASE-T Gigabit Ethernet over UTP

The IEEE standard for 1000 Mbps Ethernet over CAT 5 UTP was IEEE 802.3ab; it was approved in June 1999. It is now included in IEEE 802.3-2002. This standard uses the four pairs in the cable. (100BASE-TX and 10BASE-T Ethernet use only two pairs.) The specifications are as follows:

- It uses CAT 5 four-pair UTP.

- The maximum length is 100 meters.

- The encoding defined is a five-level coding scheme.

- One byte is sent over the four pairs at 1250 MHz.

## 10 Gigabit Ethernet Design Rules

The IEEE 802.3ae supplement to the 802.3 standard, published in August 2002, specifies the standard for 10 Gigabit Ethernet. It is defined for full-duplex operation over optical media, UTP, and copper. The IEEE 802.3an standard provides the specifications for running 10 Gigabit Ethernet over UTP cabling. Hubs or repeaters cannot be used because they operate in half-duplex mode. It allows the use of Ethernet frames over distances typically encountered in metropolitan-area networks (MANs) and wide-area networks (WANs). Other uses include data centers, corporate backbones, and server farms.

## 10 Gigabit Ethernet Media Types

10 Gigabit Ethernet has seven physical media specifications, based on different fiber types and encodings. Multimode fiber (MMF) and single-mode fiber (SMF) are used. Table 6-4 describes the different 10 Gigabit Ethernet media types.

**Table 6-4**   10 Gigabit Ethernet Media Types

| Media Type | Wavelength and Fiber/UTP/Copper | Distance | Other Description |
|---|---|---|---|
| 10GBASE-SR | Short-wavelength MMF | To 300 m | Uses 66B encoding |
| 10GBASE-SW | Short-wavelength MMF | To 300 m | Uses the WAN interface sublayer (WIS) |
| 10GBASE-LR | Long-wavelength SMF | To 10 km | Uses 66B encoding for dark fiber use |
| 10GBASE-LW | Long-wavelength SMF | To 10 km | Uses WIS |
| 10GBASE-ER | Extra-long-wavelength SMF | To 40 km | Uses 66B encoding for dark fiber use |
| 10GBASE-EW | Extra-long-wavelength SNMP | To 40 km | Uses WIS |
| 10GBASE-LX4 | Uses division multiplexing for both MMF and SMF | To 10 km | Uses 8B/10B encoding |
| 10GBASE-CX4 | Four pairs of twinax copper | 15 m | IEEE 802.3ak |
| 10GBASE-T | CAT 6a UTP | 100 m | IEEE 802.3an |
| 10GBASE-ZR | Long-wave SMF | 80 km | Not in 802.3ae |
| 10GBASE-PR | Passive optical network | 20 km | 10G EPON 802.3av |

Short-wavelength multimode fiber is 850 nm. Long-wavelength is 1310 nm, and extra-long-wavelength is 1550 nm. The WIS is used to interoperate with Synchronous Optical Network (SONET) STS-192c transmission format.

IEEE 802.3ba is the designation given for the 802.3 standard, and speeds higher than 10 Gbps are paving the way for 40 Gbps and 100 Gbps Ethernet. Both 40 Gigabit Ethernet and 100 Gigabit Ethernet have emerged as backbone technologies for networks. Table 6-5 describes some of the physical standards.

**Table 6-5**   40 Gigabit Ethernet and 100 Gigabit Ethernet Physical Standards

| Physical Layer | 40 Gigabit Ethernet | 100 Gigabit Ethernet |
|---|---|---|
| Backplane | — | 100GBASE-KP4 |
| Improved backplane | 40GBASE-KR4 | 100GBASE-KR4 |
| 7 m over twinax copper cable | 40GBASE-CR4 | 100GBASE-CR10 |
|  |  | 100GBASE-CR4 |
| 30 m over Cat.8 UTP | 40GBASE-T | — |
| 100 m over OM3 MMF | 40GBASE-SR4 | 100GBASE-SR10 |
| 125 m over OM4 MMF |  | 100GBASE-SR4 |
| 2 km over SMF | 40GBASE-FR | 100GBASE-CWDM4 |
| 10 km over SMF | 40GBASE-LR4 | 100GBASE-LR4 |
| 40 km over SMF | 40GBASE-ER4 | 100GBASE-ER4 |

## EtherChannel

The Cisco EtherChannel implementations provide a method to increase the bandwidth between two systems by bundling Fast Ethernet, Gigabit Ethernet, or 10 Gigabit Ethernet links. When bundling Fast Ethernet links, use Fast EtherChannel. Gigabit EtherChannel bundles Gigabit Ethernet links. EtherChannel port bundles enable you to group multiple ports into a single logical transmission path between a switch and a router, a switch and a host, or a switch and another switch. EtherChannels provide increased bandwidth, load sharing, and redundancy. If a link in the bundle fails, the other links take on the traffic load. You can configure EtherChannel bundles as trunk links.

Depending on your hardware, you can form an EtherChannel with up to eight compatibly configured ports on the switch. The participating ports in an EtherChannel trunk must have the same speed and duplex mode and belong to the same VLAN. Cisco's proprietary hash algorithm calculates the way load balancing occurs, as shown in Table 6-6.

**Table 6-6**   EtherChannel Load Balancing

| Number of Ports in EtherChannel | Load Balancing Between Ports |
| --- | --- |
| 8 | 1:1:1:1:1:1:1:1 |
| 7 | 2:1:1:1:1:1:1 |
| 6 | 2:2:1:1:1:1 |
| 5 | 2:2:2:1:1 |
| 4 | 2:2:2:2 |
| 3 | 3:3:2 |
| 2 | 4:4 |

### Port Aggregation Considerations

When EtherChannel is configured to bundle Layer 2 links, it aggregates the bandwidth of these links and changes Spanning Tree Protocol behavior because all links are treated as one link and thus are all in the Spanning Tree Protocol forwarding state.

When EtherChannel is configured for Layer 3 links, it aggregates the bandwidth of multiple Layer 3 links and optimizes routing because there is only one neighbor relationship per switch interconnection.

EtherChannel can be established by using three mechanisms:

- **LACP:** Link Aggregation Control Protocol (LACP) is defined in IEEE 802.3ad. It protects against misconfiguration but adds overhead and delay when setting up a bundle.

- **PAgP:** Port Aggregation Protocol (PAgP) is a Cisco-proprietary negation protocol. PAgP aids in the automatic creation of EtherChannel links.

- **Static persistence configuration:** This does not add overhead as LACP does, but it can cause problems if not configured properly.

### PAgP

PAgP aids in the automatic creation of EtherChannel links. PAgP packets are sent between EtherChannel-capable ports in order to negotiate the formation of a channel. PAgP requires that all ports in the channel belong to the same VLAN or be configured as trunk ports. When a bundle already exists and a VLAN of a port is modified, all ports in the bundle are modified to match that VLAN. If ports are configured for dynamic VLANs, PAgP does not form a bundle.

PAgP modes are off, auto, desirable, and on. Only the combinations auto/desirable, desirable/desirable, and on/on allow the formation of a channel. The device on the other side must have PAgP set to on if a device on one side of the channel, such as a router, does not support PAgP. Note that PAgP does not group ports that operate at different speeds or port duplex. If speed and duplex change when a bundle exists, PAgP changes the port speed and duplex for all ports in the bundle.

## Comparison of Campus Media

As noted previously, several media types are used for campus networks. It is common to run UTP to end stations, use multiple multimode uplinks from access to distribution, and use single-mode fiber for longer distance and higher-bandwidth links. Table 6-7 provides a summary comparison of these media.

**Table 6-7**  Campus Transmission Media Comparison

| Factor | Copper/UTP | Multimode Fiber | Single-Mode Fiber |
|---|---|---|---|
| Bandwidth | Up to 10 Gbps | Up to 10 Gbps | Up to 10 Gbps |
| Distance | Up to 100 m | Up to 2 km (Fast Ethernet) | Up to 100 km (Fast Ethernet) |
| | | Up to 550 m (Gigabit Ethernet) | Up to 5 km (Gigabit Ethernet) |
| | | Up to 300 m (10 Gigabit Ethernet) | Up to 40 km (10 Gigabit Ethernet) |
| Price | Inexpensive | Moderate | Moderate to expensive |
| Recommended use | End stations | Building access to distribution switch uplinks; peer-to-peer switch links | Long-distance links |

## Power over Ethernet (PoE)

PoE is commonly used for powering IP phones and wireless access points (WAPs) over UTP. Other devices are increasingly being supplied power, such as video cameras, point-of-sale (PoS) machines, access control readers, and LED luminaries.

Standards-based PoE is defined in the IEEE 802.3af (2003) and IEEE 802.3at (2009) specifications. IEEE 802.3af provides 15.4 watts at the power sourcing equipment (PSE) side (LAN switch); due to power dissipation, only 12.95W is assured to the powered device (PD). IEEE 802.3at (known as PoE+) provides up to 30W on the PSE side, with 25.5.W assured to the PD. PoE and PoE+ provide power using two pairs: pins 1 and 2 and pins 3 and 6.

Cisco has developed Universal Power over Ethernet (UPOE) to provide power to higher-level devices, such as telepresence systems, digital signage, and IP turrets. Cisco UPOE uses four twisted pairs (instead of two pairs for PoE) to provide additional power. Cisco UPOE provides 30W + 30W = 60W of PSE power over Category 5e UTP, assuring 51W to the PD. Cisco UPOE+ provides 45W + 45 W = 90Wof PSE power over Category 6a UTP cabling, assuring 71.3W of power to the PD. Table 6-8 compares PoE capabilities.

**Table 6-8**   Cisco PoE and UPOE Comparison

| Category | PoE | PoE+ | Cisco UPOE | Cisco UPOE+ |
|---|---|---|---|---|
| Minimum cable type | CAT 5e | CAT 5e | CAT 5e | CAT 6a |
| IEEE standard | 802.3af | 802.3at | Cisco proprietary | Cisco proprietary |
| Maximum power to the PSE port | 15.4W | 30W | 60W | 90W |
| Maximum power to the PD | 12.95W | 25.5.W | 51W | 71.3W |
| UTP pairs | 2 | 2 | 4 | 4 |
| Distance | 100 m | 100 m | 100 m | 100 m |

### Wake on LAN (WoL)

When a PC shuts down, the NIC still receives power and is able to listen to the network. WoL allows an administrator to remotely power up sleeping machines in order to perform maintenance updates. WoL sends specially coded network packets, called *magic packets*, to systems equipped and enabled to respond to these packets. If you send WoL packets from remote networks, the routers must be configured to allow directed broadcasts.

## Spanning Tree Protocol Design Considerations

Spanning Tree Protocol is defined by IEEE 802.1D. It prevents loops from being formed when switches or bridges are interconnected via multiple paths. Spanning Tree Protocol is implemented by switches exchanging BPDU messages with other switches to detect loops, which are removed by shutting down selected bridge interfaces. This algorithm guarantees that there is one and only one active path between two network devices.

By default, the root bridge priority is 32768. If all switches have the same root bridge priority, the switch with the lowest MAC address is elected as the root of the Spanning Tree Protocol. Therefore, you should lower the root bridge priority on the switch that you want to be the Spanning Tree Protocol root: the distribution legacy switch. You should also align the FHRP gateway to be the same switch.

Spanning Tree Protocol switch ports enter the following states:

- **Blocking:** A blocking port would cause a switching loop if it were active. No user data is sent or received over a blocking port, but it may go into forwarding mode if the other links in use fail and the spanning tree algorithm determines that the port may transition to the forwarding state. BPDU data is still received in the blocking state. It prevents the use of looped paths.

- **Listening:** The switch processes BPDUs and awaits possible new information that would cause it to return to the blocking state. It does not populate the MAC address table and does not forward frames.

- **Learning:** While the port does not yet forward frames, it does learn source addresses from frames received and adds them to the filtering database (switching database). It populates the MAC address table but does not forward frames.

- **Forwarding:** A forwarding port receives and sends data in normal operation. Spanning Tree Protocol still monitors incoming BPDUs that would indicate it should return to the blocking state to prevent a loop.

- **Disabled:** A network administrator can manually disable a port, although this is not strictly part of Spanning Tree Protocol.

## Spanning Tree Protocol Metrics

IEEE 802.1d-2004 increases the path cost (used to calculate the cost to the root bridge) from the original 16-bit value to a 32-bit value to provide more granular costs for higher speed interfaces. The Cisco recommended practice is to ensure that all devices are using the 32-bit cost metrics. Table 6-9 shows IEEE 802.1d and 802.1d-2004 metrics.

**Table 6-9**   IEEE 802.1d and 802.1d-2004 Metrics

| Link Speed | 802.1d Cost Value | 802.1d-2004 Cost Value |
|------------|-------------------|------------------------|
| 1 Mbps | — | 20,000,000 |
| 4 Mbps | 250 | — |
| 10 Mbps | 100 | 2,000,000 |
| 16 Mbps | 62 | — |
| 100 Mbps | 19 | 200,000 |
| 1 Gbps | 4 | 20,000 |
| 10 Gbps | 2 | 2000 |
| 100 Gbps | — | 200 |
| 1 Tbps | — | 20 |
| 10 Tbps | — | 2 |

Cisco switches support three types of Spanning Tree Protocol:

- Per VLAN Spanning Tree Plus (PVST+)

- Rapid PVST+

- Multiple Spanning Tree (MST)

### PVST+

Per VLAN Spanning Tree Plus (PVST+) provides the same functionality as PVST using 802.1Q trunking technology rather than ISL. PVST+ is an enhancement to the 802.1Q specification and is not supported on non-Cisco devices. PVST+ is based on the IEEE 802.1D and adds Cisco-proprietary features such as BackboneFast, UplinkFast, and PortFast.

### Rapid PVST+

Rapid PVST+ is based on the Rapid Spanning Tree Protocol (RSTP) IEEE 802.1W standard. RSTP (IEEE 802.1w) natively includes most of the Cisco-proprietary enhancements to 802.1D Spanning Tree Protocol, such as BackboneFast and UplinkFast. Rapid PVST+ has these unique features:

- Uses version 2 bridge protocol data units (BPDUs), which are backward compatible with the 802.1D Spanning Tree Protocol, which in turn uses version 0 BPDUs.

- All the switches generate BPDUs and send out on all the ports every 2 seconds, whereas with 802.1D Spanning Tree Protocol, only the root bridge sends the configuration BPDUs.

Rapid PVST+ have the following roles, states, and types:

- **Port roles:** Root port, designated port, alternate port, and backup port
- **Port states:** Discarding, Learning, and Forwarding
- **Port types:** Edge Port (PortFast), Point-to-Point, and Shared port

Rapid PVST+ uses RSTP to provide faster convergence. When any RSTP port receives a legacy 802.1D BPDU, it falls back to legacy Spanning Tree Protocol, and the inherent fast convergence benefits of 802.1W are lost when it interacts with legacy bridges. Cisco recommends that Rapid PVST+ be configured for best convergence.

### Alignment of Spanning Tree Protocol with FHRP

Remember to manually assign the root bridge of a Spanning Tree Protocol network. Usually one of the distribution switches is selected as the root bridge to match the Layer 3 First-Hop Resiliency Protocol (FHRP). The root bridge is assigned by manually lowering its root bridge priority from the default.

### MST

MST, which is defined by IEEE 802.1S, is based on the Cisco Multiple Instance Spanning Tree Protocol (MISTP). MISTP (802.1S) is an IEEE standard that allows several VLANs to be mapped together. MST is used to reduce the total number of spanning-tree instances that match the physical topology of the network. This reduces the CPU load on a switch and is possible because most networks do not need more than a few logical topologies. Each instance handles multiple VLANs that have the same Layer 2 topology. For MST, do not manually prune VLANs from trunks and do not run MST on access ports between switches.

## Cisco Spanning Tree Protocol Toolkit

Spanning Tree Protocol has been the friend and enemy of network designers and network troubleshooters throughout the years. Spanning Tree Protocol is required for a Layer 2 Ethernet network to function properly for path redundancy and prevention of Layer 2 loops. Cisco recommends that you design for the use of the Cisco STP Toolkit to enhance the performance of IEEE 802.1D Spanning Tree Protocol on your network. Figure 6-10 shows where each mechanism is applied in a network.

### PortFast

PortFast causes a Layer 2 LAN access port to enter the forwarding state immediately, bypassing the listening and learning states. When configured for PortFast, a port is still running Spanning Tree Protocol and can immediately transition to the blocking state, if necessary. PortFast should be used only when connecting a single end station to the port. It can be enabled on trunk ports.

### UplinkFast

UplinkFast provides fast convergence after a direct link failure. UplinkFast cannot be configured on *individual* VLANs; it is configured on *all* VLANs of a LAN switch. It is most useful when configured on the uplink ports of closet switches connecting to distribution switches. This mechanism is enabled when RSTP is enabled on a switch.

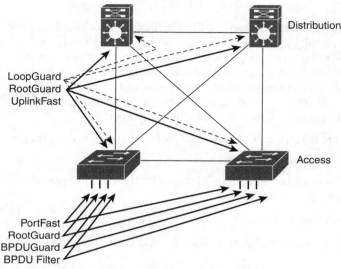

**Figure 6-10** *Cisco STP Toolkit Mechanisms*

### BackboneFast

BackboneFast provides fast failover when an indirect link failure occurs. It is initiated when a root port or blocked port on a network device receives inferior BPDUs from its designated bridge. It is configured on distribution and core switches. As with UplinkFast, this mechanism does not need to be enabled when RSTP is configured.

### Loop Guard

Loop Guard helps prevent bridging loops that could occur because of a unidirectional link failure on a point-to-point link. It detects root ports and blocked ports and ensures that they keep receiving BPDUs from the designated port on the segment. When Loop Guard is enabled, if a root or blocked port stops receiving BPDUs from its designated port, it transitions to the loop-inconsistent blocking state.

Loop Guard can be enabled on a per-port basis. It must be configured on point-to-point links only. When Loop Guard is enabled, it is automatically applied to all active instances or VLANs to which that port belongs. When enabled on an EtherChannel (link bundle) and the first link becomes unidirectional, it blocks the entire channel until the affected port is removed from the channel. Loop Guard cannot be enabled on PortFast ports, dynamic VLAN ports, or Root Guard--enabled switches. It does not affect UplinkFast or BackboneFast operation.

### Root Guard

Root Guard prevents a port from becoming a root port or blocked port. When a Root Guard port receives a superior BPDU, the port immediately goes to the root-inconsistent (blocked) state. Root Guard is configured on access switches so that they do not become a root of the spanning tree.

### BPDU Guard

BPDU Guard shuts down a port that receives a BPDU, regardless of PortFast configuration. In a valid configuration, PortFast-enabled ports do not receive BPDUs. Reception of a BPDU by a PortFast-enabled port signals an invalid configuration.

## BPDU Filter

BPDU Filter prevents a port from sending or receiving BPDUs. It can be configured on a per-port basis. When configured globally, it applies to all operational PortFast ports. Explicitly configuring PortFast BPDU filtering on a port that is not connected to a host can result in bridging loops. If a port configuration is not set to the default configuration, the PortFast setting will not affect PortFast BPDU filtering. When a PortFast port receives a BPDU, it immediately loses its operational PortFast status, BPDU filtering is automatically disabled on the port, and Spanning Tree Protocol resumes sending BPDUs on the port.

To summarize, the following are the recommended practices for Spanning Tree Protocol stability mechanisms:

- **PortFast:** Apply PortFast to all end-user ports. To secure PortFast-enabled ports, always combine PortFast with BPDU Guard.

- **Root Guard:** Apply Root Guard to all ports where a root is never expected.

- **Loop Guard:** Apply Loop Guard to all ports that are or can become non-designated ports.

Table 6-10 summarizes the mechanisms available in Cisco STP Toolkit.

**Table 6-10**    Mechanisms in Cisco STP Toolkit

| Mechanism | Improves Spanning Tree Protocol Performance or Stability? | Description |
|-----------|-----------------------------------------------------------|-------------|
| PortFast | Performance | Bypasses the listening and learning phases to transition directly to the forwarding state. Apply to all end-user ports. |
| UplinkFast | Performance | Enables fast uplink failover on an access switch. |
| BackboneFast | Performance | Enables fast convergence in distribution and core layers when Spanning Tree Protocol changes occur. |
| Loop Guard | Stability | Prevents an alternate or root port from being the designated port in the absence of bridge protocol data units (BPDUs). |
| Root Guard | Stability | Prevents external switches from becoming the root of the Spanning Tree Protocol tree. Apply to all ports where it is not expected. |
| BPDU Guard | Stability | Disables a PortFast-enabled port if a BPDU is received. |
| BPDU Filter | Stability | Suppresses BPDUs on ports. |

## Unidirectional Link Detection (UDLD) Protocol

Spanning Tree Protocol's operation relies on the reception and transmission of the bridge protocol data units (BPDUs). If the Spanning Tree Protocol process that runs on a switch with a blocking port stops receiving BPDUs from its upstream (designated) switch on the port, Spanning Tree Protocol eventually ages out the Spanning Tree Protocol information for the port and moves it to the forwarding state. This creates a forwarding loop or Spanning Tree Protocol loop. Packets start to cycle indefinitely along the looped path, and they consume more and more bandwidth. This can possibly lead to a network outage.

A Spanning Tree Protocol loop can occur on fiber networks if an SFP module fails. Unidirectional Link Detection (UDLD) can be configured on a per-port basis on all redundant links. Because Loop Guard does not work on shared links, UDLD should also be configured to prevent loops. UDLD detects unidirectional links on optical fiber links before a forwarding loop is created. Loop Guard and UDLD functionality overlap, partly in the sense that both protect against Spanning Tree Protocol failures caused by unidirectional links.

For UDLD recommended practices, Cisco recommends that UDLD aggressive mode be configured on any fiber-optic interconnection and that UDLD be enabled in global mode. Use UDLD aggressive mode for best protection. Turn on UDLD in global configuration mode so that it does not have to be enabled in every individual fiber-optic interface.

Table 6-11 compares Loop Guard and UDLD functionality.

**Table 6-11**   Loop Guard and UDLD Comparison

| Functionality | Loop Guard | UDLD |
|---|---|---|
| Configuration | Per port | Per port |
| Action granularity | Per VLAN | Per port |
| Protection against Spanning Tree Protocol failures caused by unidirectional links | Yes, when enabled on all root and alternate ports in a redundant topology | Yes, when enabled on all links in a redundant topology |
| Protection against Spanning Tree Protocol failures caused by problems in the software (designated switch does not send BPDUs) | Yes | No |
| Protection against miswiring | No | Yes |

# References and Recommended Readings

Cisco, "Campus 3.0 Virtual Switching System Design Guide," https://www.cisco.com/c/en/us/td/docs/solutions/Enterprise/Campus/VSS30dg/campusVSS_DG/VSS-dg_ch2.html.

Cisco, "Cisco TrustSec," https://www.cisco.com/c/en/us/solutions/enterprise-networks/trustsec/index.html.

Cisco, "Design Zone for Campus Wired and Wireless LAN," https://www.cisco.com/c/en/us/solutions/design-zone/networking-design-guides/campus-wired-wireless.html.

Cisco, "Power over Ethernet: Empowering Digital Transformation," https://www.cisco.com/c/dam/en/us/products/collateral/switches/catalyst-9000/nb-06-upoe-plus-wp-cte-en.pdf.

Cisco, "Understanding EtherChannel Load Balancing and Redundancy on Catalyst Switches," https://www.cisco.com/c/en/us/support/docs/lan-switching/etherchannel/12023-4.html.

## Exam Preparation Tasks

As mentioned in the section "How to Use This Book" in the Introduction, you have a couple of choices for exam preparation: the exercises here, Chapter 13, "Final Preparation," and the exam simulation questions on the companion website.

## Review All Key Topics

Review the most important topics in the chapter, noted with the Key Topic icon in the outer margin of the page. Table 6-12 lists these key topics and the page number on which each is found.

**Table 6-12**    Key Topics

| Key Topic Element | Description | Page |
|---|---|---|
| List | Hierarchical network design | 213 |
| Paragraph | Hierarchical model examples | 216 |
| Table 6-8 | Cisco PoE and UPOE Comparison | 228 |
| Table 6-10 | STP Tookit Mechanisms | 232 |

## Complete Tables and Lists from Memory

Print a copy of Appendix D, "Memory Tables," found on the companion website, or at least the section for this chapter, and complete the tables and lists from memory. Appendix E, "Memory Tables Answer Key," includes completed tables and lists to check your work.

## Define Key Terms

Define the following key terms from this chapter and check your answers in the glossary:

access layer, BackboneFast, BPDU Filter, BPDU Guard, core layer, distribution layer, Link Aggregation Control Protocol (LACP), Loop Guard, Multiple Spanning Tree (MST), Port Aggregation Protocol (PAgP), PortFast, Power over Ethernet (PoE), Root Guard, Spanning Tree Protocol, Unidirectional Link Detection (UDLD), UplinkFast, virtual local-area network (VLAN), Virtual Switching System (VSS)

## Q&A

The answers to these questions appear in Appendix A. For more practice with exam format questions, use the exam engine on the companion website.

1.    True or false: The core layer of the hierarchical model does security filtering and media translation.

2.    True or false: The access layer provides high availability and port security.

3.    True or false: You can implement a full-mesh network to increase redundancy and reduce a WAN's costs.

4.    How many links are required for a full mesh of six sites?

5.    What are four benefits of hierarchical network design?

**6.** True or false: Small to medium campus networks must always implement three layers of hierarchical design.

**7.** How many full-mesh links do you need for a network with 10 routers?

**8.** Which layer provides routing between VLANs and security filtering?

   **a.** Access layer

   **b.** Distribution layer

   **c.** Enterprise edge

   **d.** WAN module

**9.** Which of the following describe the access layer? (Choose two.)

   **a.** Transports data at high speed

   **b.** Applies network policies

   **c.** Performs network aggregation

   **d.** Concentrates user access

   **e.** Provides PoE

   **f.** Avoids data manipulation

**10.** Which of the following describe the distribution layer? (Choose two.)

   **a.** Transports data at high speed

   **b.** Applies network policies

   **c.** Performs network aggregation

   **d.** Concentrates user access

   **e.** Provides PoE

   **f.** Avoids data manipulation

**11.** Which of the following describe the core layer? (Choose two.)

   **a.** High-speed data transport

   **b.** Applies network policies

   **c.** Performs network aggregation

   **d.** Concentrates user access

   **e.** Provides PoE

   **f.** Avoids data manipulation

**12.** Which are two benefits of using a modular approach? (Choose two.)

   **a.** Simplifies the network design

   **b.** Reduces the amount of network traffic on the network

   **c.** Often reduces the cost and complexity of the network

   **d.** Simplifies the network by using full-mesh topologies

**13.** Which topology is best used for connectivity in the building distribution layer?

   **a.** Full mesh

   **b.** Partial mesh

   **c.** Hub and spoke

    **d.** Dual ring

    **e.** EtherChannel

**14.** Which are key features of the distribution layer? (Choose two.)

    **a.** Aggregates access layer switches

    **b.** Provides a routing boundary between the access and core layers

    **c.** Provides connectivity to end devices

    **d.** Provides fast switching

    **e.** Provides transport to the enterprise edge

    **f.** Provides VPN termination

**15.** Which Cisco solution allows a pair of switches to act as a single logical switch?

    **a.** HSRP

    **b.** VSS

    **c.** Spanning Tree Protocol

    **d.** GLB

**16.** What are the three layers of the hierarchical model? (Choose three.)

    **a.** WAN layer

    **b.** LAN layer

    **c.** Core layer

    **d.** Aggregation layer

    **e.** Access layer

    **f.** Distribution layer

    **g.** Edge layer

**17.** Which is the recommended design geometry for routed networks?

    **a.** Linear point-to-point networks

    **b.** Rectangular networks

    **c.** Triangular networks

    **d.** Circular networks

**18.** Which layer performs rate limiting, network access control, and broadcast suppression?

    **a.** Core layer

    **b.** Distribution layer

    **c.** Access layer

    **d.** Data link layer

**19.** Which layer performs routing between VLANs, filtering, and load balancing?

    **a.** Core layer

    **b.** Distribution layer

    **c.** Access layer

    **d.** Application layer

**20.** Which topology allows for maximum growth?

   **a.** Triangles

   **b.** Collapsed core–distribution

   **c.** Full mesh

   **d.** Core–distribution–access

**21.** Which layer performs port security and DHCP snooping?

   **a.** Core layer

   **b.** Distribution layer

   **c.** Access layer

   **d.** Application layer

**22.** Which layer handles Active Directory and messaging?

   **a.** Core layer

   **b.** Distribution layer

   **c.** Access layer

   **d.** Application layer

**23.** Which layers provide redundancy? (Choose two.)

   **a.** Core layer

   **b.** Distribution layer

   **c.** Access layer

   **d.** Data link layer

**24.** Which statement is true regarding hierarchical network design?

   **a.** It makes the network harder since there are many submodules to use.

   **b.** It provides better performance and network scalability.

   **c.** It prepares the network for migration from IPv4 to IPv6.

   **d.** It secures the network with access filters in all layers.

**25.** You need to connect a building access switch to the distribution switch. The cable distance is 135 meters. What type of cable do you recommend?

   **a.** UTP

   **b.** Coaxial cable

   **c.** Multimode fiber

   **d.** Single-mode fiber

**26.** Which of the following is an access layer best practice?

   **a.** Reduce switch peering and routing.

   **b.** Use HSRP and summarize routes.

   **c.** Disable trunking and use RPVST+.

   **d.** Offload SSL sessions and use load balancers.

**27.** Which of the following is a distribution layer best practice?

    **a.** Reduce switch peering and routing.

    **b.** Use HSRP and summarize routes.

    **c.** Disable trunking and use RPVST+.

    **d.** Offload SSL sessions and use load balancers.

**28.** Which of the following is a core layer best practice?

    **a.** Reduce switch peering and routing.

    **b.** Use HSRP and summarize routes.

    **c.** Disable trunking and use RPVST+.

    **d.** Offload SSL sessions and use load balancers.

**29.** What is the recommended method to connect the distribution switches to the core?

    **a.** Redundant triangle links

    **b.** Redundant cross-connect links

    **c.** Redundant Layer 3 squares

    **d.** Redundant Layer 2 links

**30.** Which are best practices for the access layer? (Choose four.)

    **a.** Disable trunking in host ports.

    **b.** Limit VLANs to one closet.

    **c.** Use PVST+ with multilayer switches.

    **d.** Enable trunking on host ports.

    **e.** Use VLAN spanning to speed convergence of Spanning Tree Protocol.

    **f.** Use VTP Server mode in hierarchical networks.

    **g.** Use VTP Transparent mode in hierarchical networks.

    **h.** Use RPVST+ as the Spanning Tree Protocol with multilayer switches.

**31.** Which are best practices for the distribution layer? (Choose three.)

    **a.** Use HSRP or GLBP.

    **b.** Provide fast transport.

    **c.** Use Layer 3 routing protocols to the core.

    **d.** Use Layer 2 routing protocols to the core.

    **e.** Summarize routes to the core layer.

    **f.** Summarize routes to the access layer.

**32.** Which are best practices for the core layer? (Choose three.)

    **a.** Use routing with no Layer 2 loops.

    **b.** Limit VLANs to one closet.

    **c.** Use HSRP.

    **d.** Use GLBP.

    **e.** Use Layer 3 switches with fast forwarding.

**f.** Use Layer 3 routing to the core.

**g.** Use two equal-cost paths to every destination network.

**h.** Use RPVST+ with multilayer switches.

**33.** What is a major requirement if you use a Layer 3 access layer design?

**a.** The distribution switches are configured as a VSS pair.

**b.** The core switches need to support EIGRP.

**c.** The access layer switch needs to be able to route.

**d.** HSRP is configured on the distribution switches.

**34.** What is an advantage of using the updated Layer 2 access layer design over the traditional model?

**a.** There is an increase in uplink bandwidth.

**b.** The updated model adds routing between the distribution and access layers.

**c.** The access layer switch needs to be able to route.

**d.** Layer 3 load balancing is enabled.

**35.** Which Cisco STP Toolkit mechanisms are recommended on user access ports? (Select two.)

**a.** PortFast

**b.** RootGuard

**c.** UplinkFast

**d.** Loop Guard

**e.** BPDU Guard

**36.** You want to enable physical device virtualization. Which feature provides that?

**a.** VLAN

**b.** VFR

**c.** VSS

**d.** VPN

**37.** A network has two distribution switches, A and B, connected via a Layer 2 trunk. Distribution A switch is the HSRP active gateway and Spanning Tree Protocol root. Layer 2 links are used to connect access layer switches to both distribution switches. Which version of spanning tree is recommended?

**a.** PVST+

**b.** Rapid PVST+

**c.** MST

**d.** VSS

**38.** A network has two distribution switches, A and B, connected via a Layer 2 trunk. Distribution A switch is the Spanning Tree Protocol root, and distribution B is the active HSRP gateway. Layer 2 links are used to connect access layer switches to both distribution switches. Which statement is true?

**a.** Traffic will transit from the access switches through distribution switch A through the Layer 2 trunk to distribution switch B.

    **b.**   A Spanning Tree Protocol loop will be created.

    **c.**   The access switches will not be able to communicate.

    **d.**   Loop Guard will prevent the loop from being created.

**39.**   Which is true in regard to using UDLD? (Choose three.)

    **a.**   It is used instead of Loop Guard.

    **b.**   It should be used in aggressive mode.

    **c.**   It should be enabled in global configuration mode.

    **d.**   It prevents blackholing and loops.

    **e.**   It should be used only on UTP links.

    **f.**   It cannot protect against miswiring.

**40.**   What is true regarding Spanning Tree Protocol design?

    **a.**   Best practice is for the network to determine the root bridge.

    **b.**   All ports should be configured with PortFast to enable root bridge selection.

    **c.**   The root bridge and HSRP primary router should be on the same distribution switch.

    **d.**   It is best practice to disable the toolkit when setting the root bridge.

**41.**   Match each campus design model with its description.

    **a.**   Routed access layer

    **b.**   Traditional Layer 2 access layer

    **c.**   Layer 2 access with VSS

    **d.**   Hybrid access layer

    **i.**   Legacy design

    **ii.**   Access layer using Layer 3 capabilities

    **iii.**   Layer 2 design improvement

    **iv.**   Not recommended

**42.**   Which statement is correct regarding Local VLANs? (Select two.)

    **a.**   It is the preferred design.

    **b.**   Users are grouped into VLANs depending on their physical location.

    **c.**   VLAN membership does not change if the user moves to another building within the campus.

    **d.**   VLANs are dispersed throughout the campus.

**43.**   Which statement is correct regarding end-to-end VLAN design?

    **a.**   It is the preferred design.

    **b.**   Users are grouped into VLANs based on their physical location.

    **c.**   VLAN membership does not change if the user moves to another building within the campus.

    **d.**   VLANs are dispersed throughout the campus.

**44.** You need to power a PD that requires 50 watts. Which solution is preferred?

    **a.** PoE

    **b.** PoE+

    **c.** UPOE

    **d.** UPOE+

**45.** An administrator requests a way to do remote maintenance on desktops. What solution would allow the administrator to power up end devices to do maintenance?

    **a.** PoE

    **b.** ON switch

    **c.** WoL

    **d.** Cisco UPOE

**46.** Which statement regarding campus design is correct?

    **a.** Connect access switches directly to summarize via the uplinks.

    **b.** Build using triangles rather than squares.

    **c.** Configure a security ACL in the core.

    **d.** Avoid summarization at the distribution layer.

**47.** What is the minimum cable requirement for Cisco UPOE+?

    **a.** CAT 5

    **b.** CAT 5e

    **c.** CAT 6a

    **d.** CAT 7

**48.** What is correct regarding Spanning Tree Protocol stability mechanisms?

    **a.** Apply PortFast to all end-user ports. Apply RootGuard to all ports where a root is never expected.

    **b.** Apply RootGuard to all end-user ports. Apply PortFast to all ports where a root is never expected.

    **c.** Apply PortFast to all end-user ports. Apply RootGuard to all ports where a root is expected.

    **d.** Apply Loop Guard to all end-user ports. Apply RootGuard to all ports.

6

## CHAPTER 7

# Advanced Enterprise Campus Design

**This chapter covers the following subjects:**

**Campus LAN Design and Best Practices:** This section covers best practices to consider in campus local-area network (LAN) design.

**High Availability Network Services:** This section covers high availability design for the campus LAN, from client to access switch to the core and throughout the campus network.

This chapter expands on Chapter 6, "Enterprise LAN Design and Technologies," covering advanced design of campus LANs. It covers traditional and updated Layer 2 access designs as well as Layer 3 access design. It also covers advanced redundancy solutions, first-hop redundancy protocols, and interbuilding and intrabuilding media technologies.

This chapter covers the following objectives from the ENSLD 300-420 exam:

- Design campus networks for high availability
- Design multi-campus Layer 3 infrastructures

## "Do I Know This Already?" Quiz

The "Do I Know This Already?" quiz helps you identify your strengths and deficiencies in this chapter's topics. This quiz, derived from the major sections in the "Foundation Topics" portion of the chapter, helps you determine how to spend your limited study time. Table 7-1 outlines the major topics discussed in this chapter and the "Do I Know This Already?" quiz questions that correspond to those topics. You can find the answers in Appendix A, "Answers to the 'Do I Know This Already?' Quiz Questions Q&A Questions."

**Table 7-1**  "Do I Know This Already?" Foundation Topics Section-to-Question Mapping

| Foundation Topics Section | Questions Covered in This Section |
|---|---|
| Campus LAN Design and Best Practices | 1, 3, 4, 6 |
| High Availability Network Services | 2, 5, 7–8 |

1. What is true in the Layer 3 access layer design?
   a. There is no need for an FHRP.
   b. There is no need for VLANs in the access layer.
   c. VLANs can span access switches.
   d. The SVIs are defined in the distribution layer.

**2.** Which of the following methods provide workstation-to-router redundancy in the access layer? (Choose two.)

   **a.** AppleTalk Address Resolution Protocol (AARP)

   **b.** Hot Standby Router Protocol (HSRP)

   **c.** Virtual Router Redundancy Protocol (VRRP)

   **d.** Dynamic Host Configuration Protocol (DHCP)

**3.** What is the 20/80 rule?

   **a.** 80% of the traffic is local, 20% is external

   **b.** 20% of the traffic is local, 80% is external

   **c.** 20% of the traffic is reserved for VoIP, 80% for data

   **d.** 20% of the traffic is peer-to-peer, 80% is client/server

**4.** The summarization of routes is a best practice at which layer?

   **a.** Access layer

   **b.** Distribution layer

   **c.** Core layer

   **d.** WAN layer

**5.** A design uses two Layer 2 circuits interconnecting two data centers. Spanning Tree Protocol causes the second circuit to be in blocking state. What technology can you implement to use both circuits?

   **a.** Fast IP

   **b.** MST

   **c.** STP Toolkit

   **d.** EtherChannel

**6.** Two workstations are located on separate VLANs. They exchange data directly. What type of application is this?

   **a.** Client/server

   **b.** Client/peer

   **c.** Peer-to-peer

   **d.** Client/enterprise

**7.** Which protocol is an IETF standard?

   **a.** VSS

   **b.** HSRP

   **c.** VRRP

   **d.** GLBP

**8.** Which solution allows you to expand the user capacity in the access layer without having to replace the existing switch?

   **a.** VSS

   **b.** EtherChannel

   **c.** MEC

   **d.** Stacking technology

## Foundation Topics

# Campus LAN Design and Best Practices

LANs can be classified as large-building LANs, campus LANs, or small and remote LANs. A large-building LAN typically contains a major data center with high-speed access and floor communications closets; it is usually the headquarters in a larger company. Campus LANs provide connectivity between buildings on a campus. Redundancy is usually a requirement in large-building and campus LAN deployments. Small and remote LANs provide connectivity to remote offices with a relatively small number of nodes.

Campus design factors include the following categories:

- **Network application characteristics:** Different application types
- **Infrastructure device characteristics:** Layer 2 and Layer 3 switching and hierarchy
- **Environmental characteristics:** Geography, wiring, distance, space, power, and number of nodes

## Network Requirements for Applications

A business dictates which applications need to be used, and the network must be able to support them. Applications may require high bandwidth or may be time sensitive. Infrastructure devices influence the design. Decisions on switched or routed architectures and port limitations influence the design. The actual physical distances affect the design. The selection of copper or fiber media may be influenced by the environmental or distance requirements. Table 7-2 describes different application types.

**Table 7-2**  Application Types

| Application Type | Description |
| --- | --- |
| Peer-to-peer | Peer-to-peer applications include instant messaging, file sharing, IP phone to IP phone, and video conferencing. |
| Client/local servers | Servers are located in the same segment as the clients or close by, normally on the same LAN. According to the legacy 80/20 workgroup rule, 80% of traffic is local, and 20% is not local. This rule is not followed today. |
| Client/data center | Mail servers, file servers, database servers, and business applications are located in the data center. The network needs to be reliable and provide adequate bandwidth to the data center. |
| Client/enterprise edge | External servers such as mail, web, business-to-business (B2B), and public servers are located in the enterprise-edge where off-net connectivity is located. |

There is a wide range of network requirements for applications, depending on the application type. Networks today are switched and not shared. Data centers require high-capacity links to the servers and redundant connections on the network to provide high availability. With servers now located in data centers, the 20/80 rule is applied. With 20/80, 20% of traffic is local traffic, and 80% of the traffic communicates with servers in the data center.

Costs are lower for peer-to-peer applications and become higher for applications that traverse the network with high redundancy. Table 7-3 summarizes network requirements for applications.

**Table 7-3**  Network Requirements for Application Types

| Requirement | Peer-to-Peer | Client/Local Servers | Client/Data Center | Client/ Enterprise Edge |
|---|---|---|---|---|
| Connectivity type | Switched | Switched | Switched | Switched |
| Throughput required | Medium to high | Medium | High | Medium |
| Availability | Low to high | Medium | High | High |
| Network costs | Low to medium | Medium | High | Medium |

## Best Practices for Hierarchical Layers

Each layer of the hierarchical architecture requires special considerations. The following sections describe best practices for each of the three layers of the hierarchical architecture: access, distribution, and core.

### Access Layer Best Practices

When designing the building access layer, you must consider the number of users or ports required to size up the LAN switch. Connectivity speed for each host should also be considered. Hosts might be connected using various technologies, such as Fast Ethernet, Gigabit Ethernet, and port channels. The planned VLANs enter into the design as well.

Performance in the access layer is also important. Redundancy and QoS features should be considered.

There are several options for the access layer architectures:

- Traditional Layer 2 access layer design

- Updated Layer 2 access layer design

- Layer 3 access layer design

- Hybrid access layer design

### Traditional Layer 2 Access Layer

Figure 7-1 shows the traditional Layer 2 access layer. This is the de facto model that has been used for years, where VLANs are defined in the distribution switches, HSRP gateways are configured for the VLANs with active and standby, and the Spanning Tree Protocol root bridge is configured. The access switch is configured as a Layer 2 switch that forwards traffic via trunk ports to the distribution switches. There is no load balancing because Spanning Tree Protocol blocks one of the uplink trunks, so only one uplink is active for each VLAN.

Distribution layer switches act as default gateways. Layer 3 links are used between the core and distribution switches with a routing protocol.

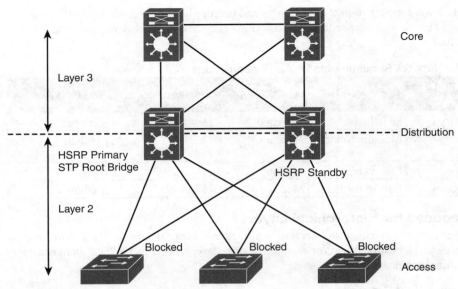

**Figure 7-1** *Traditional Layer 2 Access Layer Design*

### Updated Layer 2 Access Layer (Using VSS)

Figure 7-2 shows the updated Layer 2 access layer. In this model, the distribution switches are still the demarcation between the Layer 2 and Layer 3 boundaries. The difference now is that Virtual Switching System (VSS) is configured in the distribution layer. With VSS, the physical distribution switch pair is merged into a virtual switch. VSS is supported on Cisco 4500, 6500, and 6800 Series switches. With VSS, both access switch uplinks are used, doubling the bandwidth from access switches to the distribution pair. The bundled pair is called a *Multichassis EtherChannel (MEC)*, and it creates a loop-free topology. With Gigabit Ethernet uplinks, you have 2 Gbps of uplink bandwidth, and with 10 Gigabit Ethernet uplinks, you have 20 Gbps of uplink bandwidth.

When VSS is used, there is no need for a first-hop routing protocol (FHRP) such as HSRP. This solution provides faster convergence and higher uplink bandwidth than the traditional Layer 2 access design.

### Layer 3 Access Layer

Figure 7-3 shows the Layer 3 access layer. With this design model, the Layer 3 demarcation is pushed to the access layer. The access layer switches have VLANs defined and act as the default gateways. Notice that VLANs are not able to span access switches.

Layer 3 links are now used from the access layer to the distribution switches to the core. The use of HSRP is not necessary. In this solution, the access layer switches act as default gateways and participate in routing, and there is no need for an FHRP.

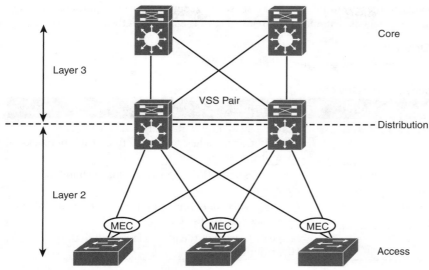

**Figure 7-2**  *Updated Layer 2 Access Layer Design*

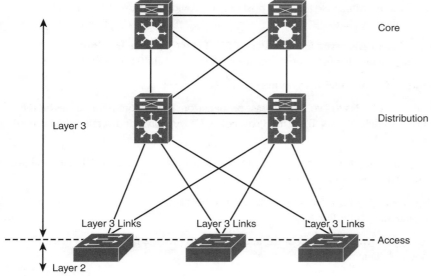

**Figure 7-3**  *Layer 3 Access Layer Design*

### Hybrid LAN Access Layer

The hybrid access layer combines the use of Layer 2 switching with Layer 3 at the access layer. In this design, some VLANs are defined in the access layer and others in the distribution layer. There are Layer 3 and Layer 2 links between the distribution switches and the access switches. With the Layer 2 links, Spanning Tree Protocol is still in the network. This design is not the preferred design because it has the added complexity of mixed Layer 2 and Layer 3 access layers per VLAN, but it is usually implemented for various reasons. One reason to implement these solutions might be sensor or security devices requiring a shared VLAN. The disadvantage is that Spanning Tree Protocol is enabled on these VLANs.

### Access Layer Designs

Table 7-4 summarizes the access layer designs.

**Table 7-4** Access Layer Designs

| Access Layer Design Model | Description |
|---|---|
| Traditional Layer 2 access layer | Layer 2 switch forwards traffic via trunk ports to distribution switches. Spanning Tree Protocol blocks one of the uplink trunks. |
| Updated Layer 2 access layer | Uses VSS and MEC to provide additional uplink bandwidth. |
| Layer 3 access layer | Layer 3 SVIs are defined in the access layer, and there is no need for an FHRP. |
| Hybrid access layer | Layer 3 routing in the access layer and in the distribution layer. |

The following are the recommended best practices for the building access layer:

- Limit VLANs to a single closet when possible to provide the most deterministic and highly available topology.

- Use Rapid Per-VLAN Spanning Tree Plus (RPVST+) if Spanning Tree Protocol is required. It provides for faster convergence than traditional 802.1d default timers.

- Set trunks to ON and ON with no-negotiate.

- Prune unused VLANs to avoid broadcast propagation; this is commonly done on the distribution switch. VLAN Trunking Protocol (VTP) version 2 and version 3 automatically prune unused VLANs.

- Use VTP Transparent mode because there is little need for a common VLAN database in hierarchical networks.

- Disable trunking on host ports because it is not necessary. Doing so provides more security and speeds up PortFast.

- Consider implementing routing in the access layer to provide fast convergence and Layer 3 load balancing.

- Use the **switchport host** command on server and end-user ports to enable PortFast and disable channeling on these ports. Alternatively, you can use the **spanning-tree portfast default** global command.

- Use the Cisco STP Toolkit, which provides the following tools:

  - **PortFast:** Bypasses the listening/learning phase for access ports.

  - **Loop Guard:** Prevents an alternate or root port from becoming designated in the absence of bridge protocol data units (BPDUs).

- **Root Guard:** Prevents external switches from becoming root.

- **Design Strategy:** Used to design a Spanning Tree Protocol priority strategy with the highest priorities hardcoded at the top layers of the Spanning Tree Protocol tree.

- **BPDU Guard:** Disables a PortFast-enabled port if a BPDU is received.

### Stacking Access Switches

Stacking is a method of joining multiple physical access switches into a single logical switch. Switches are interconnected by stackwise interconnect cables, and a master switch is selected. The switch stack is managed as a single object and uses a single IP management address and a single configuration file. This reduces management overhead. Furthermore, the switch stack can create an EtherChannel connection, and uplinks can form MECs with an upstream VSS distribution pair.

### Distribution Layer Best Practices

As shown in Figure 7-4, the distribution layer aggregates all closet switches and connects to the core layer. Design considerations for the distribution layer include providing wire-speed performance on all ports, link redundancy, and infrastructure services.

The distribution layer should not be limited in terms of performance. Links to the core must be able to support the bandwidth used by the aggregate access layer switches. Redundant links from the access switches to the distribution layer and from the distribution layer to the core layer allow for high availability in the event of a link failure. Infrastructure services include quality of service (QoS) configuration, security, and policy enforcement. Access lists are configured in the distribution layer.

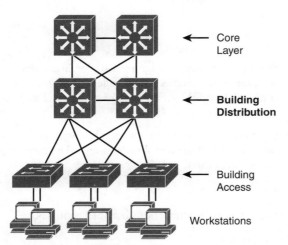

Core
Layer

**Building
Distribution**

Building
Access

Workstations

**Figure 7-4**  *Distribution Layer*

The following are recommended best practices at the distribution layer:

- Use first-hop redundancy protocols (FHRPs). Hot Standby Router Protocol (HSRP), Virtual Router Redundancy Protocol (VRRP), or Gateway Load Balancing Protocol (GLBP) should be used if you implement Layer 2 links between the Layer 2 access switches and the distribution layer.

- Use Layer 3 routing protocols between the distribution and core switches to allow for fast convergence and load balancing.

- Only peer on links that you intend to use as transit.

- Build Layer 3 triangles, not squares, as shown in Figure 7-5.

- Use the distribution switches to connect Layer 2 VLANs that span multiple access layer switches.

- Summarize routes from the distribution to the core of the network to reduce routing overhead.

- Use Virtual Switching System (VSS) to eliminate the use of Spanning Tree Protocol and the need for an FHRP.

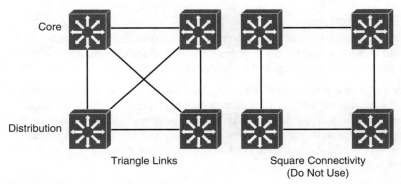

**Figure 7-5** *Layer 3 Triangles*

## Core Layer Best Practices

Depending on the network's size, a core layer might or might not be needed. For larger networks, building distribution switches are aggregated to the core. This is called a *collapsed core*. This core layer provides high-speed connectivity to the server farm or data center and to the enterprise edge (to the WAN and the Internet).

Figure 7-6 shows the criticality of the core switches. The core must provide high-speed switching with redundant paths for high availability to all the distribution points. The core must support gigabit speeds and data and voice integration.

The following are best practices for the campus core:

- Reduce switch peering by using redundant triangle connections between switches.

- Use routing that provides a loop-free topology.

- Use Layer 3 switches on the core that provide intelligent services that Layer 2 switches do not support.

- Use two equal-cost paths to every destination network.

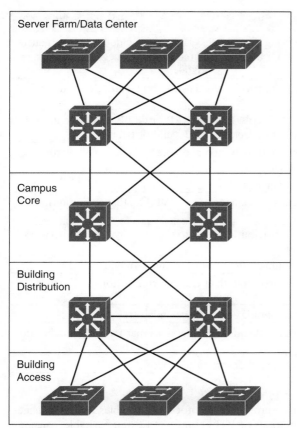

Server Farm/Data Center

Campus
Core

Building
Distribution

Building
Access

**Figure 7-6**  *Core Switches*

## Campus Layer Best Practices

Table 7-5 summarizes campus layer best practices.

**Table 7-5**  Campus Layer Design Best Practices

| Layer | Best Practices |
|---|---|
| Access layer | Limit VLANs to a single closet, when possible, to provide the most deterministic and highly available topology. |
| | Use RPVST+ if Spanning Tree Protocol is required. It provides the best convergence. |
| | Set trunks to ON and ON with no-negotiate. |
| | Manually prune unused VLANs to avoid broadcast propagation. |
| | Use VTP Transparent mode because there is little need for a common VLAN database in hierarchical networks. |
| | Disable trunking on host ports because it is not necessary. Doing so provides more security and speeds up PortFast. |

| Layer | Best Practices |
|-------|----------------|
|  | Consider implementing routing in the access layer to provide fast convergence and Layer 3 load balancing. Or use the Updated Layer 2 access layer design with VSS. |
|  | Use Cisco STP Toolkit, which provides PortFast, Loop Guard, Root Guard, and BPDU Guard. |
| Distribution layer | Use first-hop redundancy protocols. HSRP, VRRP, or GLBP should be used if you implement Layer 2 links between the access and distribution. |
|  | Use Layer 3 links between the distribution and core switches to allow for fast convergence and load balancing. |
|  | Build Layer 3 triangles, not squares. |
|  | Use the distribution switches to connect Layer 2 VLANs that span multiple access layer switches. |
|  | Summarize routes from the distribution layer to the core layer of the network to reduce routing overhead. |
|  | Use VSS as an option to eliminate the use of Spanning Tree Protocol. |
| Core layer | Reduce switch peering by using redundant triangle connections between switches. |
|  | Use routing that provides a topology with no spanning-tree loops. |
|  | Use Layer 3 switches that provide intelligent services that Layer 2 switches do not support. |
|  | Use two equal-cost paths to every destination network. |

### VTP Considerations

VLAN Trunking Protocol (VTP) is a Cisco-proprietary protocol that enables central management of the VLAN database. Implementations of VTPv1 and VTPv2 were unstable, causing the whole LAN network to go down in the event that a higher revision switch was inserted into the network. The best practice is to configure all switches in a VTPv2 domain in Transparent mode. In this mode, all VLAN changes are local.

VTP version 3 eliminated the instabilities of the previous versions. However, VTPv3 is compatible with VTPv2 only if you do not use it to propagate private or extended VLANs. If desired, you need to explicitly configure VTPv3 as the default mode in VTPv2.

## High Availability Network Services

This section covers designs for high availability network services in the access layer.

### Redundancy Models

When designing a network topology for a customer who has critical systems, services, or network paths, you should determine the likelihood that these components will fail and design redundancy where necessary. Consider incorporating one of the following types of redundancy into your design:

- Workstation-to-router redundancy in the building access layer
- Server redundancy in the data center

- Route redundancy within and between network components

- Link media redundancy in the access layer

The following sections discuss these types of redundancy.

## First-Hop Redundancy for LAN High Availability

Several protocols increase the ability of a workstation to reach its default gateway router on its network segment, including the following:

- Hot Standby Router Protocol (HSRP)

- Virtual Router Redundancy Protocol (VRRP)

- Gateway Load Balancing Protocol (GLBP)

- Virtual Switching System (VSS)

The following sections cover these methods.

### HSRP

Cisco Hot Standby Routing Protocol (HSRP) provides a way for an IP workstation that supports only one default router to keep communicating on the internetwork even if its default router becomes unavailable. HSRP works by creating a virtual router that has its own IP and MAC addresses. The workstations use this virtual IP address as their default router.

HSRP routers on a LAN communicate among themselves to designate two routers as active and standby. The active router sends periodic hello messages. The other HSRP routers listen for the hello messages. If the active router fails and the other HSRP routers stop receiving hello messages, the standby router takes over and becomes the active router. Because the new active router assumes both the phantom's IP and MAC addresses, end nodes see no change. They continue to send packets to the phantom router's MAC address, and the new active router delivers those packets.

The default HSRP timers are 3 seconds for the hello timer and 10 seconds for the dead timer. You can achieve subsecond failover with HSRP by setting the hello timer to 200 milliseconds and the dead timer to 750 milliseconds. It is recommended to configure HSRP with preemption. With preemption, the primary HSRP router reassumes the primary role when it comes back online. HSRP preemption should be explicitly configured because by default it is disabled. HSRP does not support load sharing as part of the protocol specification. In order to use both uplink paths to the distribution switches, different HSRP groups are configured for different VLANs, with the primary router configured for Switch A for some VLANs and the primary router configured for Switch B for other VLANs. HSRP has a native interface tracking mechanism that is used to track an uplink. If the uplink fails, the HSRP priority is reduced.

HSRP also works for proxy ARP. When an active HSRP router receives an ARP request for a node that is not on the local LAN, the router replies with the phantom router's MAC address instead of its own. If the router that originally sent the ARP reply later loses its connection, the new active router can still deliver the traffic.

Figure 7-7 shows a sample implementation of HSRP.

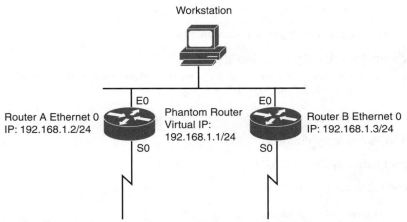

**Figure 7-7**   *HSRP: The Phantom Router Represents the Real Routers*

In Figure 7-7, the following sequence occurs:

**Step 1.**   The workstation is configured to use the phantom router (192.168.1.1) as its default router.

**Step 2.**   Upon booting, the routers elect Router A as the HSRP active router. The active router does the work for the HSRP phantom. Router B is the HSRP standby router.

**Step 3.**   When the workstation sends an ARP frame to find its default router, Router A responds with the phantom router's MAC address.

**Step 4.**   If Router A goes offline, Router B takes over as the active router and continues the delivery of the workstation's packets. The change is transparent to the workstation.

### VRRP

Virtual Router Redundancy Protocol (VRRP) is a router redundancy protocol defined in RFC 3768. VRRPv2 only supports IPv4. RFC 5798 defines VRRPv3 for both IPv4 and IPv6 networks. VRRP is based on Cisco's HSRP but is not compatible with it. VRRP specifies an election protocol that dynamically assigns responsibility for a virtual router to one of the VRRP routers on a LAN. The VRRP router controlling the IP addresses associated with a virtual router is called the *master*, and it forwards packets sent to these IP addresses. The election process provides dynamic failover in the forwarding responsibility in the event that the master become unavailable. This allows any of the virtual router IP addresses on the LAN to be used as the default first-hop router by end hosts. The virtual router backup assumes the forwarding responsibility for the virtual router if the master fails. The default VRRP hello timer is 1 second, and the dead timer is 3 seconds. Unlike in HSRP, VRRP preemption is enabled by default. Similar to HSRP, to configure load balancing, different VRRP groups are configured for different VLANs. VRRP can also be configured to track the uplink to decrement the VRRP priority of the primary router.

## GLBP

Global Load Balancing Protocol (GLBP) is a Cisco-proprietary FHRP that allows packet load sharing among a group of routers. GLBP protects data traffic from a failed router or circuit, such as HSRP, while allowing packet load sharing between a group of redundant routers. Methods for load balancing with HSRP and VRRP work with small networks, but GLBP automatically allows for first-hop load balancing on larger networks.

Unlike HSRP, GLBP provides for load balancing between multiple redundant routers—up to four gateways in a GLBP group. It balances the load by using a single virtual IP address and multiple virtual MAC addresses. All the hosts are configured with the same virtual IP address, and all routers in the virtual router group participate in forwarding packets. By default, all routers in a group forward traffic and do load balancing automatically. GLBP members communicate between each other through hello messages sent every 3 seconds to the multicast address 224.0.0.102, User Datagram Protocol (UDP) port 3222.

Benefits of GLBP include the following:

- **Load sharing:** GLBP can be configured in such a way that traffic from LAN clients can be shared by multiple routers.

- **Multiple virtual routers:** GLBP supports up to 1024 virtual routers (GLBP groups) on each physical interface of a router.

- **Preemption:** GLBP enables you to preempt an active virtual gateway with a higher-priority backup.

- **Authentication:** Simple text password authentication is supported.

## VSS

Virtual Switching System (VSS) solves the Spanning Tree Protocol unused blocked links problem by converting the distribution switching pair into a logical single switch. With VSS, the physical topology changes because each access switch has a single upstream distribution switch rather than having two upstream distribution switches. The bundled access switch pair is called a Multichassis EtherChannel (MEC), and it creates a loop-free topology eliminating Spanning Tree Protocol. VSS is configured only on Cisco 4500, 6500, and 6800 Series switches.

In Figure 7-8, the two switches are connected to each other via virtual switch links (VSLs), which makes them seem like a single switch. The key benefits of VSS include the following:

- Layer 3 switching toward the access layer

- Simplified management of a single configuration of the VSS distribution switch

- Better return on investment (ROI) via increased bandwidth between the access layer and the distribution layer

- No need to configure an FHRP such as HSRP or VRRP

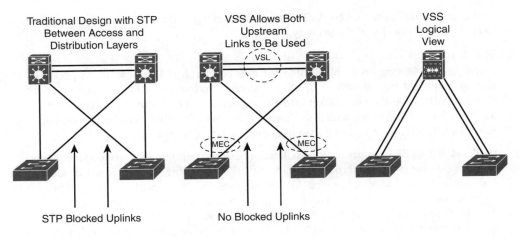

**Figure 7-8**   *Virtual Switching System*

## Server Redundancy

Some environments need fully redundant (mirrored) file and application servers. For example, in a brokerage firm where traders must access data to buy and sell stocks, two or more redundant servers can replicate the data. Also, you can deploy Cisco Unified Communications Manager (CUCM) servers in clusters for redundancy. The servers should be on different networks and should use redundant power supplies. To provide high availability in the server farm module, you have the following options:

- **Single attachment:** This is not recommended because it lacks link-level redundancy.

- **Dual attachment:** This solution increases availability by using redundant network interface cards (NICs).

- **Fast EtherChannel (FEC) and Gigabit EtherChannel (GEC) port bundles:** This solution bundles 2, 4, or 8 Fast Ethernet or Gigabit Ethernet links to increase bandwidth.

## Route Redundancy

Designing redundant routes has two purposes: balancing loads and increasing availability.

### Load Balancing

Most IP routing protocols can balance loads across parallel links that have equal cost. Use the **maximum-paths** command to change the number of links over which the router balances for IP; the default is four, and the maximum is six. To support load balancing, keep the bandwidth consistent within a layer of the hierarchical model so that all paths have the same cost. (Cisco Enhanced Interior Gateway Routing Protocol [EIGRP] is an exception because it can balance loads across multiple routes that have different metrics by using a feature called *variance*.)

A hop-based routing protocol does load balancing over unequal-bandwidth paths as long as the hop count is equal. After the slower link becomes saturated, packet loss at the saturated link prevents full utilization of the higher-capacity links; this scenario is called *pinhole congestion*. You can avoid pinhole congestion by designing and provisioning equal-bandwidth links within one layer of the hierarchy or by using a routing protocol that takes bandwidth into account.

IP load balancing in a Cisco router depends on which switching mode the router uses. Process switching balances loads on a packet-by-packet basis. Fast, autonomous, silicon, optimum, distributed, and NetFlow switching do load balancing on a destination-by-destination basis because the processor caches information used to encapsulate the packets based on destination for these types of switching modes.

### Increasing Campus Availability

In addition to facilitating load balancing, redundant routes increase network availability.

You should keep bandwidth consistent within a given design component to facilitate load balancing. Another reason to keep bandwidth consistent within a layer of a hierarchy is that routing protocols converge much faster on multiple equal-cost paths to a destination network.

By using redundant, meshed network designs, you can minimize the effect of link failures. With such designs, depending on the convergence time of the routing protocols, it is unlikely that a single link failure will have a catastrophic effect.

You can design redundant network links to provide a full mesh or a well-connected partial mesh. In a full-mesh network, every Layer 3 switch has a link to every other Layer 3 switch, as shown in Figure 7-9. A full-mesh network provides complete redundancy and provides good performance because there is just a single-hop delay between any two campus sites. The number of links in a full mesh is $n(n - 1)/2$, where $n$ is the number of routers. Each switch is connected to every other switch. A well-connected partial-mesh network provides every switch with links to at least two other routing devices in the network.

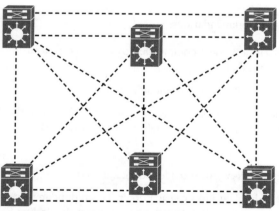

**Figure 7-9**  *Full-Mesh Network: Every Router Has a Link to Every Other Router in the Network*

A full-mesh network can be expensive to implement because of the number of links required. In addition, groups of Layer 3 switches or routers that broadcast routing updates or service advertisements have practical limits in terms of scaling. As the number of routing peers increases, the amount of bandwidth and the CPU resources devoted to processing broadcasts increase.

A suggested guideline is to keep broadcast traffic at less than 20% of the bandwidth of each link; this amount limits the number of peer routers that can exchange routing tables or service advertisements. When designing for link bandwidth, reserve 80% of the bandwidth for data, voice, and video traffic so that the rest can be used for routing and other link traffic. When planning redundancy, follow guidelines for simple hierarchical design.

Figure 7-10 illustrates a classic hierarchical and redundant campus enterprise design that uses a partial-mesh design between switches rather than a full-mesh topology.

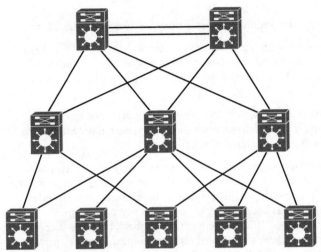

**Figure 7-10**   *Partial-Mesh Design with Redundancy*

The following are oversubscription design recommendations:

- When implementing data oversubscription, the recommended practice is for 20-to-1 oversubscription for access-to-distribution links.

- For distribution-to-core, the oversubscription recommendation is 4 to 1.

- You can increase bandwidth by adding more links and aggregating them. Between the campus, these links can be 10 Gigabit Ethernet or 40 Gigabit Ethernet fiber links.

## Link Media Redundancy

In mission-critical applications, it is often necessary to provide redundant media.

In switched networks, switches can have redundant links to each other. This redundancy is good because it minimizes downtime, but it can result in broadcasts continuously circling the network; this is called a *broadcast storm*. Cisco switches implement the IEEE 802.1d spanning-tree algorithm, which aids in avoiding the looping that occurs in broadcast networks. The spanning-tree algorithm guarantees that only one path is active between two network stations. The algorithm permits redundant paths that are automatically activated when the active path experiences problems.

You can use EtherChannel to bundle links for load balancing. Links are bundled in powers of 2 (for example, 2, 4, 8) groups. EtherChannel aggregates the bandwidth of the links. Hence, two 10 Gigabit Ethernet ports provide 20 Gbps of bandwidth when they are bundled. For more granular load balancing, use a combination of source and destination per-port load balancing, if available on the switch. In current networks, EtherChannel uses Link Aggregation Control Protocol (LACP), which is a standard-based negotiation protocol that is defined in IEEE 802.3ad. (An older solution included the Cisco-proprietary PAgP protocol.) LACP helps protect against Layer 2 loops that are caused by misconfiguration. One downside is that it introduces overhead and delay when setting up a bundle.

### Redundancy Models Summary

Table 7-6 summarizes the four main redundancy models.

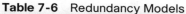

**Table 7-6**   Redundancy Models

| Redundancy Type | Description |
| --- | --- |
| Workstation-to-router redundancy | Uses HSRP, VRRP, GLBP, and VSS. |
| Server redundancy | Uses dual-attached NICs, FEC, or GEC port bundles. |
| Route redundancy | Provides load balancing and high availability. |
| Link redundancy | Uses multiple links that provide primary and secondary failover for higher availability. On LANs, uses EtherChannel. |

## Large-Building LANs

Large-building LANs are segmented by floors or departments. The building-access component serves one or more departments or floors. The building-distribution component serves one or more building-access components. Campus and building backbone devices connect the data center, the building-distribution components, and the enterprise edge-distribution component. The access layer typically uses Layer 2 switches to contain costs, with more expensive Layer 3 switches in the distribution layer to provide policy enforcement. Current best practice is to also deploy multilayer switches in the campus and building backbone. Figure 7-11 shows a typical large-building design.

Each floor can have more than 200 users. Following the hierarchical model of building access, building distribution, and core, Fast Ethernet nodes can connect to the Layer 2 switches in the communications closet. Fast Ethernet or Gigabit Ethernet uplink ports from closet switches connect back to one or two (for redundancy) distribution switches. Distribution switches can provide connectivity to server farms that provide business applications, Dynamic Host Configuration Protocol (DHCP), Domain Name System (DNS), intranet, and other services.

For intrabuilding structure, user port connectivity is provided via unshielded twisted-pair (UTP) run from cubicle ports to floor communication closets, where the access switches are located. These are Gigabit Ethernet ports. Wireless LANs are also used for user client devices. Optical fiber is used to connect the access switches to the distribution switches with new networks utilizing 10 Gigabit Ethernet ports.

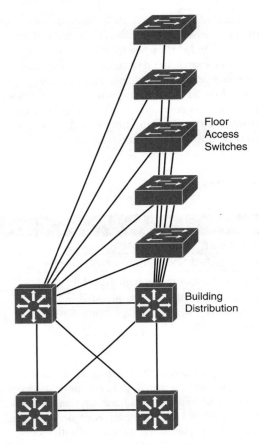

Floor
Access
Switches

Building
Distribution

**Figure 7-11**  *Large-Building LAN Design*

## Enterprise Campus LANs

A campus LAN connects two or more buildings within a local geographic area using a high-bandwidth LAN media backbone. Usually the enterprise owns the medium (copper or fiber). High-speed switching devices minimize latency. In today's networks, 10 Gigabit Ethernet or 40 Gigabit Ethernet campus backbones are the standard for new installations. In Figure 7-12, Layer 3 switches with fiber-optic media connect campus buildings.

Ensure that you implement a hierarchical design on a campus LAN and assign network layer addressing to control broadcasts on the networks. Each building should have addressing assigned in such a way as to maximize address summarization. Apply contiguous subnets to buildings at the bit boundary to apply summarization and ease the design. Campus networks can support high-bandwidth applications such as video conferencing. Remember to use Layer 3 switches with high-switching capabilities in the campus backbone design. In smaller installations, it might be desirable to collapse the building-distribution component into the campus backbone. An increasingly viable alternative is to provide building access and distribution on a single device selected from among the smaller Layer 3 switches now available.

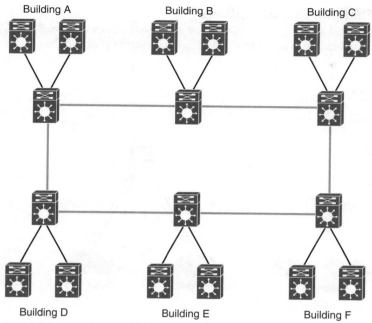

**Figure 7-12**  *Campus LAN*

As a CCNP designer, you should think about interbuilding structure considerations. Modern applications, video requirements, and distance requirements drive the use of fiber technologies for interbuilding connectivity. These include the following:

- **10GBASE-SR:** Multimode fiber for up to 400 meters (short range)

- **10GBASE-LR:** Single mode fiber for up to 10 kilometers (long range)

- **10GBASE-ER:** Single-mode fiber for up to 80 kilometers (extended range)

As shown in the previous sections, each individual module has different requirements. The building access layer is the only layer that uses Layer 2 switching. Both the campus core and the server farm have requirements for high availability and high performance.

Table 7-7 shows network requirements for application types.

**Table 7-7**  Network Requirements for Application Types

| Specification | Building Access | Distribution Layer | Campus Core | Server Farm |
|---|---|---|---|---|
| Technology | Layer 2 and Layer 3 switches | Layer 3 switches | Layer 3 switches | Layer 3 switches |
| Scalability | High | Medium | Low | Medium |
| Availability | Medium | Medium | High | High |
| Performance | Medium | Medium | High | High |
| Cost per port | Low | Medium | High | High |

## Small and Medium Campus Design Options

A medium-sized campus would have between 200 to 1000 end devices. Such a network consists of building access switches that connect to a pair of campus distribution switches, as shown in Figure 7-13.

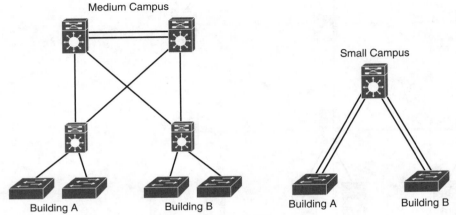

Medium Campus

Small Campus

Building A     Building B          Building A          Building B

**Figure 7-13** *Small and Medium Campus LANs*

A small campus would have fewer than 200 end devices. Switches in a small campus might not require much scaling capability. A single distribution switch would connect campus building access switches.

## Campus LAN QoS Considerations

For the access layer of a campus LAN, you can classify and mark frames or packets to apply quality of service (QoS) policies in the distribution layer or at the enterprise edge. Classification is a fundamental building block of QoS and involves recognizing and distinguishing between different traffic streams. For example, you distinguish between HTTP/HTTPS, FTP, and VoIP traffic. Without classification, all traffic is treated the same.

Marking (also called coloring or tagging) sets certain bits in a packet or frame that has been classified. Layer 2 has two methods to mark frames for CoS:

- **Inter-Switch Link (ISL):** This method is obsolete.

- **IEEE 802.1p/802.1Q:** This is the recommended method. The IEEE 802.1D-1998 standard describes IEEE 802.1p traffic class expediting.

Both methods provide 3 bits for marking frames. Cisco ISL is a proprietary trunk-encapsulation method for carrying VLANs over Fast Ethernet or Gigabit Ethernet interfaces. It is now an obsolete solution.

ISL appends tags to each frame to identify the VLAN it belongs to. As shown in Figure 7-14, the tag is a 30-byte header and CRC trailer added around the Fast Ethernet frame; it includes a 26-byte header and 4-byte CRC. The header includes a 15-bit VLAN ID that identifies each VLAN. The user field in the header also includes 3 bits for the class of service (CoS).

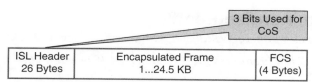

**Figure 7-14**  *ISLFrame*

The IEEE 802.1Q standard trunks VLANs over Fast Ethernet and Gigabit Ethernet interfaces, and you can use it in a multivendor environment. IEEE 802.1Q uses one instance of Spanning Tree Protocol for each VLAN allowed in the trunk. Like ISL, IEEE 802.1Q uses a tag on each frame with a VLAN identifier. Figure 7-15 shows the IEEE 802.1Q frame. Unlike ISL, 802.1Q uses an internal tag. IEEE 802.1Q also supports the IEEE 802.1p priority standard, which is included in the 802.1D-1998 specification. A 3-bit Priority field is included in the 802.1Q frame for CoS.

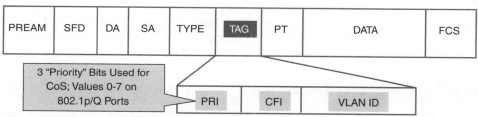

**Figure 7-15**  *IEEE 802.1Q Frame*

The preferred location to mark traffic is as close as possible to the source. Figure 7-16 shows a segment of a network with IP phones. Most workstations send packets with CoS or IP precedence bits (ToS) set to 0. If a workstation supports IEEE 802.1Q/p, it can mark packets. VoIP traffic from the phone is sent with a Layer 2 CoS set to 5. The phone also reclassifies data from the PC to a CoS/ToS of 0. With Differentiated Services Codepoint (DSCP) at Layer 3, VoIP bearer traffic is set to Expedited Forwarding (EF) (which implies a ToS set to 5), with binary value 101110 (hexadecimal 2E). Signaling traffic is set to DSCP AF31.

As shown in Figure 7-16, switch capabilities vary in the access layer. If the switches in this layer are capable, configure them to accept the markings or remap them. The advanced switches in the distribution layer can mark traffic, accept the CoS/DSCP markings, or remap the CoS/DSCP values to different markings.

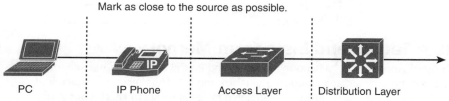

**Figure 7-16**  *Marking of Frames or Packets*

# References and Recommended Readings

RFC 3768: *Virtual Router Redundancy Protocol (VRRP)*, https://tools.ietf.org/html/rfc3768.

RFC 5798: *Virtual Router Redundancy Protocol (VRRP) Version 3 for IPv4 and IPv6*, https://tools.ietf.org/html/rfc5798.

10Gigabit Alliance, www.10gea.org.

Cisco, "Cisco Network for High Availability Design Guide," https://www.cisco.com/c/en/us/td/docs/solutions/Enterprise/Campus/HA_campus_DG/hacampusdg.html.

Cisco, "Cisco Spanning Tree Toolkit," http://www.cisco.com/c/dam/en_us/solutions/industries/docs/gov/turniton_stpt.pdf.

Cisco, "Spanning Tree from PVST+ to Rapid_PVST Migration," http://www.cisco.com/c/en/us/support/docs/switches/catalyst-6500-series-switches/72836-rapidpvst-mig-config.html.

Cisco, "Spanning Tree Protocol Enhancements Using Loop Guard and BPDU Skew Detection Features," http://www.cisco.com/c/en/us/support/docs/lan-switching/ spanning-tree-protocol/10596-84.html.

## Exam Preparation Tasks

As mentioned in the section "How to Use This Book" in the Introduction, you have a couple of choices for exam preparation: the exercises here, Chapter 13, "Final Preparation," and the exam simulation questions on the companion website.

## Review All Key Topics

Review the most important topics in the chapter, noted with the Key Topic icon in the outer margin of the page. Table 7-8 lists these key topics and the page number on which each is found.

**Table 7-8** Key Topics

| Key Topic Element | Description | Page |
|---|---|---|
| Paragraph | Best practices for hierarchical layers | 245 |
| Table 7-4 | Access layer designs | 248 |
| Table 7-5 | Campus layer design best practices | 251 |
| Paragraph | Redundancy models | 252 |
| Table 7-6 | Redundancy Models | 259 |

## Complete Tables and Lists from Memory

Print a copy of Appendix D, "Memory Tables," found on the companion website, or at least the section for this chapter, and complete the tables and lists from memory. Appendix E, "Memory Tables Answer Key," includes completed tables and lists to check your work.

## Define Key Terms

Define the following key terms from this chapter and check your answers in the glossary:

10GBASE-ER, 10GBASE-LR, 10GBASE-SR, 20/80 rule, Fast EtherChannel (FEC), first-hop routing protocol (FHRP), Gigabit EtherChannel (GEC), Global Load Balancing Protocol

(GLBP), Hot Standby Routing Protocol (HSRP), Virtual Router Redundancy Protocol (VRRP), Virtual Switching System (VSS), Virtual Trunking Protocol (VTP)

# Q&A

The answers to these questions appear in Appendix A. For more practice with exam format questions, use the exam engine on the companion website.

1. Which of the following is an example of a peer-to-peer application?

   a. IP phone call

   b. Client accessing a file server

   c. Web access

   d. Using a local server on the same segment

2. An enterprise network has grown to span multiple buildings supporting multiple departments. Clients access servers that are in local and other buildings. The company security assessment has identified policies that need to be applied. What do you recommend?

   a. Move all departments to a single building to prevent unauthorized access.

   b. Move all servers to one of the LAN client segments.

   c. Move all servers to a data center server segment that is separate from client LANs.

   d. Move all servers to the building distribution switches.

3. Link redundancy and infrastructure services are design considerations for which layer?

   a. Core layer

   b. Distribution layer

   c. Access layer

   d. Application layer

4. Which of the following are server connectivity methods in the data center?

   a. Single NIC

   b. EtherChannel

   c. Content switch

   d. All of the above

5. A campus network of four buildings is experiencing performance problems. Each building contains 400 to 600 devices, all in one IP subnet. The buildings are connected in a hub-and-spoke configuration back to Building 1 using Gigabit Ethernet with multimode fiber. All servers are located in Building 1. What do you recommend to improve performance?

   a. Connect all buildings in a ring topology.

   b. Implement multiple VLANs in each building.

   c. Move servers to the buildings.

   d. Use single-mode fiber to make the Gigabit Ethernet links faster.

7

6. Match each application type with its description.

   i.   Peer-to-peer

   ii.  Client/local server

   iii. Client/server farm

   iv.  Client/enterprise edge

   a.   Server on the same segment

   b.   IM

   c.   Web access

   d.   Client accesses database server

7. Match each campus design model with its description.

   i.   Routed access layer

   ii.  Traditional Layer 2 access layer

   iii. Layer 2 access with VSS

   iv.  Hybrid access layer

   a.   Legacy design

   b.   Access layer using Layer 3 capabilities

   c.   Improves Layer 2 design

   d.   Not recommended.

8. Which network application type is most stringent in terms of the network resources?

   a.   Peer-to-peer

   b.   Client/local server

   c.   Client/data center server farm

   d.   Client/enterprise edge

9. Company departments are located across several buildings. These departments use several common servers. Network policy and security are important. Where should servers be placed?

   a.   Within all department buildings, and they should duplicate the common servers in each building

   b.   Connecting the common servers to the campus core

   c.   The data center

   d.   Connecting the servers to the distribution layer

10. A large company has a campus core. What is the best practice for the core campus network?

   a.   Use triangles.

   b.   Use squares.

   c.   Use rectangles.

   d.   Use point-to-point mesh.

**11.** A company has five floors. It has Layer 2 switches on each floor with servers. It plans to move servers to a new computer room and create a server farm. What should it do?

    **a.** Replace all Layer 2 switches with Layer 3 switches.

    **b.** Connect the Layer 2 switches to a Layer 3 switch in the computer room.

    **c.** Connect the Layer 2 switches to a new Layer 2 switch in the computer room.

    **d.** Connect the Layer 2 switches to each other.

**12.** A link is running at 80% utilization. Business-critical applications are used. What can be done to minimize packet delay and loss?

    **a.** Implement QoS with classification and policing in the distribution layer.

    **b.** Add additional VLANs so that the business applications are used on PCs on that VLAN.

    **c.** Perform packet bit rewrites in the distribution switches.

    **d.** Classify users in the access layer with different priority bits.

**13.** Which are four best practices for the access layer? (Choose four.)

    **a.** Disable trunking in host ports.

    **b.** Limit VLANs to one closet.

    **c.** Use PVST+ with multilayer switches.

    **d.** Enable trunking on host ports.

    **e.** Use VLAN spanning to speed convergence of Spanning Tree Protocol.

    **f.** Use VTP Server mode in hierarchical networks.

    **g.** Use VTP Transparent mode in hierarchical networks.

    **h.** Use RPVST+ with multilayer switches.

**14.** Which are three best practices for the distribution layer? (Choose three.)

    **a.** Use HSRP, VRRP, or GLBP.

    **b.** Provide fast transport.

    **c.** Use Layer 3 routing protocols to the core.

    **d.** Use Layer 2 routing protocols to the core.

    **e.** Summarize routes to the core layer.

    **f.** Summarize routes to the access layer.

**15.** Which are four best practices for the distribution layer? (Choose four.)

    **a.** Disable trunking in host ports.

    **b.** Limit VLANs to one closet.

    **c.** Use HSRP.

    **d.** Use GLBP.

    **e.** Use VLAN spanning to speed convergence of Spanning Tree Protocol.

    **f.** Use Layer 3 routing to the core.

    **g.** Summarize routes.

    **h.** Use RPVST+ with multilayer switches.

7

**16.** Which are three best practices for the core layer? (Choose three.)

   **a.** Use routing with no Layer 2 loops.

   **b.** Limit VLANs to one closet.

   **c.** Use HSRP.

   **d.** Use GLBP.

   **e.** Use Layer 3 switches with fast forwarding.

   **f.** Use Layer 3 routing to the core.

   **g.** Use two equal-cost paths to every destination network.

   **h.** Use RPVST+ with multilayer switches.

**17.** What is a major requirement if you use a Layer 3 access layer design?

   **a.** The distribution switches need to be configured as a VSS pair.

   **b.** The core switches need to support EIGRP.

   **c.** The access layer switch needs to be able to route.

   **d.** HSRP needs to be configured on the distribution switches.

**18.** What is an advantage of using the updated Layer 2 access layer design over the traditional model?

   **a.** There is an increase in uplink bandwidth.

   **b.** The updated model adds routing between distribution and access layers.

   **c.** The access layer switch can route.

   **d.** Layer 3 load balancing is enabled.

**19.** Which Cisco IOS feature simplifies spanning-tree topology?

   **a.** Rapid PVST+

   **b.** MST

   **c.** MISTP 802.1W

   **d.** VSS

**20.** You implement the updated Layer 2 access layer design. What advantage have you obtained?

   **a.** Additional uplink bandwidth by using both uplinks

   **b.** No need for FHRP

   **c.** Mix of Layer 2 and Layer 3 in the access layer

   **d.** Spanning Tree Protocol blocking uplink ports

**21.** You implement the Layer 3 access layer design. What advantage have you obtained?

   **a.** Additional uplink bandwidth by using both uplinks

   **b.** No need for FHRP

   **c.** Mix of Layer 2 and Layer 3 in the access layer

   **d.** Spanning Tree Protocol blocking uplink ports

**22.** Which VTP version is enabled by default?

    **a.** VTPv1

    **b.** VTPv2

    **c.** VTPv3

    **d.** None of the above; VTP version has to be explicitly configured

**23.** You want to configure subsecond failover for HSRP. What settings do you configure?

    **a.** Hello timer = 3 seconds, dead timer = 10 seconds

    **b.** Hello timer = 3 ms, dead timer = 10 ms

    **c.** Hello timer = 200 ms, dead timer = 750 ms

    **d.** Hello timer = 200 seconds, dead timer = 750 seconds

**24.** What are the default timers for VRRP?

    **a.** Hello timer = 3 seconds, dead timer = 10 seconds

    **b.** Hello timer = 1 second, dead timer = 3 seconds

    **c.** Hello timer = 200 ms, dead timer = 750 ms

    **d.** Hello timer = 1 ms, dead timer = 10 ms

**25.** What are the default timers for HRSP?

    **a.** Hello timer = 3 seconds, dead timer = 10 seconds

    **b.** Hello timer = 1 second, dead timer = 3 seconds

    **c.** Hello timer = 200 ms, dead timer = 750 ms

    **d.** Hello timer = 1 ms, dead timer = 10 ms

**26.** Which protocol allows for load sharing among a group of routers?

    **a.** HSRP

    **b.** VRRP

    **c.** FHRP

    **d.** GLBP

**27.** What is the recommended oversubscription ratio for distribution links to core links?

    **a.** 4 to 1

    **b.** 10 to 1

    **c.** 15 to 1

    **d.** 20 to 1

**28.** What is the recommended oversubscription ratio for access links to distribution links?

    **a.** 4 to 1

    **b.** 10 to 1

    **c.** 15 to 1

    **d.** 20 to 1

7

**29.** What is the maximum number of links that can be bundled in an EtherChannel?

    **a.** 2

    **b.** 4

    **c.** 8

    **d.** 16

**30.** You need to connect sites that are 8 kilometers apart by using fiber. Which media do you recommend?

    **a.** 10GBASE-T

    **b.** 10GBASE-ER

    **c.** 10GBASE-LR

    **d.** 10GBASE-SR

**31.** You need to connect access switches to the distribution switch pair within a building. Which media do you recommend?

    **a.** 10GBASE-T

    **b.** 10GBASE-ER

    **c.** 10GBASE-LR

    **d.** 10GBASE-SR

**32.** You need to connect switches in the data center racks. Which media do you recommend?

    **a.** 10GBASE-T

    **b.** 10GBASE-ER

    **c.** 10GBASE-LR

    **d.** 10GBASE-SR

# CHAPTER 8

# WAN for the Enterprise

## This chapter covers the following subjects:

**WAN Overview:** This section describes wide-area networks (WANs) and discusses WAN and enterprise edge modules.

**WAN Transport Technologies:** This section compares and discusses WAN technology characteristics.

**Site-to-Site VPN Design:** This section discusses design considerations and characteristics of virtual private networks (VPNs).

This chapter reviews wide-area network (WAN) technologies. Expect the ENSLD 300-420 exam to include plenty of questions about the selection and use of WAN technologies in enterprise networks. A CCNP enterprise designer must understand WAN transport technology options and when to use them during the design process. This chapter starts with a WAN overview and then looks at WAN edge and enterprise modules. Next, it reviews WAN technologies, including Layer 2 VPNs and Layer 3 VPNs with MPLS, and then it explores Ethernet and fiber options, along with Cisco SD-WAN in the enterprise edge. This chapter also covers VPN site-to-site network design and provides several options for use with enterprise networks.

## "Do I Know This Already?" Quiz

The "Do I Know This Already?" quiz helps you identify your strengths and deficiencies in this chapter's topics. This quiz, derived from the major sections in the "Foundation Topics" portion of the chapter, helps you determine how to spend your limited study time. Table 8-1 outlines the major topics discussed in this chapter and the "Do I Know This Already?" quiz questions that correspond to those topics. You can find the answers in Appendix A, "Answers to the 'Do I Know This Already?' Quiz Questions Q&A Questions."

**Table 8-1** "Do I Know This Already?" Foundation Topics Section-to-Question Mapping

| Foundation Topics Section | Questions Covered in This Section |
|---|---|
| WAN Overview | 1–2 |
| WAN Transport Technologies | 3–6 |
| Site-to-Site VPN Design | 7–10 |

1. What are two modules or blocks used in the enterprise edge?

   a. Internet and campus core

   b. Core and building access

   c. Internet and DMZ

   d. WAN and building distribution

2. Which enterprise edge module is used for e-commerce applications and remote-access VPNs?

   a. Data center

   b. WAN

   c. Service provider

   d. DMZ

3. How much bandwidth does a 4G LTE Advanced download connection provide?

   a. 100 Mbps

   b. 300 Mbps

   c. 600 Mbps

   d. 10 Gbps

4. Which of the following are Layer 2 VPN options from service providers? (Choose two.)

   a. VPWS

   b. GPRS

   c. MPLS Layer 3 VPN

   d. VPLS

5. What technology delivers IP services using labels to forward packets from the source to the destination?

   a. 4G LTE

   b. SD-WAN

   c. Metro Ethernet

   d. MPLS

6. Which of the following technologies increases the bandwidth capabilities of fiber by using different wavelengths of light?

   a. Dark fiber

   b. Metro Ethernet

   c. GSM

   d. DWDM

7. Which of the following VPN options does not work on public networks that use NAT?

   a. GETVPN

   b. Extranet VPN

   c. Remote-access VPN

   d. Site-to-site VPN

8. Which Layer 2 VPN technology provides a point-to-point WAN link between two sites over an MPLS backbone?

   a. DWDM

   b. GRE

   c. VPLS

   d. VPWS

9. What VPN technology uses a combination of IPsec and GRE?

   a. DMVPN

   b. GETVPN

   c. MPLS Layer 3 VPN

   d. IKE

10. What VPN technology uses traffic engineering to override routing tables with specific paths through the network?

   a. GETVPN

   b. GRE

   c. DMPVN

   d. MPLS Layer 3 VPN

## Foundation Topics

This chapter describes the WAN topics you need to master for the ENSLD 300-420 exam. These topics include the WAN modules included in the enterprise edge, WAN technologies, WAN technology selection, and VPN design benefits and considerations. In addition, this chapter covers site-to-site VPN design options such as IPsec, GRE, DMVPN, and GETVPN.

# WAN Overview

WANs provide network connectivity for the enterprise core and remote branch locations. The enterprise edge, on the other hand, securely connects the enterprise core to the Internet in order to provide DMZ-type services such as VPN connectivity and other cloud-related services. Many WAN and Internet transport options are available, and new ones are continually emerging. When you are selecting WAN transport technologies, it is important to consider factors such as cost, bandwidth, reliability, and manageability, in addition to the hardware and software capabilities of the equipment. Moreover, enterprise branch offices can take advantage of a shared network such as MPLS WAN or use the Internet for secure VPN connectivity back to the headquarters or main office, which many are using today as a backup to their high-cost WAN circuits.

## WAN Defined

Wide-area networks (WANs) are communications networks used to connect geographically disperse network locations. Generally, service providers or telecommunication carriers offer WAN services. WANs can transport data, voice, and video traffic between the locations of a business. Service providers charge fees, called *tariffs*, for providing WAN services or communications to their customers. The term *service* is used to refer to the WAN communications provided by a service provider or carrier.

When designing a WAN, you should become familiar with the design's requirements, which typically derive from these two important goals:

■ **Service-level agreement (SLA):** An SLA defines the availability of the network. Networked applications rely on the underlying network between the client and server to provide their functions. An SLA negotiated with a service provider can include multiple levels of application availability. Organizations have to work with a carrier to define what level of service—including bandwidth, allowed latency, and loss—is acceptable to the organization.

- **Cost and usage:** To select the correct reliable WAN service, you must consider the budget and usage requirements of the WAN service.

There are three key objectives of an effective WAN design:

- The WAN needs to support the goals and policies of the organization.

- The WAN technologies selected need to meet the current application requirements and provide for growth of the organization in the future.

- The proposed design should incorporate security throughout and ensure high availability where applicable while staying within budget.

Figure 8-1 shows a typical enterprise with Multiprotocol Label Switching (MPLS) WAN and Internet connections.

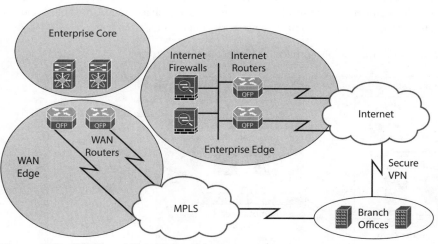

**Figure 8-1** *WAN and Enterprise Edge*

## WAN Edge Module

Enterprises can have multiple WAN interconnections. WAN connectivity between an organization's headquarters and remote sites is generally across a service provider network, such as with an MPLS WAN. Alternative options for connecting branch offices involve using broadband technologies, coupled with IPsec VPNs over the Internet, such as DMVPN or newer approaches such as SD-WAN.

WAN technologies can be point-to-point (P2P) or multipoint, such as MPLS WAN services. Most WAN service providers offer MPLS WAN solutions, where the enterprise edge router interacts with service providers at Layer 3. Public WAN connections over the Internet are available, ranging from 4G wireless technologies all the way up to multigigabit connectivity wired WAN options. Typically, these services do not provide any guarantee of network availability, so they are considered "best effort" service. MPLS network solutions usually have a much higher degree of reliability and availability.

**Note** When you are seeking a WAN service, the options can vary depending on the service provider's offerings, and it is recommended to review options from multiple WAN service providers.

### Enterprise Edge Modules

The enterprise edge modules include the demilitarized zone (DMZ) and SP edge. Internet service providers (ISPs) offer many connectivity options for the SP edge and DMZ modules in the enterprise edge:

- **Demilitarized zone (DMZ):** DMZs are used to further divide network applications and are deployed with firewall policy protections. Common DMZs include Internet DMZs for e-commerce applications, remote-access VPNs for corporate users, and site-to-site VPNs for connections to remote sites.

- **Service provider (SP) edge:** The SP edge is used to connect to ISPs and provide reliable Internet connectivity. Internet service sometimes needs high availability and is frequently deployed with multiple ISP connections as well as redundant routers and switches for aggregating the multiple network connections.

Figure 8-2 illustrates the use of modules, or blocks, in the enterprise.

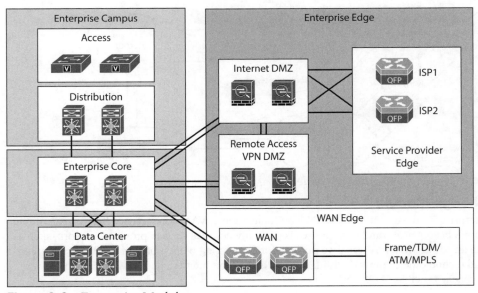

**Figure 8-2** *Enterprise Modules*

## WAN Transport Technologies

Several factors should be considered when selecting a WAN transport technology. Some WAN options are public Internet based, and some are private WAN based. Geography also plays a key role in what WAN technologies are available in a given area. Major cities have the most WAN transport options, and rural areas are more limited as to the availability of WAN service options.

Table 8-2 lists some WAN technologies and highlights some common factors used to make WAN technology selections. The information in this table reflects the different characteristics of each WAN technology. However, keep in mind that your service provider offerings limit the WAN technology choices available to you.

The following sections offer more details about the WAN technologies covered in Table 8-2.

**Table 8-2**   WAN Comparison

| WAN Technology | Bandwidth | Reliability | Latency | Cost |
|---|---|---|---|---|
| Layer 2 VPN | High | High | Low | High |
| 4G/5G | Low/medium | Low | Medium | Medium |
| Metro Ethernet | Medium/high | High | Low | Medium |
| MPLS Layer 3 VPN | High | High | Low | High |
| SD-WAN with two transports (Internet/MPLS) | Medium/high | Medium | Medium | Medium/high |
| DWDM | High | High | Low | High |

## Layer 2 VPN

Service provider VPN offerings typically include Layer 2 or Layer 3 connectivity options. Layer 2 VPNs are more expensive than Layer 3 VPNs, but they serve a couple of important use cases. Layer 2 VPNs are useful for application requirements that need Layer 2 adjacencies between sites or direct routing between edge routers at multiple locations. Layer 3 options, on the other hand, are lower cost and more scalable than Layer 2 options; however, the customer routers need to exchange routes with provider edge routers at each site.

Layer 2 VPN service can connect your HQ with one or more of your branches at Layer 2 across the SP backbone network. Layer 2 VPN services allow for attached routers at each site to connect using the same IP subnet. Interior Gateway Protocol (IGP) routing protocols such as Open Shortest Path First (OSPF) and Enhanced Interior Gateway Routing Protocol (EIGRP) can then establish neighbor adjacencies and exchange routes directly. This is useful if the business wants to manage the routing in-house instead of having the provider manage it. Layer 2 VPN provider options include Virtual Private LAN Service (VPLS) and Virtual Private Wire Service (VPWS), discussed later in this chapter.

## MPLS Layer 3 VPN

Multiprotocol Label Switching (MPLS) is a technology for the delivery of IP services using labels (numbers) to forward packets. In normal routed environments, packets are forwarded hop by hop from the source to the destination. Each router in the path performs a Layer 3 destination address lookup, rewrites the Layer 2 address, and forwards the packet to the destination. However, MPLS functions by marking packet headers that include label information. As soon as a packet is marked with a label, specific paths through the network can be designed to correspond to that distinct label and provide forwarding. MPLS labels can be set on parameters such as source addresses, Layer 2 circuit IDs, or QoS values. Packets that are destined to the same endpoint with the same requirements can be forwarded based on

8

the labels, without a routing decision at every hop. Typically, the labels correspond to the Layer 3 destination address, which makes MPLS very similar to destination-based routing.

MPLS labels can also be used to implement traffic engineering by overriding the routing tables with specific paths through the network. MPLS packets can run over most Layer 2 technologies, such as ATM, Packet over SONET (POS), and Metro Ethernet. The goal of MPLS is to maximize switching using labels and minimize Layer 3 routing.

In MPLS implementations, there are customer edge (CE) routers, provider edge (PE) routers, and provider (P) routers. A CE router resides at the customer premises, and that is typically where internal and external routing information is exchanged. A CE router connects to a PE router, which is the ingress to the MPLS service provider network. PE routers connect to P routers in the core of the service provider network. To exit the MPLS network, the process is reversed, with the last router being the CE router at the other customer premises.

Figure 8-3 shows end-to-end MPLS WAN connectivity with CE, PE, and P routers.

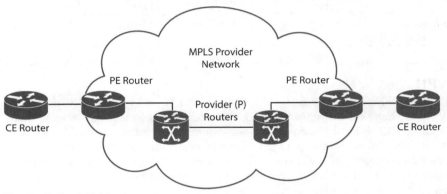

**Figure 8-3** *MPLS*

## Metro Ethernet

Demand for bandwidth in metropolitan-area networks (MANs) is increasing due to the high throughput requirements of data-intensive applications. Today, many SPs are offering Metro Ethernet services to fulfill the demand; these offerings are based on Ethernet, IP, and optical technologies such as dense wavelength-division multiplexing (DWDM) or coarse wavelength-division multiplexing.

Metro Ethernet uses Ethernet to deliver low-cost and high-speed MAN/WAN connectivity for organizations. Many service providers now offer Metro Ethernet solutions to deliver a wide range of converged network services, such as data, voice, and video, on the same wire. Metro Ethernet provides enterprise LAN type functionality out in the MAN and WAN, increasing the throughput available for applications. Metro Ethernet bandwidths can range from 100 Mbps to 10 Gbps (and even higher in some cases), supporting higher performance and increased QoS requirements. In contrast to the rigid nature of traditional circuit provisioning, Metro Ethernet services are much easier to deploy and scale due to the flexible bandwidth increments. Metro Ethernet technology is appealing to many customers who are already comfortable using Ethernet throughout their LAN environments.

Table 8-3 shows the benefits that Ethernet handoffs at the customer edge provide.

**Table 8-3**  Benefits of Ethernet Handoffs at the Customer Edge

| Benefit | Description |
| --- | --- |
| Service-enabling solution | Layering value-added services in addition to the network |
| Flexible architecture | No need for a truck roll for increasing port speeds |
|  | No need for new customer premises equipment (CPE) |
|  | Evolving existing WAN services to an IP-based solution |
| Seamless enterprise integration | Ease of integration with existing LAN network equipment |

## SONET/SDH

SONET/SDH is circuit based and delivers high-speed services over an optical network. SONET is defined by the American National Standards Institute (ANSI) specification, and the International Telecommunications Union (ITU) defines SDH. SONET/SDH guarantees bandwidth and has line rates of 155 Mbps to more than 10 Gbps. Common circuit sizes are OC-3, or 155 Mbps, and OC-12, or 622 Mbps.

SONET/SDH uses a ring topology to connect sites and provide automatic recovery capabilities, and it has self-healing mechanisms. SONET/SDH rings support ATM or POS IP encapsulations. The Optical Carrier (OC) rates are the digital bandwidth hierarchies that are part of the SONET/SDH standards. The Optical Carrier speeds supported are as follows:

- OC-1 = 51.85 Mbps

- OC-3 = 155.52 Mbps

- OC-12 = 622.08 Mbps

- OC-24 = 1.244 Gbps

- OC-48 = 2.488 Gbps

- OC-192 = 9.952 Gbps

- OC-255 = 13.21 Gbps

Figure 8-4 shows an OC-48 SONET ring with connections to three sites that share the ring.

## Dense Wavelength-Division Multiplexing

Dense wavelength-division multiplexing (DWDM) increases the bandwidth capabilities of fiber by using different wavelengths of light called *channels* over the same fiber strand. Each fiber channel is equivalent to several 10 Gigabit Ethernet links. It maximizes the use of the installed base of fiber used by service providers and is a critical component of optical networks. DWDM enables service providers to increase the services offered to customers by adding new bandwidth to existing channels on the same fiber. DWDM lets a variety of devices access the network, including IP routers, Ethernet switches, and SONET terminals.

8

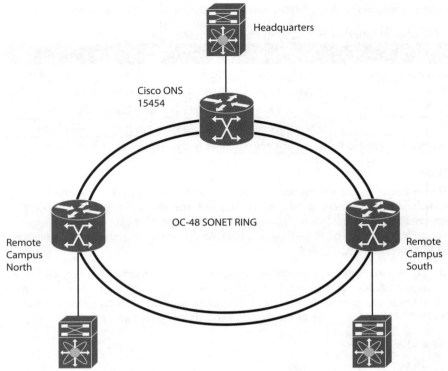

**Figure 8-4**   *SONET/SDH*

Figure 8-5 illustrates the use of DWDM using Cisco Nexus and Cisco ONS devices with a SONET/SDH ring.

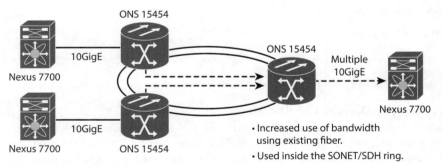

**Figure 8-5**   *DWDM*

## Dark Fiber

Dark fiber is fiber-optic cable that has been installed in the ground and where right-of-way issues are evident. To maintain signal integrity and jitter control over long distances, signal regenerators are used in some implementations. The framing for dark fiber is determined by the enterprise, not the provider. The edge devices can use the fiber just like within the enterprise, which allows for greater control of the services provided by the link. Dark fiber is owned by service providers in most cases and can be purchased similarly to leased-lined circuits for use in both MANs and WANs. The reliability of these types of links needs to be designed by the enterprise and is not provided by the service provider. High availability using dark fiber needs to be designed with multiple links; this differs from SONET/SDH technology, which has redundancy built into the architecture.

## Wireless: 4G/5G

Wireless technology uses electromagnetic waves to carry signals between endpoints. Everyday examples of wireless technology include cell phones, wireless LANs, cordless computer equipment, and the Global Positioning Systems (GPS).

Here are some examples of wireless implementations:

- **Mobile wireless:** Mobile wireless consists of cellular applications and mobile phones. Most wireless technologies, such as the third and fourth generations, are migrating to faster digital services to take advantage of the higher speeds with 5G. 3GPP is a standards body that provides standards for mobile telephony, including 3G/4G/5G cellular standards. Mobile wireless technologies include GSM, GPRS, and UMTS:

  - **Global System for Mobile Communications (GSM):** GSM is a digital mobile radio standard that uses Time Division Multiple Access (TDMA) technology in three bands (900, 1800, and 1900 MHz). The data transfer rate is 9600 bps, and GSM enables international roaming.

  - **General Packet Radio Service (GPRS):** BPRS extends the capability of GSM speeds from 64 kbps to 128 kbps.

  - **Universal Mobile Telecommunications Service (UMTS):** UMTS, also known as 3G broadband, provides packet-based transmission of digitized voice, video, and data at rates up to 2.0 Mbps. UMTS also provides a set of services available to mobile users, location-independent throughout the world.

- **Long Term Evolution (LTE):** LTE, also known as 4G LTE, is based on GSM and UMTS network technologies but increases the capacity and speed using a different radio along with network improvements. Download peak rates are up to 300 Mbps, and upload peak rates are up to 50 Mbps.

- **LTE Advanced:** LTE Advanced is the next step for 4G LTE based on Release 10/11 Category 6–12 standards from the 3GPP standards organization. Improvements such as carrier aggregation allow for carriers to transmit data to a wireless router over multiple network bands simultaneously through a single aggregated data pipe. Download peak rates are up to 600 Mbps, and upload peak rates are up to 100 Mbps.

- **LTE Advance Pro:** LTE Advance Pro/Gigabit LTE is the next standard on the path to 5G based on Release 12/13 Category 13–20 standards from the 3GPP standards organization. Estimated download peak rates of 1.1 Gbps are possible, and upload peak rates of 200 Mbps are possible.

- **5G:** 5G is an emerging wireless standard based on Release 15 Category NR from the 3GPP standards organization. It offers improvements such as carrier aggregation, sub-6 GHz, and power enhancements. Download peak rates are up to 20 Gbps, and upload peak rates are up to 10 Gbps.

8

Figure 8-6 shows examples of LTE Advanced as a primary WAN link.

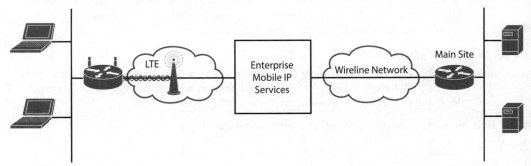

**Figure 8-6**   *LTE Primary WAN Link*

Figure 8-7 shows examples of LTE Advanced as a backup WAN link.

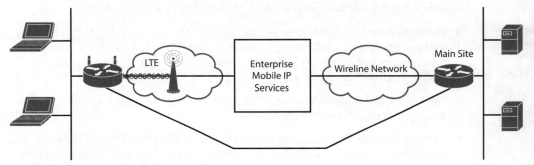

**Figure 8-7**   *LTE Backup WAN Link*

## SD-WAN Customer Edge

SDN is a centralized approach to managing a network that abstracts away the underlying network infrastructure from its applications. SD-WAN is part of the overall software-defined networking (SDN) paradigm. The Cisco SD-WAN solution is an enterprise-class WAN archi-tecture overlay that fully integrates routing, security, orchestration, and centralized policy into next-generation networks. Cisco SD-WAN is transport independent and allows for a mix of transports, including MPLS, 4G/5G, and low-cost Internet links in many combinations that extend to the data center, branch, and cloud.

The Cisco SD-WAN solution separates functions into four planes for operation:

■ **Control:** The control plane builds and maintains the network topology and informs the data plane about where traffic flows using the vSmart controller.

■ **Data:** The data plane is responsible for forwarding packets with instructions from the control plane through the vEdge router, which can be physical or virtual.

■ **Management:** The management plane is responsible for centralized management and monitoring through the use of vManage.

■ **Orchestration:** The orchestration plane helps with the onboarding of the SD-WAN routers into the SD-WAN overlay using the vBond orchestrator.

Figure 8-8 provides an overview of the Cisco SD-WAN solution.

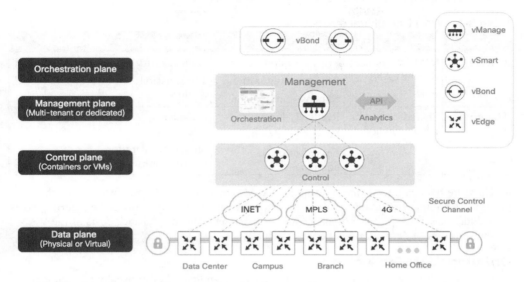

**Figure 8-8**  *Overview of a Cisco SD-WAN Solution*

The SD-WAN customer edge platforms options for the data plane or vEdge consist of physical or software devices. There are physical device options consisting of branch services routers or vEdge appliances. For the software devices, you have three different options of vEdge cloud devices. Depending on the requirements for your data center, campus, and branch or home office vEdge solution, there are several options with various speed and WAN transport characteristics. Table 8-4 lists the SD-WAN physical and software device options.

**Table 8-4**  SD-WAN Platform Options

| Physical Devices | | Software Devices | | |
|---|---|---|---|---|
| **Branch Services/Data Center** | **vEdge Appliances for Branch/Data Center** | **Universal CPE** | **Private Cloud** | **Public Cloud** |
| ISR 1000 200 Mbps | vEdge 100 100 Mbps | ENCS 5100 vEdgeCloud: ISRv Up to 250 Mbps | OpenStack vEdgeCloud: CSR1000v | Microsoft Azure vEdgeCloud: CSR1000v |
| ISR 4000 Up to 2 Gbps | vEdge 1000 Up to 1 Gbps | ENCS 5400 vEdgeCloud: ISRv 250 Mbps–2 Gbps | ESXi CSR1000v | Amazon Web Services vEdgeCloud: CSR1000v |
| ASR 1000 Fixed 2.5 Gbps and up | vEdge 2000 10 Gbps | | KVM CSR1000v | |

## WAN Link Categories

WAN link characteristics generally fall into two broad categories: private and shared. When selecting a WAN technology, there are many factors to consider, such as how the WAN is going to be used, costs, advantages, and what technology options are available in a given area. Table 8-5 identifies various WAN link characteristics.

**Table 8-5**   WAN Link Characteristics

| | Use | Cost | Advantages | Examples |
|---|---|---|---|---|
| Private | WAN to connect distant LANs | Private equipment<br>Private configuration<br>Expensive to maintain | High security<br>Transmission quality | Metro Ethernet using dark fiber |
| Shared | Shared-circuit or label-switched WAN | Relatively low cost<br>Leased bandwidth<br>Leased or private equipment | Provider maintenance<br>Shared network for multiple sites | MPLS |

There are fixed and recurring costs in most WAN environments. Fixed costs include the network equipment, circuit provisioning, and network management tools. The recurring costs include the service provider monthly WAN service fees, the maintenance costs of the WAN, and the costs of network operations personnel.

### Ordering WAN Technology

When you order WAN transport technology, early planning is key. It usually takes at least 60 days for the carrier to provision circuits. Generally, the higher a circuit's capacity, the more lead time required for provisioning. When ordering bandwidth overseas or between hemispheres, a lead time of 60 to 120 days is fairly common.

WAN transport in most cases includes an access circuit charge and, at times, distance-based charges. Metro Ethernet availability has long lead times. In rare cases, construction is necessary to provide fiber access, which requires more cost and time delays. You should compare pricing and available WAN technology options from competing carriers.

When you are selecting a standard carrier package, it takes about a month to contract a WAN circuit. If you want to negotiate a detailed SLA, expect to take another five months or more, including discussions with the service provider's legal department. The bigger the customer, the more influence it has over the SLAs and the contract negotiations.

Contract periods for most WAN services are one to five years. Contracts are usually not written for longer durations because the technology is changing quickly. An exception is dark fiber, which is generally contracted for a 20-year term. In this case, you also want to have the right of non-reversion written in the SLA. This means that no matter what happens to the service provider, the fiber is yours for the 20-year period. The process to repair a fiber cut should be defined within the SLA.

Tariffed commercial WAN services are available at published rates but are subject to restrictions. However, carriers are moving toward unpublished rates to be more competitive and to offer more options.

## Site-to-Site VPN Design

VPNs are typically deployed over some kind of shared or public infrastructure. VPNs are similar to tunnels in that they carry traffic over an existing IP infrastructure. VPN technologies use the Internet, Layer 3 MPLS WANs, and point-to-point connected IP infrastructures to transport data from end to end. A disadvantage of using VPNs over public networks is that the connectivity is best effort in nature, and troubleshooting is difficult because visibility is limited into the service provider's infrastructure.

## VPN Benefits

The major benefits of using VPNs are flexibility, cost, and scalability. VPNs are easy to set up and deploy over an existing infrastructure in most cases. VPNs enable network access to remote users, remote sites, and extranet business partners. VPNs lower the cost of ownership by reducing the WAN recurring monthly charges and standardizing VPN security policies. The geographic coverage of VPNs is nearly everywhere Internet access is available, which makes VPNs highly scalable. In addition, VPNs simplify WAN operations because they can be deployed in a secure and consistent manner.

Site-to-site VPN types include the following:

- **Intranet VPNs:** Site-to-site VPNs over the Internet offer an alternative WAN transport for interconnecting sites. Generally, the remote sites use their Internet connection to establish the VPN connection back to the corporate headend office. Site-to-site VPNs can also use an IP backbone provided by the service provider. The main use cases for site-to-site VPNs are primary WAN transport, lower-cost MPLS WAN backup, and connection to secure cloud services. Cisco ASA, Cisco ISR, and Cisco ASR Series routers are commonly used for site-to-site VPNs with IPsec over GRE to support the deployment of IGPs.

- **Extranet VPNs:** This is another form of site-to-site VPN infrastructure for business partner connectivity that also uses the Internet or a private infrastructure for network access. Keep in mind that it is important to have secure extranet network policies to restrict the business partners' access. Typically, these types of VPNs terminate in a partner-designated firewalled DMZ.

Figure 8-9 shows VPN examples for home users, mobile users, and site-to-site VPNs.

## IPsec

Internet Protocol Security (IPsec) is a network layer protocol suite for encrypting IP packets between two hosts and thereby creating a secure "tunnel." The IETF defined IPsec in RFC 4301. IPsec uses open standards and provides secure communication between peers to ensure data confidentiality, integrity, and authenticity through network layer encryption. IPsec connections are commonly configured between firewalls, VPN appliances, or routers that have IPsec features enabled. IPsec can scale from small to very large networks.

The IPsec protocols include Internet Security Association and Key Management Protocol (ISAKMP) and two other IPsec IP protocols: Encapsulating Security Payload (ESP) and Authentication Header (AH). IPsec uses symmetrical encryption algorithms to provide data protection. These algorithms need a secure method to exchange keys to ensure that the data is protected. Internet Key Exchange (IKE) ISAKMP protocols provide these functions. There are two versions of IKE: IKEv1 and IKEv2. IKEv1 works in two modes: Main mode (with six messages) and Aggressive mode (which uses three messages). IKEv2 is an enhancement to IKEv1 and uses four messages. IKEv1 requires symmetric authentication, whereas IKEv2 uses asymmetric authentication. ESP is used to provide confidentiality, data origin authentication, connectionless integrity, and anti-replay services. AH is used to provide integrity and data origin authentication, usually referred to as just authentication.

8

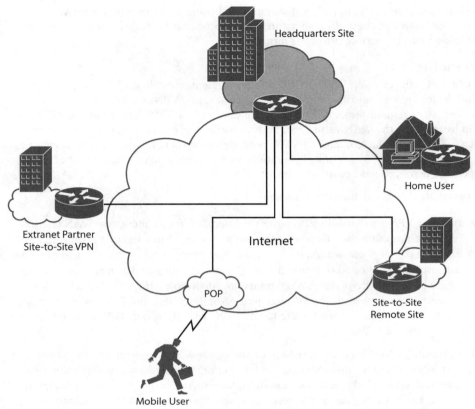

**Figure 8-9** *VPN Examples*

IPsec can secure data from eavesdropping and modification using transform sets, which give you varying levels of strength for data protection. IPsec also has several hash message authentication codes (HMACs) available to provide protection from attacks such as man-in-the-middle, packet-replay, and data-integrity.

### IPsec Direct Encapsulation

IPsec's tunnel mode enables it to be used as a standalone connection method; this is the most fundamental VPN design model. When you are using IPsec direct encapsulation, dynamic routing protocols and IP multicast are not supported. The headend IPsec terminating device needs to use static IP addressing, but the remote IPsec endpoints can use static or dynamic IP addressing. Redundancy can be provided at the headend by using multiple IPsec terminating devices, and each remote IPsec endpoint can be populated with a list of headend endpoints to make connections with.

IPsec packet payloads can be encrypted, and IPsec receivers can authenticate packet origins. Internet Key Exchange (IKE) and Public Key Infrastructure (PKI) can also be used with IPsec. IKE is the protocol used to set up a security association (SA) with IPsec. PKI is an arrangement that provides for third-party verification of identities.

Figure 8-10 shows the topology for IPsec direct encapsulation with multiple headend sites to provide resiliency for the branch offices.

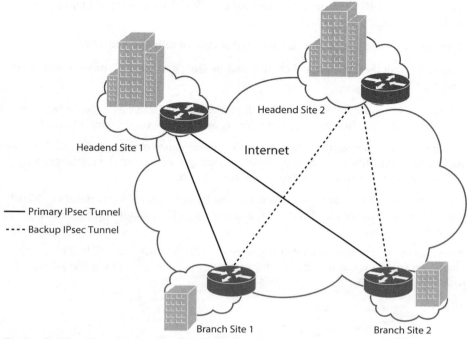

**Figure 8-10** *IPsec Direct Encapsulation Example*

## DMVPN

Dynamic Multipoint VPN (DMVPN) is a Cisco IOS solution for building IPsec over GRE VPNs in a dynamic and scalable manner.

DMVPN relies on two key technologies:

- **Next Hop Resolution Protocol (NHRP):** NHRP creates a mapping database for all spoke tunnels to real public addresses.

- **Multipoint GRE (mGRE):** mGRE is a single GRE interface that provides support for multiple GRE and IPsec tunnels to reduce the complexity and the size of the configuration.

DMVPN supports a reduced configuration framework and supports the following features:

- Hub router configuration reduction, with a single mGRE interface and a single IPsec profile to manage all spoke routers

- Automatic IPsec initiation and auto-creation of GRE tunnels without any IPsec peering configuration

- IP unicast, IP multicast, and dynamic routing protocol support without the need for a service provider

- Remote spoke routers with dynamic IP addressing

- Spoke routers behind dynamic Network Address Translation (NAT) and hub routers behind static NAT

- Dynamic spoke-to-spoke tunnels for partial scaling or fully meshed VPNs

- Support for all the GRE tunnel benefits, such as QoS, deterministic routing, and redundancy scenarios

Each remote site is connected using a P2P GRE tunnel interface to a single mGRE headend interface. The headend mGRE interface dynamically accepts new tunnel connections.

Redundancy can be achieved by configuring spokes to terminate to multiple headends at one or more hub locations. IPsec tunnel protection is typically used to map the cryptographic attributes to the tunnel that is originated by the remote peer.

Dead peer detection (DPD) can be used to detect the loss of a peer IPsec connection. NHRP is configured on both the headend and the spoke routers and is a requirement for using mGRE interfaces.

Figure 8-11 shows an example of a DMVPN network with two different DC hub locations along with two spoke locations that are using certificate authentication via a PKI infrastructure with a Microsoft CA.

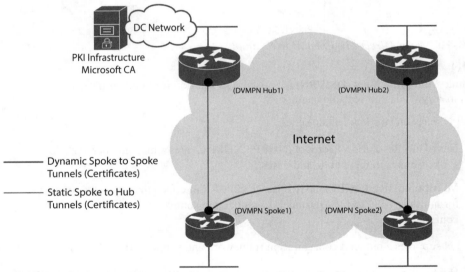

**Figure 8-11**  *DMVPN Example*

## Service Provider VPNs: Layer 2 Versus Layer 3

Layer 3 VPN service provides routed Layer 3 connections between sites. With Layer 3 VPNs, you exchange routes with the provider. Customer routes are exchanged from the customer edge (CE) routers to the provider edge (PE) router before entering the Layer 3 VPN. The service provider uses Border Gateway Protocol (BGP) for routing inside the Layer 3 VPN, and then routes are exchanged at each remote site from the PE router back to the CE router. Routing protocols such as OSPF and EIGRP are normally used at the exchange point between the CE and PE routers, but static or BGP routing can also be used. Multiprotocol Label Switching (MPLS) is an example of a Layer 3 VPN service.

## Virtual Private Wire Services

Virtual Private Wire Service (VPWS) is a Layer 2 VPN technology commonly referred to as *pseudowires*. VPWS provides a point-to-point WAN link between two sites over an MPLS provider backbone. It's similar in concept to leased-line service, except that the provider transports multiple customer VPNs on the MPLS equipment connecting your sites. Two popular VPWS use cases are connecting a pair of data centers and using point-to-point WAN transport for legacy services.

### VPWS Layer 2 VPN Considerations

There are several traffic considerations to think about with the VPWS Layer 2 VPN service. It is important to understand whether the service will transparently pass all traffic, such as Spanning Tree Protocol frames as well as broadcast, unknown unicast, and multicast (BUM) type traffic. Also, does the provider offer quality of service (QoS) mechanisms to prioritize voice, video, and critical traffic over best-effort traffic? Another consideration is the maximum transmission unit (MTU) size throughout the provider network for the Layer 2 VPN. If you are using VPWS for Data Center Interconnect (DCI), you might need to support jumbo frames within the provider network. In addition, you will want to make sure the provider is passing link loss signaling from end to end. This way, you can detect when the far side link is down.

### Virtual Private LAN Service

Virtual Private LAN Service (VPLS) expands on VPWS and defines an architecture that enables Ethernet Multipoint Service (EMS) over an MPLS network. VPLS allows for connecting Layer 2 domains over an IP/MPLS network, which emulates an IEEE Ethernet bridge.

Figure 8-12 depicts a VPLS topology in an MPLS network.

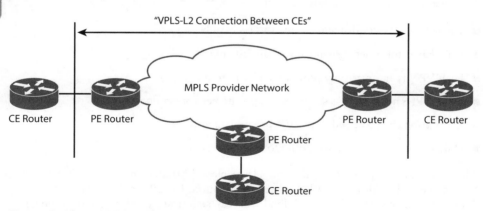

**Figure 8-12**  *VPLS Topology Example*

VPLS is a type of VPN that allows for the connection of multiple sites into a single Layer 2 domain over a managed IP/MPLS network. VPLS presents an Ethernet interface, which simplifies the LAN/WAN demarcation for service providers. This enables rapid and flexible service provisioning because the service bandwidth is not tied to the physical interface. All the VPLS services appear to be on the same VLAN, regardless of the physical locations in the WAN.

VPLS uses edge routers that learn Layer 2 domains, bridge them, and replicate them through the VPN. Within the IP/MPLS cloud is a collection of full-mesh connections providing any-to-any connectivity between sites. VPLS supports many of the new applications and services that need to be on the same Layer 2 network to function properly. Some services lack network layer addressing or are transparent to the upper-layer protocols.

### VPLS Layer 2 VPN Considerations

Because VPLS provides a Layer 2 switched segment between sites, you can choose to control the Layer 3 routing between the sites rather than leave it to the provider. That means you can use routing protocols such as EIGRP, OSPF, and BGP. However, you can run into scalability problems with IGP routing protocols if you try to connect hundreds of routers to the same Layer 2 segment. With VPLS providing the connectivity, BGP is the only routing protocol that you should use in larger Layer 2 domains.

## MPLS Layer 3 VPNs

MPLS is a technology for the delivery of IP services using an efficient encapsulation mechanism. MPLS uses labels appended to IP packets or Layer 2 frames for the transport of data. The labels can be used as designators to identify IP prefixes and ATM Virutal Circuits (VC) and to guarantee bandwidth. MPLS can run on many Layer 2 technologies, including Layer 2 VPNs and Metro Ethernet.

MPLS is an economical solution that can be easily integrated over any existing infrastructure because MPLS is independent of access technologies. SPs can offer intelligent network services to their customers over a single infrastructure. Each of the SP's customers can have one or more VPNs within the overall MPLS network, called virtual routing and forwarding (VRF) instances.

### MPLS Layer 3 Design Overview

MPLS Layer 3 VPNs have the following characteristics:

- The MPLS network distributes labels to each VPN.

- Only labels for other VPN members are distributed.

- Each VPN is automatically provisioned by IP routing.

- Each MPLS network is as secure as the private network connections.

- Encryption can be added to the VPN to provide privacy.

- Only one label is needed for both QoS and a VPN.

MPLS Layer 3 VPNs represent the most popular deployed MPLS technology. MPLS Layer 3 VPNs leverage BGP to distribute VPN-related information. The SP typically manages the BGP routing domain within the MPLS cloud. This can significantly reduce the operational costs and complexities for enterprise environments.

Inside the MPLS cloud, network routes are learned with a dynamic IGP routing protocol such as OSPF, EIGRP, or BGP, or with static routes that are manually configured.

### MPLS Layer 3 VPN Considerations

MPLS VPNs use labels to specify the VRF instance and the corresponding VPN destination networks, which prevent the overlapping of addresses between VPNs. With MPLS Layer 3 VPNs, other valued-added services can be layered on, such as QoS and traffic engineering.

These services might offer enhanced network services such as voice, video, and data, for example. In addition, MPLS TE and Fast Reroute (FRR) features can be used to provide tight SLAs, including up to five levels of QoS.

## Generic Routing Encapsulation

Cisco developed Generic Routing Encapsulation (GRE) to encapsulate a variety of protocols inside IP tunnels. This approach consists of minimal configuration for basic IP VPNs but lacks both security and scalability. In fact, GRE tunnels do not use encryption to secure the packets during transport.

Using IPsec with GRE tunnels provides for secure VPN tunnels by encrypting the GRE tunnels. There are many advantages with this approach, such as support for dynamic IGP routing protocols, non-IP protocols, and IP multicast. Other advantages include support for QoS policies and deterministic routing metrics for headend IPsec termination points. Because all the primary and backup GRE over IPsec tunnels are preestablished, there is built-in redundancy to support failure scenarios. The remote sites can have dynamic or static IP addressing, but the headend site requires static IP addressing. Primary tunnels can be differentiated from backup tunnels by modifying the routing metrics slightly to prefer the one or the other.

## GETVPN

Group Encrypted Transport VPN (GETVPN) is a technology for creating tunnel-less VPNs over private WANs. GETVPN uses Group Domain of Interest (GDOI; see RFC 6407) to distribute the IPsec keys to a group of VPN gateway devices. With GETVPN, key servers create and maintain the control plane and define the encryption policies that are pushed to the IKE authenticated group members during registration. The group members handle the encryption and decryption in the data plane, based on defined policy.

GETVPN is similar to the technology in IPsec VPNs; however, it differs in that it preserves the original IP addresses in the outer IP header of the packets. Because the original IP source and destination addresses are preserved, no overlay routing control plane is needed, thereby allowing routing and multicast to route natively within the underlying network.

GETVPN is not typically used on the Internet because NAT does not work with it due to the original IP addressing preservation. However, GETVPN can be a good solution on private MPLS networks or where you have control of the end-to-end private IP address space.

# References and Recommended Readings

RFC 4301: IPsec, https://www.ietf.org/rfc/rfc4301.txt.

RFC 6407: GDIO, https://www.ietf.org/rfc/rfc4301.txt.

Cisco, "10GE DWDM Interconnections in Enterprise Campus Networks," www.cisco.com/c/en/us/products/collateral/interfaces-modules/transceiver-modules/prod_white_paper0900aecd8054d53d.html.

Cisco, "Cisco IOS Quality of Service Solutions Configuration Guide Library, Cisco IOS Release 15M&T," https://www.cisco.com/c/en/us/td/docs/ios-xml/ios/qos/config_library/15-mt/qos-15-mt-library.html.

Cisco, "Cisco LTE Advanced 3.0 Network Interface Modules Wireless WAN Interface Cards," https://www.cisco.com/c/en/us/products/collateral/routers/4000-series-integrated-services-routers-isr/datasheet_C78-738511.html.

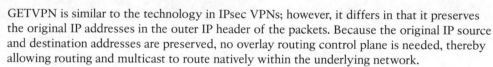

Cisco, "Cisco SD-WAN Design Guide," https://www.cisco.com/c/dam/en/us/td/docs/solutions/CVD/SDWAN/CVD-SD-WAN-Design-2018OCT.pdf.

Cisco, "Deploying 5G and LTE for Enterprise and IoT Last Mile," https://www.ciscolive.com/c/dam/r/ciscolive/us/docs/2019/pdf/BRKSPM-2129.pdf.

Cisco, "Module 4: Enterprise Network Design," Designing for Cisco Internetwork Solution Course (DESGN) v3.0.

Cisco, "WAN Architectures and Design Principles," https://www.ciscolive.com/c/dam/r/ciscolive/us/docs/2019/pdf/BRKRST-2041.pdf.

Wikipedia, "LTE: LTE (telecommunications)," https://en.wikipedia.org/wiki/LTE_(telecommunication).

## Exam Preparation Tasks

As mentioned in the section "How to Use This Book" in the Introduction, you have a couple of choices for exam preparation: the exercises here, Chapter 13, "Final Preparation," and the exam simulation questions on the companion website.

## Review All Key Topics

Review the most important topics in the chapter, noted with the Key Topic icon in the outer margin of the page. Table 8-6 lists these key topics and the page number on which each is found.

**Table 8-6**    Key Topics

| Key Topic Element | Description | Page |
|---|---|---|
| Paragraph | WAN edge module | 275 |
| List | Enterprise edge modules | 276 |
| Table 8-2 | WAN comparison | 277 |
| Paragraph | MPLS Layer 3 VPN | 278 |
| Table 8-3 | Benefits of Ethernet handoffs | 279 |
| List | Wireless implementations | 281 |
| List | SD-WAN | 282 |
| Table 8-4 | SD-WAN platform options | 283 |
| Table 8-5 | WAN link characteristics | 284 |
| List | Site-to-site VPN types | 285 |
| Paragraph | IPsec | 285 |
| List | DMVPN | 287 |
| Paragraph | VPLS | 289 |
| List | MPLS Layer 3 VPN | 290 |
| Paragraph | GRE | 291 |
| Paragraph | GETVPN | 291 |

## Complete Tables and Lists from Memory

Print a copy of Appendix D, "Memory Tables," found on the companion website, or at least the section for this chapter, and complete the tables and lists from memory. Appendix E, "Memory Tables Answer Key," includes completed tables and lists to check your work.

## Define Key Terms

Define the following key terms from this chapter and check your answers in the glossary:

5G, dense wavelength-division multiplexing (DWDM), Dynamic Multipoint VPN (DMVPN), enterprise edge module, Group Encrypted Transport VPN (GETVPN), IP Security (IPsec), Multiprotocol Label Switching (MPLS) Layer 3 VPN, SONET/SDH, Virtual Private LAN Service (VPLS), Virtual Private Wire Service (VPWS)

## Q&A

The answers to these questions appear in Appendix A. For more practice with exam format questions, use the exam engine on the companion website.

**1.** With the Cisco SD-WAN solution, the control plane builds and maintains the network topology and informs the data plane on where traffic flows by using the _____ controller.

   **a.** vEdge

   **b.** vSmart

   **c.** vManage

   **d.** vBond

**2.** Which module is within the enterprise edge module?

   **a.** Data center module

   **b.** Campus core

   **c.** Building distribution

   **d.** Remote-access VPN DMZ

**3.** What technology forms tunnel-less VPNs over private WANs?

   **a.** MPLS Layer 3 VPN

   **b.** VPLS

   **c.** GETVPN

   **d.** DMVPN

**4.** What two modules are found in the enterprise edge? (Choose two.)

   **a.** Campus core

   **b.** Building access

   **c.** Internet

   **d.** DMZ

**5.** Which of the following tunneling technologies lacks security and scalability?

   **a.** MPLS Layer 3 VPN

   **b.** DMVPN

8

    **c.** GRE

    **d.** GETVPN

  **6.** What is the most popular VPN technology that leverages BGP to distribute VPN-related information?

    **a.** IPsec

    **b.** GETVPN

    **c.** DMVPN

    **d.** MPLS Layer 3 VPN

  **7.** Which of the following best describes the operation of VPLS?

    **a.** Allows for connecting Layer 2 domains over an IP/MPLS network

    **b.** Creates point-to-point WAN links between two sites over an MPLS backbone

    **c.** Creates a mapping database for all spoke tunnels to real public addresses

    **d.** Secures data from eavesdropping and modification of transform sets

  **8.** Which of the following modules belongs in the enterprise edge?

    **a.** Building distribution

    **b.** Campus core

    **c.** Network management

    **d.** DMZ/e-commerce

  **9.** Which network module connects to ISPs in the enterprise edge?

    **a.** Building distribution

    **b.** Campus core

    **c.** WAN edge

    **d.** Service provider edge

  **10.** Which network module connects using MPLS connectivity?

    **a.** Remote-access VPN

    **b.** Campus core

    **c.** Building access

    **d.** WAN edge

  **11.** Which network module connects using SD-WAN?

    **a.** Remote-access VPN

    **b.** WAN edge

    **c.** Building distribution

    **d.** Server farm

  **12.** What IPsec protocol is used to provide confidentiality, data origin authentication, connectionless integrity, and anti-replay services?

    **a.** ISAKMP

    **b.** ESP

    **c.** AH

    **d.** HMAC

**13.** What functional area provides connectivity between the central site and remote sites?

   **a.** Access

   **b.** Campus core

   **c.** Building distribution

   **d.** WAN edge

**14.** What WAN technology allows the enterprise to control framing?

   **a.** SONET/SDH

   **b.** Wireless

   **c.** DWDM

   **d.** Dark fiber

**15.** Which 4G standard is pushing download rates of 1 Gbps?

   **a.** LTE Advanced

   **b.** UMTS

   **c.** LTE Advance Pro

   **d.** LTE

**16.** Which WAN technology is circuit based and delivers high-speed services using Optical Carrier rates?

   **a.** SONET/SDH

   **b.** DWDM

   **c.** UTMS

   **d.** Dark fiber

**17.** Which emerging wireless standard uses sub-6 GHz and download rates of 20 Gbps?

   **a.** LTE

   **b.** LTE Advanced

   **c.** 5G

   **d.** UMTS

**18.** _____ improves the utilization of optical-fiber strands.

**19.** Which of the following best describes the advantages of private WAN links?

   **a.** Provider responsibility for maintenance

   **b.** High security and transmission quality

   **c.** Only best-effort bandwidth guarantees

   **d.** Support for dynamic routing protocols

**20.** What are two benefits of Ethernet handoffs at the customer edge? (Choose two.)

   **a.** No need for new customer premises equipment

   **b.** Ease of integration with existing LAN equipment

   **c.** Longer contract periods

   **d.** No need for NAT in connecting to public networks

8

**21.** With the Cisco SD-WAN solution, the data plane is responsible for forwarding packets with instructions from the control plane through what router?

   **a.** vEdge

   **b.** vSmart

   **c.** vManage

   **d.** vBond

**22.** What do service providers use to define their network availability at different levels?

   **a.** SD-WAN

   **b.** WAN tiers

   **c.** WWAN

   **d.** SLAs

**23.** With the Cisco SD-WAN solution, the management plane is responsible for centralized management and monitoring through the use of _____.

   **a.** vEdge

   **b.** vSmart

   **c.** vManage

   **d.** vBond

**24.** With MPLS implementations, which of the following router types handles the exchange of customer routing information with the service provider?

   **a.** P routers

   **b.** CE routers

   **c.** PE routers

   **d.** FE routers

**25.** Which of the following are key objectives of an effective WAN design? (Choose three.)

   **a.** The WAN needs to support the goals and policies of the organization.

   **b.** The WAN needs to be fully meshed with PKI and certificate authentication.

   **c.** WAN technologies need to meet the current application requirements and provide for growth.

   **d.** WAN design should incorporate security throughout and ensure high availability where applicable while staying within budget.

**26.** With GETVPN, what maintains the control plane and defines the encryption policies that are pushed to IKE authenticated group members?

   **a.** GDOI

   **b.** GRE

   **c.** Key servers

   **d.** PKI

**27.** Which VPN technology uses a Multipoint GRE (mGRE) interface to provide support for multiple GRE and IPsec tunnels?

   **a.** MPLS Layer 3 VPN

   **b.** VPLS

   **c.** GETVPN

   **d.** DMVPN

**28.** Which IPsec protocol is used to provide integrity and data origin authentication?

   **a.** AH

   **b.** ESP

   **c.** ISAKMP

   **d.** IKE

**29.** What within IPsec provides protection from attacks such as man-in-the-middle, packet-replay, and data-integrity attacks?

   **a.** AH

   **b.** ESP

   **c.** ISAKMP

   **d.** HMAC

**30.** With IPsec, what is used to detect the loss of a peer IPsec connection?

   **a.** DPD

   **b.** ESP

   **c.** mGRE

   **d.** NAT

8

## CHAPTER 9

# WAN Availability and QoS

## This chapter covers the following subjects:

**WAN Design Methodologies:** This section discusses the processes of identifying business and technology strategies, assessing the existing network, and creating a design that is scalable, flexible, and resilient.

**Design for High Availability:** This section covers removing the single points of failure from a network design by using software features or hardware-based resiliency.

**Internet Connectivity:** This section discusses public network access and securely connecting business locations.

**Backup Connectivity:** This section discusses providing an alternative WAN path between locations when primary paths are unavailable.

**QoS Strategies:** This section discusses design models for providing QoS service differentiation.

**Designing End-to-End QoS Policies:** This section discusses options for QoS mechanisms such as queuing, policing, and traffic shaping.

This chapter covers WAN design and QoS. Expect plenty of questions on the ENSLD 300-420 exam about the selection and use of WAN designs in enterprise networks. A CCNP enterprise designer must understand WAN availability and the QoS models that are available to protect traffic flows in the network. This chapter starts with WAN methodologies and then covers WAN availability with deployment models using MPLS, hybrid, and Internet designs. This chapter also explores backup connectivity and failover designs. Finally, it covers QoS strategies and designing end-to-end QoS policies.

## "Do I Know This Already?" Quiz

The "Do I Know This Already?" quiz helps you identify your strengths and deficiencies in this chapter's topics. This quiz, derived from the major sections in the "Foundation Topics" portion of the chapter, helps you determine how to spend your limited study time. Table 9-1 outlines the major topics discussed in this chapter and the "Do I Know This Already?" quiz questions that correspond to those topics. You can find the answers in Appendix A, "Answers to the 'Do I Know This Already?' Quiz Questions Q&A Questions."

**Table 9-1** "Do I Know This Already?" Foundation Topics Section-to-Question Mapping

| Foundation Topics Section | Questions Covered in This Section |
|---|---|
| WAN Design Methodologies | 1–2 |
| Design for High Availability | 3 |

| Foundation Topics Section | Questions Covered in This Section |
|---|---|
| Internet Connectivity | 4–5 |
| Backup Connectivity | 6 |
| QoS Strategies | 7–8 |
| Designing End-to-End QoS Policies | 9–10 |

1. Which of the following is a measure of data transferred from one host to another in a given amount of time?

   a. Reliability

   b. Response time

   c. Throughput

   d. Jitter

2. Which of the following is a description of the key design principle scalability?

   a. Modularity with additional devices, services, and technologies

   b. Redundancy through hardware, software, and connectivity

   c. Ease of managing and maintaining the infrastructure

   d. Providing enough capacity and bandwidth for applications

3. What percentage of availability allows for four hours of downtime in a year?

   a. 99.5%

   b. 99.99%

   c. 99.999%

   d. 99.95%

4. What Internet connectivity option provides the highest level of resiliency for services?

   a. Single-router dual-homed

   b. Single-router single-homed

   c. Dual-router dual-homed

   d. Shared DMZ

5. Which of the following eliminates single points of failures with the router and the circuit?

   a. Dual-router dual-homed

   b. Single-router dual-homed

   c. Shared DMZ

   d. Single-router single-homed

6. What backup option allows for both a backup link and load-sharing capabilities using the available bandwidth?

   a. Dial backup

   b. Secondary WAN link

   c. IPsec tunnel

   d. GRE tunnel

7. Which of the following adds a strict priority queue to modular class-based QoS?

   a. FIFO

   b. CBWFQ

   c. WFQ

   d. LLQ

8. Which of the following is a mechanism to handle traffic overflow using a queuing algorithm with QoS?

   a. Congestion management

   b. Traffic shaping and policing

   c. Classification

   d. Link efficiency

9. Which QoS model uses Resource Reservation Protocol (RSVP) to explicitly request QoS for the application along the end-to-end path through devices in the network?

   a. DiffServ

   b. IntServ

   c. CBWFQ

   d. BE

10. What technique does traffic shaping use to release the packets into the output queue at a preconfigured rate?

    a. Token bucket

    b. Leaky bucket

    c. Tagging

    d. Interleaving

# Foundation Topics

This chapter describes the WAN design and QoS topics you need to master for the ENSLD 300-420 exam. These topics include WAN methodologies in the enterprise edge, WAN availability, and WAN designs including backup and failover options. In addition, this chapter describes quality of service (QoS) and how it can be used to prioritize network traffic and better utilize the available WAN bandwidth.

## WAN Design Methodologies

WAN design methodologies should be used when designing enterprise edge networks. Some keys to WAN design are the following processes:

- **Identifying the network requirements:** This includes reviewing the types of applications, the traffic volume, and the traffic patterns in the network.

- **Assessing the existing network:** This involves reviewing the technologies used and the locations of hosts, servers, network equipment, and other end nodes.

- **Designing the topology:** This is based on the availability of technology as well as the projected traffic patterns, technology performance, constraints, and reliability.

When designing the WAN topology, remember that the design should describe the functions that the enterprise modules should perform. The expected service levels provided by each WAN technology should be explained. WAN connections can be characterized by the cost of renting the transmission media from the service provider to connect two or more sites.

New network designs should be flexible and adaptable to future technologies and should not limit the customer's options going forward. For example, collaboration applications such as VoIP and video are common now, and most enterprise network designs should be able to support them. The customer should not have to undergo major hardware upgrades to implement these types of technologies. The ongoing support and management of the network is another important factor, and the design's cost-effectiveness is important as well.

Table 9-2 lists key design principles that can help serve as the basis for developing network designs.

**Table 9-2**   Key Design Principles

| Design Principle | Description |
| --- | --- |
| High availability | Redundancy through hardware, software, and connectivity |
| Scalability | Modularity with additional devices, services, and technologies |
| Security | Measures to protect business data |
| Performance | Enough capacity and bandwidth for applications |
| Manageability | Ease of managing and maintaining the infrastructure |
| Standards and regulations | Compliance with applicable laws, regulations, and standards |
| Cost | Appropriate security and technologies given the budget |

High availability is what most businesses and organizations strive for in sound network designs. The key components of application availability are response time, throughput, and reliability. Real-time applications such as voice and video are not very tolerant of jitter and delay.

Table 9-3 identifies various application requirements for data, voice, and video traffic.

**Table 9-3**   Application Requirements for Data, Voice, and Video Traffic

| Characteristic | Data File Transfer | Interactive Data Application | Real-Time Voice | Real-Time Video |
| --- | --- | --- | --- | --- |
| **Response time** | Reasonable | Within a second | One-way delay less than 150 ms with low delay and jitter | Minimum delay and jitter |
| **Throughput and packet loss tolerance** | High/medium | Low/low | Low/low | High/medium |
| **Downtime (high reliability = low downtime)** | Reasonable | Low | Low | Minimum |

9

### Response Time

Response time is a measure of the time between a client user request and a response from the server host. An end user will be satisfied with a certain level of delay in response time. However, there is a limit to how long the user will wait. This amount of time can be measured and serves as a basis for future application response times. Users perceive the network communication in terms of how quickly the server returns the requested information and how fast the screen updates. Some applications, such as a request for an HTML web page, require short response times. On the other hand, a large FTP transfer might take a while, but this is generally acceptable.

### Throughput

In network communications, throughput is a measure of data transferred from one host to another in a given amount of time. Bandwidth-intensive applications have a greater impact on a network's throughput than does interactive traffic such as a Telnet session. Most high-throughput applications involve some type of file-transfer activity. Because throughput-intensive applications have longer response times, you can usually schedule them when time-sensitive traffic volumes are lower, such as after hours.

### Reliability

Reliability is a measure of a given application's availability to its users. Some organizations require rock-solid application reliability, such as five nines (99.999%); this level of reliability has a higher price than most other applications. For example, financial and security exchange commissions require nearly 100% uptime for their applications. These types of networks are built with a large amount of physical and logical redundancy. It is important to ascertain the level of reliability needed for a network that you are designing. Reliability goes further than availability by measuring not only whether the service is there but whether it is performing as it should.

### Bandwidth Considerations

Table 9-4 compares several WAN technologies in terms of speeds and media types.

**Table 9-4**    Physical Bandwidth Comparison

| WAN Connectivity | Bandwidth: Up to 100 Mbps | Bandwidth: 1 Gbps to 10 Gbps |
| --- | --- | --- |
| Copper | Fast Ethernet | Gigabit Ethernet, 10 Gigabit Ethernet |
| Fiber | Fast Ethernet | Gigabit Ethernet, 10 Gigabit Ethernet, SONET/SDH, dark fiber |
| Wireless | 802.11a/g | 802.11n/ac Wave1/Wave2 |
| LTE/5G | LTE/LTE Advanced | LTE Advance Pro/5G |

A WAN designer must engineer the network with enough bandwidth to support the needs of the users and applications that will use the network. How much bandwidth a network needs depends on the services and applications that will require network bandwidth. For example, VoIP requires more bandwidth than interactive Secure Shell (SSH) traffic. A large number of graphics or CAD drawings require an extensive amount of bandwidth compared to file or print sharing information being transferred on the network. A big driver in increasing demand for bandwidth is the expanded use of collaboration applications that utilize video interactively.

When designing bandwidth for a WAN, remember that implementation and recurring costs are important factors. It is best to begin planning for WAN capacity early. When the link utilization reaches around 50% to 60%, you should consider increases and closely monitor the capacity. When the link utilization reaches around 75%, immediate attention is required to avoid congestion problems and packet loss that will occur when the utilization nears full capacity.

QoS techniques become increasingly important when delay-sensitive traffic such as VoIP is using the limited bandwidth available on the WAN. LAN bandwidth, on the other hand, is generally inexpensive and plentiful; in the age of robust real-time applications, however, QoS can be necessary. To provide connectivity on the LAN, you typically need to be concerned only with hardware and implementation costs.

# Design for High Availability

Most businesses need a high level of availability, especially for their critical applications. The goal of high availability is to remove the single points of failure in the network design by using software features or hardware-based resiliency. Redundancy is critical in providing high levels of availability for the enterprise. Some technologies have built-in techniques that enable them to be highly available. For technologies that do not have high availability, other techniques can be used, such as additional WAN circuits or backup power supplies.

## Defining Availability

System availability is a ratio of the expected uptime to the amount of downtime over the same period of time. Let's take an example of 4 hours of downtime per year. There are 365 days in a year, which equals 8760 hours (365 × 24 = 8760). Now, if we subtract 4 hours from the annual total of 8760 hours, we get 8756. Then, if we figure 8756 / 8760 × 100, we get the amount of availability percentage, which in this case is 99.95%.

Table 9-5 shows the availability percentages from 99% to 99.999999%, along with amounts of downtime per year.

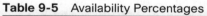

**Table 9-5**   Availability Percentages

| Availability | Downtime per Year | The Nines of Availability | Targets |
|---|---|---|---|
| 99.000000% | 3.65 days | Two nines | |
| 99.900000% | 8.76 hours | Three nines | |
| 99.990000% | 52.56 minutes | Four nines | Branch WAN high availability |
| 99.999000% | 5.256 minutes | Five nines | Branch WAN high availability |
| 99.999900% | 31.536 seconds | Six nines | Ultra high availability |
| 99.999990% | 3.1536 seconds | Seven nines | Ultra high availability |
| 99.999999% | .31536 seconds | Eight nines | Ultra high availability |

Figure 9-1 illustrates WAN router paths and the impacts to availability depending on the level of redundancy used.

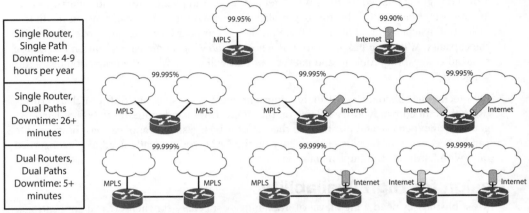

**Figure 9-1** *Router Paths and Availability Examples*

## Deployment Models

There are three common deployment models for WAN connectivity, each with pros and cons:

- **MPLS WAN:** Single- or dual-router MPLS VPN

- **Hybrid WAN:** MPLS VPN and Internet VPN

- **Internet WAN:** Single- or dual-router Internet VPN

An MPLS WAN involves single or dual routers for the MPLS VPN connections. It provides for the highest in SLA guarantees for both QoS capabilities and network availability. However, this option is the most expensive, and it ties the organization to the service provider.

A hybrid WAN combines an MPLS VPN and an Internet VPN on a single router or on a pair of routers. This deployment model offers a balanced cost option between the higher-cost MPLS VPN connection and the lower-cost Internet VPN for backup. With a hybrid WAN, traffic can be split between the MPLS VPN for higher-priority-based traffic and Internet VPN for lower-priority-based traffic. Newer WAN designs are also using SDWAN with both MPLS and Internet-based transports.

An Internet WAN includes a single router or dual routers using Internet-based VPN only. This deployment model is the lowest-cost option but lacks the SLAs and QoS capabilities offered by carriers. The enterprise would be responsible for providing SLAs to the end users.

## Redundancy Options

Depending on the cost of downtime for an organization, different levels of redundancy can be implemented for a remote site. The more critical WAN sites will use higher levels of redundancy. With any of the deployment options—MPLS WAN, hybrid WAN, or Internet WAN—you can design redundant links with redundant routers, a single router with redundant links, or a single router with a single link.

For the most critical WAN sites, you typically want to eliminate single points of failure by designing with dual routers and dual WAN links along with dual power supplies. However, this highly available option comes with a higher price tag and is more complex to manage; however, it offers failover capabilities. Another option available to reduce cost is to use a single router with dual power supplies and multiple WAN links providing power and link redundancy. Non-redundant, single-homed sites are the lowest cost, but they have multiple single points of failure inherent with the design, such as the WAN carrier or WAN link.

## Single-Homed Versus Multi-Homed WANs

The advantages of working with a single WAN carrier are that you only have one vendor to manage, and you can work out a common QoS model that can be used throughout your WAN. The major drawback with a single carrier is that if the carrier has an outage, it can be catastrophic to your overall WAN connectivity. This also makes it difficult to transition to a new carrier because all your WAN connectivity is with a single carrier.

On the other hand, if you have dual WAN carriers, the fault domains are segmented, and there are typically more WAN offerings to choose from because you are working with two different carriers. This also allows for greater failover capabilities with routing and software redundancy features. The disadvantages with dual WAN carriers are that the overall design is more complex to manage, and there will be higher recurring WAN costs.

## Single-Homed MPLS WANs

In a single-MPLS-carrier design, each site is connected to a single MPLS VPN from one provider. For example, you might have some sites that are single-homed and some sites that are dual-homed to the MPLS VPN. Each site will consist of CE routers peering with the provider using eBGP, and iBGP will be used for any CE-to-CE peering. Each CE will advertise any local prefixes to the provider with BGP and redistribute any learned BGP routes from the provider into the IGP or use default routing. Common IGPs are standard-based OSPF and EIGRP.

Figure 9-2 illustrates a single-MPLS-carrier design with single- and dual-homed sites.

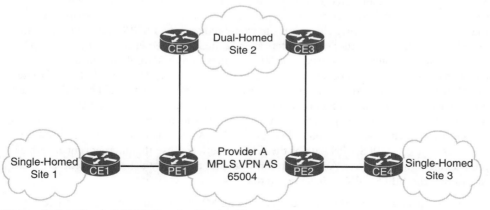

**Figure 9-2**  *Single-MPLS-Carrier Design Example*

## Multi-Homed MPLS WANs

In a dual-MPLS-carrier design, each site is connected to both provider A and provider B. Some sites might have two routers for high availability, and others might have only a single router but with two links for link and provider redundancy. For example, each CE router would redistribute local routes from EIGRP into BGP. Routes from other sites would be redistributed from BGP into EIGRP as external routes. For sites that have two routers, filtering or tagging of the routes in and out of BGP would be needed to prevent routing loops.

Figure 9-3 illustrates a dual-MPLS-carrier design with single and dual routers.

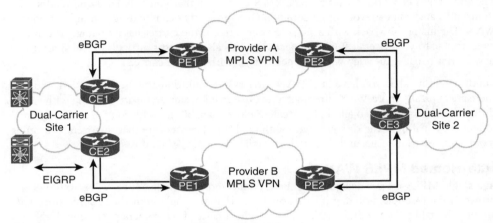

**Figure 9-3** *Dual-MPLS-Carrier Design Example*

## Hybrid WANs: Layer 3 VPN with Internet Tunnels

Hybrid WAN designs involve using an MPLS VPN for the primary connection and an Internet tunnel for the backup connection. In this design, eBGP would be used to peer with the MPLS VPN provider, and EIGRP would be used for routing for the IGP internally. At each site, the CE router would learn routes from the MPLS VPN via BGP and redistribute the routes from BGP into EIGRP. Then each site would redistribute EIGRP routes into BGP and use EIGRP to peer with other local routers at each site. The Internet tunnel routers would use EIGRP to exchange routes inside the VPN tunnels, and they would not need to redistribute routing information because they would run only EIGRP. On the MPLS VPN router, BGP-learned routes would be preferred because the BGP routes that would be redistributed into EIGRP routes would have a lower administrative distance. In this case, if you want the MPLS VPN router to be the primary path, you need to run an FHRP between the dual-homed routers, with the active router being the MPLS VPN-connected router. That way, it would choose the MPLS VPN path as the primary path and use the Internet tunnel path as the backup path for failover. Another option would be to modify the routing protocol metrics so that the MPLS VPN path is preferred.

Figure 9-4 illustrates a hybrid WAN design with an MPLS VPN and an Internet VPN.

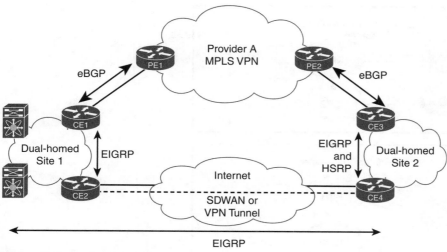

**Figure 9-4** *Hybrid WAN Design Example*

# Internet Connectivity

Most enterprises have multiple sites with different numbers of users at the sites, but they are usually grouped into two site types: larger central WAN sites and smaller branch WAN sites. The larger site types typically host more of the users and services. The smaller branch offices tend to have a low user count and a smaller number of hosted services. Both central and branch sites typically need Internet access, but there are high availability considerations to think about when selecting the Internet access design for a given site type. When choosing an Internet connectivity option, remember to consider the business requirements and the budget allocated for the design.

Internet connectivity options include the following:

- **Dual-router dual-homed:** Provides the highest level of resiliency for Internet connectivity with full redundancy in hardware, links, and Internet service providers.

- **Single-router dual-homed:** Provides a good level of redundancy for Internet connectivity through the use of multiple links and multiple Internet service providers.

- **Single-router single-homed:** Provides the bare minimum for Internet connectivity, providing no levels of redundancy for the hardware, links, or Internet service providers.

Figure 9-5 shows Internet connectivity options with different levels of redundancy.

Because central sites have larger user populations, they normally have higher Internet bandwidth connectivity and centralized access control for the Internet traffic flows. Although most branch offices have Internet connections, many of them still have their Internet traffic backhauled over the WAN to the central site, where centralized access control can occur.

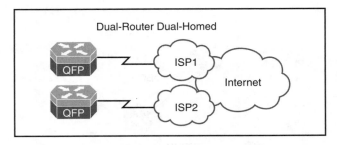

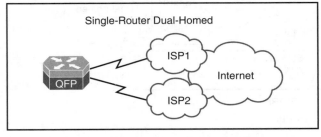

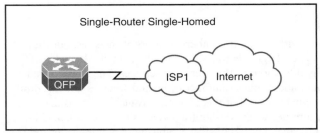

**Figure 9-5**   *Internet Connectivity Options*

## Internet for Remote Sites

When designing the Internet traffic flows for remote site locations, you have two main options to consider. One option, referred to as centralized Internet access, involves tunneling all the Internet traffic back to the data center or main site. With this option, you have more control over the Internet traffic with centralized security services such as URL filtering, firewalling, and intrusion prevention. However, there are some drawbacks with this approach because the bandwidth requirements and cost will be higher for your WAN links to the branch locations, and it increases the delay for any Internet-based traffic. Another option is to allow Internet-destined traffic at each branch to use the dedicated local Internet connection or VPN split tunneling. There are some advantages with this approach; your bandwidth requirements and the cost for your MPLS VPN links will be lower for your branch locations because you do not need to transport Internet traffic on them. This approach does have some drawbacks, however, because the local Internet access may violate your security policy by exposing more Internet points within your organization that need protection with security services.

Here are some pros and cons of each of these options:

- **Centralized Internet for each remote site:** Higher bandwidth is available, and security policies are centralized, but traffic flows are suboptimal. This option might require additional redundancy at the Internet edge, which may or may not be present.

■ **Direct Internet for remote site:** Traffic flows are optimal, but it is more difficult to manage distributed security policies. This option also has a higher risk of Internet attacks due to the greater number of attachment points.

## High Availability for the Internet Edge

When you have decided to have two Internet routers, each with a link to two different Internet service providers, you need to think about the logical design for the routers, including failover options. Logical Internet high availability design considerations include the following:

■ Use a public BGP AS number for eBGP connections to the ISPs.

■ Use provider-independent IP address space to allow for advertisement to both ISPs.

■ Receive full or partial Internet routing tables to optimize forwarding outbound.

■ Use HSRP/GLBP or an IGP such as EIGRP or OSPF internally.

# Backup Connectivity

Redundancy is a critical component of WAN design for the remote site because of the unreliable nature of WAN links compared to the LANs that they connect. Many enterprise edge solutions require high availability between the primary and remote sites. Because many remote site WAN links have lower reliability and lack bandwidth, they are good candidates for most WAN backup designs.

Remote site offices should have some type of backup strategy to deal with primary link failures. Backup links can either be permanent WAN or Internet-based connections.

WAN backup options are as follows:

■ **Secondary WAN link:** Adding a secondary WAN link makes the network more fault tolerant. This solution offers two key advantages:

   ■ **Backup link:** The backup link provides for network connectivity if the primary link fails. Dynamic or static routing techniques can be used to provide routing consistency during backup events. Application availability can also be increased because of the additional backup link.

   ■ **Additional bandwidth:** Load sharing allows both links to be used at the same time, increasing the available bandwidth. Load balancing can be achieved over the parallel links using automatic routing protocol techniques.

■ **IPsec tunnel across the Internet:** An IPsec VPN backup link can redirect traffic to the corporate headquarters when a network failure has been detected on the primary WAN link.

■ **SDWAN with MPLS and Internet tunnel:** With SDWAN using two transports, an Internet link can carry traffic to the corporate headquarters by load balancing with the MPLS link or during a failover event when a network failure has occurred.

9

### Failover

An option for network connectivity failover is to use the Internet as the failover transport between sites. However, keep in mind that this type of connection does not support bandwidth guarantees. The enterprise also needs to set up the tunnels and advertise the company's networks internally so that remote offices have reachable IP destinations. IP SLA monitoring can be leveraged along with a floating static route to provide failover.

Security is of great importance when you rely on the Internet for network connectivity, so a secure tunnel using IPsec needs to be deployed to protect the data during transport.

Figure 9-6 illustrates connectivity between the headend or central site and a remote site using traditional MPLS Layer 3 VPN IP connections for the primary WAN link. The IPsec tunnel is a failover tunnel that provides redundancy for the site if the primary WAN link fails.

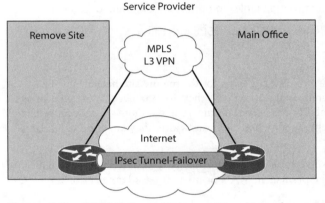

**Figure 9-6**   *WAN Failover Using an IPsec Tunnel*

IPsec tunnels are configured between the source and destination routers using tunnel interfaces. Packets that are destined for the tunnel have the standard formatted IP header. IP packets that are forwarded across the tunnel need an additional GRE/IPsec header placed on them, as well. As soon as the packets have the required headers, they are placed in the tunnel with the tunnel endpoint as the destination address. After the packets cross the tunnel and arrive on the far end, the GRE/IPsec headers are removed. The packets are then forwarded normally, using the original IP packet headers. An important design consideration to keep in mind is that you might need to modify the MTU sizes between the source and destination of the tunnel endpoints to account for the larger header sizes of the additional GRE/IPsec headers.

## QoS Strategies

Quality of service (QoS) is a fundamental network technology that has been around for over 20 years and is still relevant in today's networks, even though bandwidth has been increasing rapidly over the years. QoS gives network operators techniques to help manage the contention for network resources and in turn provide better application experiences for end users. To help us with this, Cisco supports three main models for providing QoS service differentiation: best-effort (BE), Differentiated Services (DiffServ), and Integrated Services (IntServ). These three models are different in how they enable applications to be prioritized throughout the network and how they handle the delivery of data packets with a specified level of service.

## Best-Effort QoS

The best-effort (BE) QoS model is typically the default QoS model and does not implement any QoS behaviors to prioritize traffic before other QoS traffic classes. This is the easiest of the three models because there is nothing you really need to do for it to work. You would not want to use best-effort QoS for any real-time applications such as voice or video traffic. It is a last-resort QoS model that you use after you have already prioritized all other important traffic classes that are sensitive to delay, jitter, and/or bandwidth within the network.

## DiffServ

The DiffServ QoS model separates traffic into multiple classes that can be used to satisfy varying QoS requirements. A packet's class can be marked directly inside the packet that classifies packets into different treatment categories.

With the DiffServ model, packets are classified and marked to receive a per-hop behavior (PHB) at the edge of the network. Then the rest of the network along the path to the destination uses the DSCP value to provide proper treatment. Each network device then treats the packets according to the defined PHB. The PHB can be specified in different ways, such as by using the 6-bit Differentiated Services Code Point (DSCP) setting in IP packets or by using ACLs with source and destination addresses.

Priorities are marked in each packet using DSCP values to classify the traffic according to the specified QoS policy for the traffic class. Typically, the marking is performed per packet at the QoS domain boundaries within the network. Additional policing and shaping operations can be implemented to enable greater scalability.

Table 9-6 maps applications to DSCP and decimal values.

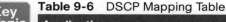

**Table 9-6**  DSCP Mapping Table

| Application | DSCP | Decimal Value |
|---|---|---|
| Network control | CS7 | 56 |
| Internetwork control | CS6 | 48 |
| VoIP | EF | 46 |
| Broadcast video | CS5 | 40 |
| Multimedia conferencing | AF4 | 34–38 |
| Real-time interaction | CS4 | 32 |
| Multimedia streaming | AF3 | 26–30 |
| Signaling | CS3 | 24 |
| Transactional data | AF2 | 18–22 |
| Network management | CS2 | 16 |
| Bulk data | AF1 | 10–14 |
| Scavenger | CS1 | 8 |
| Best-effort | Default | 0 |

9

### IntServ

The IntServ QoS model was designed for the needs of real-time applications such as video, multimedia conferencing, and virtual reality. It provides end-to-end QoS treatment that real-time applications require by explicitly reserving network resources and giving QoS treatment to user packet flows. The IntServ model applications ask the network for an explicit resource reservation per flow and use admission control mechanisms as key building blocks to establish end-to-end QoS throughout the network.

IntServ uses Resource Reservation Protocol (RSVP) to explicitly request QoS for the application along the end-to-end path through devices in the network. Before an application begins transmitting, it requests that each network device reserve the necessary bandwidth along the path. The network, in turn, accepts or rejects the reservation per flow based on available network resources.

IntServ requires several functions on each of the routers and switches between the source and destination of the packet flow:

- **Admission control:** Determines whether the requested flows can be accepted without impacting existing reservations

- **Classification:** Identifies traffic that requires different levels of QoS

- **Policing:** Allows or drops packets when traffic does not conform to the QoS policy

- **Queuing and Scheduling:** Forwards traffic for permitted QoS reservations

## Designing End-to-End QoS Policies

Cisco has developed many different QoS mechanisms, such as queuing, policing, and traffic shaping, to enable network operators to manage and prioritize the traffic flowing on a network. Applications that are delay sensitive, such as VoIP, require special treatment to ensure proper application functionality.

### Classification and Marking

For a flow to have priority, it must be classified and marked. Classification is the process of identifying the type of traffic. Marking is the process of setting a value in the IP header based on the classification. The following are examples of technologies that support classification:

- **Network-based application recognition (NBAR):** This technology uses deep packet content inspection to identify network applications. An advantage of NBAR is that it can recognize applications even when they do not use standard network ports. Furthermore, it matches fields at the application layer. Before NBAR, classification was limited to Layer 4 TCP and User Datagram Protocol (UDP) port numbers.

- **Committed access rate (CAR):** CAR uses a rate limit to set precedence and allows customization of the precedence assignment by user, source or destination IP address, and application type.

### Shaping

Traffic shaping and policing are mechanisms that inspect traffic and take action based on the traffic's characteristics, such as DSCP or IP precedence bits set in the IP header.

Traffic shaping involves slowing down the rate at which packets are sent out an interface (egress) by matching certain criteria. Traffic shaping uses a token bucket technique to release the packets into the output queue at a preconfigured rate. Traffic shaping helps eliminate potential bottlenecks by throttling back the traffic rate at the source. In enterprise environments, traffic shaping is used to smooth the flow of traffic going out to the provider. This is desirable for several reasons. For example, in provider networks, it prevents the provider from dropping traffic that exceeds the contracted rate.

## Policing

Policing involves tagging or dropping traffic, depending on the match criteria. Generally, policing is used to set the limit of traffic coming into an interface (ingress) and uses a "leaky bucket mechanism." Policing can be used to forward traffic based on conforming traffic and to drop traffic that violates the policy. Policing is also referred to as *committed access rate* (*CAR*). One example of using policing is giving preferential treatment to critical application traffic by elevating to a higher class and reducing best-effort traffic to a lower-priority class.

When you contrast traffic shaping with policing, remember that traffic shaping buffers packets, while policing can be configured to drop packets. In addition, policing propagates bursts, but traffic shaping does not.

## Queuing

Queuing refers to the buffering process used by routers and switches when they receive traffic faster than it can be transmitted. Different queuing mechanisms can be implemented to influence the order in which the different queues are serviced (that is, how different types of traffic are emptied from the queues).

QoS is an effective tool for managing a WAN's available bandwidth. Keep in mind that QoS does not add bandwidth; it only helps you make better use of the existing bandwidth. For chronic congestion problems, QoS is not the answer; in such situations, you need to add more bandwidth. However, by prioritizing traffic, you can make sure that your most critical traffic gets the best treatment and available bandwidth in times of congestion. One popular QoS technique is to classify your traffic based on a protocol type or a matching access control list (ACL) and then give policy treatment to the class. You can define many classes to match or identify your most important traffic classes. The remaining unmatched traffic then uses a default class in which the traffic can be treated as best-effort.

Table 9-7 describes QoS options for optimizing bandwidth.

**Table 9-7**  QoS Options

| QoS Category | Description |
|---|---|
| Classification | Identifies and marks flows |
| Congestion management | Handles traffic overflow using a queuing algorithm |
| Link-efficiency mechanisms | Reduce latency and jitter for network traffic on low-speed links |
| Traffic shaping and policing | Prevent congestion by policing ingress and egress flows |

## Congestion Management

Two types of output queues are available on routers: the hardware queue and the software queue. The hardware queue uses the first-in, first-out (FIFO) strategy. The software queue schedules packets first and then places them in the hardware queue. Keep in mind that the

9

software queue is used only during periods of congestion. The software queue uses QoS techniques such as priority queuing, custom queuing, weighted fair queuing, class-based weighted fair queuing, low-latency queuing, and traffic shaping and policing.

### Priority Queuing

Priority queuing (PQ) is a queuing method that establishes four interface output queues that serve different priority levels: high, medium, default, and low. Unfortunately, PQ can starve other queues if too much data is in one queue because higher-priority queues must be emptied before lower-priority queues.

### Custom Queuing

Custom queuing (CQ) uses up to 16 individual output queues. Byte size limits are assigned to each queue so that when the limit is reached, CQ proceeds to the next queue. The network operator can customize these byte size limits. CQ is fairer than PQ because it allows some level of service to all traffic. This queuing method is considered legacy due to improvements in the other queuing methods.

### Weighted Fair Queuing

Weighted fair queuing (WFQ) ensures that traffic is separated into individual flows or sessions without requiring that you define ACLs. WFQ uses two categories to group sessions: high bandwidth and low bandwidth. Low-bandwidth traffic has priority over high-bandwidth traffic. High-bandwidth traffic shares the service according to assigned weight values. WFQ is the default QoS mechanism on interfaces below 2.0 Mbps.

### Class-Based Weighted Fair Queuing

Class-based weighted fair queuing (CBWFQ) extends WFQ capabilities by providing support for modular user-defined traffic classes. CBWFQ lets you define traffic classes that correspond to match criteria, including ACLs, protocols, and input interfaces. Traffic that matches the class criteria belongs to that specific class. Each class has a defined queue that corresponds to an output interface.

After traffic has been matched and belongs to a specific class, you can modify its characteristics, such as by assigning bandwidth and specifying the maximum queue limit and weight. During periods of congestion, the bandwidth assigned to the class is the guaranteed bandwidth that is delivered to the class.

One of the key advantages of CBWFQ is its modular nature, which makes it extremely flexible for most situations. It is often referred to as Modular QoS CLI (MQC), which is the framework for building QoS policies. Many classes can be defined to separate network traffic as needed in the MQC.

### Low-Latency Queuing

Low-latency queuing (LLQ) adds a strict priority queue to CBWFQ. The strict priority queue allows delay-sensitive traffic such as voice to be sent first, before other queues are serviced. That gives voice preferential treatment over the other traffic types. Unlike PQ, LLQ provides for a maximum threshold on the priority queue to prevent lower-priority traffic from being starved by the priority queue.

Without LLQ, CBWFQ would not have a priority queue for real-time traffic. The additional classification of other traffic classes is done using the same CBWFQ techniques. LLQ is the standard QoS method for many VoIP networks.

## Link Efficiency

With Cisco IOS, several link-efficiency mechanisms are available. Link fragmentation and interleaving (LFI), Multilink PPP (MLP), and Real-Time Transport Protocol (RTP) header compression can provide for more efficient use of bandwidth.

Table 9-8 describes Cisco IOS link-efficiency mechanisms.

**Table 9-8**   Link-Efficiency Mechanisms

| Mechanisms | Description |
|---|---|
| Link fragmentation and interleaving (LFI) | Reduces delay and jitter on slower-speed links by breaking up large packet flows and inserting smaller data packets (Telnet, VoIP) in between them. |
| Multilink PPP (MLP) | Bonds multiple links between two nodes, which increases the available bandwidth. MLP can be used on analog or digital links and is based on RFC 1990. |
| Real-Time Transport (RTP) header compression | Provides increased efficiency for applications that take advantage of RTP on slow links. Compresses RTP/UDP/IP headers from 40 bytes down to 2–5 bytes. |

## Window Size

The window size defines the upper limit of frames that can be transmitted without getting a return acknowledgment. Transport protocols such as TCP rely on acknowledgments to provide connection-oriented reliable transport of data segments. For example, if the TCP window size is set to 8192, the source stops sending data after 8192 bytes if no acknowledgment has been received from the destination host. In some cases, the window size might need to be modified because of unacceptable delay for larger WAN links. If the window size is not adjusted to coincide with the delay factor, retransmissions can occur, which affects throughput significantly. It is recommended that you adjust the window size to achieve better connectivity conditions.

# References and Recommended Readings

9

RFC 1990: The PPP Multilink Protocol, https://tools.ietf.org/html/rfc1990.

Cisco, "Campus QoS Design Simplified," https://www.ciscolive.com/c/dam/r/ciscolive/emea/docs/2018/pdf/BRKCRS-2501.pdf.

isco, "Cisco IOS Quality of Service Solutions Configuration Guide Library, Cisco IOS Release 15M&T," http://www.cisco.com/c/en/us/td/docs/ios-xml/ios/qos/config_library/15-mt/qos-15-mt-library.html.

Cisco, "DSCP and Precedence Values," https://www.cisco.com/c/en/us/td/docs/switches/datacenter/nexus1000/sw/4_0/qos/configuration/guide/nexus1000v_qos/qos_6dscp_val.pdf.

Cisco, "Highly Available Wide Area Network Design," https://www.ciscolive.com/c/dam/r/ciscolive/us/docs/2019/pdf/BRKRST-2042.pdf.

Cisco, "Module 4: Enterprise Network Design," Designing for Cisco Internetwork Solution Course (DESGN) v3.0.

Wikipedia, "LTE: LTE (telecommunications)," en.wikipedia.org/wiki/LTE_(telecommunication).

## Exam Preparation Tasks

As mentioned in the section "How to Use This Book" in the Introduction, you have a couple of choices for exam preparation: the exercises here, Chapter 13, "Final Preparation," and the exam simulation questions on the companion website.

## Review All Key Topics

Review the most important topics in the chapter, noted with the Key Topic icon in the outer margin of the page. Table 9-9 lists these key topics and the page number on which each is found.

**Table 9-9**   Key Topics

| Key Topic Element | Description | Page |
|---|---|---|
| List | WAN design methodologies | 300 |
| Table 9-2 | Key design principles | 301 |
| Table 9-3 | Application requirements for data, voice, and video traffic | 301 |
| Table 9-4 | Physical bandwidth comparison | 302 |
| Table 9-5 | Availability percentages | 303 |
| List | Deployment models | 304 |
| Paragraph | Single-homed MPLS WANs | 305 |
| Paragraph | Dual-homed MPLS WANs | 306 |
| Paragraph | Hybrid WANs: Layer 3 VPN with Internet tunnels | 306 |
| List | Internet for remote sites | 308 |
| List | WAN backup options | 309 |
| Paragraph | Failover | 310 |
| Paragraph | DiffServ | 311 |
| Table 9-6 | DSCP mapping table | 311 |
| Paragraph | IntServ | 312 |
| List | Classification technologies | 312 |
| Paragraph | Shaping | 313 |
| Paragraph | Policing | 313 |
| Paragraph | Queuing | 313 |
| Table 9-7 | QoS options | 313 |
| Table 9-8 | Link-efficiency mechanisms | 315 |

## Complete Tables and Lists from Memory

Print a copy of Appendix D, "Memory Tables," found on the companion website, or at least the section for this chapter, and complete the tables and lists from memory. Appendix E, "Memory Tables Answer Key," includes completed tables and lists to check your work.

## Define Key Terms

Define the following key terms from this chapter and check your answers in the glossary:

class-based weighted fair queuing (CBWFQ), classification, congestion management, DiffServ, IntServ, low-latency queuing (LLQ), reliability, response time, throughput, traffic shaping and policing, window size

## Q&A

The answers to these questions appear in Appendix A. For more practice with exam format questions, use the exam engine on the companion website.

1. Which of the following is based on the availability of technology as well as the projected traffic patterns, technology performance, constraints, and reliability?

   a. Designing the topology

   b. Assessing the existing network

   c. Identifying the network requirements

   d. Characterize the existing network

2. Which design principle involves redundancy through hardware, software, and connectivity?

   a. Performance

   b. Security

   c. Scalability

   d. High availability

3. Which application requires round-trip times of less than 400 ms with low delay and jitter?

   a. Data file transfer

   b. Real-time voice

   c. Real-time video

   d. Interactive data

4. Which of the following is a measure of a given application's availability to its users?

   a. Response time

   b. Throughput

   c. Reliability

   d. Performance

5. Which of the following defines the upper limit of frames that can be transmitted without a return acknowledgment?

   a. Throughput

   b. Link efficiency

   c. Window size

   d. Low-latency queuing

9

**6.** Which of the following is the availability target range for branch WAN high availability?

  **a.** 99.9900%

  **b.** 99.9000%

  **c.** 99.0000%

  **d.** 99.9999%

**7.** Which WAN deployment model provides for the best SLA guarantees?

  **a.** MPLS WAN with dual routers

  **b.** Hybrid WAN with MPLS and Internet routers

  **c.** Internet WAN with dual routers

  **d.** Internet WAN with a single router

**8.** Which Internet connectivity option provides for the highest level of resiliency?

  **a.** Single-router single-homed

  **b.** Single-router dual-homed

  **c.** Dual-router dual-homed

  **d.** GRE tunnels

**9.** When designing Internet for remote sites, which option provides control for security services such as URL filtering, firewalling, and intrusion prevention?

  **a.** Centralized Internet

  **b.** Direct Internet

  **c.** Direct Internet with split tunnel

  **d.** IPsec with split tunnel

**10.** Which design considerations are most important for Internet high availability design? (Choose two.)

  **a.** Using a public BGP AS number for eBGP connections to ISPs

  **b.** Using provider-independent IP address space for advertisements to ISPs

  **c.** Using BGP communities

  **d.** Using extended ACLs

**11.** Which WAN backup option provides for redundancy and additional bandwidth?

  **a.** Backup link

  **b.** IPsec tunnel

  **c.** GRE tunnel

  **d.** NAT-T

**12.** Which failover option can be used to back up the primary MPLS WAN connection?

  **a.** BGP

  **b.** GLBP

  **c.** HSRP

  **d.** IPsec tunnel

**13.** Which of the following is not a model for providing QoS?

   **a.** Best-effort

   **b.** DiffServ

   **c.** IntServ

   **d.** NSF

**14.** In QoS markings, what DSCP value is used for VoIP traffic?

   **a.** AF4

   **b.** CS2

   **c.** EF

   **d.** CS5

**15.** Which QoS method uses a strict priority queue in addition to modular traffic classes?

   **a.** CBWFQ

   **b.** Policing

   **c.** WFQ

   **d.** LLQ

**16.** Within RSVP, what function is used to determine whether the requested flows can be accepted?

   **a.** Admission control

   **b.** Classification

   **c.** Policing

   **d.** Queuing and scheduling

**17.** Which of the following slows down the rate at which packets are sent out an interface (egress) by matching certain criteria?

   **a.** Policing

   **b.** CAR

   **c.** Shaping

   **d.** NBAR

**18.** What is the buffering process that routers and switches use when they receive traffic faster than it can be transmitted?

   **a.** Policing

   **b.** Queuing

   **c.** NBAR

   **d.** Shaping

**19.** What do service providers use to define their service offerings at different levels?

   **a.** SWAN

   **b.** WAN tiers

   **c.** WWAN

   **d.** SLA

9

**20.** Which of the following has mechanisms to handle traffic overflow using a queuing algorithm?

   **a.** Link-efficiency mechanisms

   **b.** Classification

   **c.** Congestion management

   **d.** Traffic shaping and policing

**21.** Which QoS category identifies and marks flows?

   **a.** Congestion management

   **b.** Traffic shaping and policing

   **c.** Link-efficiency mechanisms

   **d.** Classification and marking

**22.** Which design principle balances the amount of security and technologies with the budget?

   **a.** Performance

   **b.** Standards and regulations

   **c.** Cost

   **d.** Security

**23.** Which application type has requirements for low throughput and response time within a second?

   **a.** Real-time video

   **b.** Interactive data

   **c.** Real-time voice

   **d.** Interactive video

**24.** Which of the following WAN connectivity options has bandwidth capabilities of 1 Gbps to 10 Gbps?

   **a.** 802.11a

   **b.** LTE

   **c.** LTE Advance Pro

   **d.** LTE Advanced

**25.** How many days of downtime per year occur with 99.00000% availability?

   **a.** 8.76 days

   **b.** 5.2 days

   **c.** 3.65 days

   **d.** 1.2 days

**26.** With dual-router and dual-path availability models, how much downtime is expected per year?

   **a.** 4 to 9 hours per year

   **b.** 26 hours per year

   **c.** 5 hours per year

   **d.** 5 minutes per year

**27.** Which deployment model for WAN connectivity has a single router or dual routers and uses both MPLS and an Internet VPN?

   **a.** Hybrid WAN

   **b.** Internet WAN

   **c.** MPLS WAN

   **d.** VPLS WAN

**28.** When designing the Internet with high availability, which of the following is a design consideration ?

   **a.** Use public address space for internal addressing

   **b.** Use private address space for route advertising to the ISPs

   **c.** Block all Internet routes

   **d.** Use HSRP/GLBP or an IGP internally

**29.** Which of the following is an important design consideration when using IPsec over GRE tunnels?

   **a.** QoS classification

   **b.** MTU size

   **c.** Header type

   **d.** Payload length

**30.** When using DSCP to classify traffic, which of the following is prioritized the most?

   **a.** Signaling

   **b.** Transactional data

   **c.** Real-time interaction

   **d.** VoIP

9

## CHAPTER 10

# SD-Access Design

**This chapter covers the following subjects:**

**SD-Access Architecture:** This section discusses an intent-based networking solution for the enterprise built on Cisco DNA.

**SD-Access Fabric Design Considerations for Wired and Wireless Access:** This section covers several key factors, including overlay, fabric design, control plane design, border design, segmentation, virtual networks, and fabric wireless.

This chapter covers SD-Access architecture and SD-Access fabric design considerations for wired and wireless access. The ENSLD 300-420 exam will test your understanding of these SD-Access design concepts from a networking and security perspective. CCNP enterprise designers must take into account the new SD-Access design models when designing new campus environments. This chapter starts by covering SD-Access architecture for the underlay, overlay, control/data planes, and automation. Next, it explores fabric considerations for overlay and fabric design. It wraps up with an overview of SD-Access border design, segmentation, and wireless access.

## "Do I Know This Already?" Quiz

The "Do I Know This Already?" quiz helps you identify your strengths and deficiencies in this chapter's topics. This quiz, derived from the major sections in the "Foundation Topics" portion of the chapter, helps you determine how to spend your limited study time. Table 10-1 outlines the major topics discussed in this chapter and the "Do I Know This Already?" quiz questions that correspond to those topics. You can find the answers in Appendix A, "Answers to the 'Do I Know This Already?' Quiz Questions Q&A Questions."

**Table 10-1** "Do I Know This Already?" Foundation Topics Section-to-Question Mapping

| Foundation Topics Section | Questions Covered in This Section |
|---|---|
| SD-Access Architecture | 1–5 |
| SD-Access Fabric Design Considerations for Wired and Wireless Access | 6–10 |

1. Which of the following is not a key benefit of SD-Access?

   a. Compatibility

   b. Automation

   c. Policy

   d. Assurance

2. What are the main components of SD-Access architecture? (Choose two.)

   a. SD-Access fabric

   b. Redundancy

    **c.** Cisco DNA Center

    **d.** Modularity

**3.** Which of the following describes the logical mapping and resolution of the endpoint ID to its location in the SD-Access control plane?

    **a.** VXLAN

    **b.** SGT

    **c.** Scalable groups

    **d.** LISP

**4.** How does Cisco DNA Center make changes on Cisco ISE?

    **a.** LISP

    **b.** pxGRID

    **c.** REST API

    **d.** VXLAN

**5.** Which wireless integration with SD-Access uses CAPWAP for both the control plane and the data plane?

    **a.** Fabric wireless

    **b.** Over-the-top

    **c.** Local mode

    **d.** FlexConnect

**6.** Which of the following segmentation options uses SGTs to manage group-based polices between groups of endpoints with a VN?

    **a.** Microsegmentation

    **b.** pxGRID

    **c.** Local mode

    **d.** Macrosegmentation

**7.** Which of the following best describes a medium site with many wiring closets or multiple buildings?

    **a.** 10,000 endpoints and 32 VNs

    **b.** 50,000 endpoints and 64 VNs

    **c.** 75,000 endpoints and 96 VNs

    **d.** 25,000 endpoints and 64 VNs

**8.** Which of the following multicast protocols is used for RP redundancy in SD-Access?

    **a.** SSM

    **b.** IGMP

    **c.** VXLAN

    **d.** MSDP

**9.** How many VNI segments are possible with VXLAN?

    **a.** 16 million

    **b.** 8092

   **c.** 8 million

   **d.** 4092

**10.** What device fuses the SD-Access VNs into the GRT of the external network?

   **a.** Border node

   **b.** DNA Center

   **c.** Core switch

   **d.** Fusion router

## Foundation Topics

This chapter describes SD-Access architecture and the SD-Access fabric design considerations, which are topics you need to master for the ENSLD 300-420 exam. SD-Access architecture topics include underlay, overlay, control and data planes, automation, wireless, and security. In addition, this chapter describes SD-Access fabric design considerations for wired and wireless access, including overlay, fabric design, control plane design, border design, segmentation, virtual networks, scalability, over-the-top wireless, fabric wireless, and multicast.

## SD-Access Architecture

Cisco Software-Defined Access (SD-Access) is an intent-based networking solution for the enterprise that is built on the foundation of Cisco Digital Network Architecture (DNA). The SD-Access solution provides automated end-to-end segmentation for users and devices from the edge of the network to applications. SD-Access leverages Cisco DNA Center to provide the design settings, policy definition, and automated provisioning of network devices, along with assurance analytics for both wired and wireless networks.

The following are some of the key benefits of SD-Access:

- **Automation:** Automation simplifies deployment of network devices and enables consistent management of both wired and wireless network configurations.

- **Policy:** Automated configuration enables group-based security policies and network segmentation.

- **Assurance:** Contextual insights enable quick issue resolution and capacity planning.

- **Integration:** SD-Access is open and programmable for third-party integrated solutions.

Two main components make up SD-Access architecture:

- **Cisco DNA Center:** Cisco DNA Center has a rich set of features and benefits that are grouped into these core areas: automation, design, policy, provision, and assurance.

- **SD-Access fabric:** The SD-Access fabric consists of the physical and logical network infrastructure.

Figure 10-1 illustrates SD-Access with Cisco DNA Center at the top providing network services to the physical and logical infrastructure below it.

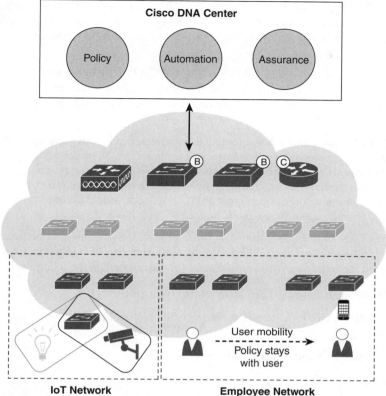

**Figure 10-1**  *SD-Access Architecture Overview*

## SD-Access Fabric

Two different layers make up the SD-Access fabric:

- **Underlay:** This layer is responsible for physical devices and traffic forwarding.

- **Overlay:** This is a logical layer that consists of wired and wireless users where services and policies are applied.

The layered separation between the overlay and underlay allows for one or more logical networks to be provisioned to meet the design intent without changing anything on the underlay.

The use of overlay and fabric has been around for quite some time. Networks that are built with MPLS, GRE, and DMVPN are examples of technologies that use tunneling to create overlay networks. SD-WAN is another example of a WAN technology that creates overlay networks over physical transports using Internet and MPLS circuits.

## Underlay

The underlay network is a collection of physical switches and routers running a dynamic Layer 3 routing protocol used as the underlying transport for the SD-Access network. The underlay implementation uses a deterministic Layer 3 routed design to ensure resiliency, performance, and scalability. Client traffic and endpoints are not part of the underlay network; instead, they are part of the configured overlay networks.

Each network device used in the underlay network needs to establish IPv4 connectivity with neighboring devices. Technically, any routing protocol can be used in the underlay network, but the use of a link-state protocol is highly recommended to ensure good performance, scalability, and resiliency.

Using a routed access design prevents the need to run STP, VTP, and FHRP in the underlay network. Instead, you can use a logical fabric over the top of the underlay, which provides routing protocol benefits such as multipath routing, fast convergence, and ease of management.

Cisco DNA Center has a feature called LAN automation for automatically provisioning switch configurations for the underlay network based on best practices. However, underlay network switch configurations can also be done manually. LAN automation can provision the CLI/SNMP credentials for the switches and upgrade the device to the desired software version. In addition, LAN automation can configure MTU, loopbacks, routed point-to-point links, ECMP, BFD, and routed access for the fabric nodes.

The Cisco DNA Center LAN automation feature uses the Intermediate System-to-Intermediate System (IS-IS) routing protocol; however, OSPF can also be used with manual configurations. IS-IS and OSPF are used for underlay switch configuration for reasons such as the following:

- IS-IS and OSPF are standards-based link-state routing protocols.

- IS-IS is used in large service provider networks and is the protocol of choice for fabric-based networks.

- OSPF is used in enterprise and campus environments.

- Link-state routing protocols coverage more quickly than distance vector routing protocols.

- Link-state routing protocols use areas and advertise information about the network topology instead of advertising the complete routing table.

- Link-state routing protocols use the SPF routing algorithm to find the shortest path to each node in the routing topology.

## Overlay

The overlay network is a logical network built on top of the underlay in order to create virtualized networks. These virtualized networks are created in the SD-Access fabric by encapsulating user traffic in the overlay networks using IP packets on the boundary edge switches.

The SD-Access fabric overlay has three main components:

- **Fabric control plane:** This plane provides logical mapping and resolution of endpoint IDs of users/devices using Locator/ID Separation Protocol (LISP).

- **Fabric data plane:** This plane provides a logical overlay created by Virtual Extensible LAN (VXLAN) packet encapsulation along with a Group Policy Object (GPO).

- **Fabric policy plane:** Within this plane, network security policy is applied through scalable group tags (SGTs) and group-based policies.

LISP simplifies routing environments by removing the need for routers to know every possible IP destination. LISP moves the remote destination information to a centralized map database that allows each router to manage only its local routes and queries the map database to find destination endpoints when needed.

VXLAN with GPO provides support for both Layer 2 and Layer 3 virtual overlays and the ability to use VRF instances or virtual networks along with SGTs for secure policy.

## Control Plane

SD-Access uses LISP for a control plane protocol to handle the mapping and resolution of endpoint addresses. The two main things that LISP keeps track of are the routing locator (RLOC) or attached router and the endpoint identifier (EID), which is the IP address or MAC address. Together, the RLOC and EID provide the information needed for traffic forwarding even if the IP address moves within the edge of the network. LISP enables the decoupling of the EID and the RLOC, which provides mobility to the endpoint. This technology differs from older collapsed core designs where the endpoints were tied to the IP subnet and the location where they were attached to the network.

LISP is an IETF standard protocol (defined in RFC 6830) that runs on a control plane node within the SD-Access fabric. The control plane node contains the settings, protocols, and tables to provide the endpoint-to-location mapping system for the fabric overlay. LISP provides many advantages, such as less CPU usage, smaller routing tables, host mobility, address mapping (IPv4, IPv6, or MAC), and VRF awareness.

Figure 10-2 illustrates the host mobility capability of LISP as two laptops move from SW1 on Floor 1 to SW8 on Floor 3 and preserve their IP addresses. Keep in mind that these switches are routed access switches at the SD-Access fabric edge.

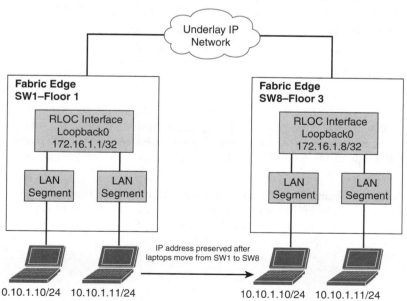

**Figure 10-2**  *LISP Host Mobility*

## Data Plane

The SD-Access fabric uses VXLAN encapsulation for the fabric data plane over the top of the underlay network. VXLAN encapsulations are IP/UDP based, using port 4789, which effectively creates the overlay within the SD-Access fabric. VXLAN is an IETF standard defined in RFC 7348 as a way to overlay a Layer 2 network over a Layer 3 network. Inside the VXLAN header is a VXLAN network identifier (VNI) that defines the virtual network that the data plane traffic is a part of. In addition, scalable group tags (SGTs) are defined in the Group ID field of the VXLAN header as part of the group-based policy option.

Figure 10-3 shows the VXLAN GPO header along with the packet payload and associated packet headers.

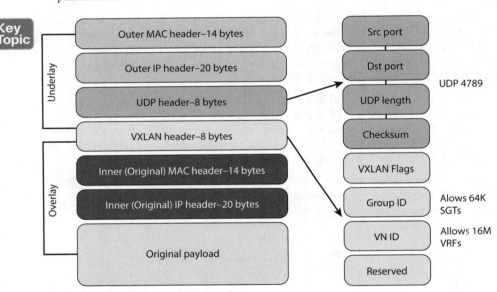

**Figure 10-3** *VXLAN GPO Header*

## Automation

The automation and orchestration features of the SD-Access solution are provided by Cisco DNA Center, which really brings to life the *software-defined* nature of the solution into the campus environment. The Cisco DNA Center appliance exposes all controller functionality through northbound REST APIs to enable automation and integration possibilities.

The SD-Access solution integrates with Cisco ISE through Cisco Platform Exchange Grid (pxGrid) and REST APIs for the exchange of client information and automation of fabric-related configurations. In addition, third-party IPAM solutions with Infoblox and BlueCat can be integrated with Cisco DNA Center.

Cisco DNA Center has a set of network underlay workflows and fabric overlay workflows related to automation:

- Underlay

  - **Global and site settings:** Hierarchical structure for the management of network settings

  - **Device discovery:** Automated discovery and inventory of network devices

  - **LAN automation:** Automatic deployment of the underlay configurations of switches

- Overlay

  - **Fabric sites:** Automated configuration of a group of fabric-enabled network devices with the same control/data plane

  - **Fabric device roles:** Automated configuration of network devices providing fabric functions (edge, border, and so on)

  - **Virtual networks:** Automated configuration for VRF segmentation

  - **Transits:** Connectivity between multiple SD-Access sites

  - **Group-based policies:** Automated configuration to enable group-based security policies

## Wireless

There are two methods of integrating wireless into an SD-Access network. The preferred method, referred to as fabric mode wireless, extends the SD-Access benefits for wired users over to wireless users. The alternative method, over-the-top (OTT), uses the traditional Cisco Unified Wireless local-mode configurations for wireless access.

Fabric mode wireless requires fabric mode–enabled WLCs and fabric mode–enabled APs. The fabric mode APs are the latest 802.11ac Wave 2 and Wave 1 APs associated with the WLCs that are configured with fabric-enabled SSIDs. The WLCs configured for fabric mode communicate with the fabric control plane by registering MAC addresses, SGTs, and virtual networks. APs use a CAPWAP tunnel to the WLC for the control plane communication, much like traditional Cisco Unified Wireless. However, the client traffic in the data plane is VXLAN encapsulated and decapsulated by the fabric mode APs. The WLC integration within the SD-Access control plane supports wireless client roaming between APs in the fabric.

Figure 10-4 illustrates an SD-Access wireless fabric integration.

If you need to support older model APs, you still can use the over-the-top method of wireless integration with the SD-Access fabric. When you use this method, the control plane and data plane traffic from the APs continue to use CAPWAP-based tunnels. In this mode, the SD-Access fabric provides only a transport to the WLC. This method can also be used as a migration step to full SD-Access in the future.

Figure 10-5 depicts the over-the-top (OTT) wireless integration.

10

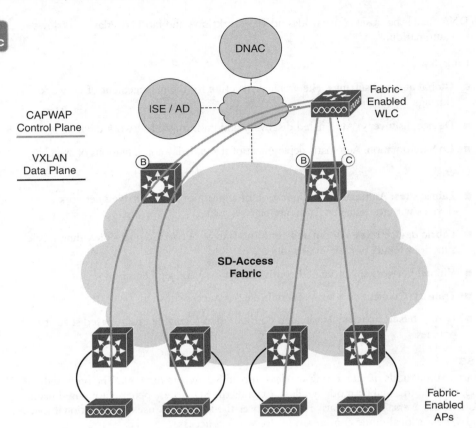

**CAPWAP**
**Control Plane**

**VXLAN**
**Data Plane**

**Figure 10-4**  *SD-Access Wireless*

## Security and ISE

Cisco ISE is a secure network access platform that enables control, visibility, and consistency for users and devices accessing the network. Within the SD-Access fabric, Cisco ISE provides all the identity and policy services. Cisco ISE is a critical component of SD-Access for policy enforcement; it allows for the dynamic mapping of users and endpoints to scalable groups, thereby simplifying the end-to-end security policy in the fabric. To support group-based policy end-to-end, Cisco TrustSec is leveraged to enable SGT information to be inserted into the VXLAN headers in the data plane traffic while also supporting multiple virtual networks (VNs). Cisco ISE supports AAA services, groups, policy, and endpoint profiling, and Cisco DNA Center orchestrates the policy workflows to use the functionality. The integration of ISE and DNA Center is done by establishing trust through ISE pxGRID services and by enabling External RESTful Services (ERS) to allow policies and contracts to flow between systems. Cisco DNA Center can create SGTs and send them to Cisco ISE via REST APIs.

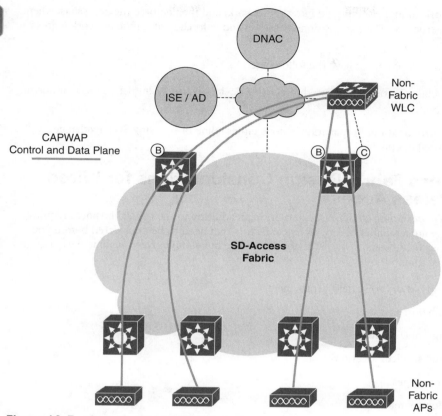

**Figure 10-5**  *Over-the-Top (OTT) Wireless*

Figure 10-6 illustrates the DNA Center and ISE integration using REST APIs and pxGRID.

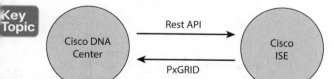

**Figure 10-6**  *DNA Center and ISE Integration*

A scalable group tag (SGT) consists of a 16-bit value contained in the VXLAN header. SGTs are also known as security groups. Cisco ISE manages the SGTs for a given SD-Access fabric. Although Cisco DNA Center drives the management of the policies, Cisco ISE is tightly integrated with DNA Center through REST APIs to provide the SGT information needed to enforce policy.

The deployment of Cisco ISE can occur through a standalone appliance or through a distributed set of appliances based on functionality.

TrustSec is a complementary enforcement technology that allows endpoint security management without the need to maintain access lists on all the network devices where the endpoints are connected. The ultimate goal of TrustSec is to assign an SGT to a user's or device's traffic at ingress (inbound into the network) and then enforce the access elsewhere in the infrastructure. The tag is assigned at login and enforced within the network (egress enforcement).

Each TrustSec design must have the following:

- **SGT classification:** ISE is used to classify devices based on authentication/authorization policies.

- **SGT propagation:** Propagation is done either inline or by using SGT Exchange Protocol (SXP).

# SD-Access Fabric Design Considerations for Wired and Wireless Access

When you're designing an SD-Access solution, in addition to the typical business requirements, there are a number of key technical factors that need to be considered before you develop your final design. This list is not exhaustive but should give you some design guidance to keep in mind:

- Greenfield or brownfield deployment

- Number of users

- Geographic location

- Shared services location

- Transit types

- Fusion routers

- WAN and Internet connectivity

- Security policy

- High availability

## Overlay Design

The overlay network within the SD-Access fabric is used to transport all of the user traffic, including all VNs that are defined in the fabric. As the user traffic is transported via VXLAN encapsulation, additional SGT information contained inside the frames can be used to provide segmentation for users and devices within the fabric. Here are some design considerations to think about when designing virtual networks:

- **Macrosegmentation:** Use macrosegmentation when you want to group many like users or devices together. The outcome of macrosegmentation is the creation of a virtual network. Macrosegmentation provides path isolation at both the control and the data planes for a group of user traffic. To enable any inter-VN traffic communication, the use of an external firewall or fusion router is required.

- **Microsegmentation:** Use microsegmentation for data plane isolation within a VN using SGTs. This type of segmentation provides data plane isolation and provides a simple way to manage group-based policies between groups of endpoints in a VN.

- **Reduce IP subnets:** Larger IP subnets can be used since they do not have the same broadcast flooding issues common with standard large Layer 2 networks. This can reduce the number of DHCP scopes and simplify IP address management for the SD-Access fabric.

- **Avoid overlapping IP subnets:** Although using multiple VNs allows for overlapping IP subnets, you should try to avoid this because many deployments require shared services that need inter-VN communications.

## Fabric Design

When you design SD-Access, each fabric site has its own set of control plane nodes, border nodes, and edge nodes.

Here are some key characteristics of a fabric site:

- An IP pool or subnet part of a single fabric site

- Layer 2/Layer 3 mobility within the single fabric site

- Layer 2 extension/anycast gateways within a single fabric site

- A fabric site that is separate from other fabrics that may exist externally

Figure 10-7 shows an example of an SD-Access fabric site.

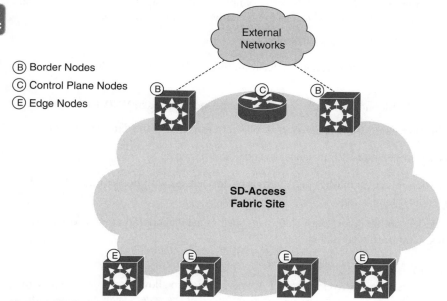

**Figure 10-7**   *SD-Access Fabric Site*

## Control Plane Design

The database for identifying endpoints is the responsibility of the fabric control plane nodes in the SD-Access fabric. This is an important function for the fabric to operate well. If the control plane node were down for whatever reason, fabric endpoints would have to rely on the local database information for connectivity, which might or might not work.

Cisco DNA Center helps to automate the control plane functions in the SD-Access fabric. It is recommended when designing the control plane to deploy the functionality on two nodes for high availability. Each control plane node contains a copy of the control plane information in the database that can be used to respond to requests for endpoint location information.

You can collocate the fabric control functions within the border nodes if the border nodes can support the endpoint-scale requirements. Some border nodes that are core switches do not support the requirements, and additional control plane nodes such as physical or virtual routers need to be used.

SD-Access fabrics can support up to six control plane nodes in a wired deployment, and WLCs and can communicate with up to four control plane nodes.

## Border Design

The border design for the SD-Access fabric involves connectivity to the outside or external networks. The next hop after the borders or the edge of the fabric for inter-VRF instance routing is to use a fusion router or firewall. These devices perform inter-VRF instance route leaking in order to fuse or tie the VRF instances together.

There are some design options to consider, depending on the locations of the shared services. DNA Center, AD, DHCP, and DNS are examples of shared services. These services can be in the global routing table (GRT) or can be in another separate VRF instance.

Shared services in the GRT include the following:

- The fabric border node exchanges GRT routes using External BGP (eBGP) with the fusion routers.

- The fabric border nodes handle the routing adjacencies for each VN/VRF instance.

- The fusion router fuses the SD-Access VNs into the GRT of the external network.

Shared services in separate VRF instances include the following:

- The fusion router establishes per-VN routing adjacencies with border nodes for each BGP address family.

- This design option comes with challenges such as manual configurations, loss of SGT context, and traffic hairpinning.

## Segmentation

Unified policy was a major driver in the SD-Access solution to allow for the same policy to be applied to both wired and wireless networks enforced at the access layer. Segmentation adds to unified policy by enabling VRF instance/VN (macro) and SGT (micro) segmentation to be deployed in the SD-Access fabric.

VRF instance/VN segmentation involves creation of a separate VRF instance for each group of devices/users contained inside it. To extend segmentation beyond the single fabric site, transits are used. SD-Access can use distributed campus and SD-WAN transits, which allow for the VN information to be natively carried inside the packets. On the other hand, IP transits allow for WAN connectivity, but the packets are decapsulated into native IP packets, which causes a loss of SGT/VN policy information.

SGT segmentation uses metadata to assign tags in order to enforce group policy. In SD-Access fabrics, edge and border nodes get security group access control lists (SGACLs) downloaded from ISE to enforce policy based on SGTs. Within DNA Center, SGTs are referred to as *scalable groups* (*SGs*).

Figure 10-8 provides an example of microsegmentation within the SD-Access fabric. Although Sales and Marketing security groups coexist on the same fabric, they are restricted from talking to each other.

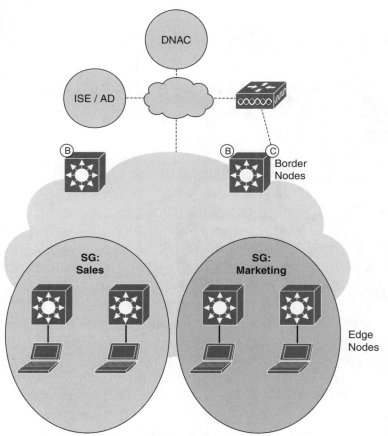

**Figure 10-8**   *Microsegmentation in SD-Access*

## Virtual Networks

A virtual network (VN) is a separate VRF instance that provides isolation for host pools or IP subnets. VNs serve the same basic purpose as VRF instances in traditional networks. Within SD-Access, the LISP control plane assigns to every endpoint a VN. Any communication between endpoints in different VNs must go through a fusion router or firewall. VN assignment is based on the attached host pool.

VNs are configured on all of the border and edge nodes in the SD-Access fabric. In addition, a default VN is used for any pools that are not assigned specific VNs. Inside the VXLAN header is a field that includes the VN identifier (VNI), which is used for traffic inside the fabric. There are 16 million VNI segments possible, so the VNs can be separate from one another, and VRF-based routing or firewall policy enforcement is possible.

Figure 10-9 show the use of three VNs for macrosegmentation along with scalable groups/SGTs for microsegmentation.

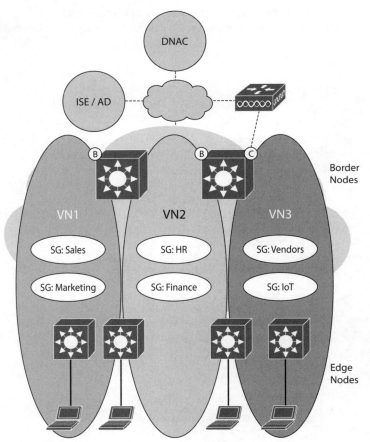

**Figure 10-9** *Virtual Networks and Scalable Groups*

## Scalability

Site reference models can be leveraged to scale the SD-Access fabric from very small to large site sizes. The following scaling numbers are to be used as guidelines only and are not intended to be size limits for SD-Access:

- **Very small site:** A single switch stack covering one wiring closet with fewer than 2000 endpoints, up to 8 VNs, and up to 100 APs. All border, control plane, edge, and WLC nodes are in a single platform.

- **Small site:** A single office building to support fewer than 10,000 endpoints, up to 32 VNs, and up to 200 APs. The border and control plane nodes are in one or two nodes, and a WLC has an optional redundancy node.

- **Medium site:** A medium-size building with many wiring closets or multiple buildings to support fewer than 25,000 endpoints, up to 64 VNs, and up to 1000 APs. All border, control plane, and WLC nodes are on distributed devices with high availability configurations.

- **Large site:** A large building with many wiring closets or multiple buildings to support fewer than 50,000 endpoints, up to 64 VNs, and up to 2000 APs. All border, control plane, and WLC nodes are on distributed devices with high availability configurations along with multiple border exits.

## Very Small Site Design Considerations

In very small sites, high availability and site survivability requirements are not common. Shared services are present in all reference designs for DHCP, DNS, WLC, and ISE. These services can be deployed in a remote data center and connected to the fabric through a fusion router, or they can be deployed locally with direct connections. High availability can be deployed in the design through StackWise technology with stackable switches or with multiple supervisors if chassis-based switches are used. WLCs can be attached to the fabric, or an embedded Catalyst 9800 WLC can be used.

Table 10-2 shows reference guidelines for very small sites.

**Table 10-2**   SD-Access Very Small Site Guidelines

| SD-Access Component Description | Size |
| --- | --- |
| Endpoints | Up to 2000 |
| IP pools | Up to 8 |
| Virtual networks | Up to 8 |
| Border nodes | Up to 1 |
| Control plane nodes | Up to 1 |
| Edge nodes | Up to 1 |
| Wireless LAN controllers | Up to 1 |
| Access points | Up to 100 |

## Small Site Design Considerations

High availability with small sites typically colocates border and control plane node functions on a pair of collapsed core switches. Multiple link connections should be used between the core switches for link redundancy and added resiliency. Since the endpoint counts are usually higher with small sites than with very small sites, embedded WLCs are not recommended unless there are fewer than 200 APs and 4000 endpoints. The higher endpoint and access point counts use physical WLCs deployed with high availability connected to the fabric. The WLCs should be connected using a service switch directly to the border nodes or attached to the fusion router locally at the fabric site.

Table 10-3 shows reference guidelines for small sites.

**Table 10-3** SD-Access Small Site Guidelines

| SD-Access Component Description | Size |
| --- | --- |
| Endpoints | Up to 10,000 |
| IP pools | Up to 100 |
| Virtual networks | Up to 32 |
| Border nodes | Up to 2 |
| Control plane nodes | Up to 2 |
| Edge nodes | Up to 25 |
| Wireless LAN controllers | Up to 2 |
| Access points | Up to 200 |

## Medium Site Design Considerations

In medium sites, dedicated border and control plane nodes are used for high availability. Inter-switch links should be used between the core switches for link redundancy and added resiliency. The control plane nodes would also connect to the core switches. Embedded WLCs are not used in medium-sized sites due to the larger endpoint counts. Because these sites are larger, physical WLCs are needed and are typically deployed in a high availability pair for redundancy. The WLCs should be connected using a service switch directly to the border nodes or attached to the fusion router locally at the fabric site.

Table 10-4 shows reference guidelines for medium sites.

**Table 10-4** SD-Access Medium Site Guidelines

| SD-Access Component Description | Size |
| --- | --- |
| Endpoints | Up to 25,000 |
| IP pools | Up to 300 |
| Virtual networks | Up to 64 |
| Border nodes | Up to 2 |
| Control plane nodes | Up to 4 |
| Edge nodes | Up to 250 |
| Wireless LAN controllers | Up to 2 |
| Access points | Up to 1000 |

## Large Site Design Considerations

Typically, a large site is designed with a three-tier network that consists of separate core, distribution, and access layers. These larger site networks are designed to support up to 50,000 endpoints. Multiple service exits points with dedicated data center connections, a shared services block, and Internet services are common.

In a multi-fabric deployment, the headquarters location might use a large site design. There may also be a perimeter edge firewall used to filter Internet traffic for the site. Cisco DNA Center and ISE may be deployed at the site or at a data center that has dedicated connections to the site.

High availability pairs for both the border and the control plane nodes with extra control plane nodes dedicated to guests can be used. Physical WLCs with high availability should be deployed for large sites. The WLCs usually have connectivity to the service switch or through the border nodes.

Table 10-5 lists reference guidelines for large sites.

**Table 10-5**   SD-Access Large Site Guidelines

| SD-Access Component Description | Size |
| --- | --- |
| Endpoints | Up to 50,000 |
| IP pools | Up to 500 |
| Virtual networks | Up to 64 |
| Border nodes | Up to 4 |
| Control plane nodes | Up to 6 |
| Edge nodes | Up to 1000 |
| Wireless LAN controllers | Up to 2 |
| Access points | Up to 2000 |

## Over-the-Top

SD-Access supports over-the-top wireless as another option when dedicated WLCs and newer fabric mode APs are not an option. This is the traditional Cisco Unified Wireless design model, which uses local mode but lacks the advantages of the SD-Access fabric integration.

With OTT, you still get features like mobility with roaming, IP address management, and simplified configuration and troubleshooting. Typically the WLC is located in the data center or in a services block near the enterprise network that is running SD-Access. The wireless traffic uses CAPWAP between the APs and the WLCs. In this mode, APs can exist both inside and outside the SD-Access fabric because the SD-Access fabric benefits are not being leveraged.

## Fabric Wireless

Fabric wireless is the best option for SD-Access if you have local WLCs and new fabric mode APs. This option allows wireless traffic to take advantage of security benefits with using SGTs with the SD-Access fabric. With fabric wireless, APs are responsible for delivering wireless traffic into and out of the wired network. The WLC control plane still uses CAPWAP and continues to utilize low-latency connections between the WLC and the APs. The colocation requirement of the WLCs is per SD-Access fabric, so other remote SD-Access fabrics still need their own WLCs.

Considerations for fabric placement of the WLCs are important when integrating wireless into SD-Access. Larger deployments typically have a shared services block in which the WLCs can connect and integrate near the core of the fabric. However, the preferred connectivity for WLCs involves multiple chassis connections with VSS or switch stacks using Stack-Wise technology to implement *Multichassis EtherChannels* for link and switch redundancy.

Fabric mode APs use the INFRA VRF instance, which is the same VRF instance that is used for the underlay in the SD-Access fabric. The INFRA VRF instance uses the global routing table (GRT) and provides connectivity for the network between the edge switches and the border switches.

10

Figure 10-10 shows the fabric wireless components in SD-Access.

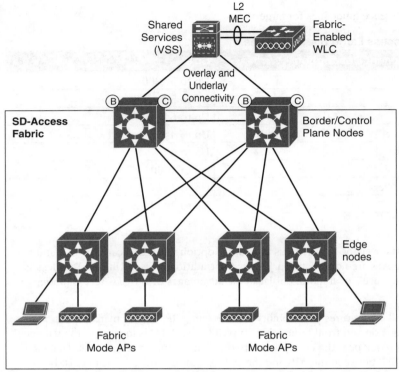

**Figure 10-10**  *Fabric Wireless Components in SD-Access*

## Multicast

In the earlier versions of SD-Access, headend replication of multicast packets into the fabric was standard. This meant that the headend (border) had to receive and replicate all the multicast packets from the edge switches and forward them on. However, recent versions of SD-Access have multicast features that can be configured manually within the fabric switches or done through LAN automation. This reduces headend replication overhead on the border switches.

Multicast sources can be supported both inside and outside the SD-Access fabric. With PIM implementations, a rendezvous point (RP) is used on the border for all multicast clients in the overlay. The multicast protocol configurations can be done within Cisco DNA Center.

Both PIM Source-Specific Multicast (SSM) and PIM–Sparse Mode are supported with SD-Access. When using IP multicast in the overlay, the use of a RP is required. Multicast Source Discovery Protocol (MSDP) can be used for RP redundancy, if desired.

# References and Recommended Readings

RFC 5415: *Control and Provisioning of Wireless Access Points (CAPWAP)*, https://tools.ietf.org/html/rfc5415.

RFC 6830: *The Locator/ID Separation Protocol (LISP)*, https://tools.ietf.org/html/rfc6830.

RFC 7348: *Virtual Extensible Local Area Network (VXLAN)*, https://tools.ietf.org/html/rfc7348.

Cisco, "Cisco Software-Defined Access: Enabling Intent-Based Networking," https://www.cisco.com/c/dam/en/us/products/se/2018/1/Collateral/nb-06-software-defined-access-ebook-en.pdf.

Cisco, "Cisco Software-Defined Access Solution Overview," https://www.cisco.com/c/en/us/solutions/collateral/enterprise-networks/software-defined-access/solution-overview-c22-739012.html.

Cisco, "Software-Defined Access 1.0" white paper, https://www.cisco.com/c/dam/en/us/solutions/collateral/enterprise-networks/software-defined-access/white-paper-c11-740585.pdf.

Cisco, "Software-Defined Access Solution Design Guide," https://www.cisco.com/c/en/us/td/docs/solutions/CVD/Campus/sda-sdg-2019oct.pdf.

# Exam Preparation Tasks

As mentioned in the section "How to Use This Book" in the Introduction, you have a couple of choices for exam preparation: the exercises here, Chapter 13, "Final Preparation," and the exam simulation questions on the companion website.

## Review All Key Topics

Review the most important topics in the chapter, noted with the Key Topic icon in the outer margin of the page. Table 10-6 lists these key topics and the page number on which each is found.

**Table 10-6**   Key Topics

| Key Topic Element | Description | Page |
|---|---|---|
| List | Key benefits of SD-Access | 324 |
| List | Main components of SD-Access | 324 |
| Figure 10-1 | SD-Access architecture overview | 325 |
| List | Overlay components | 326 |
| Figure 10-2 | LISP host mobility | 327 |
| Figure 10-3 | VXLAN GPO header | 328 |
| List | DNA Center automation workflows | 329 |
| Figure 10-4 | SD-Access wireless | 330 |
| Figure 10-5 | Over-the-top (OTT) wireless | 331 |
| Figure 10-6 | DNA Center and ISE integration | 331 |
| List | Virtual network design considerations | 332 |
| List | Fabric site characteristics | 333 |
| Figure 10-7 | SD-Access fabric site | 333 |
| Figure 10-8 | Microsegmentation in SD-Access | 335 |
| Figure 10-9 | Virtual networks and scalable groups | 336 |

10

| Key Topic Element | Description | Page |
|---|---|---|
| Table 10-2 | SD-Access very small site guidelines | 337 |
| Table 10-3 | SD-Access small site guidelines | 338 |
| Table 10-4 | SD-Access medium site guidelines | 338 |
| Table 10-5 | SD-Access large site guidelines | 339 |
| Figure 10-10 | Fabric wireless components in SD-Access | 340 |

## Complete Tables and Lists from Memory

Print a copy of Appendix D, "Memory Tables," found on the companion website, or at least the section for this chapter, and complete the tables and lists from memory. Appendix E, "Memory Tables Answer Key," includes completed tables and lists to check your work.

## Define Key Terms

Define the following key terms from this chapter and check your answers in the glossary:

assurance, automation, Cisco DNA Center, fabric control plane, fabric data plane, fabric policy plane, fabric wireless, overlay, policy, scalable group, SD-Access fabric, underlay, virtual network

## Q&A

The answers to these questions appear in Appendix A. For more practice with exam format questions, use the exam engine on the companion website.

1. Which of the following multicast protocols are supported with SD-Access? (Choose two.)
   a. SSM
   b. RP
   c. PIM
   d. CAPWAP

2. What is the preferred connectivity for WLCs? (Choose two.)
   a. Cisco DNA Center
   b. SGTs
   c. VSS
   d. Switch stacks

3. Which of the following best describes the limits for a very small site for SD-Access?
   a. 2000 endpoints and 8 VNs
   b. 3000 endpoints and 12 VNs
   c. 1000 endpoints and 4 VNs
   d. 4000 endpoints and 16 VNs

4. Which of the following gives you contextual insights for quick issue resolution and capacity planning?
   a. Integration
   b. Assurance

    **c.** Policy

    **d.** Automation

**5.** Which of the following is not an example of a technology that is used to create overlay networks?

    **a.** OSPF

    **b.** MPLS

    **c.** GRE

    **d.** DMVPN

**6.** What is used for endpoints in different VNs to communicate with each other?

    **a.** VXLAN

    **b.** SGTs

    **c.** VRFs

    **d.** Fusion router

**7.** Which VRF instance do fabric mode APs use? (*Hint:* It is the same VRF instance that is used for the underlay in the SD-Access fabric.)

    **a.** INFRA

    **b.** MGMT

    **c.** SGT

    **d.** GRE

**8.** Edge and border nodes get _____ downloaded from ISE to enforce policy based on SGTs.

    **a.** scalable groups

    **b.** VNs

    **c.** VRF instances

    **d.** SGACLs

**9.** What SD-Access site size supports up to 10,000 endpoints, 32 VNs, and up to 200 APs?

    **a.** Very small site

    **b.** Small site

    **c.** Medium site

    **d.** Large site

**10.** Which of the following APs is supported for fabric mode wireless in SD-Access?

    **a.** 802.11n

    **b.** 802.11g

    **c.** 802.11ac Wave 1

    **d.** 802.11a

**11.** Within the VXLAN header, how may SGTs are supported in the Group ID section?

    **a.** 16 million

    **b.** 4000

    **c.** 8 million

    **d.** 64,000

**10**

**12.** What technology is leveraged to enable SGT information to be inserted into the VXLAN headers in the data plane?

    **a.** GRT

    **b.** Cisco TrustSec

    **c.** ISE

    **d.** IPsec

**13.** Which of the following best describes data plane isolation with a VN using SGTs?

    **a.** Microsegmentation

    **b.** Macrosegmentation

    **c.** VRFs

    **d.** VNs

**14.** What SD-Access wireless method uses VXLAN in the data plane?

    **a.** Over-the-top

    **b.** Local mode

    **c.** Fabric wireless

    **d.** FlexConnect

**15.** The routing locator (RLOC) and the _____ are the two main things that LISP keeps track of.

    **a.** mapping database

    **b.** group ID (GID)

    **c.** global routing table (GRT)

    **d.** endpoint identifier (EID)

**16.** During the integration of ISE and DNA Center, which of the following are used to establish trust through ISE?

    **a.** REST APIs

    **b.** pxGRID services

    **c.** Scalable groups

    **d.** SGACLs

**17.** What routing protocol does Cisco DNA Center LAN automation use to deploy underlay routing configurations?

    **a.** BGP

    **b.** RIPv2

    **c.** EIGRP

    **d.** IS-IS

**18.** Open and programmable for third-party integrated solutions best describes which key benefit of SD-Access?

    **a.** Integration

    **b.** Assurance

    **c.** Policy

    **d.** Automation

**19.** Which of the following involves a collection of physical switches and routers running a dynamic Layer 3 routing protocol used for the transport in SD-Access?

   **a.** Overlay

   **b.** LAN automation

   **c.** Underlay

   **d.** LISP

**20.** Which of the following solutions can be integrated with Cisco DNA Center for IPAM? (Choose two.)

   **a.** Infoblox

   **b.** SolarWinds

   **c.** Microsoft DHCP

   **d.** BlueCat

**21.** Which key benefit of SD-Access can be described as automated configurations that help enable group-based security policies and network segmentation?

   **a.** Automation

   **b.** Assurance

   **c.** Policy

   **d.** Integration

**22.** Which of the following is used in the SD-Access control plane to handle the mapping and resolving of endpoint addresses?

   **a.** VXLAN

   **b.** LISP

   **c.** SGTs

   **d.** RLOCs

**23.** Which type of routing protocols use areas and advertise information about the network topology instead of advertising the complete routing table?

   **a.** Distance vector

   **b.** Hybrid

   **c.** Link state

   **d.** Path vector

**24.** Which of the following supports AAA services, groups, policy, and endpoint profiling?

   **a.** ISE

   **b.** DNA Center

   **c.** Cisco TrustSec

   **d.** VXLAN

**25.** What is the next hop after the border nodes to external networks?

   **a.** Edge nodes

   **b.** WLC

   **c.** Fusion routers

   **d.** Transit routers

10

**26.** Which of the following provides the logical overlay created by Virtual Extensible VLAN (VXLAN) packet encapsulation along with a Group Policy Object (GPO)?

    **a.** Fabric data plane

    **b.** Fabric control plane

    **c.** Fabric policy plane

    **d.** Security policy plane

**27.** Which of the following is a separate routing and forwarding instance that provides isolation for host pools?

    **a.** VXLAN

    **b.** SGT

    **c.** Virtual network

    **d.** Scalable group

**28.** Which site reference model supports up to 50,000 endpoints and 64 VNs?

    **a.** Very small site

    **b.** Small site

    **c.** Medium site

    **d.** Large site

**29.** Which underlay workflow provides a hierarchical structure for the management of network settings?

    **a.** Device discovery

    **b.** LAN automation

    **c.** Fabric sites

    **d.** Global and site settings

**30.** What moves the remote destination information to a centralized map database?

    **a.** VXLAN

    **b.** LISP

    **c.** Fabric data plane

    **d.** ISE

# CHAPTER 11

# SD-WAN Design

## This chapter covers the following subjects:

**SD-WAN Architecture:** This section describes the orchestration, management, control, and data planes of SD-WAN, Overlay Management Protocol, and provisioning.

**SD-WAN Design Considerations:** This section covers high-availability and scalability design, LAN design, security, migration to SD-WAN, and multicast over SD-WAN.

This chapter covers SD-WAN architecture and SD-WAN design considerations. The ENSLD 300-420 exam will test your understanding of SD-WAN architecture concepts related to the orchestration plane, management plane, control plane, and data plane. It will also test your knowledge of SD-WAN design considerations such as control plane design, overlay design, availability, redundancy, and scalability.

This chapter covers the following objectives from the ENSLD 300-420 exam:

- Describe Cisco SD-WAN architecture (orchestration plane, management plane, control plane, data plane, onboarding plane and provisioning, and security)

- Describe Cisco SD-WAN design considerations (control plane design, overlay design, LAN design, high availability, redundancy, scalability, security design, QoS, and multicast over SD-WAN fabric)

This chapter covers SD-WAN architecture and SD-WAN design considerations. The ENSLD 300-420 exam will test your understanding of SD-WAN architecture concepts related to the orchestration plane, management plane, control plane, and data plane. It will also test your knowledge of SD-WAN design considerations such as control plane design, overlay design, availability, redundancy, and scalability.

## "Do I Know This Already?" Quiz

The "Do I Know This Already?" quiz helps you identify your strengths and deficiencies in this chapter's topics. This quiz, derived from the major sections in the "Foundation Topics" portion of the chapter, helps you determine how to spend your limited study time. Table 11-1 outlines the major topics discussed in this chapter and the "Do I Know This Already?" quiz questions that correspond to those topics. You can find the answers in Appendix A, "Answers to the 'Do I Know This Already?' Quiz Questions Q&A Questions."

**Table 11-1** "Do I Know This Already?" Foundation Topics Section-to-Question Mapping

| Foundation Topics Section | Questions Covered in This Section |
| --- | --- |
| SD-WAN Architecture | 1–4 |
| SD-WAN Design Considerations | 5–8 |

1. Which device is the brains in SD-WAN?

   a. vEdge

   b. vSmart

   c. vBond

   d. vManage

2. What is the function of vBond?

   a. To bond vEdge devices to each other

   b. To establish OMP connectivity

   c. To establish control channels with vSmart controllers

   d. To perform initial authentication of vEdge devices

3. You configure a new vEdge manually with IP address, gateway, and vBond IP address. What method of onboarding are you using?

   a. Bootstrapping

   b. Manual configuration

   c. ZTP

   d. PnP

4. What are three types of OMP routes?

   a. Static, dynamic, and redundant

   b. Static, OSPF, and BGP

   c. Prefix routes, TLOC routes, and service routes

   d. ZTP, DTLS, and OMP

5. Two vEdge routers are used at a branch site. If Layer 2 redundancy is implemented on the LAN, which of the following will take care of failover?

   a. BGP

   b. OSPF

   c. Static

   d. VRRP

6. Which of the following gathers information about latency, jitter, and packet loss?

   a. SNMP

   b. BFD

   c. IPFIX

   d. Probes

7. Which of the following increases availability and scalability in the control plane?

   a. Creating a vManage cluster

   b. Adding vSmart controllers

   c. Adding vEdge devices at the branch

   d. Adding vBond orchestrators

**8.** Which multicast protocol is supported by Cisco SD-WAN?

   **a.** MSDP

   **b.** SSM

   **c.** PIM-SM

   **d.** BIDIR-PIM

## Foundation Topics

Software-defined Wide Area Networking (SD-WAN) is a Cisco software-defined networking (SDN) technology, which abstracts the underlying network infrastructure away from its applications. SDN decouples the forwarding plane from the control and management planes, allowing centralization of network intelligence. SD-WAN applies SDN principles to the WAN.

This chapter describes SD-WAN architecture and SD-WAN design considerations, which are topics you need to master for the ENSLD 300-420 exam. These topics include orchestration, management, control, data planes, onboarding, provisioning, and security. This chapter also covers control plane design, overlay design, redundancy, scalability, multicast, and SD-WAN security.

## SD-WAN Architecture

Cisco SD-WAN is an enterprise-grade WAN architecture overlay that enables digital and cloud transformation for enterprises. It fully integrates routing, security, centralized policy, and orchestration into large-scale networks. It is a multi-tenant, cloud-delivered, highly automated, secure, scalable, and application-aware solution with rich analytics. The Cisco SD-WAN technology addresses the problems and challenges of common WAN deployments. Some of the benefits include:

   ■ Centralized management and policy management

   ■ Ability to mix MPLS, Internet, and any combination of transport technology in active/active fashion

   ■ Transport-independent overlay

   ■ Deployment flexibility

   ■ Robust security, including strong encryption of data, end-to-end network segmentation, a router and controller zero-trust model, control plane protection, and an application firewall

   ■ Application visibility and recognition and application-aware policies

   ■ Analytics with visibility into applications and infrastructure

**Key Topic**

As shown in Figure 11-1, Cisco's SD-WAN architecture is divided into the following planes:

   ■ **Orchestration plane:** This plane assists in the automatic onboarding of SD-WAN routers into the SD-WAN overlay.

   ■ **Management plane:** This plane is responsible for central configuration and monitoring.

- **Control plane:** This plane builds and maintains the network topology and makes decisions on where traffic flows.

- **Data plane:** This plane is responsible for forwarding packets based on decisions from the control plane.

## Management Plane

The vManage component resides in the management plane. vManage is the centralized network management system (NMS) that provides a GUI interface to monitor, configure, and maintain all Cisco SD-WAN devices and links in the underlay and overlay networks. vManage supports web console, REST API, CLI, syslog, SNMP, and NETCONF. The vManage dashboard provides:

- **Transport independence:** vManage automates flexibility over multiple connections, such as MPLS, Internet, and 5G.

- **Network services:** vManage provides WAN optimization, cloud security, firewalling, intrusion prevention services, and URL filtering.

- **Endpoint flexibility:** vManage simplifies connectivity across branches, campuses, data centers, and cloud environments.

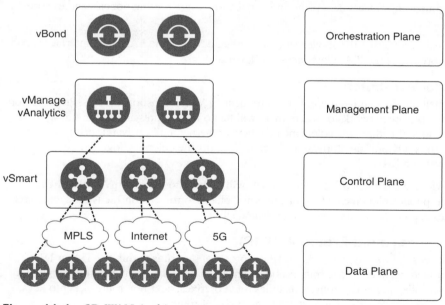

**Figure 11-1**  *SD-WAN Architecture*

The vAnalytics engine, which is accessed through vManage, is also a management plane component. vAnalytics allows end-to-end visibility of applications and infrastructure across the entire SD-WAN fabric with real-time information about failure correlation and application scores, ability to see "what-if" scenarios for performance forecasting, application QoS categorization, and policy changes for predictable performance, and assistance is planning application provisioning, bandwidth increases, and branch expansions.

## Orchestration Plane

The vBond component resides in the orchestration plane. vBond is a software-based component that performs the initial authentication of vEdge devices and orchestrates vSmart and vEdge connectivity. In other words, it tells vEdge routers how to connect with vManage and vSmart controllers, and it tells vSmart controllers about the new vEdge devices.

Because vManage also performs orchestration functions, it is included in this plane.

## Control Plane

The vSmart component resides in the control plane. vSmart controllers provide routing, enforce data plane policies, and enforce network-wide segmentation. Because policies are created on vManage, vSmart is the component responsible for enforcing these policies centrally. It is the "brains" of the architecture. vEdge routers communicate their routing information with the vSmart controllers, not to each other. Overlay Management Protocol (OMP) is used for this vEdge-to-vSmart communication.

## Data Plane

The vEdge component resides in the data plane. vEdge routers are responsible for establishing the network fabric and forwarding traffic; they bring up IPsec and GRE tunnels between sites. vEdge routers can be virtual or physical. vEdge routers establish a control channel to vSmart controllers and IPsec tunnels to other vEdge devices to form the overlay network. A vEdge router implements data plane and application-aware routing policies and exports performance statistics.

For nomenclature clarity, the service side of a vEdge device is the LAN side (interfaces), and the transport side is the WAN interfaces (MPLS/IPsec).

## vEdge Color Attributes

A color attribute on a vEdge router is used to identify WAN transport tunnels. Private colors are used for private networks or where there will be no NAT addressing of the transport IP endpoints. Predefined private colors include metro-ethernet, mpls, private1, private2, private3, private4, private5, and private6. When using a private color, a vEdge device is using a native private underlay IP.

vEdge devices use public colors where tunnels will be built to the post-NAT IP address. Predefined public colors include 3g, biz, internet, blue, bronze, custom1, custom2, custom3, default, gold, green, lte, public-internet, red, and silver.

## Overlay Management Protocol (OMP)

OMP manages the overlay network. OMP is a protocol that runs within the TLS or DTLS tunnels formed between vEdge routers and a vSmart controller. Communication between a vSmart controller and vEdge routers includes route prefixes, next-hop routes, crypto keys, and policy information. OMP advertises three types of routes:

- **OMP routes:** OMP advertises prefixes learned at the local site, including static, OSPF, or BGP routes. These routes are also called vRoutes.

- **TLOC routes:** Transport location (TLOC) routes are logical tunnel termination points on WAN edge routers that connect to the transport network.

- **Service routes:** OMP advertises routes for services such as firewalls, intrusion prevention, application optimization, and VPN labels.

OMP routes include the following attributes:

- **TLOC:** This is the transport location identifier of the next hop for OMP routes. It is similar to the BGP NEXT_HOP attribute. A TLOC consists of three components:

  - System IP address of the OMP speaker that originates the OMP route

  - Color to identify the link type (for example, mpls, metro-ethernet)

  - Encapsulation type on the transport tunnel (IPsec or GRE)

- **Origin:** This is the source of the route, such as BGP, OSPF, connected, or static, and the metric associated with the original route.

- **Originator:** This is the OMP identifier of the originator of the route, which is the IP address from which the route was learned.

- **Preference:** This is the degree of preference for an OMP route. A higher preference value is more preferred.

- **Service:** This is the network service associated with the OMP route.

- **Site ID:** This ID identifies a site within the SD-WAN overlay network domain to which the OMP route belongs.

- **Tag:** This is an optional transitive path attribute that an OMP speaker can use to control the routing information it accepts, prefers, or redistributes.

- **VPN:** This is the VPN or network segment to which the OMP route belongs.

TLOC routes contain the following attributes:

- **TLOC private address:** This is the private IP address of the interface associated with the TLOC.

- **TLOC public address:** This is the NAT-translated address of the TLOC.

- **Carrier:** This is an identifier of the carrier type, which is generally used to indicate whether the transport is public or private.

- **Color:** The color identifies the link type.

- **Encapsulation type:** This is the tunnel encapsulation type.

- **Preference:** This is the degree of preference that is used to differentiate between TLOCs that advertise the same OMP route.

- **Site ID:** This ID identifies a site within the SD-WAN overlay network domain to which the TLOC belongs.

- **Tag:** This is an optional transitive path attribute that an OMP speaker can use to control the flow of routing information toward a TLOC. When an OMP route is advertised along with its TLOC, both or either can be distributed with a community tag, to be used to decide how to send traffic to or receive traffic from a group of TLOCs.

- **Weight:** This value is used to discriminate among multiple entry points if an OMP route is reachable through two or more TLOCs.

**11**

## Onboarding and Provisioning

vEdge devices can be onboarded via two methods: Zero Touch Provisioning (ZTP) or manual configuration. ZTP does require some initial steps on Cisco's Plug and Play (PnP) Connect portal:

**Step 1.** Use the PnP Connect portal, which is linked to Cisco Commerce Workspace (CCW), to place an order for SD-WAN devices with PnP licenses.

**Step 2.** Configure the vBond controller IP address or domain name.

**Step 3.** Define the vBond controller in PnP Connect.

**Step 4.** PnP will automatically send the data to ZTP.

**Step 5.** Upload a provisioning file to vManage.

Once these steps are complete, the device is available in vManage for ZTP.

### Zero Touch Provisioning (ZTP)

Cisco makes its ZTP automatic provisioning software available as a service (SaaS). The ZTP process involves the following considerations:

- The edge or gateway router at the site where the hardware vEdge router is located must be able to reach public DNS servers. It is recommended that they be configured to reach the Google public DNS servers 8.8.8.8 and 8.8.4.4.

- The edge or gateway router at the site must be able to reach ztp.viptela.com.

- A network cable must be plugged into the interface that the hardware router uses for ZTP. These interfaces are:

  - **For vEdge 1000 routers:** ge0/0

  - **For vEdge 2000 routers:** ge2/0

  - **For vEdge 100 series routers:** ge0/4

Onboarding vEdge routers involves the following steps:

**Step 1.** Build a configuration template on vManage for the vEdge routers that will be joining the SD-WAN overlay network.

**Step 2.** Cable and power on the vEdge routers. The vEdge devices use their circuits to connect with the Cisco-hosted PnP Connect server, which redirects the vEdge devices to the vBond server to authenticate these devices. The template configuration from vManage is then loaded onto the vEdge routers.

**Step 3.** Once configured, the vEdge routers build secure channels to the vSmart controller.

**Step 4.** The vEdge routers set up OMP peering with vSmart controllers.

**Step 5.** Once OMP peers are established, the vEdge routers learn routing information to other sites and information required to establish IPsec connections to other locations.

**Step 6.** IPsec tunnels are established to other locations to form the SD-WAN overlay network, based on the configured policies the vEdge routers for BFD adjacencies with each other.

## Onboarding a vEdge Router via Manual Configuration

With the manual configuration method, a site network administrator manually configures minimal information that allows the vEdge devices to connect with the vBond orchestrator. The following information is configured:

- IP address and gateway IP address (or use DHCP)

- The vBond IP address or the vBond hostname (if in DNS) and DNS server IP address

- The organization name, system IP address, and site ID

## Onboarding Cisco IOS XE SD-WAN Routers

Cisco IOS XE devices can be onboarded in three different ways:

- **PnP Connect:** The Day 0 PnP Connect process discovers, installs, and provisions the Cisco IOS XE device to the SD-WAN overlay network.

- **Bootstrap:** In this scenario, the configuration is loaded onto a USB key that is inserted into the Cisco IOS XE device. The configuration file is created with vManage.

- **Manual configuration:** It is possible for a network administrator to connect to the console port to configure parameters.

## SD-WAN Security

Cisco's SD-WAN solution provides security for the management plane, control plane, and data plane. The control plane uses a Zero Trust model, the management plane uses role-based access control (RBAC) and access control lists (ACLs), and the data plane has integrated on-premises and cloud security layers.

The Cisco SD-WAN fabric incorporates a Zero Trust model in the control plane. As shown in Figure 11-2, all elements in the SD-WAN fabric are authenticated and authorized with each other prior to admission to the network. Digital certificates are used to establish secure Transport Layer Security 1.2 or Datagram Transport Layer Security (TLS/DTLS) control channels between vEdge routers and the controllers. TLS 1.2 is defined in RFC 5246. DTLS 1.2 is defined in RFC 6347. The hashing algorithm used in the control plane is SHA256, and the encryption algorithm is AES-256-GCM.

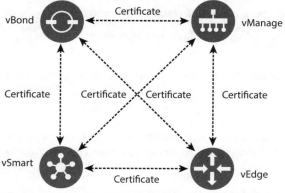

**Figure 11-2**  *SD-WAN Certificate-Based Authentication*

OMP and Network Configuration Protocol (NETCONF) run over these TLS/DLTS channels. OMP ensures the propagation of encryption keys used by the data plane. NETCONF allows the controllers to propagate configuration and networking information inside the control channel.

The vManage component uses RBAC to control the permission for users based on their privileges. RBAC controls who can access, read, and modify configurations and policies. Users are authenticated using authentication, authorization, and accounting (AAA) via SAML SSO, RADIUS, or TACACS.

vManage has some predefined user groups assigned with different levels of privileges:

- **Basic group:** Permissions to view interface and system information

- **Operator group:** Permission to view information

- **Netadmin group:** Permission to perform all operations

Remote access to the vManage server can be further controlled by using white-list access control lists (ACLs) to specify the only allowed IP subnets that can access the vManage server.

As mentioned earlier, vEdge routers use Advanced Encryption Standard (AES) with a 256-bit key length with the preferred operation Galois/Counter Mode (GCM)—hence AES-256-GCM. A secondary mode, cipher block chaining (CBC), can be used when required, such as in multicast applications.

# SD-WAN Design Considerations

An enterprise designer should consider design options in deploying SD-WAN components to account for scalability, high availability, security, and QoS.

## Control Plane Design

SD-WAN vManage, vSmart, and vBond can be deployed in one of three cloud-delivered control methods. The design option chosen depends on the company's IT policies on network infrastructure. A company might want to manage all devices with its internal IT team. Another company might consider the cloud infrastructure services of Cisco or a service provider (SP). Controller deployment models include the following:

- **On-premises:** An enterprise IT administrator can deploy the vManage, vSmart, and vBond components and manage all configuration of vEdge routers and overlay policy.

- **Managed SP:** In this model, a service provider deploys the vManage, vSmart, and vBond components in the SP's cloud infrastructure.

- **Cisco cloud deployment:** In this model, the vManage, vSmart, and vBond components are deployed in Cisco's cloud infrastructure.

### Scalability

To increase the availability and growth of the orchestration, management, and control planes, it is important to implement horizontal solution scaling. As shown in Figure 11-3, the following can be done to scale a solution:

- Add vBond orchestrators to increase vEdge bring-up capacity.

- Create a vManage cluster to support more vEdge routers.

- Add vSmart controllers to increase the capacity of the control plane.

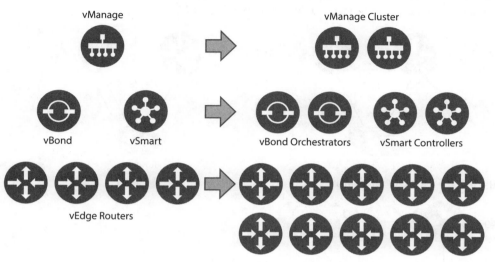

**Figure 11-3**  *Horizontal Solution Scaling*

## High Availability and Redundancy

Cisco SD-WAN provides many solutions that provide high availability and redundancy. These solutions can be divided into the following categories:

- Site redundancy

- Transport redundancy

- Network/headend redundancy

- Control redundancy

### Site Redundancy

Site redundancy provides redundancy in the event that one of the vEdge routers fails at a site. It can be accomplished by using VRRP from the switched infrastructure or Layer 3 routing from a Layer 3 switch or router. In Figure 11-4, for example, if there is a failure of the vEdge router on the left, VRRP will fail over, and traffic will flow to the vEdge router on the right. If OSPF or BGP is running between the vEdge devices and the router, if the vEdge device on the left fails, the routing protocol will handle the rerouting of traffic to the vEdge router on the right.

### Transport Redundancy

Transport redundancy allows you to fail over from your primary WAN transport to a secondary transport. For example, in Figure 11-5, if the MPLS circuit fails, traffic is diverted to the Internet transport.

11

### Network/Headend Redundancy

SD-WAN provides network/headend redundancy so that in the event of loss of connectivity via the primary network headend vEdge router at the data center, the vEdge router can connect to a redundant headend vEdge router (see Figure 11-6).

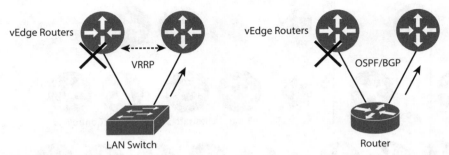

**Figure 11-4**  *Site Redundancy*

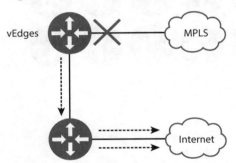

**Figure 11-5**  *Transport Redundancy*

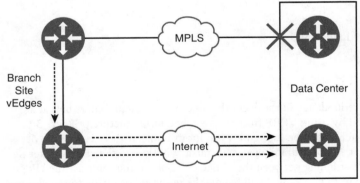

**Figure 11-6**  *Network/Headend Redundancy*

### Controller Redundancy

As mentioned previously, you can increase the number of vSmart controllers to increase the scalability and redundancy of the control plane.

## LAN Design

Site LAN designs vary based on size and other requirements. A site can be a simple Layer 2 access switch or a large hierarchical network with multiple distribution and access switches with a Layer 3 core network. Furthermore, SD-WAN can handle separate LAN networks as VPNs (that is, multiple VPNs). Separate VPNs can be implemented to separate regular corporate traffic from, say, PCI traffic and guest wireless. This way, each VPN can be given separate policies. Layer 2 design options include the following:

- Layer 2 with a single vEdge router

- Layer 2 with VRRP for dual vEdge routers

- Layer 2 with a single vEdge router and multiple VPNs

- Layer 2 with VRRP for dual vEdge router and multiple VPNs

Figure 11-7 shows a Layer 2 access switch connected to a single vEdge router, which is a common setup for small branch sites. When additional redundancy is required, dual vEdge routers are implemented, and VRRP is used as the first-hop gateway protocol. VRRP specifies an election protocol that dynamically assigns responsibility for a virtual master router to one of the VRRP routers on a LAN. The virtual router backup assumes the forwarding responsibility for the virtual router if the master fails. VRRP is covered in more detail in Chapter 7, "Advanced Enterprise Campus Design."

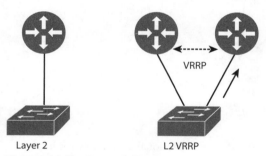

**Figure 11-7**   *Layer 2 Design*

Figure 11-8 shows the Layer 2 design but with separate LAN networks (separate IP subnets) that are placed in separate VPNs. When two vEdge routers are used, separate VRRP instances are used to support each VPN.

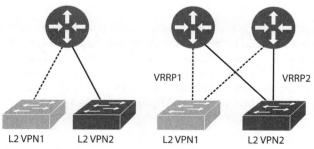

**Figure 11-8**   *Layer 2 Design with Multiple VPNs*

11

Figure 11-9 shows a Layer 3 design where static routes, OSPF, or BGP can be used to exchange routes between the vEdge routers and the Layer 3 switch. At a branch site, a single static route might be enough. Larger sites might use OSPF to exchange routes, and a data center would use BGP.

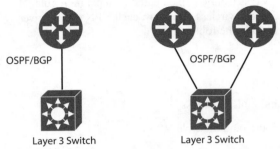

**Figure 11-9**   *Layer 3 LAN Design for SD-WAN*

Figure 11-10 shows a Layer 3 LAN design with multiple VPNs. Routes between the VPNs are not exchanged.

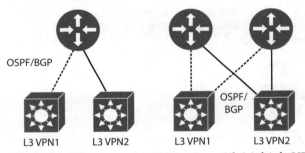

**Figure 11-10**   *Layer 3 LAN Design with Multiple VPN*

## vEdge DHCP Server

vEdge routers can be configured to provide DHCP server functionality to allow for host IP address assignments to be made directly from a vEdge device on a customer site. DHCP servers are configurable for the service side interface.

DHCP relay (IP helper) functionality is also supported for forwarding requests from the service side network to the IP address defined as the DHCP server in a different subnet.

## Direct Internet Access (DIA)

With DIA, Internet-bound traffic or public cloud traffic from the branch is routed directly to the Internet, avoiding the latency involved in tunneling Internet-bound traffic to a central site. Benefits of using DIA include reduced bandwidth consumption, latency, and costs (thanks to offloading Internet traffic from the private WAN circuit). Employees at remote branch offices experience improved connectivity to Internet sites via DIA. IP NAT is enabled on the Internet transport interface to handle private-to-public IP address translations.

## Security Design

Cisco SD-WAN offers four security categories for both integrated on-premises and cloud deployments: network segmentation, enterprise firewall, secure web gateway, and DNS-layer security. The following security features are included:

- IPsec encryption
- Intrusion prevention system
- App controls
- Malware protection
- SSL/TLS decryption

vEdge routers are also equipped with a stateful firewall to ensure that user traffic is restricted to authorized destinations and to provide auditing of security incidents.

### VPN Segmentation

Segmentation via VPNs is another security feature of the Cisco SD-WAN solution. It is similar to virtual routing and forwarding (VRF) segmentation on Cisco IOS routers. Segmentation is initiated in the control plane and enforced in the data plane. Each VPN is assigned a value from 0 to 65530, where 0 and 512 are reserved for system use. Each VPN has traffic and has its own forwarding table.

VPN 0 is the transport VPN and contains the interfaces that connect to the WAN transports (MPLS and IPsec). DTLS/TLS connections to vSmart or between vSmart and vBond are initiated from VPN 0. VPN 512 is the management VPN; it carries out-of-band management traffic. This VPN is not carried across the overlay network.

Figure 11-11 shows an example in which different VPN segments are available at different sites. Some sites have VPN 1, which is carried over to only two other sites. VPN 2 is available and transported between three sites. VPN 3 is only carried by the SD-WAN overlay between two sites.

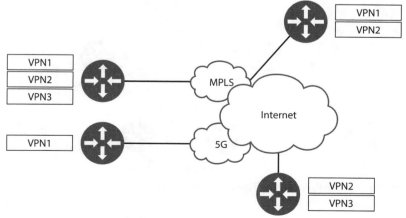

**Figure 11-11** *SD-WAN VPN Segmentation*

11

### VPN Topology Design

Each VPN is independent of every other VPN. You might separate VPNs in order to separate business traffic from guest wireless traffic. Or you might want to separate manufacturing or extranet traffic. Some traffic might be site-to-site traffic, and other traffic might be site-to-data center traffic. VPNs can be configured with several different topologies:

- **Full-mesh:** All sites connect to each other (site-to-site traffic).

- **Hub-and-spoke:** Remote sites connect to a single central site (data center).

- **Partial-mesh:** Most sites are interconnected with one another.

- **Point-to-point:** One site connects to another.

Figure 11-12 shows full-mesh and hub-and-spoke VPN topologies.

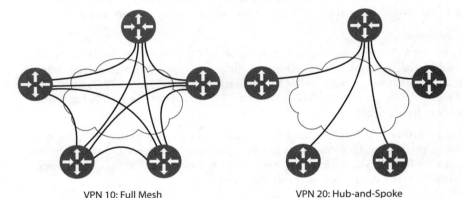

VPN 10: Full Mesh    VPN 20: Hub-and-Spoke

**Figure 11-12**   *VPN Topologies: Full-Mesh and Hub-and-Spoke*

Figure 11-13 shows partial-mesh and point-to-point VPN topologies.

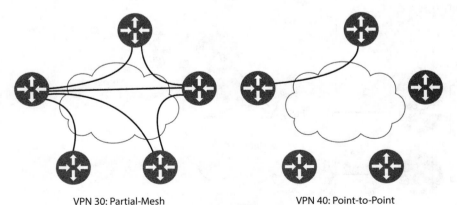

VPN 30: Partial-Mesh    VPN 40: Point-to-Point

**Figure 11-13**   *VPN Topologies: Partial-Mesh and Point-to-Point*

### Access Control Lists (ACLs)

ACLs can be created and applied to particular interfaces in order to police traffic in either the ingress or the egress directions. An ACL allows a sequenced list of "match" statements to be defined; traffic is then matched against these statements, and the defined actions are taken (for example, drop, log). Any packets not matching a statement in the ACL are explicitly dropped as the default action of last resort.

Standard ACL options allow for matching of packets based on 5-tuple traffic definitions or DSCP. Advanced ACL options allow for matching based on a more granular set of parameters, such as packet length and TCP flag parameters.

## SD-WAN Migration Strategy

SD-WAN leverages existing infrastructure and WAN transports and can be seamlessly integrated. A common strategy is to place the new vEdge overlay network in parallel with the existing WAN and then cut over the infrastructure.

As shown in Figure 11-14, the first step is to install the parallel SD-WAN infrastructure. This leaves the existing MPLS infrastructure intact. In the next step, the SD-WAN fabric leverages the MPLS transport, allowing the vEdge device to establish an overlay network over both the MPLS and the Internet transport. The final step is to replace the MPLS routers with vEdge devices to allow full SD-WAN overlay transport with full transport and headend redundancy.

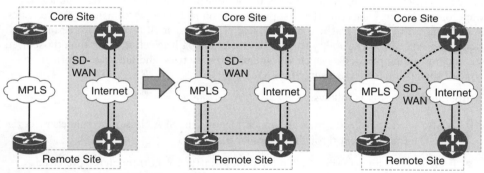

**Figure 11-14** *SD-WAN Migration*

## QoS in SD-WAN

Cisco's SD-WAN solution has many QoS features that provide advanced prioritization of traffic and network policies. These features include Bidirectional Forwarding Detection (BFD), application-aware routing, and interface queuing with low-latency queueing (LLQ).

### Bidirectional Forwarding Detection (BFD)

WAN edge routers use Bidirectional Forwarding Detection (BFD) to probe and measure the performance of the transport links. BFD probes provide information about latency, jitter, and loss on all the transport links, which aids in the determination of best paths. Information on interface up/down and IPsec tunnel MTU is also gathered. Path liveliness and quality measurements run on all WAN edge routers (and WAN edge cloud routers) in the network. BFD in SD-WAN has the following characteristics:

- Runs inside IPsec tunnels

- Operates in echo mode

- Is automatically invoked during IPsec tunnel establishment

- Cannot be disabled

11

## Policies

Policies can be configured to influence the flow of traffic in the overlay network. Policies can be control plane or data plane policies, and they can be configured centrally on the vSmart controller or locally on the vEdge routers.

Centralized control policies operate on the routing and TLOC information and allow for customization of routing decisions and determination of routing paths through the overlay network. These policies can be used in configuring traffic engineering, path affinity, service insertion, and different types of VPN topologies.

Data policies influence the flow of data traffic through the network based on fields in the IP packet headers and VPN membership. Centralized data policies can be used in configuring application firewalls, service chaining, traffic engineering, and QoS. Localized data policies allow you to configure how data traffic is handled at a specific site, such as through ACLs, QoS, mirroring, or policing.

## Application-Aware Routing

Application-aware routing policies are key centralized policies that affect the traffic on a vEdge router that is flowing from the LAN to the transport tunnel WAN side. Application-aware routing involves selecting the best path based on real-time performance characteristics for different traffic types. Traffic is matched and placed into an SLA class, with certain loss, jitter, and delay values. The ability to consider factors in path selection other than those used by standard routing protocols—such as route prefixes, metrics, and link-state information—is one of the main benefits of using SD-WAN.

The routing behavior is as follows:

- Traffic is load balanced across all tunnels meeting the SLA class. If no tunnels meet the SLA, the traffic is sent through any available tunnel.

- If preferred colors are specified in the policy, traffic is sent through the preferred color tunnels as long as the SLA is met. If no tunnels meet the SLA, the traffic is sent through any available tunnel.

- If a backup SLA-preferred color is specified, then that tunnel is used when there are no paths that meet the SLA. Another path is used if the backup tunnel is unavailable.

- A strict keyword can be used in the policy. If a strict keyword is used and no tunnel can meet the SLA, the traffic is dropped.

- The policy can be configured with no default action. In this case, if traffic does not match any sequence in the list, it is routed normally according to the routing protocol. Alternatively, this default traffic can be placed into an SLA class.

## vEdge Interface Queues

Each vEdge interface has eight queues. Of these queues, queue 0 uses LLQ. By default, control and BFD traffic use queue 0. Control and BFD traffic is marked as DSCP 48 decimal. LLQ traffic is transmitted before packets in any of the other queues. The only congestion-avoidance algorithm used for this queue is tail drop, which treats all traffic equally and does not differentiate between classes of service. When the output queue 0 is full and tail drop is in effect, packets are dropped until the congestion is eliminated and the queue is no longer full.

Queues 1 through 7 use Weighted Round Robin (WRR) for scheduling. By default, user traffic uses queue 2.

When a packet passes from the service LAN to the transport, the following packet flow occurs on the vEdge router:

1. Local policy and configuration checks occur (including the policer, admission control, and classification marking).

2. Centralized application-aware routing policy is applied, with path selection based on the SLA.

3. Centralized data policy is enforced (including policer admission control, classification marking, and path selection).

4. Routing and forwarding occurs.

5. Packets are scheduled and queued (using LLQ, WRR, and RED).

6. Local policy shaping and ACLs are enforced (including shaping, a re-marking policer, and ACLs).

## Multicast over SD-WAN

The Cisco SD-WAN solution supports PIM–Sparse Mode (PIM-SM) for multicast traffic over the overlay network. The Cisco SD-WAN solution optimizes multicast packet distribution by eliminating packet replication on the ingress router. The ingress router is the router that is connected to the multicast source. The ingress router forwards multicast streams to a vEdge router that is configured as a replicator.

As shown in Figure 11-15, the replicator vEdge forwards streams to multicast receivers. The PIM rendezvous point (RP) is not an SD-WAN device; vEdge routers do not support RP functionality. For distributing RP-to-group mapping information to local-site PIM routers, auto-RP is supported. vEdge routers support Internet Group Management Protocol (IGMP) version 2 to process receiver membership report for hosts in a particular VPN to determine if traffic should be forwarded. PIM-SM, RP, and IGMPv2 are covered in Chapter 5, "IP Multicast and Network Management."

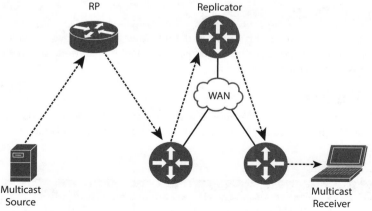

**Figure 11-15**  *Multicast Traffic Flow over SD-WAN*

# References and Recommended Readings

RFC 5246: *The Transport Layer Security (TLS) Protocol Version 1.2*, https://tools.ietf.org/html/rfc5246.

RFC 6347: *Datagram Transport Layer Security Version 1.2*, https://tools.ietf.org/html/rfc6347.

Cisco, "Cisco Multicast Overlay Routing Overview," https://sdwan-docs.cisco.com/@api/deki/pages/8693/pdf/Multicast%2bOverlay%2bRouting%2bOverview.pdf?stylesheet=default.

Cisco, "Cisco Plug and Play Support Guide for Cisco SD-WAN Products," https://www.cisco.com/c/dam/en_us/services/downloads/SD-WAN_pnp_support_guide.pdf.

Cisco, "Cisco SD-WAN," https://www.cisco.com/c/en/us/solutions/enterprise-networks/sd-wan/index.html?dtid=osscdc000283.

Cisco, "Cisco SD-WAN Cloud Scale Architecture," https://www.cisco.com/c/dam/en/us/solutions/collateral/enterprise-networks/sd-wan/nb-06-cisco-sd-wan-ebook-cte-en.pdf.

Cisco, "Cisco SD-WAN: Enabling Direct Internet Access Deployment Guide," https://www.cisco.com/c/dam/en/us/td/docs/solutions/CVD/SDWAN/sdwan-dia-deploy-2019nov.pdf.

Cisco, "Cisco SD-WAN End-to-End Deployment Guide," https://www.cisco.com/c/dam/en/us/td/docs/solutions/CVD/SDWAN/SD-WAN-End-to-End-Deployment-Guide.pdf.

Cisco, "Cisco SD-WAN: WAN Edge Onboarding," https://www.cisco.com/c/dam/en/us/td/docs/solutions/CVD/SDWAN/sd-wan-wan-edge-onboarding-deploy-guide-2020jan.pdf.

Cisco, "Cisco Validated Design Cisco SD-WAN Design Guide," https://www.cisco.com/c/dam/en/us/td/docs/solutions/CVD/SDWAN/CVD-SD-WAN-Design-2018OCT.pdf?oid=dsgen013910.

Cisco, "Delivering Cisco Next Generation SD-WAN with Viptela," CiscoLive BRKCRS-2110.

# Exam Preparation Tasks

As mentioned in the section "How to Use This Book" in the Introduction, you have a couple of choices for exam preparation: the exercises here, Chapter 13, "Final Preparation," and the exam simulation questions on the companion website.

# Review All Key Topics

Review the most important topics in the chapter, noted with the Key Topic icon in the outer margin of the page. Table 11-2 lists these key topics and the page number on which each is found.

**Table 11-2**  Key Topics

| Key Topic Element | Description | Page |
|---|---|---|
| List | SD-WAN architecture | 350 |
| Paragraph | OMP | 352 |
| Paragraph | SD-WAN security | 355 |

| Key Topic Element | Description | Page |
|---|---|---|
| List | Scalability | 356 |
| Section | High availability and redundancy | 357 |
| Paragraph | LAN design | 359 |
| Paragraph | VPN topology design | 362 |

## Complete Tables and Lists from Memory

There are no memory tables for this chapter.

## Define Key Terms

Define the following key terms from this chapter and check your answers in the glossary:

Bidirectional Forwarding Detection (BFD), Network Configuration Protocol (NETCONF), Overlay Management Protocol (OMP), role-based access control (RBAC), SD-WAN, software-defined networking (SDN), vBond, vManage, vEdge, vSmart

## Q&A

The answers to these questions appear in Appendix A. For more practice with exam format questions, use the exam engine on the companion website.

1. What is the function of vSmart?

   a. Provides routing and enforces policies

   b. Bonds vEdge devices to each other

   c. Establishes control channel to controllers

   d. Performs initial authentication of vEdge devices

2. Which plane is responsible for central configuration?

   a. Orchestration

   b. Management

   c. Control

   d. Data

3. In Cisco SD-WAN overlay networks, multicast streams are sent to what device?

   a. RP

   b. Replicator

   c. PIM-SM

   d. vSmart controller

4. Which plane is responsible for maintaining the network topology?

   a. Orchestration

   b. Management

   c. Control

   d. Data

11

**5.** Which component provides end-to-end visibility of applications with real-time information of application scores?

   **a.** vSmart

   **b.** vManage

   **c.** vEdge

   **d.** vAnalytics

**6.** In SD-WAN, what are gold, blue, bronze, green ?

   **a.** vSmart rainbow colors

   **b.** Private colors

   **c.** Public colors

   **d.** VPN colors

**7.** True or false: A vEdge device uses a native underlay IP address when using a private color.

   **a.** True

   **b.** False

**8.** In SD-WAN, what are mpls, metro-ethernet, and private1?

   **a.** vSmart rainbow colors

   **b.** Private colors

   **c.** Public colors

   **d.** VPN colors

**9.** Which route type contains firewall and VPN labels?

   **a.** OMP routes

   **b.** TLOC routes

   **c.** Service routes

   **d.** BGP routes

**10.** Which route type contains static and OSPF routes?

   **a.** OMP routes

   **b.** TLOC routes

   **c.** Service routes

   **d.** BGP routes

**11.** Attributes such as transport location identifier, origin, preference, and site ID are part of which type of routes?

   **a.** OMP routes

   **b.** TLOC routes

   **c.** Service routes

   **d.** BGP routes

**12.** Attributes such as TLOC private address, carrier, encapsulation type, and weight are part of which type of routes?

   **a.** OMP routes

   **b.** TLOC routes

   **c.** Service routes

   **d.** BGP routes

**13.** Which of the following are requirements for ZTP? (Choose two.)

   **a.** PnP Connect portal linked to CCW

   **b.** Provisioning file uploaded to vManage

   **c.** Configuration of the IP address, gateway IP address, and vBond IP address

   **d.** Configuration of the organization name, system IP address, and site ID

**14.** Which of the following are requirements for manual configuration? (Choose two.)

   **a.** PnP Connect portal linked to CCW

   **b.** Provisioning file uploaded to vManage

   **c.** Configuration of the IP address, gateway IP address, and vBond IP address

   **d.** Configuration of the organization name, system IP address, and site ID

**15.** What security model is used in the control plane?

   **a.** RBAC

   **b.** Hierarchical model

   **c.** Segmentation

   **d.** Zero Trust

**16.** What security feature is used in the management plane?

   **a.** RBAC

   **b.** Hierarchical model

   **c.** Segmentation

   **d.** Zero Trust

**17.** What is not a predefined vManage user group?

   **a.** Basic

   **b.** Operator

   **c.** SuperUser

   **d.** Netadmin

**18.** What are the hashing algorithm and preferred encryption with TLS/DTLS for SD-WAN? (Choose two.)

   **a.** SHA256

   **b.** SHA512

   **c.** AES-256-GCM

   **d.** CBC

**19.** Which of the following deploys vManage, vSmart, and vBond in a service provider's cloud infrastructure?

   **a.** On-premises deployment

   **b.** Managed SP deployment

   **c.** Cisco cloud deployment

   **d.** Hybrid deployment

11

**20.** Which of the following scales the orchestration, management, and control planes?

    **a.** Hierarchical network

    **b.** Data center

    **c.** Horizontal solution scaling

    **d.** vManage cluster

**21.** A site has two vEdge routers. Which of the following provides site redundancy for a Layer 2 LAN?

    **a.** OSPF

    **b.** VRRP

    **c.** Multiple vSmart controllers

    **d.** vManage cluster

**22.** A site has two vEdge routers. Which of the following provides site redundancy for a Layer 3 LAN?

    **a.** OSPF

    **b.** VRRP

    **c.** Multiple vSmart controllers

    **d.** vManage cluster

**23.** Which type of redundancy fails over to a second vEdge device at the data center?

    **a.** Site redundancy

    **b.** Transport redundancy

    **c.** Headend redundancy

    **d.** Controller redundancy

**24.** How are VPNs identified in SD-WAN?

    **a.** Color

    **b.** Number

    **c.** Name

    **d.** Interface

**25.** Which VPN is identified as VPN 512?

    **a.** System

    **b.** DTLS/TLS

    **c.** Management

    **d.** OMP

**26.** How are headers appended to an original packet in SD-WAN?

    **a.** IP-UDP-VPN-ESP-Packet

    **b.** IP-UDP-ESP-VPN-Packet

    **c.** VPN-IP-ESP-UDP-Packet

    **d.** ESP-VPN-IP-UDP-Packet

**27.** Which VPN topology connects all sites to each other?

    **a.** Point-to-point

    **b.** Hub-and-spoke

    **c.** Partial-mesh

    **d.** Full-mesh

**28.** Which VPN topology connects remote sites to a single site?

    **a.** Point-to-point

    **b.** Hub-and-spoke

    **c.** Partial-mesh

    **d.** Full-mesh

**29.** Which VPN topology connects one site to another single site?

    **a.** Point-to-point

    **b.** Hub-and-spoke

    **c.** Partial-mesh

    **d.** Full-mesh

**30.** Which VPN topology connects most sites directly to all other sites?

    **a.** Point-to-point

    **b.** Hub-and-spoke

    **c.** Partial-mesh

    **d.** Full-mesh

**31.** What technology gathers information about latency, jitter, and packet loss to measure performance of transport links in SD-WAN?

    **a.** SNMP

    **b.** BFD

    **c.** IPFIX

    **d.** Probes

**32.** The use of ACLs and QoS at a site is an example of which policy type?

    **a.** Centralized control policy

    **b.** Centralized data policy

    **c.** Localized data policy

    **d.** Localized control policy

**33.** The use of service chaining and traffic engineering for a site is an example of which policy type?

    **a.** Centralized control policy

    **b.** Centralized data policy

    **c.** Localized data policy

    **d.** Localized control policy

**34.** The customization of routing decisions is an example of which policy type?

    **a.** Centralized control policy

    **b.** Centralized data Policy

    **c.** Localized data policy

    **d.** Localized control policy

11

**35.** Which solution selects the optimal path based on real-time performance for different traffic types?

   **a.** BGP

   **b.** AAR

   **c.** OSFP

   **d.** LLQ

**36.** Which queuing technique is used in vEdge interface queue 2?

   **a.** WFQ

   **b.** LLQ

   **c.** WRR

   **d.** Tail drop

**37.** Which queuing technique is used in vEdge interface queue 0?

   **a.** WFQ

   **b.** LLQ

   **c.** WRR

   **d.** Tail drop

**38.** Which congestion-avoidance algorithm is used in queue 0?

   **a.** WFQ

   **b.** LLQ

   **c.** WRR

   **d.** Tail drop

**39.** By default, how are control and BFD traffic marked in SD-WAN?

   **a.** DSCP 48

   **b.** DSCP 46

   **c.** DSCP 30

   **d.** DSCP 34

**40.** How is multicast traffic routed in an SD-WAN overlay network?

   **a.** Via the RP

   **b.** Via the MPLS RP

   **c.** Via IGMPv2

   **d.** Via the replicator

**41.** Which of the following are benefits of DIA? (Choose two.)

   **a.** Reduced bandwidth and costs on the private WAN circuit

   **b.** Prioritized overlay traffic to the headend

   **c.** Improved user branch experience

   **d.** Linking of the underlay to the overlay

# CHAPTER 12

# Automation

**This chapter covers the following subjects:**

**Introduction to Network APIs and Protocols:** Application programming interfaces (APIs) enable software systems to talk to one another, and protocols are used to transport information between the systems.

**YANG, NETCONF, and RESTCONF Explored:** Yet Another Next Generation (YANG) is a data modeling language used to describe the data for network configuration protocols such as NETCONF and RESTCONF.

**IETF, OpenConfig, and Cisco YANG Models:** YANG data models are developed by industry standards bodies, such as the IETF and OpenConfig, and by specific vendors, such as Cisco.

**Model-Driven Telemetry:** Model-driven telemetry is a new concept for network monitoring in which data is streamed from network devices to subscribers, providing real-time configuration and state information.

This chapter covers automation, including network APIs, protocols, YANG, and model-driven telemetry. Expect plenty of questions on the ENSLD 300-420 exam about the selection and use of YANG with NETCONF and RESTCONF in enterprise networks. This chapter starts with an introduction to APIs and protocols and then looks at YANG, NETCONF, and RESTCONF. Next, it explores standards bodies and their impact on data models. Finally, this chapter covers model-driven telemetry and examines dial-in/dial-out approaches.

## "Do I Know This Already?" Quiz

The "Do I Know This Already?" quiz helps you identify your strengths and deficiencies in this chapter's topics. This quiz, derived from the major sections in the "Foundation Topics" portion of the chapter, helps you determine how to spend your limited study time. Table 12-1 outlines the major topics discussed in this chapter and the "Do I Know This Already?" quiz questions that correspond to those topics. You can find the answers in Appendix A, "Answers to the 'Do I Know This Already?' Quiz Questions Q&A Questions."

**Table 12-1** "Do I Know This Already?" Foundation Topics Section-to-Question Mapping

| Foundation Topics Section | Questions Covered in This Section |
|---|---|
| Introduction to Network APIs and Protocols | 1–2 |
| YANG, NETCONF, and RESTCONF Explored | 3–6 |
| IETF, OpenConfig, and Cisco YANG Models | 7–8 |
| Model-Driven Telemetry | 9–10 |

1. What data encoding format uses tags such as <> and </>?
   a. JSON
   b. XML
   c. BER
   d. Base64
2. Which of the following is an HTTP-based protocol that provides a programmatic interface for accessing YANG modeled data?
   a. SSH
   b. JSON
   c. NETCONF
   d. RESTCONF
3. Which of the following is a data modeling language used to describe the data for network configuration protocols such as NETCONF and RESTCONF?
   a. YANG
   b. SOAP
   c. Express
   d. gRPC
4. Inside the YANG data model, which of the following is used to group related nodes?
   a. Lists
   b. Attributes
   c. Containers
   d. Types
5. What network management protocol defined by the IETF supports running, candidate, and startup configuration data stores?
   a. NETCONF
   b. JSON
   c. RESTCONF
   d. SSH
6. Which of the following uses HTTP operations to provide create, retrieve, update, and delete (CRUD) operations on a NETCONF data store containing YANG data?
   a. XML
   b. JSON
   c. NETCONF
   d. RESTCONF
7. Which Internet standards body develops open standards by using open processes and working groups?
   a. OpenConfig
   b. IETF

    **c.** IANA

    **d.** ARIN

  **8.** Which of the following is a group of network operators working on developing programmable interfaces and tools for managing networks in a vendor-neutral way?

    **a.** IETF

    **b.** IANA

    **c.** ARIN

    **d.** OpenConfig

  **9.** Model-driven telemetry is a new concept for network monitoring in which data is streamed from network devices continuously to subscribers using a push model via which protocol?

    **a.** NETCONF

    **b.** RESTCONF

    **c.** XML

    **d.** HTML

  **10.** What type of subscription is useful for situations in which a data value changes occasionally but the information needs to be sent in a timely manner?

    **a.** On-change publication

    **b.** Dial-out

    **c.** Periodic publication

    **d.** Dial-in

## Foundation Topics

This chapter covers automation, data models, and protocol information that you need to master for the ENSLD 300-420 exam. It covers the YANG data models with IETF and Open-Config, along with NETCONF and RESTCONF protocols. In addition, this chapter describes model-driven telemetry and how it can be used to gather information from network devices.

# Introduction to Network APIs and Protocols

Application programming interfaces (APIs) are simply interfaces for software systems to talk to one another. An API has a set of requirements that describe how applications can communicate between themselves. For years, users have been communicating with applications through user interfaces (UIs) by viewing information and requesting data from the application. When a software system wants to communicate with another software system, that is where APIs come into play. However, we as users can also use APIs to talk to applications—just in a more software way instead of in a traditional UI way. Protocols are used to transport information between the systems using NETCONF and RESTCONF. We will explore these protocols in more detail in the coming sections.

## Network APIs and Protocol Concepts

APIs can help application developers enable features that end up helping end users. For example, a mobile application such as Yelp pulls location data from Google Maps via API calls to provide lists of locations of restaurants for Yelp's end users. Again, this is an example of a software system that wants to communicate with another software system. As another example, network management systems (NMSs) communicate via Simple Network Management Protocol (SNMP) to request and receive information from SNMP-enabled devices.

Simple Object Access Protocol (SOAP) is a mature standard from Microsoft that is used to build web services on the Internet. SOAP uses HTTP to transport messages using XML syntax.

Representational State Transfer (REST) is an API framework for simple web services that also uses HTTP methods such as GET, POST, PUT, and DELETE. REST is popular due to its performance, reliability, simplicity, and scalability.

The Network Configuration (NETCONF) protocol, which was standardized in 2006, leverages SSH- and XML-based encoding. NETCONF defines the transport and communication protocol and uses YANG for data.

The RESTCONF protocol provides a REST-like API for a network. RESTCONF, which was standardized in 2017, supports both XML and JSON representations and uses YANG for data.

Google RPC (gRPC) provides a general (open-source) framework. It is a functional subset of NETCONF and uses JSON representation. gRPC also supports unstructured data using the CLI and offers high performance.

## Evolution of Programmability

Back in 2003, RFC 3535 was published to provide an overview of a workshop held by the Internet Architecture Board (IAB) on network management. The goal was to continue the dialogue started between network operators and protocol developers. One of the notable recommendations from the network operators and developers was that the IETF should focus resources on the standardization of configuration management mechanisms.

Next, in 2006, NETCONF was defined in RFC 4741 and again in 2011, it was further defined in RFC 6241. The NETCONF protocol provides mechanisms to install, change, and delete network device configurations.

## Data Encoding Formats

As systems communicate with each other, there needs to be a structure behind what is communicated. Simple formatted text that is presented with **show** commands on a Cisco device will not work. However, systems can easily parse and work with data that is encoded in XML and JSON formats.

### JSON

JavaScript Object Notation (JSON) is a lightweight data-interchange text format. It is fairly easy to read and write and fairly easy for systems to understand and process. For example, take a look at the syntax that JSON uses for objects and arrays:

- Collections name/value pairs
  - Object { }
- Ordered list of values
  - Array [ ]

**12**

Figure 12-1 shows a simple example of JSON-formatted text.

```
[
    {
        "first_name": "John",
        "last_name": "Smith"
    },
    {
        "first_name": "James",
        "last_name": "Jordan"
    }
]
```

**Figure 12-1** *JSON Example*

## XML

Extensible Markup Language (XML) is a markup language similar to HTML that was designed to store and transport data. XML is data wrapped in tags and is both human readable and system readable. For example, notice the tags used to start and end text:

- Beginning and ending tags

    - <text>Hello, world!</text>

- Hierarchy of tags

    - Start tags <tx><houston>

    - End tags </Houston></tx>

Figure 12-2 shows an example of XML for a Gigabit Ethernet interface.

```
<GigabitEthernet>
    <name>1</name>
    <ip>
        <address>
            <primary>
                <address>10.0.0.1</address>
                <mask>255.255.255.0</mask>
            </primary>
        </address>
    </ip>
</GigabitEthernet>
```

**Figure 12-2** *XML Example*

## Data Models

A data model can be thought of as a well-understood and agreed upon way of describing something. A data model describes a controlled set of data, using well-defined parameters to standardize the representation of data. Let's consider an example of houses for sale. Here is a possible data model for houses for sale:

- **Location:** Houston, TX or Austin, TX

- **Bedrooms:** 3–5 bedrooms

- **Square feet:** 2500 to 5500

- **Total Bathrooms:** 2–3 Full and 1-2 Half

- **Lot size:** .25 acres to 7 or more acres

- **Property Type:** Singe Family, Condo, or Multi-Family

- **Price:** $149,000 to $675,000

## Model-Driven Programmability Stack

Model-driven programmability provides several advantages, including flexibility and modularity. Model-driven programmability is model based, structured, and system friendly. It provides support for multiple model types, from native and common to OpenConfig and IETF industry standards. Furthermore, models are decoupled from transport, protocols, and encoding. Model-driven APIs allow for abstraction and simplification.

In Figure 12-3, the model-driven programmability stack consists of six layers. At the bottom are YANG data models that are both native and open. Next are two transport protocols: SSH and HTTP. Above that is the protocol layer, including NETCONF, RESTCONF, and gRPC. The encoding layer has both JSON and XML. The API layer is next, with model-driven APIs using YANG. Finally, apps are at the top of the stack. We will further explore several of these components in this chapter.

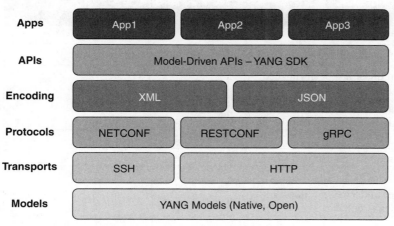

**Figure 12-3**  *Model-Driven Programmability Stack*

## REST

Web browsers use REST to get and post information to web servers or other systems that use HTTP. The same HTTP request methods and response codes are used.

Figure 12-4 shows a create, retrieve, update, and delete (CRUD) example with a client using HTTP POST, GET, PUT, and DELETE calls along with the response codes coming back from the server.

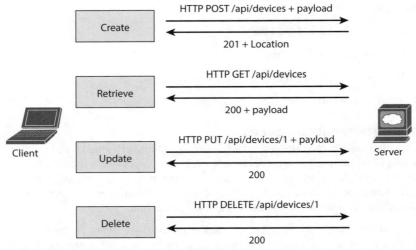

**Figure 12-4**  *Create, Retrieve, Update, and Delete (CRUD)*

Table 12-2 lists some common HTTP response codes.

**Table 12-2**   Common HTTP Response Codes

| Response Code | Description | | |
|---|---|---|---|
| *Success Messages (2xxx)* | | | |
| 200 | Request succeeded | | |
| 201 | The request has been fulfilled; new resource created | | |
| 204 | The server fulfilled the request but does not return a body | | |
| *Client Errors (4xx)* | | | |
| 400 | Bad request; malformed syntax | | |
| 401 | Unauthorized | | |
| 403 | Server understood request but refuses to fulfill it | | |
| *Server Errors (5xx)* | | | |
| 500 | Internal server error | | |
| 501 | Not implemented | | |

# YANG, NETCONF, and RESTCONF Explored

YANG is intertwined with NETCONF and RESTCONF, as they are all protocols used to manage configuration and state data.

Table 12-3 lists the Cisco-supported products for YANG, NETCONF, and RESTCONF.

**Table 12-3**   Cisco-Supported Products for YANG, NETCONF, and RESTCONF

| Cisco-Supported Products | YANG, NETCONF, and/or RESTCONF |
|---|---|
| Tail-f Network Control System | NETCONF/YANG |
| Tail-f Confd Agent | NETCONF/YANG |
| Open SDN Controller/OpenDaylight | NETCONF/YANG/RESTCONF |
| IOS XR | NETCONF/YANG |
| NX-OS | NETCONF |
| IOS XE | NETCONF |

## YANG Concepts

Yet Another Next Generation (YANG) is an IETF standard (RFC 6020) data modeling language used to describe the data for network configuration protocols such as NETCONF and RESTCONF. YANG is extensible, enabling the addition of new content to existing data models and new statements to the YANG language. YANG also has a limited scope: It is intended to describe network concepts in a tree structure along with data and types. YANG is intended to be very readable compared to other schema languages.

YANG data models can be displayed and represented in a variety of formats, including the following:

- YANG language

- Clear text

- XML

- JSON

- HTML/JavaScript

Figure 12-5 illustrates the NETCONF/YANG stack.

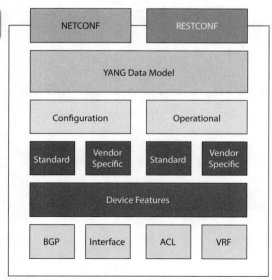

**Figure 12-5**   *NETCONF/YANG Stack*

A YANG module is a self-contained top-level hierarchy of nodes. A YANG module can also use submodules. It uses linkage statements such as **import** and **include**. Within a module, containers are used to group related nodes. Within a container, lists are used to identify nodes that are stored in a sequence. Inside lists, each individual attribute is referred to as a *leaf*, and attributes are used for things like names or descriptions. Each leaf also needs to have an associated type, such as Boolean or string.

Table 12-4 lists the common attributes for leaf values.

**Table 12-4**   Leaf Attributes

| Attribute | Description |
| --- | --- |
| config | Specifies whether this leaf is a configurable value ("true") or an operational value ("false") and is inherited from the parent container if not specified. |
| default | Specifies the default value for this leaf and implies that the leaf is optional. |
| mandatory | Specifies whether the leaf is mandatory ("true") or optional ("false"). |
| must | Specifies the XPath constraint that will be enforced for this leaf. |
| type | Specifies the data type (and range) of this leaf. |
| when | Indicates a conditional leaf, which is present only if the XPath expression is true. |
| description | Provides a human-readable definition and help text for the leaf. |
| reference | Provides a human-readable reference to some other element or spec. |
| units | Provides a human-readable unit specification (for example, Hz, Mbps, °F). |
| status | Indicates whether this leaf is current, deprecated, or obsolete. |

When versioning YANG modules, consider the following:

- Add a revision statement at the top.

- Update the organization, contact, and other information.

- Do not rename a module or namespaces.

- Do not remove obsolete definitions.

- Do not reorder data definitions.

YANG is used to describe both device data models and service data models. The following are examples of the device data model:

- Interface

- VLAN

- ACL

The following are examples of the service data model:

- Layer 3 MPLS VPN

- VRF

- Network ACL

## NETCONF Concepts

Network Configuration Protocol (NETCONF) is a network management protocol defined by the IETF in RFC 6241. NETCONF provides rich functionality for managing configuration and state data. The protocol operations are defined as remote procedure calls (RPCs) for requests and replies in XML-based representation. NETCONF supports running, candidate, and startup configuration data stores. The NETCONF capabilities are exchanged during session initiation. Transaction support is also a key NETCONF feature.

Figure 12-6 lists some key points for three NETCONF data stores: running, startup, and candidate.

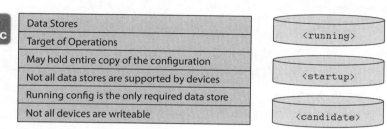

**Figure 12-6**  *NETCONF Data Stores*

Figure 12-7 shows the NETCONF model, which has four layers, and how NETCONF details map to it.

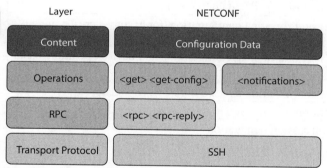

**Figure 12-7**  *The NETCONF Model*

NETCONF is a client/server protocol and is connection oriented over TCP. All NETCONF messages are encrypted with SSH and encoded with XML. A NETCONF manager is a client, and a NETCONF device is a server. The initial contents of the <hello> message define the NETCONF capabilities that each side supports. The YANG data model defines capabilities for the supported devices. In addition, other standards bodies and proprietary specifications define capabilities.

Figure 12-8 provides an example of the NETCONF <hello> operation. Notice that the capabilities are listed, and each one has either ietf or tail-f noted to indicate whether IETF or Tail-F proprietary specifications define the YANG data for that capability.

**12**

```
<?xml version="1.0" encoding="UTF-8"?>
<hello xmlns="urn:ietf:params:xml:ns:netconf:base:1.1">
<capabilities>
<capability>urn:ietf:params:netconf:base:1.1</capability>
<capability>urn:ietf:params:netconf:capability:writable-running:1.0</capability>
<capability>urn:ietf:params:netconf:capability:candidate:1.0</capability>
<capability>urn:ietf:params:netconf:capability:confirmed-commit:1.0</capability>
<capability>urn:ietf:params:netconf:capability:xpath:1.0</capability>
<capability>urn:ietf:params:netconf:capability:validate:1.0</capability>
<capability>urn:ietf:params:netconf:capability:rollback-on-error:1.0</capability>
<capability>http://tail-f.com/ns/netconf/with-defaults/1.0</capability>
<capability>http://tail-f.com/ns/netconf/actions/1.0</capability>
<capability>http://tail-f.com/ns/netconf/commit/1.0</capability>
<capability>http://tail-f.com/ns/example/dhcpd?module=dhcpd</capability>
<capability>urn:ietf:params:xml:ns:yang:ietf-inet-types?revision=2010-09-24&amp;module=ietf-inet-
types</capability>
</capabilities>
<session-id>5</session-id>
</hello>
```

**Figure 12-8** *NETCONF <hello> Operation*

Table 12-5 lists NETCONF protocol operations, which, as you can see, use XML-based encoding.

**Table 12-5** NETCONF Protocol Operations

| Operation | Description |
|---|---|
| <get-config> | Retrieves all or part of a specified configuration |
| <edit-config> | Loads all or part of a specified configuration (for example, create, merge, replace, delete) |
| <get> | Retrieves all or part of a running configuration and device operational data |
| <get-schema> | Retrieves the device schema |
| <lock> | Locks the entire configuration data store (that is, candidate) |
| <unlock> | Removes the lock on the entire configuration data store (that is, candidate) |
| <close-session> | Requests graceful session termination |

## RESTCONF Concepts

RESTCONF, which is defined in RFC 8040, is an HTTP-based protocol that provides a programmatic interface for accessing YANG modeled data. RESTCONF uses HTTP operations to provide create, retrieve, update, and delete (CRUD) operations on a NETCONF data store containing YANG data. RESTCONF is tightly coupled to the YANG data model definitions. IT supports HTTP-based tools and programming libraries. RESTCONF can be encoded in either XML or JSON.

Here is an example of a RESTCONF uniform resource identifier (URI):

`/restconf/<resource-type>/<yang-module:resource>`

RESTCONF uses data and operations (RPCs) for resource types within a RESTCONF URI.

Figure 12-9 shows JSON-formatted RESTCONF data and RPC operations and their associated URIs.

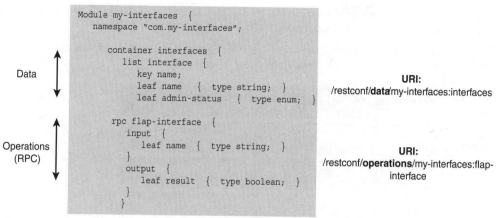

**Figure 12-9**  *RESTCONF API: URIs for Data or Operations*

Figure 12-10 shows JSON RESTCONF data illustrating containers and lists with URIs.

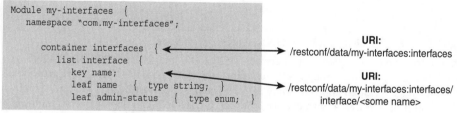

**Figure 12-10**  *RESTCONF API: Containers and Lists*

Table 12-6 shows the RESTCONF API CRUD operations GET, POST, PUT, and DELETE and associated URIs.

**Table 12-6**   RESTCONF CRUD Operations

| Operation | Description | URI |
|-----------|-------------|-----|
| GET | Gets a resource | *GET /restconf/data/my-interfaces:interfaces/ interface/<some name>* |
| POST | Creates a resource or invokes an operation | *POST /restconf/data/my-interfaces:flap-interface + JSON/XML Form Data* |
| PUT | Replaces a resource | *PUT /restconf/data/my-interfaces:interfaces/ interface/<some name>* <br> *+ JSON/XML Form Data* |
| DELETE | Removes a resource | *DELETE /restconf/data/ my-interfaces:interface/<some name>* |

## NETCONF and RESTCONF Compared

In many respects, NETCONF and RESTCONF are very similar. They both use the YANG data model and YANG development kits. They both are client/server based, with the controller being the client or the initiator and the server or receiver being the network element. They both use **ietf-yang-library** to either discover server capabilities (NETCONF) or list the features the server supports (RESTCONF). NETCONF and RESTCONF both use the concept of data stores, but RESTCONF uses the data stores defined in NETCONF.

Figure 12-11 shows a stack comparison of NETCONF and RESTCONF. As you can see, there are many similarities, especially in terms of YANG.

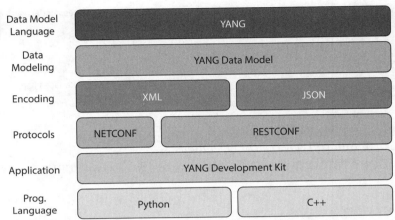

**Figure 12-11** *NETCONF and RESTCONF Stack Comparison*

Let's consider some of the differences between NETCONF and RESTCONF. NETCONF was developed first, in 2006, using XML encoding, and it uses SSH as a transport protocol. RESTCONF was developed approximately 10 years later to support both XML and JSON encoding, and it uses HTTP as a transport protocol. NETCONF can deploy across multiple devices by using a networkwide transaction. RESTCONF, on the other hand, has no concept of a transaction. A RESTCONF call uses HTTP PUT, POST, UPDATE, or DELETE methods to edit data resources represented by YANG data models. NETCONF includes the concept of a lock to stop operations while editing the configuration in the candidate data store; RESTCONF does not provide the concept of a lock; changes are directly applied.

Figure 12-12 illustrates the TCP/IP network frame format showing where NETCONF, RESTCONF, gRPC, and YANG are present within an IP packet.

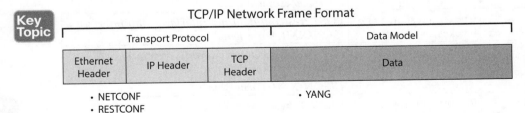

**Figure 12-12** *TCP/IP Network Frame Format*

# IETF, OpenConfig, and Cisco YANG Models

YANG data models are developed by industry standards bodies such as the IETF and OpenConfig or specific vendors such as Cisco.

## IETF

The Internet Engineering Task Force (IETF) is an Internet standards body that develops open standards through open processes. The IETF is a large international group of network designers, operators, vendors, and researchers who are focused on the evolution of Internet architecture. Their technical work within the IETF is done in working groups organized by topic into several areas. The YANG Model Coordination Group, for example, has been spending time on the inventory of YANG models in the industry, tooling aspects, training and education of NETCONF, YANG, pyang, and the model coordination for the IETF.

IETF data models are available on GitHub, at https://github.com/YangModels/yang.

## OpenConfig

OpenConfig is a group of network operators working on developing programmable interfaces and tools for managing networks in a vendor-neutral way using software-defined networking concepts and model-driven management and operations. OpenConfig focuses on building consistent sets of vendor-neutral data models written in YANG to support operational needs and requirements from various network operators. The data models are developed by OpenConfig or complied from third-party modules that use OpenConfig requirements. The developed YANG data models combine both configuration and operational data with support from multiple routing vendors, such as Cisco, Juniper, and Arista. OpenConfig collaborates with standards bodies and network equipment manufacturers; the goal is for the developed data models to become industry-standard interfaces that are widely adopted.

OpenConfig data models are available on GitHub, at https://github.com/openconfig/public.

## Cisco YANG Models

A Cisco YANG model is a collection of Cisco native, IETF, and OpenConfig YANG models that can be used with Cisco-based platforms. As of this writing, Cisco has YANG models that are specific to the IOS XR, NX-OS, and IOS XE Cisco platforms, divided into subdirectories on GitHub. Each subdirectory has further OS/platform information in a README file.

Cisco data models are available on GitHub, at https://github.com/YangModels/yang/tree/master/vendor/cisco.

# Model-Driven Telemetry

Model-driven telemetry is a new concept in network monitoring; it involves continuously streaming data from network devices to subscribers using a push model and providing real-time configuration and state information. You can define what data you want to subscribe to by using standard YANG models and the NETCONF protocol. Structured data is published at a defined cadence or as things change, based on the subscription criteria and data type.

Third-party applications can be used to collect data for monitoring and troubleshooting. Telemetry application subscriptions and their updates are transmitted over the NETCONF protocol. A NETCONF session is established using an SSH session to a network device.

## Streaming Telemetry Data

Streaming telemetry data can be used for analysis and troubleshooting purposes to maintain the health of the network. Streaming telemetry allows users to direct data to configured

12

receivers, where DevOps engineers can use the real-time operational information to find problems, look into issues, and optimize networks.

Using traditional models for collecting network data limits scalability and efficiency. Network administrators have been using tools like SNMP and CLI to get operational data from routers and switches for years. However, these methods do not provide automation and do not make it easy to gather useful data from network devices. One of the limitations is the use of the pull model, in which a client must request data from network devices. The pull model does not scale when there are several network management stations within the network.

A push model continuously streams data out of the network devices and sends it to the client. Telemetry makes the push model possible and enables near-real-time access to data monitoring.

There are two areas where streaming real-time telemetry data is useful:

- **Traffic optimization:** When things like link utilization and packet drops in the network are occurring quickly, traffic optimization allows for traffic rerouting, adding and removing links, and making modifications to QoS policies. This is faster than with SNMP polling intervals and enables quicker response times.

- **Preventive troubleshooting:** This type of troubleshooting helps detect and avoid failure situations faster after problematic network events occur.

Table 12-7 describes the three methods of steaming telemetry data.

**Table 12-7** Telemetry Methods

| Method | Description |
|---|---|
| Model-driven telemetry | Provides a mechanism to stream data from a model-driven telemetry–capable device to a receiver |
| Cadence-based telemetry | Continuously streams operational statistics and state transitions at a configured cadence or time frame |
| Policy-based telemetry | Streams data to a receiver using a policy file that defines the data to stream and the frequency for getting the data |

## Model-Driven Telemetry Concepts

Telemetry is an automated communication process by which measurements are collected and transmitted to receivers for monitoring of the data. Model-driven telemetry replaces the need for periodic polling of network elements using SNMP. Instead, it involves a continuous request for information to be delivered to a subscriber or receiver that has an established session with the network device. Data is received either periodically or as objects change via a subscribed set of YANG objects.

RFC 6241: Network Configuration Protocol (NETCONF) explains a YANG push model, which is a subscription and push mechanism for access to YANG databases. The YANG push model encompasses all of the data in the configuration and operational databases using the YANG model on the network device. However, a filter needs to be used for the data, as the subscription to all data is not supported.

All sessions in telemetry use NETCONF sessions, which impose any session limitation specific to the NETCONF implementation. High availability in telemetry for NETCONF sessions uses SSH to the active switch or a member in a switch stack. If a NETCONF session is broken, a new NETCONF session must be established, including sessions that carry telemetry subscriptions.

## Subscription Explained

To stream data in model-driven telemetry, the client application requests a subscription to a data set in YANG from the network device. A subscription is an agreement between the subscriber and the subscription service that describes the data to be pushed out. The subscription service allows clients to subscribe to the desired YANG data models, and then the network device pushes the data to the receiver per the agreed upon subscription model. There are two types of subscriptions: periodic and on-change publications. We will take a look at both of them in the upcoming sections.

Figure 12-13 illustrates subscriptions in model-driven telemetry.

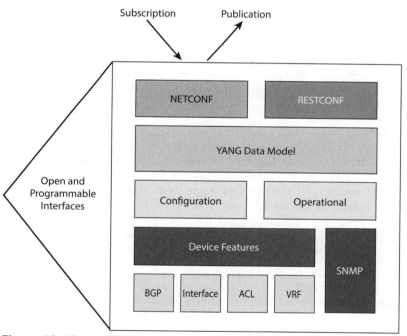

**Figure 12-13**  *Model-Driven Telemetry Subscriptions*

## Periodic Publication

Subscriptions that are periodic are streamed out to the receivers at specified intervals, such as every five seconds. With periodic publications, the network device continuously sends data for the lifetime of that configured subscription. A typical example where this type of periodic subscription is useful is for receiving data from PDU counters on a device.

Figure 12-14 shows sample output from the **show telemetry ietf subscription** command, using a period of 10 seconds. The period configuration in Figure 12-14 is for time and is in centiseconds, which is 1/100 of a second between updates.

12

```
ATL-DIST-SW01#  show telemetry ietf subscription 2147483668 detail

Telemetry subscription detail:

  Subscription ID: 2147483668
  State: Valid
  Stream: yang-push
  Encoding: encode-xml
  Filter:
    Filter type: xpath
    XPath: /cpu-usage/cpu-utilization/five-sconds
  Update policy:
    Update Trigger: periodic
    Period: 1000
  Notes:
```

**Figure 12-14** *Telemetry Subscription Detail from a Switch CLI*

### On-Change Publication

An on-change subscription streams out data only when a change in the data has occurred, such as when an interface or a neighbor relationship goes down. This type of subscription is useful for when a data value changes occasionally but the information needs to be sent in a timely manner. An on-change subscription capability must be described in a YANG module definition in order to prevent erroneous association to a YANG subscription. It is not recommended to use on-change subscriptions for frequently changing data values such as counters incrementing on an interface.

## Dial-In Approaches

In dial-in mode, a network device listens until the receiver dials in and sends the initial SYN packet to start the TCP connection. After the initial TCP connection is established, the network device pushes data out to the receiver at the configured interval. The network device acts as the server, and the receiver is the client. Don't let the direction of the SYN packet throw you off, as there is no polling mechanism in model-driven telemetry. The dial-in mode of the subscription is dynamic and terminates only when the receiver cancels the subscription or when the session is terminated. Dial-in mode uses a single channel to communicate via a single transport and protocol for both configuration data and streaming operational data.

Here are two examples of methods to request sensor paths in a dynamic subscription:

■ **OpenConfig RPC:** The **subscribe RPC** command is used to specify sensor paths and frequency. A subsequent **cancel RPC** command is used to remove the existing dynamic subscription.

■ **IOS XR MDT RPC:** With IOS XR, RPCs are used to subscribe or cancel configured subscriptions. The sensor paths and frequency are part of the telemetry configuration.

## Dial-Out Approaches

With dial-out mode, a network device dials out and sends the initial SYN packet to start the TCP connection to the receiver. This is the default mode of operation. In this mode, the network device acts as the client, and the receiver acts as the server. The network device continually attempts to establish a session and stream data to the receiver that has a valid subscription. The dial-out mode of subscriptions is persistent. If a session terminates for some reason, the network device continuously tries to establish a new session with the receiver every 30 seconds.

When using TCP dial-out, open a TCP socket on your receiver, and the network device starts the three-way TCP handshake and starts pushing telemetry data across the session. No complicated programming libraries are required on the receiver. If you are using Python, you need a simple **bind** command for the port. TCP dial-out takes advantage of the benefits of TCP, such as reliability, fragmentation, and reordering, and is a great place to start with model-driven telemetry.

## References and Recommended Readings

RFC 3535: *Overview of the 2002 IAB Network Management Workshop*, https://tools.ietf.org/html/rfc3535.

RFC 4741: *Network Configuration Protocol (NETCONF)*, https://tools.ietf.org/html/rfc4741.

RFC 6020: *YANG, A Data Modeling Language for the Network Configuration Protocol*, https://tools.ietf.org/html/rfc6020.

RFC 6241: *Network Configuration Protocol (NETCONF)*, https://tools.ietf.org/html/rfc6241.

RFC 8040: *RESTCONF Protocol*, https://tools.ietf.org/html/rfc8040.

Benoit Claise, "NETCONF Versus RESTCONF," https://www.claise.be/netconf-versus-restconf-capability-comparisons-for-data-model-driven-management-2/.

Cisco, "Advanced Topics in Cisco IOS Telemetry," https://www.ciscolive.com/c/dam/r/ciscolive/us/docs/2019/pdf/BRKSPG-2503.pdf.

Cisco, "Coding 1001: Intro to APIs and REST," https://www.ciscolive.com/c/dam/r/ciscolive/emea/docs/2018/pdf/DEVNET-3607.pdf.

Cisco, "Data Models Configuration Guide," https://www.cisco.com/c/en/us/td/docs/ios-xml/ios/datamodels/configuration/xe-16/data-models-xe-16-book/yang-netconf.html.

Cisco, "Getting Started with Model-Driven Programmability on Cisco Nexus 9000 Series Switches White Paper," https://www.cisco.com/c/en/us/products/collateral/switches/nexus-9000-series-switches/white-paper-c11-741518.html.

Cisco, "Getting the 'YANG' of It with Standard Data Models," https://developer.cisco.com/video/net-prog-basics/02-network_device_apis/yang.

Cisco, "A Model-Driven Approach to SDN with YANG, NETCONF/RESTCONF," https://www.ciscolive.com/c/dam/r/ciscolive/us/docs/2015/pdf/BRKSDN-1903.pdf.

Cisco, "Cisco Nexus 9000 Series NX-OS Programmability Guide, Release 9.2(x)," https://www.cisco.com/c/en/us/td/docs/switches/datacenter/nexus9000/sw/92x/programmability/guide/b-cisco-nexus-9000-series-nx-os-programmability-guide-92x/b-cisco-nexus-9000-series-nx-os-programmability-guide-92x_chapter_0100011.html.

Cisco, "Model-Driven Programmability," https://www.cisco.com/c/dam/m/en_us/service-provider/ciscoknowledgenetwork/files/586_05_03-16-saalvare-xr-mdp-ckn-may-2016-v8.pdf.

12

IETF, https://ietf.org.

Openconfig, http://openconfig.net/.

## Exam Preparation Tasks

As mentioned in the section "How to Use This Book" in the Introduction, you have a couple of choices for exam preparation: the exercises here, Chapter 13, "Final Preparation," and the exam simulation questions on the companion website.

## Review All Key Topics

Review the most important topics in the chapter, noted with the Key Topic icon in the outer margin of the page. Table 12-8 lists these key topics and the page number on which each is found.

**Table 12-8** Key Topics

| Key Topic Element | Description | Page |
|---|---|---|
| Paragraph | Network APIs and protocol concepts | 377 |
| Figure 12-1 | JSON example | 378 |
| Figure 12-2 | XML example | 378 |
| Paragraph | Data models | 378 |
| Figure 12-3 | Model-driven programmability stack | 379 |
| Figure 12-4 | Create, retrieve, update, and delete (CRUD) | 379 |
| Table 12-2 | Common HTTP response codes | 380 |
| Table 12-3 | Cisco-supported products for YANG, NETCONF, and RESTCONF | 381 |
| List | YANG concepts | 381 |
| Figure 12-5 | NETCONF/YANG stack | 381 |
| Table 12-4 | Leaf attributes | 382 |
| List | Device data model examples | 382 |
| Figure 12-6 | NETCONF data stores | 383 |
| Figure 12-7 | The NETCONF model | 383 |
| Figure 12-8 | NETCONF <hello> operation | 383 |
| Table 12-5 | NETCONF protocol operations | 384 |
| Figure 12-9 | RESTCONF API: URIs for data or operations | 384 |
| Figure 12-10 | RESTCONF API: Containers and lists | 385 |
| Table 12-6 | RESTCONF API: CRUD operations | 385 |
| Figure 12-11 | NETCONF and RESTCONF stack comparison | 386 |
| Figure 12-12 | TCP/IP network frame format | 386 |
| Paragraph | IETF, OpenConfig, and Cisco YANG models | 387 |
| List | Streaming real-time telemetry | 388 |

| Key Topic Element | Description | Page |
|---|---|---|
| Table 12-7 | Telemetry methods | 388 |
| Figure 12-13 | Model-driven telemetry subscriptions | 389 |
| Figure 12-14 | Telemetry subscription detail from a switch CLI | 390 |
| Paragraph | On-change publication | 390 |

## Complete Tables and Lists from Memory

Print a copy of Appendix D, "Memory Tables," found on the companion website, or at least the section for this chapter, and complete the tables and lists from memory. Appendix E, "Memory Tables Answer Key," includes completed tables and lists to check your work.

## Define Key Terms

Define the following key terms from this chapter and check your answers in the glossary:

dial-in mode, dial-out mode, Extensible Markup Language (XML), model-driven telemetry, Network Configuration Protocol (NETCONF), OpenConfig, periodic publication, RESTCONF, Yet Another Next Generation (YANG)

## Q&A

The answers to these questions appear in Appendix A. For more practice with exam format questions, use the exam engine on the companion website.

1.  Which of the following does Simple Object Access Protocol (SOAP) use to transport messages using XML-based syntax?

    a.  HTML

    b.  SSH

    c.  NETCONF

    d.  HTTP

2.  Which of the following is an open-source framework project and is a functional subset of NETCONF with JSON representation?

    a.  XML

    b.  SOAP

    c.  gRPC

    d.  YANG

3.  Which of the following is a lightweight data-interchange text format that is fairly easy to read and write and easy for systems to understand?

    a.  JSON

    b.  REST

    c.  NETCONF

    d.  RESTCONF

12

4. What network management protocol uses protocol operations that are defined as remote procedure calls (RPCs) for requests and replies in XML-based representation?

   a. XML

   b. SSH

   c. JSON

   d. NETCONF

5. Which of the following is a data modeling language used to describe the data for network configuration protocols such as NETCONF and RESTCONF?

   a. YANG

   b. RPC

   c. REST

   d. XML

6. Which of the following are service data models? (Choose two.)

   a. Interface

   b. Layer 3 MPLS VPN

   c. ACL

   d. VRF

7. Select the three data stores that NETCONF uses? (Choose three.)

   a. running

   b. archive

   c. candidate

   d. startup

8. What are the resource types in a RESTCONF URI? (Choose two.)

   a. schema

   b. data

   c. operations

   d. edit-config

9. Which of the following CRUD operations creates a resource or invokes an operation?

   a. GET

   b. PUT

   c. POST

   d. DELETE

10. What group is focused on building consistent sets of vendor-neutral data models written in YANG to support operational needs and requirements from various network operators?

    a. IETF

    b. IANA

    c. ARIN

    d. OpenConfig

**11.** What protocol provides a programmatic interface for accessing YANG modeled data with either XML or JSON encoding?

**a.** RESTCONF

**b.** NETCONF

**c.** OpenConfig

**d.** REST

**12.** With model-driven telemetry, which mode initiates the connection from the network device to start the TCP connection to the receiver?

**a.** Dial-in

**b.** On-change

**c.** Dial-out

**d.** Periodic

**13.** With a dynamic subscription, which methods are used to request sensor paths? (Choose two.)

**a.** IOS XR MDT RPC

**b.** IETF RPC

**c.** OpenConfig RPC

**d.** Cisco YANG RPC

**14.** Which subscriptions are streamed out to the receivers at specified intervals such as 5 seconds?

**a.** OpenConfig RPCs

**b.** IOS XR MDT RPCs

**c.** On-change publications

**d.** Periodic publications

**15.** What method of telemetry streams data to a receiver using a policy file that defines the data to stream and the frequency to get the data?

**a.** Policy-based telemetry

**b.** Cadence-based telemetry

**c.** Model-driven telemetry

**d.** Periodic publication

**16.** Which of the following is a new concept in network monitoring in which data is continuously streamed from network devices to subscribers using a push model, providing real-time configuration and state information?

**a.** Cisco YANG models

**b.** Model-driven telemetry

**c.** NETCONF

**d.** RESTCONF

**17.** What API call uses HTTP PUT, POST, UPDATE, or DELETE methods to edit data resources represented by YANG data models?

**a.** NETCONF

**b.** REST

12

    **c.** RESTCONF

    **d.** Postman

**18.** What do NETCONF and RESTCONF have in common?

    **a.** JSON encoding

    **b.** Use of **ietf-yang-library**

    **c.** Lock operations

    **d.** Transactions

**19.** Where in the TCP/IP network frame format does the YANG data model reside?

    **a.** Ethernet header

    **b.** IP header

    **c.** TCP header

    **d.** Data

**20.** Which of the following CRUD operations gets a resource?

    **a.** GET

    **b.** POST

    **c.** PUT

    **d.** DELETE

**21.** Which of the following NETCONF protocol operations retrieves all or part of a running configuration and device operational data?

    **a.** <get-config>

    **b.** <edit-config>

    **c.** <get>

    **d.** <get-schema>

**22.** Inside a YANG data model, what are used to identify nodes that are stored in a sequence?

    **a.** Attributes

    **b.** Lists

    **c.** Submodules

    **d.** Leafs

**23.** Which of the following Cisco products supports NETCONF, YANG, and RESTCONF?

    **a.** NX-OS

    **b.** IOS XE

    **c.** IOS XR

    **d.** Open SDN Controller/OpenDaylight

**24.** Which of the following is a TCP transport protocol that RESTCONF and gRPC use?

    **a.** HTTP

    **b.** SSH

    **c.** FTP

    **d.** SFTP

**25.** Which of the following is an API framework for simple web services that uses GET, POST, PUT, and DELETE methods?

  **a.** RESTCONF

  **b.** NETCONF

  **c.** REST

  **d.** JSON

**26.** Which of the following is data wrapped in tags that is both human readable and system readable?

  **a.** JSON

  **b.** NETCONF

  **c.** RESTCONF

  **d.** XML

**27.** Inside a YANG data model, what is used inside lists to describe things like a name or a description?

  **a.** Leafs

  **b.** Containers

  **c.** Modules

  **d.** Submodules

**28.** Which of the following is a collection of Cisco native, IETF, and OpenConfig YANG models that can be used with Cisco-based platforms?

  **a.** REST model

  **b.** SOAP model

  **c.** Tail-f model

  **d.** Cisco YANG model

**29.** Which of the following streams out data only when a change in the data has occurred, such as when an interface or a neighbor relationship goes down?

  **a.** Dial-in

  **b.** On-change publication

  **c.** Periodic publication

  **d.** Dial-out

**30.** With model-driven telemetry, which mode listens until the receiver sends the initial SYN packet to start the TCP connection?

  **a.** Dial-in

  **b.** Dial-out

  **c.** Periodic

  **d.** On-change

12

# CHAPTER 13

# Final Preparation

The first 12 chapters of this book cover the technologies, protocols, design concepts, and considerations required to be prepared to pass the 300-420 CCNP Designing Cisco Enterprise Networks ENSLD exam. While those chapters supply the detailed information, most people need more preparation than simply reading the first 12 chapters of this book. This chapter provides a set of tools and a study plan to help you complete your preparation for the exams.

This short chapter has three main sections. The first section helps you get ready to take the exam, and the second section lists the exam preparation tools useful at this point in the study process. The third section provides a suggested study plan you can use now that you have completed all the earlier chapters in this book.

## Getting Ready

Here are some important tips to keep in mind to ensure that you are ready for this rewarding exam:

- **Build and use a study tracker:** Consider using the exam objectives shown in this chapter to build a study tracker for yourself. Such a tracker can help ensure that you have not missed anything and that you are confident for your exam. As a matter of fact, this book offers a sample study planner as a website supplement.

- **Think about your time budget for questions on the exam:** When you do the math, you will see that, on average, you have one minute per question. While this does not sound like a lot of time, keep in mind that many of the questions will be very straightforward, and you will take 15 to 30 seconds on those. This leaves you extra time for other questions on the exam.

- **Watch the clock:** Check in on the time remaining periodically as you are taking the exam. You might even find that you can slow down pretty dramatically if you have built up a nice block of extra time.

- **Get some earplugs:** The testing center might provide earplugs, but get some just in case and bring them along. There might be other test takers in the center with you, and you do not want to be distracted by their screams. I personally have no issue blocking out the sounds around me, so I never worry about this, but I know it is an issue for some.

- **Plan your travel time:** Give yourself extra time to find the center and get checked in. Be sure to arrive early. As you test more at a particular center, you can certainly start cutting it closer time-wise.

- **Online testing:** If participating in online testing ensure that you have performed and passed the online system check. For more information, check here: https://www.cisco.com/c/en/us/training-events/training-certifications/online-exam-proctoring.html#~requirements

- **Get rest:** Most students report that getting plenty of rest the night before the exam boosts their success. All-night cram sessions are not typically successful.

- **Bring in valuables, but get ready to lock them up:** The testing center will take your phone, your smartwatch, your wallet, and other such items and will provide a secure place for them.

- **Take notes:** You will be given note-taking implements and should not be afraid to use them. I always jot down any questions I struggle with on the exam. I then memorize them at the end of the test by reading my notes over and over again. I always make sure I have a pen and paper in the car, and I write down the issues in my car just after the exam. When I get home—with a pass or fail—I research those items!

# Tools for Final Preparation

This section lists some information about the available tools and how to access them.

## Pearson Cert Practice Test Engine and Questions on the Website

Register this book to get access to the Pearson IT Certification test engine (software that displays and grades a set of exam-realistic multiple-choice questions). Using the Pearson Cert Practice Test Engine, you can either study by going through the questions in Study mode or take a simulated (timed) 300-420 CCNP Designing Cisco Enterprise Networks ENSLD exam.

The Pearson Test Prep practice test software comes with two full practice exams. These practice tests are available to you either online or as an offline Windows application. To access the practice exams that were developed with this book, please see the instructions in the card inserted in the sleeve in the back of the book. This card includes a unique access code that enables you to activate your exams in the Pearson Test Prep software.

### Accessing the Pearson Test Prep Software Online

The online version of this software can be used on any device with a browser and connectivity to the Internet, including desktop machines, tablets, and smartphones. To start using your practice exams online, simply follow these steps:

**Step 1.** Go to http://www.PearsonTestPrep.com.

**Step 2.** Select **Pearson IT Certification** as your product group.

**Step 3.** Enter your email and password for your account. If you don't have an account on PearsonITCertification.com or CiscoPress.com, you need to establish one by going to PearsonITCertification.com/join.

**Step 4.** In the **My Products** tab, click the **Activate New Product** button.

**Step 5.** Enter the access code printed on the insert card in the back of your book to activate your product. The product is then listed in your My Products page.

**Step 6.** Click the Exams button to launch the exam settings screen and start the exam.

### Accessing the Pearson Test Prep Software Offline

If you wish to study offline, you can download and install the Windows version of the Pearson Test Prep software. You can find a download link for this software on the book's companion website, or you can just enter this link in your browser:

http://www.pearsonitcertification.com/content/downloads/pcpt/engine.zip

To access the book's companion website and the software, simply follow these steps:

**Step 1.**  Register your book by going to PearsonITCertification.com/register and entering the ISBN **9780136575191**.

**Step 2.**  Respond to the challenge questions.

**Step 3.**  Go to your account page and select the Registered Products tab.

**Step 4.**  Click on the Access Bonus Content link under the product listing.

**Step 5.**  Click the Install Pearson Test Prep Desktop Version link in the Practice Exams section of the page to download the software.

**Step 6.**  When the software finishes downloading, unzip all the files onto your computer.

**Step 7.**  Double-click the application file to start the installation and follow the onscreen instructions to complete the registration.

**Step 8.**  When the installation is complete, launch the application and click the Activate Exam button on the My Products tab.

**Step 9.**  Click the Activate a Product button in the Activate Product Wizard.

**Step 10.**  Enter the unique access code from the card in the sleeve in the back of your book and click the Activate button.

**Step 11.**  Click Next and then click the Finish button to download the exam data to your application.

**Step 12.**  You can now start using the practice exams by selecting the product and clicking the Open Exam button to open the exam settings screen.

Note that the offline and online versions sync together, so saved exams and grade results recorded on one version will be available to you in the other version as well.

## Customizing Your Exams

When you are in the exam settings screen, you can choose to take exams in one of three modes:

- Study mode
- Practice Exam mode
- Flash Card mode

Study mode allows you to fully customize an exam and review answers as you are taking the exam. This is typically the mode you use first to assess your knowledge and identify information gaps. Practice Exam mode locks certain customization options in order to present a realistic exam experience. Use this mode when you are preparing to test your exam readiness. Flash Card mode strips out the answers and presents you with only the question stem. This mode is great for late-stage preparation, when you really want to challenge yourself to provide answers without the benefit of seeing multiple-choice options. This mode does not provide the detailed score reports that the other two modes provide, so it is not the best mode for helping you identify knowledge gaps.

In addition to these three modes, you will be able to select the source of your questions. You can choose to take exams that cover all of the chapters, or you can narrow your selection to just a single chapter or the chapters that make up specific parts in the book. All chapters are selected by default. If you want to narrow your focus to individual chapters, simply deselect all the chapters and then select only those on which you wish to focus in the Objectives area.

You can also select the exam banks on which to focus. Each exam bank comes complete with a full exam of questions that cover topics in every chapter. The two exams printed in the book are available to you, as are two additional exams of unique questions. You can have the test engine serve up exams from all four banks or just from one individual bank by selecting the desired banks in the exam bank area.

There are several other customizations you can make to your exam from the exam settings screen, such as the time allowed for taking the exam, the number of questions served up, whether to randomize questions and answers, whether to show the number of correct answers for multiple-answer questions, and whether to serve up only specific types of questions. You can also create custom test banks by selecting only questions that you have marked or questions on which you have added notes.

## Updating Your Exams

If you are using the online version of the Pearson Test Prep software, you should always have access to the latest version of the software as well as the exam data. If you are using the Windows desktop version, every time you launch the software, it will check to see if there are any updates to your exam data and automatically download any changes since the last time you used the software. This requires that you be connected to the Internet at the time you launch the software.

Sometimes, due to a number of factors, the exam data might not fully download when you activate your exam. If you find that figures or exhibits are missing, you might need to manually update your exams.

To update a particular exam you have already activated and downloaded, simply select the **Tools** tab and click the **Update Products** button. Again, this is only an issue with the desktop Windows application.

If you wish to check for updates to the Windows desktop version of the Pearson Test Prep exam engine software, simply select the **Tools** tab and click the **Update Application** button. Doing so allows you to ensure that you are running the latest version of the software engine.

### Premium Edition

In addition to the free practice exam provided on the website, you can purchase additional exams with expanded functionality directly from Pearson IT Certification. The Premium Edition of this title contains an additional two full practice exams and an eBook (in both

13

PDF and ePub format). In addition, the Premium Edition title has remediation for each question to the specific part of the eBook that relates to that question.

Because you have purchased the print version of this title, you can purchase the Premium Edition at a deep discount. There is a coupon code in the book sleeve that contains a one-time-use code and instructions for where you can purchase the Premium Edition.

To view the premium edition product page, go to www.informit.com/title/9780136590750.

### Chapter-Ending Review Tools

Chapters 1 through 12 each have several features in the "Exam Preparation Tasks" section at the end of the chapter. You might have already worked through these in each chapter. It can also be useful to use these tools again as you make your final preparations for the exam.

## Suggested Plan for Final Review/Study

This section lists a suggested study plan from the point at which you finish reading through Chapter 12 until you take the 300-420 CCNP Designing Cisco Enterprise Networks ENSLD exam. You can ignore this plan, use it as is, or take suggestions from it.

The plan involves two steps:

**Step 1.**   **Review key topics and "Do I Know This Already?" (DIKTA?) questions:** You can use the table that lists the key topics in each chapter or just flip the pages, looking for key topics. Also, reviewing the DIKTA? questions from the beginning of the chapter can be helpful for review.

**Step 2.**   **Use the Pearson Cert Practice Test engine to practice:** The Pearson Cert Practice Test engine allows you to study using a bank of unique exam-realistic questions available only with this book.

## Summary

The tools and suggestions listed in this chapter have been designed with one goal in mind: to help you develop the skills required to pass the 300-420 CCNP Designing Cisco Enterprise Networks ENSLD exam. This book has been developed from the beginning to not just tell you the facts but help you learn how to apply the facts. No matter what your experience level leading up to when you take the exam, it is our hope that the broad range of preparation tools, and even the structure of the book, will help you pass the exam with ease. We hope you do well on the exam.

# Answers to the "Do I Know This Already?" Quiz Questions Q&A Questions

## "Do I Know This Already?" Answers

### Chapter 1

1. B. Private IPv4 address blocks are 10.0.0.0 to 10.255.255.255, 172.16.0.0 to 172.31.255.255.255, and 192.168.0.0 to 192.168.255.255.0.

2. B. There are 5 host bits: $2^5 - 2 = 30$ hosts.

3. D. Loopback addresses should have a /32 mask so that address space is not wasted.

4. C. The precedence bits are located in the Type of Service field of the IPv4 header.

5. B. Multicast addresses range from 224.0.0.1 to 239.255.255.255.

6. D. The summary route summarizes subnetworks from 150.10.192.0/24 to 150.10.199.0/24. Answer D is the only one that includes them.

7. D. Point-to-point links need only two host addresses. They use a /30 mask, which provides $2^2 - 2 = 2$ host addresses.

8. C. DHCP assigns IP addresses dynamically.

9. C. Static NAT is used to statically translate public IP addresses to private IP addresses.

10. C. The DS field allocates 6 bits in the ToS field, thus making it capable of 64 distinct codepoints.

### Chapter 2

1. C. IPv6 uses 128 bits for addresses, and IPv4 uses 32 bits, so the difference is 96.

2. C. The IPv6 header is 40 bytes in length.

3. C. The defining first hexadecimal digits for link-local addresses are FE8.

4. D. IPv6 addresses can be unicast, anycast, or multicast.

5. B. Answers A and C are incorrect because you cannot use the double colons (::) twice. Answers C and D are also incorrect because you cannot reduce b100 to b1.

6. C. DNS64 is a DNS mechanism that synthesizes AAAA records from A records.

7. B. The IPv6 multicast address type handles broadcasts.

8. B. The IPv6 loopback address is ::1.

9. A. IPv4-compatible IPv6 addresses have the format ::d.d.d.d.

10. C. The DNS maps fully qualified domain names to IPv6 addresses using (AAAA) records.

11. B. IPv6 increases the address space, which allows globally unique IP addresses. Broadcasts are no longer used.

12. C.

13. D.

14. B. IP Migrate is not an IPv4-to-IPv6 migration strategy

## Chapter 3

1. B. The default metric for interfaces for IS-IS is 10.

2. D. Both Level 2 and Level 1/2 routers are used to interconnect IS-IS areas.

3. A. RIPv2 is a classless distance-vector routing protocol.

4. B. Distance-vector routing protocols send periodic updates.

5. B. In IS-IS, every interface has a default metric of 10.

6. B. If bandwidth is used, the path with the highest bandwidth is selected. If cost is used, the path with the lowest cost is selected.

7. B. OSPF has an administrative distance of 110. EIGRP has an administrative distance of 90. The route with the lower administrative distance is selected: EIGRP.

8. B. The feasible successor satisfies the feasibility condition and is maintained as a backup route.

9. B. The default metrics for EIGRP are bandwidth and delay.

10. C. EIGRP implements DUAL.

## Chapter 4

1. C. In OSPF, summarization of internal routes is performed on the ABRs.

2. D. Weight is assigned locally on a router to specify a preferred path if multiple paths exist out of a router for a destination.

3. B. OSPF defines the ASBR as the router that injects external routes into the OSPF autonomous system.

4. E. OSPFv2 Type 5 LSAs are autonomous system external LSAs.

5. C. OSPFv2 routers use 224.0.0.6 to communicate with DRs.

6. A. Type 1 LSAs (router LSAs) are forwarded to all routers within an OSPF area.

7. D. Intra-area-prefix LSAs carry IPv6 prefixes associated with a router, a stub network, or an associated transit network segment.

8. B. You use External Border Gateway Protocol (eBGP) to exchange routes between autonomous systems.

9. B. It is a best practice to summarize routes on the distribution routers toward the core.

10. A. The administrative distance of eBGP routes is 20. The administrative distance of Internal BGP (iBGP) routes is 200.

## Chapter 5

1. B. You use IGMP between hosts and local routers to register with multicast groups.
2. B. The lower 23 bits of the IP multicast address are mapped to the last 23 bits of the Layer 2 MAC address.
3. C. SNMPv3 introduces authentication and encryption for SNMP.
4. A. Managed devices contain SNMP agents.
5. C. An OOB management network uses separate infrastructure.
6. C. SSM eliminates the RPs and shared trees and only builds a SPT.
7. C. The NMS manager uses the GetBulk operation to retrieve large blocks of data, such as multiple rows in a table.
8. A. RMON1 is focused on the data link and physical layers of the OSI model.
9. B. Community is not an SNMP operation.
10. A. Source trees are also called shortest-path trees (SPTs) because they create paths without having to go through a rendezvous point (RP).

## Chapter 6

1. B. The core layer is responsible for fast transport.
2. C. The maximum distance for 100BASE-T is 100 meters.
3. C. The distribution layer is responsible for security filtering, address and area aggregation, and media translation.
4. C. Multimode fiber provide a cost-effective solution for that distance. Single-mode fiber is more expensive. UTP's maximum distance is 100 meters.
5. C. PortFast bypasses the listening/learning phase for access ports and goes directly to the port-forwarding state.
6. C. The maximum power per PSE port for Cisco UPOE is 60W; for PoE it is 15.4W, for PoE+ it is 30W, and for Cisco UPOE+ it is 90W.
7. B. Wake on LAN (WoL) is a combination of hardware and software technologies to wake up sleeping systems. The WoL feature allows an administrator to remotely power up all sleeping machines so that they can receive updates.
8. D. The access layer functions are high availability, port security, rate limiting, ARP inspection, and trust classification.

## Chapter 7

1. A. In the Layer 3 access layer, there is no need for an FHRP.
2. B and C. HSRP and VRRP provide default gateway redundancy.
3. B. 20% of traffic is local and 80% is external to the local LAN.
4. B. Routes are summarized at the distribution layer.
5. D. Use EtherChannel to merge the two physical units into one.
6. C. This is a peer-to-peer application.

Appendix A: Answers to the "Do I Know This Already?" Quiz Questions Q&A Questions   407

A

**7.** C. Virtual Router Redundancy Protocol (VRRP) is an IETF standard.

**8.** D. Stacking switch technology allows you to increase the number of ports in the access layer while still using the same uplinks and ports in the distribution layer.

## Chapter 8

**1.** C. Internet, remote-access DMZ, and service provider edge are the only modules or blocks used in the enterprise edge.

**2.** D. E-commerce and remote-access services use the DMZ in the enterprise edge.

**3.** C. 4G LTE Advanced download peak rates are up to 600 Mbps, and upload peak rates are up to 100 Mbps.

**4.** A and D. Both VPWS and VPLS are Layer 2 VPN technologies that service providers offer.

**5.** D. Multiprotocol Label Switching (MPLS) uses labels appended to IP packets or Layer 2 frames for the transport of data.

**6.** D. Dense wavelength-division multiplexing (DWDM) increases the bandwidth capabilities of fiber by using different wavelengths of light called *channels* over the same fiber strand.

**7.** A. GETVPN is not typically used on the Internet because NAT does not work due to the original IP addressing preservation.

**8.** D. VPWS provides a point-to-point WAN link between two sites over an MPLS provider backbone.

**9.** A. Dynamic Multipoint VPN (DMVPN) is a Cisco IOS solution for building IPsec over GRE VPNs in a dynamic and scalable manner.

**10.** D. MPLS labels can be used to implement traffic engineering by overriding the routing tables with specific paths through the network.

## Chapter 9

**1.** C. Throughput is the measure of data transferred from one host to another in a given amount of time.

**2.** A. Modularity with additional devices, services, and technologies is a description of the key design principle scalability.

**3.** D. 8756 / 8760 × 100 yields the availability percentage, which is 99.95%.

**4.** C. The highest level of resiliency for services avoids single points of failures for both the router and the circuits by using dual routers with one circuit per router.

**5.** A. To eliminate single points of failures on both routers and circuits, you need dual routers with one circuit per router.

**6.** B. Adding a secondary WAN link makes the network more fault tolerant by allowing for both a backup link and load sharing.

**7.** D. Low-latency queuing (LLQ) adds a strict priority queue to CBWFQ.

**8.** A. Congestion management is a mechanism to handle traffic overflow using a queuing algorithm.

9.  B. IntServ uses Resource Reservation Protocol (RSVP) to explicitly request QoS for the application along the end-to-end path through devices in the network.

10.  A. The token bucket technique uses traffic shaping to release the packets into the output queue at a preconfigured rate.

## Chapter 10

1.  A. Automation, policy, and assurance are key benefits of SD-Access; compatibility is not.

2.  A and C. The SD-Access fabric and Cisco DNA Center are two main components of SD-Access architecture.

3.  D. The two main things that LISP keeps track of are the routing locator (RLOC) or router location and the endpoint identifier (EID), which is the IP address or MAC address.

4.  C. Cisco ISE is tightly integrated with DNA Center through REST APIs to provide the SGT information needed to enforce policy.

5.  B. With the over-the-top method of wireless integration with the SD-Access fabric, the control plane and data plane traffic from the APs use CAPWAP-based tunnels.

6.  A. Microsegmentation enables data plane isolation and provides a simple way to manage group-based policies between groups of endpoints with a VN.

7.  D. Medium sites can support up to 25,000 endpoints and up to 64 VNs.

8.  D. Multicast Source Discovery Protocol (MSDP) can be used for RP redundancy.

9.  A. There are 16 million VNI segments possible with VXLAN.

10.  D. The fusion router fuses the SD-Access VNs into the organization's GRT of the external network.

## Chapter 11

1.  B. vSmart is the brains of the SD-WAN architecture.

2.  D. vBond performs the initial authentication of vEdge devices and orchestrates vSmart and vEdge connectivity.

3.  B. With manual configuration, a site network administrator manually configures minimal information that allows a vEdge device to connect with the vBond orchestrator.

4.  OMP advertises prefix, TLOC, and service routes.

5.  D. VRRP is used for Layer 2 redundancy.

6.  B. The BFD probes provide information about latency, jitter, and loss on all the transport links.

7.  B. In the control plane, add a vSmart controller to increase capacity.

8.  C. Cisco SD-WAN supports only PIM-SM.

Appendix A: Answers to the "Do I Know This Already?" Quiz Questions Q&A Questions    409

A

## Chapter 12

1.  B. XML is the data encoding format that uses these tags.
2.  D. RESTCONF is an HTTP-based protocol that provides a programmatic interface for accessing YANG data.
3.  A. YANG is a data modeling language used to describe the data for network configuration protocols.
4.  C. Containers are used to group related nodes in a YANG data model.
5.  A. NETCONF is defined by the IETF and supports running, candidate, and startup configuration data stores.
6.  D. RESTCONF uses HTTP operations to provide create, retrieve, update, and delete (CRUD) operations on a NETCONF data store.
7.  B. The IETF is an Internet standards body that develops open standards using open processes and working groups.
8.  D. OpenConfig is a group of network operators working on developing programmable interfaces and tools for managing networks in a vendor-neutral way.
9.  A. Model-driven telemetry is a new concept for network monitoring in which data is streamed from network devices continuously to subscribers using NETCONF.
10. C. A periodic publication is a subscription that is useful for when a data value changes occasionally but the information needs to be sent in a timely manner.

# Quiz Answers

## Chapter 1

1.  10/8, 172.16/12 (172.16.0.0 to 172.31.255.255), and 192.168/16.
2.  True. You can use DHCP to specify several host IP configuration parameters, including IP address, mask, default gateway, DNS servers, and TFTP server.
3.  False. The bit-number representation of 255.255.255.248 is /29. /28 is the same mask as 255.255.255.240.
4.  True.
5.  20 (bytes).
6.  DSCP uses 6 bits, which provides 64 levels of classification.
7.  True.
8.  False. The header checksum field only includes a checksum of the IP header; it does not check the data portion.
9.  The subnet is 172.56.4.0/22, the address range is from 172.56.4.1 to 172.56.7.254, and the subnet broadcast is 172.56.7.255.
10. The IP layer in the destination host.
11. B. DHCP configures the IP address, subnet mask, default gateway, and other optional parameters.
12. C. Class B networks have 16 bits for host addresses with the default mask: $2^{16} - 2 = 65,534$.

**13.**   B. A /26 mask has 26 network bits and 6 host bits.

**14.**   C. Network 192.170.20.16 with a prefix of /29 summarizes addresses from 192.170.20.16 to 192.170.20.23.

**15.**   B. AF3 is backward compatible with IP precedence priority traffic with a binary of 011.

**16.**   A. IPv4 packets can be fragmented by the sending host and routers.

**17.**   B. Multicast addresses are received by a set of hosts subscribed to the multicast group.

**18.**   B, D, and E. The three types of IPv4 address are unicast, broadcast, and multicast.

**19.**   A, C, and D. End-user workstations, Cisco IP phones, and mobile devices should have their IP addresses assigned dynamically.

**20.**   B. Dynamic name resolution reduces administrative overhead. Name-to-IP address tables do not need to be configured.

**21.**   B. There are 4 bits to determine the number of host addresses: $2^4 - 2 = 16 - 2 = 14$.

**22.**   B. Answer B allows up to 6 hosts. Answer A allows only 2 hosts, which is too small. Answer C allows 14 hosts, which is larger than Answer B.

**23.**   D, G, and I.

**24.**   C. PAT.

**25.**   C. RIPE.

**26.**   B. VLSM.

**27.**   C. The American Registry for Internet Numbers allocates IP address blocks for the United States, Canada, several parts of the Caribbean region, and Antarctica.

**28.**   D. The Asia-Pacific Network Information Centre allocates IP address blocks for Asia, Australia, New Zealand, and neighboring counties.

**29.**   C. Subnet 172.16.45.224.

**30.**   B. The networks in Answer B provide 126 addresses for hosts in each LAN at Site B.

**31.**   A. Network 192.168.15.0/25 provides 126 addresses for LAN 1, network 192.168.15.128/26 provides 62 addresses for LAN 2, and network 192.168.15.192/27 provides 30 addresses for LAN 3.

**32.**   D. You need only two addresses for the WAN link, and the /30 mask provides only two.

**33.**   A. Private addresses are not announced to Internet service providers.

**34.**   B. NAT translates internal private addresses to public addresses.

**35.**   D. VLSM provides the ability to use different masks throughout the network.

## Chapter 2

**1.**   False. OSPFv3 supports IPv6. OSPFv2 is used in IPv4 networks.

**2.**   True.

**3.**   ARP.

**4.**   16.

Appendix A: Answers to the "Do I Know This Already?" Quiz Questions Q&A Questions   411

A

5. 0110. The first field of the IPv6 header is the Version field. It is set to binary 0110 (6).

6. False.

7. 0xFF (1111 1111 binary).

8. FE8/10.

9. True.

10. Version, Traffic Class, Flow Label, Payload Length, Next Header, Hop Limit, IPv6 Source Address, and IPv6 Destination Address.

11. B. IPv6 address types are unicast, anycast, and multicast.

12. False. The longer set of zeros should be compressed. The valid representation is 2001:0:0:1234::abcd.

13. 2001:1:0:ab0::/64.

14. 32.

15. It is a multicast address. All IPv6 multicast addresses begin with hexadecimal FF.

16. C. Answers A, B, and D are incorrect because 0100 does not compact to 01. Answer B is also incorrect because 0010 does not compact to 001.

17. A. The dual-stack backbone routers handle packets between IPv4 hosts and IPv6 hosts.

18. B. DNS indicates which stack to use. DNS A records return IPv4 addresses. DNS AAAA records return IPv6 addresses.

19. B.

20. A and D.

21. D. IPv4 packets can be fragmented by the sending host and routers. IPv6 packets are fragmented by the sending host only.

22. A. Anycast addresses reach the nearest destination in a group of hosts.

23. D.

24. D.

25. C and D.

26. A.

27. D.

28. C. Running dual-stack IPv4 and IPv6 on hosts and routers allows for full flexibility for communications for the corporation internally, with partners, and with the Internet.

29. B.

30. B.

31. A and C.

32. A.

33. C.

34. A.

35. D.

36. A. All the networks can be summarized with a 52-bit mask.

**37.**   C. SLAAC is used first to assign the IPv6 address, and then DHCPv6 is used to assign additional options.

**38.**   C. Link-local and site-local addresses are unicast addresses, and multicast addresses are sent to a group of hosts. Anycast addresses are routed to the nearest receiver from a group of hosts.

**39.**   B. A packet with a link-local source address remains with the local link.

**40.**   B and D. Only OSPF and IS-IS are link-state routing protocols.

**41.**   A, C, and E. Dual-stack, tunneled, and translation are strategies for transitioning to IPv6.

**42.**   B. ISATAP uses a well-defined IPv6 address format composed of any unicast prefix of 64 bits, which can be a link-local or global IPv6 unicast prefix. It then uses the 32 bits 0000:5EFE that define the ISATAP address ending with the 32-bit IPv4 address of the ISATAP link.

**43.**   C. IPv6 multicast "all-nodes" addresses replace IPv4 broadcasts.

**44.**   D. Unique local unicast IPv6 addresses use the FC00::/7 prefix.

**45.**   C. NAT64 is a transition mechanism that does translation where the IPv6 client can reach IPv4-only servers.

**46.**   D. 2001:4C::9A:0:0:1 is the correct representation since the first set of 16-bit pairs is the set that should be compressed.

**47.**   D. ::FFFF:0:0/96 addresses are IPv4-mapped IPv6 addresses. 2000::/3 addresses are global unicast addresses, FE80::/10 addresses are link local addresses, and 0000::/96 addresses were IPv4-compatible IPv6 addresses that have been deprecated.

**48.**   C. Stateful NAT64.

**49.**   B. 6RD tunnels allow an SP to provide unicast IPv6 service to its customers over its IPv4 network.

**50.**   A. If an AAAA query is returned empty, the DNS64 server queries the IPv4 DNS authoritative server for an A record.

**51.**   E. Both answers B and C are correct. The WKP 64:ff9b::/96 is not globally routable, and an NSP needs to be defined. 2001:FF9b::/96 is not a NAT64 WKP.

**52.**   Implement a dual-stack backbone or implement IPv6 over IPv4 tunnels.

**53.**   NAT64 is used to provide translation between IPv6 and IPv4 hosts.

**54.**   If a dual-stack backbone is implemented, only the WAN routers require an IPv6/IPv4 dual stack. End hosts do not need a dual stack.

**55.**   No. All WAN routers still run the IPv4 stack, with two exceptions: the WAN routers at Sites A and B. These routers speak IPv6 within their sites and speak IPv4 to the WAN.

## Chapter 3

**1.**   False. Distance-vector routing protocols send periodic routing updates.

**2.**   True. The lowest cost is preferred.

**3.**   True. The higher value for reliability is preferred.

Appendix A: Answers to the "Do I Know This Already?" Quiz Questions Q&A Questions    413

A

4.  False. The link with the lower load is preferred.

5.  The EIGRP route. EIGRP routes have an administrative distance of 90, and OSPF routes have an administrative distance of 100. The lower administrative distance is preferred.

6.  The IS-IS route. IS-IS routes have an administrative distance of 115, and RIP routes have an administrative distance of 120. The lower administrative distance is preferred.

7.  The OSPF route is used to reach the destination because it is a more specific route.

8.  A. The best reliability is 255/255 (100%), and the best load is 1/255 (approximately 0%).

9.  C and E. IS-IS and OSPF permit an explicit hierarchical topology.

10. Delay is based on the amount of time it takes a packet to travel from one end to another in an internetwork.

11. i = C, ii = A, iii = D, iv = B.

12. B. OSPFv3 is the only standards-based routing protocol in the list that supports large networks. RIPng has limited scalability.

13. C, D, and E. Link-state routing protocols plus EIGRP's hybrid characteristics converge faster.

14. C. EIGRP supports large networks and does not require a hierarchical network.

15. F. BGP is used to connect to ISPs.

16. D. OSPFv3 is the only correct answer. RIPv2 is for IPv4 networks. EIGRP is not a standards-based protocol. BGPv6 and RIPv3 do not exist.

17. B and C. IGPs converge faster than EGPs.

18. C. Faster routing convergence means more accurate information.

19. B and C. EIGRP uses DUAL for fast convergence and supports VLSMs.

20. i = D, ii = B, iii = A, iv = C.

21. i = B, ii = D, iii = A, iv = C.

22. i = C, ii = A, iii = D, iv = B.

23. B. The EIGRP route has a lower administrative distance.

24. D. IS-IS.

25. B. The default IS-IS cost metric for any interface type is 10.

26. D. IS-IS does not define BDRs.

27. C. EIGRP.

28. C. EIGRP.

29. C and E.

30. A, B, D, and F.

31. B and C.

32. A and C.

33. B and C.

34. C. EIGRP for IPv6.

35. C. 1900.6500.0001 is the system ID, 49 is the AFI, and 0001 is the area ID.

**36.** B. 2. The **variance** command configures EIGRP to accept unequal-cost routes with a metric of less than $2 \times 20 = 40$. The route with a metric of 35 is added.

**37.** A. Administrative distances are BGP = 20, EIGRP = 90, OSPF = 110, IS-IS = 115, and RIP = 120.

**38.** B. Administrative distances are EIGRP = 90, OSPF = 110, IS-IS = 115, RIP = 120, and iBGP = 200.

**39.** A is EIGRP for IPv6, B is OSPFv2, C is RIPv2, D is EIGRP for IPv4, and E is OSPFv3.

**40.** B. Path 2 has greater bandwidth.

**41.** C. Load sharing is enabled with the **variance** command.

**42.** B. By default, Path 2 has higher bandwidth and thus has the better metric.

**43.** A. IS-IS chooses Path 1 with a metric of 10 over Path 2 with a metric of 30.

**44.** D. The EIGRP successor is the path with the lowest metric.

**45.** C. The feasible successor is the backup route.

**46.** B. The EIGRP delay does not affect other routing protocols.

**47.** B. The passive route is stable.

**48.** D. IS-IS supports routing of OSI, IPv4, and IPv6 protocols.

## Chapter 4

**1.** False. A router with one or more interfaces in Area 0 is considered an OSPF backbone router.

**2.** True.

**3.** 224.0.0.5 for ALLSPFRouters and 224.0.0.6 for ALLDRouters.

**4.** FF02::5 for ALLSPFRouters and FF02::6 for ALLDRouters.

**5.** The administrative distance of OSPF is 110.

**6.** OSPF ABRs generate the Type 3 summary LSA for ABRs.

**7.** OSPF DRs generate Type 2 network LSAs.

**8.** Included are the router's links, interfaces, link states, and costs.

**9.** False. The router with the highest priority is selected as the OSPF designated router.

**10.** False. You use eBGP to exchange routes between different autonomous systems.

**11.** True.

**12.** 20, 200.

**13.** i = C, ii = B, iii = A, iv = D.

**14.** OSPF. Although RIPv2 and EIGRP support VLSM, RIPv2 is no longer recommended. EIGRP is not supported on non-Cisco routers.

**15.** You do not need to flood external LSAs into the stub area, and not doing this flooding reduces LSA traffic.

**16.** All traffic from one area must travel through Area 0 (the backbone) to get to another area.

**17.** OSPFv3 is identified as IPv6 Next Header 89.

Appendix A: Answers to the "Do I Know This Already?" Quiz Questions Q&A Questions   415

A

18. F. EIGRP and OSPFv2 are recommended for large enterprise networks.

19. C. Link LSAs are flooded to the local link.

20. E. EIGRP and OSPFv2 have fast convergence.

21. F. EIGRP for IPv6 and OSPFv3 have fast convergence for IPv6 networks.

22. H. RIPv1 and RIPv2 generate periodic routing traffic. IS-IS is used in SP networks. BGP is used for external networks.

23. B. From Router A, the OSPF cost for Path 1 is $10^8$ / 256 kbps = 390. The OSPF cost for Path 2 is ($10^8$ / 1536 kbps) + ($10^8$ / 1024 kbps) + ($10^8$ / 768 kbps) = 65 + 97 + 130 = 292. OSPF selects Path 2 because it has a lower cost.

24. Router A = internal; Router B = ABR; Router C = backbone; Router D = ASBR; Router E = ABR; Router F = internal.

25. i = B, ii = C, iii = D, iv = A.

26. Weight. Weight is configured locally and is not exchanged in BGP updates. On the other hand, the local preference attribute is exchanged between iBGP peers and is configured at the gateway router.

27. Route reflectors reduce the number of iBGP logical mesh connections.

28. External peers see the confederation ID. The internal private autonomous system numbers are used within the confederation.

29. BGP confederations, route reflectors.

30. B. The correct order of BGP path selection is weight, local preference, autonomous system path, origin, MED, and lowest IP address.

31. C.

32. C.

33. C.

34. D. BGP.

35. A and D.

36. B.

37. A.

38. C.

39. A and D.

40. D. R4.

41. B. BGP should be configured between AS 100 and AS 500.

42. C. Both Routers A and B perform the redistribution with route filters to prevent route feedback.

43. B. The OSPF routes are redistributed into EIGRP. Then you can redistribute EIGRP routes into BGP.

44. D. You should use filters on all routers performing redistribution.

45. D. Atomic aggregate and local preference are BGP well-known discretionary attributes.

**46.** A. AS_Path and next hop are BGP well-known discretionary BGP attributes. Origin is also a well-known discretionary BGP attribute, but MED is optional nontransitive.

**47.** C. Aggregator and community are BGP optional transitive attributes.

**48.** B. The IP address of the BGP peer might be in the OSPF routes and not in the eBGP routes.

**49.** B. When used within an AS, iBGP carries eBGP attributes that otherwise would be lost if eBGP were redistributed into an IGP.

**50.** D. OSPF metrics are not automatically converted into EIGRP metrics. If an EIGRP metric is not defined, then infinity is assigned to the redistributed routes, which are thus not injected into the routing table.

## Chapter 5

**1.** True.

**2.** False. PIM does not have a hop count limit. DVMRP has a hop count limit of 32.

**3.** True.

**4.** i = D, ii = B, iii = A, iv = C.

**5.** i = E, ii = C, iii = A, iv = B, v = D.

**6.** D.

**7.** Data link layer.

**8.** Notice level.

**9.** False.

**10.** True.

**11.** Device ID, IP address, capabilities, OS version, model number, and port ID.

**12.** D. A trap message is sent by the agent when a significant event occurs.

**13.** A. The NMS manager uses the Get operation to retrieve the value-specific MIB variable from an agent.

**14.** B. The NMS manager uses the Set operation to set values of the object instance within an agent.

**15.** C. More than 500 syslog facilities can be configured on Cisco IOS.

**16.** B. At the authNoPriv level, authentication is provided, but encryption is not.

**17.** B. CBC-DES is the encryption algorithm used by SNMPv3.

**18.** B, C, and D.

**19.** D. RMON2 provides monitoring information from the network to the application layers.

**20.** A. The authPriv level provides authentication and encryption.

**21.** i = C, ii = A, iii = D, iv = B.

**22.** A. Syslog level 0 indicates an emergency and that the system is unusable.

**23.** B. RMON2 allows for Layer 4 monitoring. NetFlow is not a long-term trending solution.

Appendix A: Answers to the "Do I Know This Already?" Quiz Questions Q&A Questions   417

A

24. C. NetFlow does network traffic analysis.

25. E. MIB is the database that stores information.

26. C. ASN.1 is used to define information being stored.

27. C. authNoPriv provides authentication and no encryption.

28. D. Community is not an SNMP operation.

29. E. Private MIBs can be used for vendor-specific information.

30. C. NetFlow allows for network planning, traffic engineering, usage-based network billing, accounting, denial-of-service monitoring, and application monitoring. One big benefit is that NetFlow provides the data necessary for billing of network usage.

31. C. NetFlow can be configured to provide timestamped data on multiple interfaces.

32. A, B, and D. NetFlow consists of three major components: NetFlow accounting, flow collector engines, and network data analyzers.

33. B. Multicast RPF is used to prevent forwarding loops.

34. C. The RP knows of all sources in the network.

35. C. (*,G) means any source to group G.

36. B. With BIDIR-PIM, the first packets from the source are not encapsulated, and there are no (S,G) states.

37. E. SSM is recommended for broadcast applications and well-known receivers.

38. C. MSDP is used to interconnect PIM-SM domains.

39. A. Network management traffic should be assigned CoS of 2.

40. B. SSM eliminates the RPs and shared trees of sparse mode and only builds an SPT.

## Chapter 6

1. False

2. True

3. False. A full-mesh network increases costs.

4. Use $n(n - 1)/2$, where $n = 6$. $6(6 - 1)/2 = (6 \times 5)/2 = 30/2 = 15$.

5. Cost savings, ease of understanding, easy network growth (scalability), and improved fault isolation.

6. False. Small campus networks can have collapsed core and distribution layers and implement a two-layer design. Medium campus networks can have two-tier or three-tier designs.

7. Use the formula $n(n - 1)/2$, where $n = 10$. $10(10 - 1)/2 = 90/2 = 45$ links.

8. B. The distribution layer provides routing between VLANs and security filtering.

9. D and E. The access layer concentrates user access and provides PoE to IP phones.

10. B and C. The distribution layer concentrates the network access switches and routers and applies network policies with access lists.

11. A and F. The core layer provides high-speed data transport without manipulating the data.

**12.** A and C.

**13.** B. Partial-mesh connectivity is best suited for the distribution layer.

**14.** A and B.

**15.** B. VSS allows a Catalyst switch pair to act as a single logical switch.

**16.** C, E, and F. Core, distribution, and access layers.

**17.** C. Build in triangles.

**18.** C.

**19.** B.

**20.** D.

**21.** C.

**22.** D.

**23.** A and B.

**24.** B.

**25.** C. Multimode fiber provides the necessary connectivity at the required distance. UTP can reach only 100 meters. Single-mode fiber is more expensive.

**26.** C. Disabling trunking on host ports and using RPVST+ are best practices at the access layer.

**27.** B. The use of HSRP and summarization of routes are best practices in the distribution layer.

**28.** A. Best practices for the core include the use of triangle connections to reduce switch peering and using routing to prevent network loops.

**29.** A. The core and the distribution layers should be connected using redundant Layer 3 triangular links.

**30.** A, B, G, and H.

**31.** A, C, and E.

**32.** A, E, and G.

**33.** C.

**34.** A.

**35.** A and E.

**36.** C.

**37.** B.

**38.** A.

**39.** B, C, and D.

**40.** C. The Spanning Tree Protocol root bridge and HSRP active router should match.

**41.** A = ii, B = i, C = iii, D = iv.

**42.** A and B.

**43.** C and D.

**44.** C. UPOE provides up to 51W to a powered device.

Appendix A: Answers to the "Do I Know This Already?" Quiz Questions Q&A Questions    419

A

**45.** C. Wake on LAN.

**46.** B. Build triangles.

**47.** C. Category 6a.

**48.** A. Apply PortFast to all end-user ports. Apply RootGuard to all ports where a root is never expected.

## Chapter 7

**1.** A. IP phone–to–IP phone communication is an example of peer-to-peer communication.

**2.** C. Create a data center server segment that enables the enforcement of security policies.

**3.** B. These are design considerations for the distribution layer.

**4.** D. All these are server connectivity options.

**5.** B. The building subnets are too large and should be further segmented to reduce the broadcast domain.

**6.** i = B, ii = A, iii = D, iv = C.

**7.** i = B, ii = A, iii = C, iv = D.

**8.** C.

**9.** C.

**10.** A. Use redundant triangle topology between the distribution and core layers.

**11.** B.

**12.** A.

**13.** A, B, G, and H.

**14.** A, C, and E.

**15.** C, D, F, and G.

**16.** A, E, and G.

**17.** C.

**18.** A.

**19.** D.

**20.** A.

**21.** B.

**22.** B. VTPv2 is the default version.

**23.** C. You can achieve subsecond failover with HSRP by setting the hello timer to 200 milliseconds and the dead timer to 750 milliseconds.

**24.** B. The default VRRP hello timer is 1 second, and the dead timer is 3 seconds.

**25.** A. The default HSRP timers are 3 seconds for hello and 10 seconds for the dead timer.

**26.** D. GLBP is a Cisco-proprietary FHRP that allows packet load sharing among a group of routers.

**27.** A. For distribution-to-core, the oversubscription recommendation is 4 to 1.

**28.** D. When implementing data oversubscription, the recommended practice is 20 to 1 oversubscription for access-to-distribution links.

**29.** C.

**30.** C. 10GBASE-LR is long-range single-mode fiber with a maximum distance of 10 kilometers.

**31.** D. 10GBASE-SR uses multimode fiber with a range of 400 meters.

**32.** A. 10BASE-T uses UTP with a range of 100 meters.

## Chapter 8

**1.** B. The control plane builds and maintains the network topology and informs the data plane on where traffic flows by using the vSmart controller.

**2.** D. Remote-access VPN DMZ resides in the Enterprise Edge.

**3.** C. GETVPN forms tunnel-less VPNs over private WANs.

**4.** C and D. Internet and DMZ are two modules found in the enterprise edge.

**5.** C. GRE is a tunneling technology that lacks security and scalability.

**6.** D. MPLS is the most popular VPN technology that leverages BGP to distribute VPN-related information.

**7.** A. VPLS allows for connecting Layer 2 domains over an IP/MPLS network.

**8.** D. DMZ/e-commerce modules belong in the enterprise edge.

**9.** D. Service provider edge network modules connect to ISPs in the enterprise edge.

**10.** D. WAN edge network modules connect using MPLS connectivity.

**11.** B. WAN edge network modules connect using SD-WAN.

**12.** B. ESP, an IPsec protocol, is used to provide confidentiality, data origin authentication, connectionless integrity, and anti-replay services.

**13.** D. The WAN edge is a functional area that provides connectivity between the central site and remote sites.

**14.** D. Dark Fiber allows the enterprise to control framing.

**15.** C. LTE Advanced Pro is a 4G standard that is pushing download rates of 1 Gbps.

**16.** A. SONET/SDN is circuit based and delivers high-speed services using Optical Carrier rates.

**17.** C. 5G is an emerging wireless standard that uses sub-6 GHz and download rates of 20 Gbps.

**18.** DWDM improves the utilization of optical-fiber strands.

**19.** B. High security and transmission quality are advantages of private WAN links.

**20.** A and B. No need for new customer premises equipment and ease of integration with existing LAN equipment are benefits of Ethernet handoffs at the customer edge.

**21.** A. The data plane is responsible for forwarding packets with instructions from the control plane through vEdge routers.

**22.** D. Service providers use SLAs to define their network availability at different levels.

A

23. C. The management plane is responsible for centralized management and monitoring through the use of vManage.

24. B. CE router types handle the exchange of customer routing information with the service provider.

25. A, C, and D. A fully meshed WAN with PKI and certificate authentication are not objectives of an effective WAN design.

26. C. Key servers maintain the control plane and define the encryption policies that are pushed to IKE authenticated group members.

27. D. DMVPN uses a Multipoint GRE (mGRE) interface to provide support for multiple GRE and IPsec tunnels.

28. A. AH is used to provide integrity and data origin authentication.

29. D. HMAC provides protection from attacks such as man-in-the-middle, packet-replay, and data-integrity.

30. A. DPD detects the loss of a peer IPsec connection.

## Chapter 9

1. A. Designing the topology is based on the availability of technology as well as the projected traffic patterns, technology performance, constraints, and reliability.

2. D. High availability is a design principle that involves redundancy through hardware, software, and connectivity.

3. B. Real-time voice is an application that requires round-trip times of less than 400 ms with low delay and jitter.

4. C. Reliability is a measure of a given application's availability to its users.

5. C. Window size defines the upper limit of frames that can be transmitted without a return acknowledgment.

6. A. The availability target range for branch WAN high availability is 99.9900%.

7. A. MPLS WAN with dual routers is a deployment model that provides the best SLA guarantees.

8. C. Dual-router dual-homed Internet connectivity provides for the highest level of resiliency.

9. A. When designing Internet for remote sites, centralized Internet provides control for security services such as URL filtering, firewalling, and intrusion prevention.

10. A and B. Using a public BGP AS number for eBGP connections and provider-independent IP address space for advertisements to ISPs are two important design considerations for a high availability design.

11. A. Backup link for WAN backup provides for redundancy and additional bandwidth.

12. D. IPsec tunnel failover can be used to back up the primary MPLS WAN connection.

13. D. NSF is not a model for providing QoS. Best-effort, DiffServ, and IntServ are QoS models.

14. C. EF is the DSCP value for VoIP traffic.

**15.**   D. LLQ uses a strict priority queue in addition to modular traffic classes.

**16.**   A. Admission control is the function used to determine whether the requested flows can be accepted.

**17.**   C. Shaping slows down the rate at which packets are sent out an interface (egress) by matching certain criteria.

**18.**   B. Queuing is the buffering process that routers and switches use when they receive traffic faster than can be transmitted.

**19.**   D. SLAs are used by service providers to define their service offerings at different levels.

**20.**   C. Congestion management mechanisms handle traffic overflow using a queuing algorithm.

**21.**   D. Classification and marking identifies and marks flows.

**22.**   C. The cost design principle balances the amount of security and technologies with the budget.

**23.**   B. Interactive data as an application type has requirements for low throughput and response time within a second.

**24.**   C. LTE Advanced Pro has bandwidth capabilities of 1 Gbps to 10 Gbps.

**25.**   C. Downtime at 99% equates to 3.65 days of availability per year.

**26.**   D. With dual-router and dual-path availability models, 5 mins of downtime is expected per year.

**27.**   A. The hybrid WAN deployment model has single routers or dual routers and uses both MPLS and an Internet VPN.

**28.**   D. HSRP/GLBP or an IGP internally are design considerations for designing Internet with high availability.

**29.**   B. MTU size is an important design consideration when using IPsec over GRE tunnels.

**30.**   D. VoIP needs to be prioritized the most.

## Chapter 10

**1.**   A and C. SSM and PIM multicast protocols are supported with SD-Access.

**2.**   C and D. VSS and Switch stacks are the preferred connectivity for WLCs.

**3.**   A. A very small site in SD-Access supports up to 2000 endpoints and 8 VNs.

**4.**   B. Assurance provides contextual insights for quick issue resolution and capacity planning.

**5.**   A. OSPF is not a technology used to create overlay networks.

**6.**   D. A Fusion router is used to allow endpoints in different VNs to communicate with each other.

**7.**   A. Fabric mode APs use the INFRA VRF instance.

**8.**   D. Edge and border nodes get SGACLs downloaded from ISE to enforce policy based on SGTs.

**9.**   B. A small site in SD-Access supports up to 10,000 endpoints and 32 VNs.

**10.** C. 802.11ac Wave 1 is supported for fabric mode wireless in SD-Access.

**11.** D. Within a VXLAN header, 64,000 SGTs are supported in the Group ID section.

**12.** B. Cisco TrustSec is leveraged to enable SGT information to be inserted into the VXLAN headers in the data plane.

**13.** A. Data plane isolation with a VN using SGTs describes microsegmentation.

**14.** C. Fabric wireless uses VXLAN in the data plane.

**15.** D. The routing locator (RLOC) and the endpoint identifier are the two main things that LISP keeps track of.

**16.** B. The integration of ISE and DNA Center uses pxGRID services to establish trust through ISE.

**17.** D. Cisco DNA Center LAN automation uses IS-IS to deploy underlay routing configurations.

**18.** A. Integration is a key SD-Access benefit for open and programmable third-party integrated solutions.

**19.** C. The underlay is a collection of physical switches and routers running a dynamic Layer 3 routing protocol used for the transport in SD-Access.

**20.** A and D. Infoblox and BlueCat IPAM solutions can be integrated with Cisco DNA Center.

**21.** C. Policy is a key benefit of SD-Access that can be described as automated configurations that help enable group-based security policies and network segmentation.

**22.** B. LISP is used in the SD-Access control plane to handle the mapping and resolving of endpoint addresses.

**23.** C. Link state routing protocols use areas and advertise information about the network topology instead of advertising the complete routing table.

**24.** A. ISE supports AAA services, groups, policy, and endpoint profiling.

**25.** C. Fusion routers are the next hop after the border nodes to external networks.

**26.** A. A fabric data plane provides the logical overlay created by Virtual Extensible VLAN (VXLAN) packet encapsulation along with a Group Policy Object (GPO).

**27.** C. A virtual network is a separate routing and forwarding instance that provides isolation for host pools.

**28.** D. A large site in SD-Access supports up to 50,000 endpoints and 64 VNs.

**29.** D. The global and site settings underlay workflow provides a hierarchical structure for the management of network settings.

**30.** B. LISP moves the remote destination information to a centralized map database.

## Chapter 11

**1.** A. vSmart controllers provide routing, enforce data plane policies, and enforce segmentation.

**2.** B. The management plane (vManage) is responsible for central configuration and monitoring.

**3.** B. The multicast stream is sent to the replicator in the SD-WAN network.

**4.** C. The control plane builds and maintains the network topology and makes decisions on where traffic flows.

**5.** D. vAnalytics, a component of vManage, provides end-to-end visibility of applications with real-time information.

**6.** C. Predefined public colors include 3g, biz, internet, blue, bronze, custom1, custom2, custom3, default, gold, green, lte, public-internet, red, and silver.

**7.** A. When using a private color, the vEdge device is using a native private underlay IP.

**8.** B. Private colors include metro-ethernet, mpls, private1, private2, private3, private4, private5, and private6.

**9.** C. Service routes contain routes for services such as firewall, intrusion prevention, application optimization, and VPN labels.

**10.** A. OMP routes include prefixes learned at the local site, including static, OSPF, and BGP routes.

**11.** A. Transport location identifier, origin, preference, and site ID are attributes of OMP routes.

**12.** B. TLOC private address, carrier, encapsulation type, and weight attributes are part of TLOC routes.

**13.** A and B.

**14.** C and D.

**15.** D. The control plane uses the Zero Trust model.

**16.** A. The management plane uses role-based access control.

**17.** C. vManage predefined user groups are basic, operator, and netadmin.

**18.** A and C. SHA256 and AES-256-GCM are used.

**19.** B.

**20.** C. To increase the availability and redundancy of the orchestration, management, and control planes, you can implement horizontal solution scaling.

**21.** B. For Layer 2 LANs, failure of VRRP on one of the vEdge routers causes failover to the second vEdge router.

**22.** A. For Layer 3 LANs, failure of OSPF on one of the vEdge routers causes failover to the second vEdge router.

**23.** B. A VPN is assigned a number between 1 and 65,530, excluding 512.

**24.** B. Each VPN is assigned a value from 0 to 65,530.

**25.** C. VPN 512 is the management VPN.

**26.** B. Headers are appended as follows: IP-UDP-ESP-VPN-Packet.

**27.** D.

**28.** B.

**29.** A.

**30.** C.

**31.** B. BFD probes provide information about latency, jitter, and loss on all the transport links, enabling the determination of best paths.

Appendix A: Answers to the "Do I Know This Already?" Quiz Questions Q&A Questions   425

A

**32.** C. Localized data policies allow you to configure how data traffic is handled at a specific site, such as through ACLs, QoS, mirroring, and policing.

**33.** B. Centralized data policies can be used in configuring application firewalls, service chaining, traffic engineering, and QoS.

**34.** A. Centralized control policies operate on the routing and TLOC information and allow for customization of routing decisions and determination of routing paths through the overlay network.

**35.** B. Application-aware routing selects the optimal path based on real-time path performance characteristics for different traffic types.

**36.** C. Queues 1 through 7 use Weighted Round Robin (WRR) for scheduling.

**37.** B. Queue 0 uses LLQ.

**38.** D. Tail drop is the congestion-avoidance algorithm used in queue 0.

**39.** A. Control and BFD traffic is marked as DSCP 48 decimal (CS6).

**40.** D. The vEdge replicator forwards streams to multicast receivers in the SD-WAN network.

**41.** A and C. Direct Internet Access (DIA) reduces bandwidth, latency, and cost on WAN links and improves branch office user experience.

# Chapter 12

**1.** D. Simple Object Access Protocol (SOAP) uses HTTP to transport messages using XML-based syntax.

**2.** C. gRPC is an open-source framework project and is a functional subset of NETCONF with JSON representation.

**3.** A. JSON is a lightweight data-interchange text format that is fairly easy to read and write and easy for systems to understand.

**4.** D. NETCONF is a network management protocol that uses protocol operations that are defined as remote procedure calls (RPCs) for requests and replies in XML-based representation.

**5.** A. YANG is a data modeling language used to describe the data for network configuration protocols such as NETCONF and RESTCONF.

**6.** B and D. Layer 3 MPLS VPN and VRF are service data models.

**7.** A, C, and D. NETCONF uses running, candidate, and startup data stores.

**8.** B and C. A RESTCONF URI uses data and operations resource types.

**9.** C. A POST operation creates a resource or invokes an operation.

**10.** D. The OpenConfig group is focused on building consistent sets of vendor-neutral data models written in YANG to support operational needs and requirements from various network operators.

**11.** A. The RESTCONF protocol provides a programmatic interface for accessing YANG modeled data with either XML or JSON encoding.

**12.** C. Dial-out mode initiates the connection from the network device to start the TCP connection to the receiver.

**13.** A and C. IOS XR MDT RPC and OpenConfig RPC are methods used to request sensor paths with a dynamic subscription.

**14.** D. Periodic publications are subscriptions that are streamed out to the receivers at specified intervals such as 5 seconds.

**15.** A. Policy-based telemetry streams data to a receiver using a policy file that defines the data to stream and the frequency to get the data.

**16.** B. Model-driven telemetry is a new concept in network monitoring in which data is continuously streamed from network devices to subscribers using a push model, providing real-time configuration and state information.

**17.** C. A RESTCONF API call uses HTTP PUT, POST, UPDATE, or DELETE methods to edit data resources represented by YANG data models.

**18.** B. Both NETCONF and RESTCONF use the ietf-yang-library.

**19.** D. The YANG data model resides in the data portion of the TCP/IP network frame.

**20.** A. The GET CRUD operations get a resource.

**21.** C. The <get> NETCONF protocol operation retrieves all or part of a running configuration and device operational data.

**22.** B. Lists inside a YANG data model are used to identify nodes that are stored in a sequence.

**23.** D. The Open SDN Controller/OpenDaylight Cisco product supports NETCONF, YANG, and RESTCONF.

**24.** A. HTTP is a TCP transport protocol that RESTCONF and gRPC use.

**25.** C. REST is an API framework for simple web services that uses GET, POST, PUT, and DELETE methods.

**26.** D. XML is data wrapped in tags that is both human readable and system readable.

**27.** A. Inside a YANG data model, leafs are used inside lists to describe things like a name or a description.

**28.** D. The Cisco YANG model is a collection of Cisco native, IETF, and OpenConfig YANG models that can be used with Cisco-based platforms.

**29.** B. On-change publication streams out data only when a change in the data has occurred, such as when an interface or a neighbor relationship goes down.

**30.** A. Dial-in mode listens until the receiver sends the initial SYN packet to start the TCP connection.

# CCNP Enterprise Design ENSLD 300-420 Official Cert Guide Exam Updates

Over time, reader feedback allows Pearson to gauge which topics give our readers the most problems when taking the exams. To assist readers with those topics, the authors create new materials clarifying and expanding on those troublesome exam topics. As mentioned in the Introduction, the additional content about the exam is contained in a PDF on this book's companion website, at http://www.ciscopress.com/title/9780136575191.

This appendix is intended to provide you with updated information if Cisco Systems makes minor modifications to the exam upon which this book is based. When Cisco Systems releases an entirely new exam, the changes are usually too extensive to provide in a simple update appendix. In those cases, you might need to consult the new edition of the book for the updated content. This appendix attempts to fill the void that occurs with any print book. In particular, this appendix does the following:

- Mentions technical items that might not have been mentioned elsewhere in the book

- Covers new topics if Cisco Systems adds new content to the exam over time

- Provides a way to get up-to-the-minute current information about content for the exam

## Always Get the Latest at the Book's Product Page

You are reading the version of this appendix that was available when your book was printed. However, given that the main purpose of this appendix is to be a living, changing document, it is important that you look for the latest version online at the book's companion website. To do so, follow these steps:

Step 1.  Browse to www.ciscopress.com/title/9780136575191 .

Step 2.  Click the Updates tab.

Step 3.  If there is a new Appendix B document on the page, download the latest Appendix B document.

> **Note** The downloaded document has a version number. Comparing the version of the print Appendix B (Version 1.0) with the latest online version of this appendix, you should do the following:
>
> - **Same version:** Ignore the PDF that you downloaded from the companion website.
>
> - **Website has a later version:** Ignore this Appendix B in your book and read only the latest version that you downloaded from the companion website.

## Technical Content

The current Version 1.0 of this appendix does not contain additional technical coverage.

# OSI Model, TCP/IP Architecture, and Numeric Conversion

The Open Systems Interconnection (OSI) model is a mandatory topic in any internetworking book. The CCNP candidate should understand the OSI model and identify which OSI layers host the different networking protocols. The OSI model provides a framework for understanding internetworking. This appendix offers an overview and general understanding of the OSI reference model.

The Transmission Control Protocol/Internet Protocol (TCP/IP) architecture provides the practical implementation of a layered model. This appendix is an overview of the TCP/IP layers and how they map to the OSI model.

Also covered in this appendix is the numeric conversion of binary, decimal, and hexadecimal numbers. The ability to covert between binary, decimal, and hexadecimal numbers helps you manipulate IP addresses in binary and dotted-decimal format. Quickly converting these numbers will help you answer test questions.

## OSI Model Overview

The International Organization for Standardization (ISO) developed the OSI model in 1984, and revisited it in 1994, to coordinate standards development for interconnected information-processing systems. The model describes seven layers that start with the physical connection and end with the application. As shown in Figure C-1, the seven layers are physical, data link, network, transport, session, presentation, and application.

The OSI model divides the tasks involved in moving data into seven smaller, more manageable layers. Each layer supplies services to the layer above, performs at least the functions specified by the model, and expects the defined services from the layer below. The model does not define the precise nature of the interface between layers or the protocol used between peers at the same layer in different instantiations of a protocol stack. The model's design encourages each layer to be implemented independently. For example, you can run an application over IP (Layer 3), Fast Ethernet (Layer 2), Frame Relay (Layer 2), or Gigabit Ethernet (Layer 2). As the packets route through the Internet, the Layer 2 media change independently from the upper-layer protocols. The OSI model helps standardize discussion of the design and construction of networks for developers and hardware manufacturers. It also provides network engineers and analysts with a framework useful in understanding internetworking.

| Layer Number | OSI Layer Name |
|:---:|:---:|
| 7 | Application |
| 6 | Presentation |
| 5 | Session |
| 4 | Transport |
| 3 | Network |
| 2 | Data Link |
| 1 | Physical |

**Figure C-1**  *Seven-Layer OSI Model*

Layered implementations of internetworking technologies do not necessarily map directly to the OSI model. For example, the TCP/IP architecture model describes only four layers, with the upper layer mapping to the three upper layers of the OSI model (application, presentation, and session). The development of IP predates the OSI model. For a more thorough discussion of the TCP/IP model, see Chapter 1, "Internet Protocol Version 4 (IPv4) Design."

The following sections describe and provide sample protocols for each OSI layer.

## Physical Layer (OSI Layer 1)

The physical layer describes the transportation of raw bits over physical media. It defines signaling specifications and media types and interfaces. It also describes voltage levels, physical data rates, and maximum transmission distances. In summary, it deals with the electrical, mechanical, functional, and procedural specifications for links between networked systems.

Examples of physical layer specifications are

- EIA/TIA-232 (Electronic Industries Association/ Telecommunications Industry Association)

- EIA/TIA-449

- V.35

- IEEE 802 LAN and metropolitan-area network (MAN) standards

- Physical layer (PHY) groups Synchronous Optical Network/Synchronous Digital Hierarchy (SONET/SDH)

- Maximum cable distances of the Ethernet standards

## Data Link Layer (OSI Layer 2)

The data link layer is concerned with the reliable transport of data across a physical link. Data at this layer is formatted into frames. Data link specifications include frame sequencing, flow control, synchronization, error notification, physical network topology, and physical addressing. This layer converts frames into bits when sending information and converts bits into frames when receiving information from the physical media. Bridges and switches operate at the data link layer.

Because of the complexity of this OSI layer, the IEEE subdivides the data link layer into three sublayers for LANs. Figure C-2 shows how Layer 2 is subdivided. The upper layer is the logical link sublayer, which manages communications between devices. The bridging layer, defined by IEEE 802.1, is the middle layer. The lowest layer is the Media Access Control (MAC) sublayer, which manages the protocol access to the physical layer and ultimately the actual media. Systems attached to a common data link layer have a unique address on that data link layer. Be aware that you might find some references describing this layer as having two sublayers: the Logical Link Control (LLC) sublayer and the MAC sublayer.

| OSI Model | IEEE 802 Specifications |
|---|---|
| Data Link Layer | 802.2 Logical Link |
| | 802.1 Bridging |
| | Media Access Control |

**Figure C-2**  *IEEE Data Link Sublayers*

Examples of data link layer technologies are

- Frame Relay
- ATM
- Synchronous Data Link Control (SDLC)
- High-Level Data Link Control (HDLC)
- Point-to-Point Protocol (PPP)
- Ethernet implementations (IEEE 802.3)
- Wireless LAN (IEEE 802.11)

## Network Layer (OSI Layer 3)

The network layer is concerned with routing information and methods to determine paths to a destination. Information at this layer is called packets. Specifications include routing protocols, logical network addressing, and packet fragmentation. Routers operate at this layer.

Examples of network layer specifications are

- Protocol
  - IPv4, IPv6
  - ICMP

- ARP

- Connectionless Network Protocol (CLNP)

- Routing protocols

  - Routing Information Protocol (RIP)

  - Open Shortest Path First (OSPF)

  - Enhanced Interior Gateway Routing Protocol (EIGRP)

  - Intermediate System-to-Intermediate System (IS-IS)

## Transport Layer (OSI Layer 4)

The transport layer provides reliable, transparent transport of data segments from upper layers. It provides end-to-end error checking and recovery, multiplexing, virtual circuit management, and flow control. Messages are assigned a sequence number at the transmission end. At the receiving end, the packets are reassembled, checked for errors, and acknowledged. Flow control manages the data transmission to ensure that the transmitting device does not send more data than the receiving device can process.

Examples of transport layer specifications are

- Transmission Control Protocol (TCP)

- Real-Time Transport Protocol (RTP)

- User Datagram Protocol (UDP)

**Note:** Although UDP operates in the transport layer, it does not perform the reliable error-checking functions that other transport layer protocols do.

## Session Layer (OSI Layer 5)

The session layer provides a control structure for communication between applications. It establishes, manages, and terminates communication connections called sessions. Communication sessions consist of service requests and responses that occur between applications on different devices.

Examples of specifications that operate at the session layer are

- DECnet's Session Control Protocol (SCP)

- H.245 and H.225

### Presentation Layer (OSI Layer 6)

The presentation layer provides application layer entities with services to ensure that information is preserved during transfer. Knowledge of the syntax selected at the application layer allows selection of compatible transfer syntax if a change is required. This layer provides conversion of character-representation formats, as might be required for reliable transfer. Voice coding schemes are specified at this layer. Furthermore, compression and encryption can occur at this layer.

An example of a specification that operates at the presentation layer is Abstract Syntax Notation 1 (ASN.1).

### Application Layer (OSI Layer 7)

The application layer gives the user or operating system access to the network services. It interacts with software applications by identifying communication resources, determining network availability, and distributing information services. It also provides synchronization between the peer applications residing on separate systems.

Examples of application layer specifications are

- Telnet
- File Transfer Protocol (FTP)
- Simple Mail Transfer Protocol (SMTP)
- Simple Network Management Protocol (SNMP)
- Network File System (NFS)
- Border Gateway Protocol (BGP)

## TCP/IP Architecture

The suite of TCP/IP protocols was developed for use by the U.S. government and research universities. The suite is identified by its most widely known protocols: TCP and IP. As mentioned, the ISO published the OSI model in 1984. However, the TCP/IP protocols had been developed by the Department of Defense's Advanced Research Projects Agency (DARPA) since 1969. TCP/IP uses only four layers (as described in RFC 791) versus the seven layers used by OSI. The TCP/IP layers are

- Application
- Host-to-host transport
- Internet
- Network interface

Figure C-3 shows how the TCP/IP layers map to the OSI model.

| OSI Model | TCP/IP Architecture | TCP/IP Protocols |
|---|---|---|
| Application | Application | Telnet, SMTP, SNMP, FTP, TFTP, HTTPS, DNS |
| Presentation | | |
| Session | | |
| Transport | Host-to-Host Transport | TCP, UDP |
| Network | Internet | IP, ARP, OSPF, ICMP |
| Data Link | Network Interface | Use of lower layer protocols such as Ethernet and Frame Relay |
| Physical | | |

**Figure C-3**  *The TCP/IP Architecture and the OSI Model*

## Network Interface Layer

The TCP/IP network interface layer (also known as network access layer) maps to the OSI data link and physical layers. TCP/IP uses the lower-layer protocols for transport.

## Internet Layer

The Internet layer is where IP resides. IP packets exist at this layer. It directly maps to the network layer of the OSI model. Other TCP/IP protocols at this layer are Internet Control Message Protocol (ICMP), Address Resolution Protocol (ARP), and Reverse ARP (RARP).

## Host-to-Host Transport Layer

The host-to-host transport layer of TCP/IP provides two connection services: TCP and UDP. TCP provides reliable transport of IP packets, and UDP provides transport of IP packets without verification of delivery. This layer maps to the OSI transport layer, but the OSI model only defines reliable delivery at this layer.

## Application Layer

The TCP/IP application layer maps to the top three layers of the OSI model: application, presentation, and session. This layer interfaces with the end user and provides authentication, compression, and formatting. The application protocol determines the data's format and how the session is controlled. Examples of TCP/IP application protocols are Telnet, FTP, BGP, and Hypertext Transfer Protocol Secure (HTTPS).

## Example of Layered Communication

Suppose that you use a Telnet application. Telnet maps to the top three layers of the OSI model. In Figure C-4, a user on Host 1 enables the Telnet application to access a remote host (Host 2). The Telnet application provides a user interface (application layer) to network services. As defined in RFC 854, ASCII is the default code format. No session layer is defined for Telnet (not an OSI protocol). Per the RFC, Telnet uses TCP for connectivity (transport layer).

The TCP segment is placed in an IP packet (network layer) with a destination IP address of Host 2. The IP packet is placed in an Ethernet frame (data link layer), which is converted into bits and sent onto the wire (physical layer).

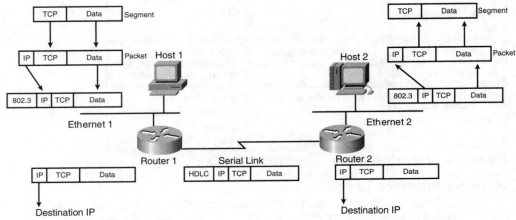

**Figure C-4**  *Telnet Example*

When the frame arrives at Router 1, it converts the bits into a frame; removes the frame headers (data link); checks the destination IP address (network); places a serial link header on the packet, making it a serial frame; and forwards the frame to the serial link (data link), which sends it as bits.

Router 2 receives the bits and converts them into a frame; removes the serial encapsulation headers; checks the destination IP address (network); adds an Ethernet header to the packet, making it a frame; and places the frame on Ethernet 2 (data link). Host 2 receives bits (physical) from the Ethernet cable and converts the bits into a frame (data link). Then the IP protocol is examined and the packet data is forwarded to TCP, which checks the segment number for errors and then forwards the segment to TCP port 23 (Telnet), which is the application.

# Numeric Conversion

This section focuses on the techniques for converting between decimal, binary, and hexadecimal numbers. Although the exam might not have a specific question about converting a binary number to decimal, you need to know how to convert these numbers to do problems on the test. An IPv4 address could be shown as binary or in traditional dotted-decimal format. MAC addresses and IPv6 addresses are represented in hexadecimal. Some **show** commands have output information in hexadecimal or binary formats.

## Hexadecimal Numbers

The hexadecimal numeric system uses 16 digits instead of the 10 digits used by the decimal system. Table C-1 shows the hexadecimal digits and their decimal equivalent values.

**Table C-1**    Hexadecimal Digits

| Hexadecimal Digit | Decimal Value |
|---|---|
| 0 | 0 |
| 1 | 1 |
| 2 | 2 |
| 3 | 3 |
| 4 | 4 |
| 5 | 5 |
| 6 | 6 |
| 7 | 7 |
| 8 | 8 |
| 9 | 9 |
| A | 10 |
| B | 11 |
| C | 12 |
| D | 13 |
| E | 14 |
| F | 15 |
| 10 | 16 |
| 11 | 17 |
| 12 | 18 |
| 13 | 19 |
| 14 | 20 |

## Hexadecimal Representation

It is common to represent a hexadecimal number with 0x before the number so that it is not confused with a decimal number. The hexadecimal number of decimal 16 is written as 0x10, not 10. Another method is to put a subscript $h$ to the right of the number, such as $10_h$. It is also common to use the term *hex* when speaking of hexadecimal. Much of the following text uses *hex*.

## Converting Decimal to Hexadecimal

First things first: Memorize Table C-1. There are two ways to convert larger numbers. The first method is to convert decimal to binary and then convert binary to hex. The second method is to divide the decimal number by 16—the residual is the rightmost hexadecimal digit—and then keep dividing until the number is not divisible anymore. For the first method, use the schemes described in later sections. For the second method, follow the examples described here.

First, divide the decimal number by 16. The remainder of the division is the least-significant (first) hexadecimal digit. Continue to divide the quotients (answer) of the divisions by 16 until the quotient is 0. The remainder value of each later division is converted to a hexadecimal digit and prepended to the previous value. The final remainder is the most-significant digit of the hexadecimal equivalent. For large numbers, you might have to divide many times. The following examples make the process clearer.

Divide by 16:

```
        1
16 |  26
     -16
      10 = Ah
```

Answer: **1Ah**

**Conversion Example C-1**   *Convert 26 to Its Hex Equivalent*

Not divisible by 256; divide by 16:

```
        6
16 |  96
     -96
       0 = 0h
```

Answer: **60h**

**Conversion Example C-2**   *Convert 96 to Its Hex Equivalent*

Divide by 16 first:

```
          23
16 |   375
      -32
        55
       -48
         7
```

Now divide 23 by 16:

```
         1
16 |   23
      -16
        7
```

Now take the residual from the first division (7) and concatentate it with the residual from the second division (7), plus the result of the second division (1), and the answer is **177h**.

**Conversion Example C-3**   *Convert 375 to Its Hex Equivalent*

Divide by 16:

```
       13 = Dh
16 |  218
     -16
       58
      -48
       10 = Ah
```

Answer: **DAh**

**Conversion Example C-4**   *Convert 218 to Its Hex Equivalent*

## Converting Hexadecimal to Decimal

To convert a hex number to decimal, take the rightmost digit and convert it to decimal (for example, 0xC = 12). Then add this number to the second rightmost digit multiplied by 16 and the third rightmost digit multiplied by 256. Do not expect to convert numbers larger than 255 on the CCNP exam, because the upper limit of IP addresses in dotted-decimal format is 255 (although Token Ring numbers reach 4096). Some examples follow.

```
1 x 256 = 256
7 x  16 = 112
7 x   1 =   7
         375d
```

**Conversion Example C-5**   *Convert $177_b$ to Decimal*

```
6 x 16 =  96
0 x  1 =   0
          96d
```

**Conversion Example C-6**   *Convert $60_b$ to Decimal*

```
1 x 256 = 256
0 x  16 =   0
0 x   1 =   0
          256d
```

**Conversion Example C-7**   *Convert $100_b$ to Decimal*

```
 1 x 256 = 256
13 x  16 = 208
10 x   1 =  10
           474d
```

**Conversion Example C-8**   *Convert $1DA_b$ to Decimal*

## Alternative Method for Converting from Hexadecimal to Decimal

Another way is to convert from hex to binary and then from binary to decimal. The following sections discuss converting from binary to decimal.

## Binary Numbers

The binary number system uses two digits: 1 and 0. Computer systems use binary numbers. IP addresses and MAC addresses are represented by binary numbers. The number of binary 1s or 0s is the number of bits, short for binary digits. For example, 01101010 is a binary number with 8 bits. An IP address has 32 bits, and a MAC address has 48 bits. As shown in Table C-2, IPv4 addresses are usually represented in dotted-decimal format; therefore, it is helpful to know how to convert between binary and decimal numbers.

MAC addresses are usually represented in hexadecimal numbers; therefore, it is helpful to know how to convert between binary and hexadecimal.

The CCNP candidate should memorize Table C-3, which shows numbers from 0 to 16 in decimal, binary, and hexadecimal formats.

**Table C-2**   Binary Representation of IP and MAC Addresses

| IPv4 Address in Binary | IPv4 Address in Dotted Decimal |
|---|---|
| 00101000 10001010 01010101 10101010 | = 40.138.85.170 |
| **MAC Address in Binary** | **MAC Address in Hexadecimal** |
| 00001100 10100001 10010111 01010001 00000001 10010001 | = 0C:A1:97:51:01:91 |

**Table C-3**   Decimal, Binary, and Hexadecimal Numbers

| Decimal Value | Hexadecimal | Binary |
|---|---|---|
| 0 | 0 | 0000 |
| 1 | 1 | 0001 |
| 2 | 2 | 0010 |
| 3 | 3 | 0011 |
| 4 | 4 | 0100 |
| 5 | 5 | 0101 |
| 6 | 6 | 0110 |
| 7 | 7 | 0111 |
| 8 | 8 | 1000 |
| 9 | 9 | 1001 |
| 10 | A | 1010 |
| 11 | B | 1011 |
| 12 | C | 1100 |
| 13 | D | 1101 |
| 14 | E | 1110 |
| 15 | F | 1111 |
| 16 | 10 | 10000 |

## Converting Binary to Hexadecimal

To convert binary numbers to hex, put the bits in groups of 4, starting with the right-justified bits. Groups of 4 bits are often called *nibbles*. Each nibble can be represented by a single hexadecimal digit. A group of two nibbles is an octet, 8 bits. Examples follow.

Group the bits:
    00 1001 1101
Answer:  **09D$_h$**

**Conversion Example C-9**   *Convert 0010011101 to Hex*

Group the bits:
    0010 1010 0101 1001 0000 1011 0001
Answer:  **2A590B1$_h$**

**Conversion Example C-10**   *Convert 0010101001011001000010110001 to Hex*

## Converting Hexadecimal to Binary

This procedure is also easy. Just change the hex digits into their 4-bit equivalents. Examples follow.

Hex:        0    D    E    A    D    0
Binary:   0000 1101 1110 1010 1101 0000
Answer: **000011011110101011010000**
**Conversion Example C-11**   *Convert 0DEAD0 to Hex*

Hex:      A    A    0    1    0    1
Binary:   1010 1010 0000 0001 0000 0001
Answer: **101010100000000100000001**
**Conversion Example C-12**   *Convert AA0101 to Hex*

## Converting Binary to Decimal

To convert a binary number to decimal, multiply each instance of 0 or 1 by the power of 2 associated with the position of the bit in the binary number. The first bit, starting from the right, is associated with $2^0 = 1$. The value of the exponent increases by 1 as each bit is processed, working leftward. As shown in Table C-4, each bit in the binary number 10101010 has a decimal equivalent from 0 to 128 based on the value of the bit multiplied by a power of 2 associated with the bit position. This is similar to decimal numbers, in which the numbers are based on powers of 10: 1s, 10s, 100s, and so on. In decimal, the number 111 is $(1*100) + (1*10) + (1*1)$. In binary, the number 11111111 is the sum of $(1*2^7) + (1*2^6) + (1*2^5) + (1*2^4) + (1*2^3) + (1*2^2) + (1*2^1) + (1*2^0) = 128 + 64 + 32 + 16 + 8 + 4 + 2 + 1 = 255$. For 10101010, the result is $128 + 0 + 32 + 0 + 8 + 0 + 2 + 0 = 170$. Examples follow.

**Table C-4**   Decimal Values of Bits in a Binary Number

| Power of 2 | $2^7 = 128$ | $2^6 = 64$ | $2^5 = 32$ | $2^3 = 8$ | $2^2 = 4$ | $2^0 = 1$ |
|---|---|---|---|---|---|---|
| Binary | 1 | 1 | 1 | 1 | 1 | 1 |

**Note:**   Just memorize 1, 2, 4, 8, 16, 32, 64, and 128. Use it as you read a binary number from right to left. This technique should be helpful in fast conversions.

Sum:  128  + 0 + 32 + 16 + 0 + 4 + 2 + 1
Answer = **183**
**Conversion Example C-13**   *Convert 10110111 to Decimal*

Sum: 16 + 8 + 0 + 2 + 1
Answer = **27**
**Conversion Example C-14**   *Convert 00011011 to Decimal*

Sum: 128 + 64 + 32 + 16 + 8 + 4 + 2 + 1
Answer = **255**
**Conversion Example C-15**   *Convert 11111111 to Decimal*

## Converting Decimal to Binary Numbers

This procedure is similar to converting from hex to decimal (by dividing), but now you divide the decimal number by 2. You use each residual to build the binary number by pre-pending each residual bit to the previous bit, starting on the right. Repeat the procedure until you cannot divide anymore. The only problem is that for large numbers, you might have to divide many times. You can reduce the number of divisions by first converting the decimal value to a hexadecimal value and then converting the intermediate result to the binary repre-sentation. After the following example, you will read about an alternate method suitable for use with decimal values between 0 and 255 that can be represented in a single octet.

```
       13                              6
  2 |  26                        2 |  13
      -26                            -12
        0                              1
```

The first bit is 0; now divide 13 by 2. [0]        The second bit is 1; now divide 6 by 2. [10]

```
        3                              1
  2 |   6                        2 |   3
       -6                             -2
        0                              1
```

The third bit is 0; now divide 3 by 2. [010]        The fourth bit is 1; the leftmost bit is the division result at the top, which is one. [11010]

Answer: **11010**

**Conversion Example C-16**   *Convert 26 to Binary*

## Alternative Method for Converting from Decimal to Binary

The dividing procedure just described works; it just takes a lot of time. Another way is to remember the bit position values within a byte—128, 64, 32, 16, 8, 4, 2, 1—and play with the bits until the sum adds up to the desired number. This method works when you convert integer values between 0 and 255, inclusive. Table C-5 shows these binary numbers and their decimal values.

**Table C-5**   Bit Values

| Binary Number | Decimal Value |
|---------------|---------------|
| 10000000 | 128 |
| 01000000 | 64 |
| 00100000 | 32 |
| 00010000 | 16 |
| 00001000 | 8 |
| 00000100 | 4 |
| 00000010 | 2 |
| 00000001 | 1 |

For example, to convert 26, you know that it is a number smaller than 128, 64, and 32, so those 3 bits are 0 (000?????). Now you need to find a combination of 16, 8, 4, 2, and 1 that adds up to 26. This method involves using subtraction to compute the remaining number. Start with the largest number, and make the bit at 16 a 1 (0001????). The difference between 26 and 16 is 10. What combination of 8, 4, 2, and 1 gives 10? 1010. Therefore, the answer is 00011010. You might think this method involves too much guesswork, but it becomes second nature after some practice.

The number is larger than 128; enable that bit. [1???????]

How far is 137 from 128: 9; enable the remaining bits for a value of 9 [1???1001].

The answer is 10001001.

**Conversion Example C-17**   *Convert 137 to Binary*

The number is larger than 128; enable that bit. [1???????]

Because 211–128 is greater than 64, enable that bit. [11??????] (Remember that

11000000 = 192.)

Because 211–192=19, enable bits 16, 2, and 1. [11?1??11]

The answer is 11010011.

**Conversion Example C-18**   *Convert 211 to Binary*

In addition to remembering the bit-position values (128, 64, 32, 16, 8, 4, 2, 1), it helps to remember network subnet mask values. Remembering them makes it easier to figure out whether you need to enable a bit. Table C-6 summarizes the binary subnet mask numbers and their decimal values.

**Table C-6**   Binary Masks and Their Decimal Values

| Binary Mask | Decimal |
| --- | --- |
| 10000000 | 128 |
| 11000000 | 192 |
| 11100000 | 224 |
| 11110000 | 240 |
| 11111000 | 248 |
| 11111100 | 252 |
| 11111110 | 254 |

# References and Recommended Readings

ISO/IEC 7498-1: 1994. "Information Processing Systems—OSI Reference—The Basic Model."

RFC 791: *Internet Protocol*, www.ietf.org/rfc.

RFC 793: *Transmission Control Protocol*, www.ietf.org/rfc.

**10GBASE-ER**  A single-mode fiber for up to 80 kilometers (extended range).

**10GBASE-LR**  A single-mode fiber for up to 10 kilometers (long range).

**10GBASE-SR**  A multimode fiber for up to 400 meters (short range).

**20/80 rule**  A rule which says that 20% of traffic is local, and 80% of traffic is to servers in the data center.

**5G**  An emerging wireless standard based on Release 15 Category NR from the 3GPP standards organization.

**6RD (IPv6 Rapid Deployment)**  A tunnel mechanism that allows a service provider to provide unicast IPv6 service to its customers over its IPv4 network by using encapsulation of IPv6 in IPv4.

**ABR (area border router)**  An OSPF router that is connected to more than one area.

**access layer**  In the hierarchical network model, the layer that provides workgroup and user access to local segments on a network.

**administrative distance**  A rating of the trustworthiness of a routing information source. A lower number is preferred.

**ASBR (autonomous system boundary router)**  An OSPF router that injects external LSAs into the OSPF database.

**assurance**  Contextual insights for quick issue resolution and capacity planning.

**automation**  A simplified deployment option for network devices, along with consistent management of network configurations for both wired and wireless access.

**BackboneFast**  A feature that enables fast convergence in the distribution and core layers when Spanning Tree Protocol changes occur.

**BFD (Bidirectional Forwarding Detection)**  A protocol that captures delay, jitter, and packet loss information.

**BGP (Border Gateway Protocol)**  An interdomain routing protocol that allows BGP speakers residing in different autonomous systems to exchange routing information.

**BIDIR-PM (Bidirectional PIM)**  A variant of PIM-SM that builds bidirectional shared trees connecting multicast sources and receivers. It never builds a shortest path tree, and it can scale well because it does not need a source-specific state.

**BPDU Filter**  A feature that suppresses BPDUs on ports.

**BPDU Guard**  A feature that disables a PortFast-enabled port if a BPDU is received.

**BW (bandwidth)**  The capacity of an interface or a link.

**CBWFQ (class-based weighted fair queuing)**  A scheduling mechanism that defines traffic classes that correspond to match criteria, including ACLs, protocols, and input interfaces.

**Cisco DNA Center**   A Cisco tool that helps with design settings, policy definition, and automated provisioning of network devices along with assurance analytics for both wired and wireless networks.

**classification**   The process of identifying the type of traffic.

**congestion management**   A mechanism to handle traffic overflow using a queuing algorithm.

**core layer**   In the hierarchical network model, the layer that provides fast transport between distribution switches in the enterprise campus. Provides a high-speed switching backbone with high reliability and redundancy.

**delay**   A metric based on how long it takes a packet to reach the destination.

**DHCP (Dynamic Host Configuration Protocol)**   A protocol that dynamically configures devices on a network.

**DHCPv6 (Dynamic Host Configuration Protocol version 6)**   A protocol used for dynamic configuration of devices in an IPv6 network.

**dial-in mode**   A mode in which a network device listens until the receiver dials in and sends the initial SYN packet to start the TCP connection.

**dial-out mode**   A mode in which a network device dials out and sends the initial SYN packet to start the TCP connection to the receiver.

**DiffServ**   A QoS model that separates traffic into multiple classes that can be used to satisfy varying QoS requirements.

**distance-vector routing protocol**   A routing protocol that advertises the entire routing table to its neighbors.

**distribution layer**   In the hierarchical network model, the layer that provides policy-based connectivity and aggregation of access layer devices. It is an isolation point between the access and core layers. Security filtering, aggregation of wiring closets, QoS, and routing between VLANs occur at this layer.

**DMVPN (Dynamic Multipoint VPN)**   A Cisco IOS solution for building IPsec over GRE VPNs in a dynamic and scalable manner.

**DNS (Domain Name System)**   An Internet-based directory system that returns the destination IP address, given a domain name.

**DNS64**   A Domain Name System (DNS) mechanism that synthesizes AAAA records from A records.

**DR (designated router)**   An OSPF router type in a multiaccess network that collects LSAs for the multiaccess network and forwards them to all non-DR routers; this arrangement reduces the amount of LSA traffic generated.

**DSCP (Differentiated Services Code Point)**   Bits in an IPv4 header that are used to identify traffic that needs priority.

**DWDM (dense wavelength-division multiplexing)**   A WAN technology used to increase the bandwidth capabilities of fiber by using different wavelengths of light called *channels* over the same fiber strand.

**EGP (exterior gateway protocol)**   A routing protocol type that exchanges routes between administrative domains (for example, BGP).

**EIGRP (Enhanced Interior Gateway Routing Protocol)**   Cisco's proprietary routing protocol.

**enterprise edge module**   Consists of the demilitarized zone (DMZ) and SP edge.

**fabric control plane**   The part of the network that provides logical mapping and resolution of endpoint IDs to users/devices using Locator/ID Separation Protocol (LISP).

**fabric data plane**   The logical overlay created by Virtual Extensible LAN (VXLAN) packet encapsulation along with a Group Policy Object (GPO).

**fabric policy plane**   The part of a network where network security policy is applied through scalable group tags (SGTs) and group-based policies.

**fabric wireless**   A technology that allows wireless traffic to take advantage of the security benefits of using SGTs with the SD-Access fabric.

**FEC (Fast EtherChannel)**   A technology that bundles 2, 4, or 8 Fast Ethernet links for increased bandwidth.

**FHRP (first-hop routing protocol)**   A protocol that deals with first hop routing. Options are HSRP, VRRP, and GLBP.

**FQDN (fully qualified domain name)**   The complete host domain name of a device.

**GEC (Gigabit EtherChannel)**   A technology that bundles 2, 4, or 8 Gigabit Ethernet links together for increased bandwidth.

**GETVPN (Group Encrypted Transport VPN)**   A technology for creating tunnel-less VPNs over private WANs.

**GLBP (Global Load Balancing Protocol)**   A Cisco-proprietary protocol that attempts to overcome the limitations of existing redundant router protocols by adding basic load balancing functionality. In addition to being able to set priorities on different gateway routers, GLBP allows a weighting parameter to be set.

**hop count**   A metric that counts the number of links between routers the packet must traverse to reach a destination.

**HSRP (Hot Standby Routing Protocol)**   A Cisco-proprietary first-hop routing protocol that provides redundancy by creating a virtual router out of two or more routers.

**IANA (Internet Assigned Numbers Authority)**   The global organization responsible for coordination of the DNS root, IP addressing, and other Internet Protocol resources.

**ICMPv6 (Internet Control Message Protocol version 6)**   A protocol that is an integral part of IPv6 and that performs error reporting and diagnostic functions.

**ID (identifier)**   A number that identifies a host network interface.

**IGMP (Internet Group Management Protocol)**   The protocol used in multicast implementations between end hosts and a local router.

**IGP (interior gateway protocol)**   A routing protocol type that exchanges routes within an administrative domain (for example, OSPF and EIGRP).

**IntServ**   A QoS model that benefits real-time applications by explicitly reserving network resources and giving QoS treatment to user packet flows.

**IPsec (IP Security)**   A security architecture that operates in a host to protect IP traffic. The IETF defined IPsec in RFC 4301. IPsec uses open standards and provides secure communication between peers to ensure data confidentiality, integrity, and authentication through network layer encryption.

**IPv4 (Internet Protocol version 4)**   A 32-bit IP addressing format used in networking.

**ISATAP (Intra-Site Automatic Tunnel Addressing Protocol)**   An IPv6 transition mechanism that involves transmitting IPv6 packets between dual-stack nodes over an IPv4 network.

**IS-IS (Intermediate System-to-Intermediate System)**   A interior gateway routing protocol defined by the OSI with link-state characteristics.

**LACP (Link Aggregation Control Protocol)**   A protocol defined in IEEE 802.3ad that provides a method to control the bundling of several physical ports to form a single logical channel.

**link-state routing protocol**   A routing protocol that uses Dijkstra's shortest path algorithm to calculate the best path.

**LLQ (low-latency queuing)**   A feature that provides a strict priority queue to delay-sensitive traffic such as voice to be sent before other queues are serviced.

**load**   A metric based on the degree to which an interface link is busy.

**Loop Guard**   A feature that prevents an alternate or root port from being the designated port in the absence of BPDUs.

**LSA (link-state advertisement)**   A message that is used to communicate network information such as router links, interfaces, link states, and costs.

**model-driven telemetry**   A mechanism to stream data from a model-driven telemetry–capable device to a receiver.

**MP-BGP (Multiprotocol Border Gateway Protocol)**   A BGP extension that is used to carry MPLS VPN information between all provider edge (PE) routers within a VPN community.

**MPLS (Multiprotocol Label Switching) Layer 3 VPN**   A technology for the delivery of IP services using an efficient encapsulation mechanism.

**MSDP (Multicast Source Discovery Protocol)**   A protocol that is used to connect multicast domains.

**MST (Multiple Spanning Tree)**   A protocol that is used to reduce the total number of spanning-tree instances that match the physical topology of the network, reducing the CPU load.

**MTU (maximum transmission unit)**   The MTU is the largest size packet or frame that can be sent.

**NAT (Network Address Translation)**   A process that involves converting IP address space into globally unique IP addresses.

**NAT64**   A Network Address Translation (NAT) transition mechanism that translates between IPv4 and IPv6 protocols.

**ND (Neighbor Discovery)**   IPv6 protocol responsible for gathering various information, including the configuration of local connections, domain name servers, and gateways used to communicate with more distant systems.

**NET (Network Entity Title)**   An address used by IS-IS that consists of the authority and format identifier (AFI), area ID, system ID, and selector (SEL).

**NETCONF (Network Configuration Protocol)**   A network management protocol defined by the IETF in RFC 6241 that provides rich functionality to manage configuration and state data.

**NMS (network management system)**   A system that runs the applications that manage and monitor managed devices.

**NSSA (not-so-stubby area)**   A stub area that contains an ASBR and generates external Type 7 LSAs.

**OMP (Overlay Management Protocol)**   A protocol that runs within the TLS or DTLS control plane tunnels formed by peering between vEdge routers and vSmart controllers.

**OOB (out-of-band) management**   Network management that uses separate infrastructure to connect to managed devices.

**OpenConfig**   A group of network operators working on developing programmable interfaces and tools for managing networks in a vendor-neutral way.

**OSPFv2 (Open Shortest Path First version 2)**   A routing protocol for IPv4 networks.

**OSPFv3 (Open Short Path First version 3)**   A link-state routing protocol that uses Dijkstra's shortest path first (SPF) algorithm to calculate paths to IPv6 destinations.

**overlay**   A logical network built on top of the underlay in order to create virtualized networks.

**PAgP (Port Aggregation Protocol)**   A Cisco-proprietary protocol used for automated logical aggregation of Ethernet switch ports (EtherChannel).

**PAT (Port Address Translation)**   A process that involves translating many IP addresses into a single IP address.

**PBR (policy-based routing)**   A method of manually modifying the next-hop addresses of packets or of marking packets to receive differential service based on source address.

**periodic publication**   A subscription that is useful for when a data value changes occasionally but the information needs to be sent in a timely manner.

**PIM-SM (Protocol Independent Multicast–Sparse Mode)**   A protocol that uses shared trees and rendezvous points to reach widely dispersed group members with reasonable protocol bandwidth efficiency.

**PoE (Power over Ethernet)**   A technology that provides power to end devices such as IP phones, wireless access points, and video cameras via UTP cabling.

**policy**   An automated configuration to enable group-based security policies and network segmentation.

**PortFast**   A feature that bypasses the listening and learning phases to transition directly to the forwarding state.

**RBAC (role-based access control)**   A policy-neutral access control mechanism defined around roles and privileges. The components of RBAC such as role/permissions, user/role, and role/role relationships make it simple to perform user assignments.

**reliability**   A measure of a given application's availability to its users.

**response time**   A measure of the time between a client user request and the response from the server host.

**RESTCONF**   An HTTP-based protocol defined in RFC 8040 that provides a programmatic interface for accessing YANG modeled data.

**RIPng (Routing Information Protocol next generation)**   A distance-vector routing protocol for IPv6 networks.

**RMON (Remote Monitoring)**   A standard monitoring specification that enables network monitoring devices and console systems to exchange network monitoring data.

**Root Guard**   A feature that prevents external switches from becoming the root of the Spanning Tree Protocol tree.

**scalable group**   A group defined in the Group ID field of the VXLAN header as part of group-based policy.

**SD-Access fabric**   The physical and logical network infrastructure.

**SDN (software-defined networking)**   A form of networking that abstracts the underlying network infrastructure away from its applications. SDN decouples the forwarding plane from the control and management planes to enable centralization of network intelligence.

**SD-WAN**   A Cisco enterprise-grade software-based WAN architecture overlay that enables digital and cloud transformation for enterprises. It fully integrates routing, security, centralized policy, and orchestration into largescale networks. It is a multi-tenant, cloud-delivered, highly automated, secure, scalable, and application-aware solution with rich analytics.

**SNMP (Simple Network Management Protocol)**   An IP application layer protocol that has become the standard for the exchange of management information between network devices.

**SONET/SDH**   A circuit-based technology that delivers high-speed services over an optical network.

**Spanning Tree Protocol**   A protocol that prevents loops from being formed when switches are interconnected via multiple paths.

**SSM (Source-Specific Multicast)** A variant of PIM-SM that builds trees, each rooted in just one source. SSM eliminates the rendezvous points and shared trees of sparse mode and only builds a source path tree.

**throughput** A measure of the data transferred from one host to another in a given amount of time.

**ToS (Type of Service)** An IP header field that is used to specify QoS parameters.

**traffic shaping and policing:** Mechanisms that avoid congestion by policing ingress and egress flows.

**UDLD (Unidirectional Link Detection)** A Cisco protocol that is used on unidirectional links (optical fiber) to prevent traffic blackholing and loops.

**underlay** A collection of physical switches and routers running a dynamic Layer 3 routing protocol used as the underlying transport for the SD-Access network.

**UplinkFast** A feature that enables fast uplink failover on an access switch.

**vBond** A software-based component that performs initial authentication of vEdge devices.

**vEdge** A routing component of the SD-WAN architecture that delivers WAN, security, and multi-cloud capabilities. These components can be delivered as hardware, software, cloud, or virtual components.

**virtual network** A separate routing and forwarding instance that provides isolation for host pools or IP subnets.

**VLAN (virtual local-area network)** A broadcast domain that is isolated within Layer 2 and defined logically. Ports in a LAN switch are assigned to different VLAN numbers.

**VLSM (variable-length subnet masking)** The process of dividing a network into subnets of various sizes.

**vManage** A centralized network management system that provides a GUI interface to monitor, configure, and maintain all Cisco SD-WAN devices and links in the underlay and overlay networks.

**VPLS (Virtual Private LAN Service)** A Cisco VPN technology that allows for the connection of multiple sites into a single Layer 2 domain over a managed IP/MPLS network.

**VPWS (Virtual Private Wire Service)** A Layer 2 VPN technology commonly referred to as *pseudowires*.

**VRRP (Virtual Router Redundancy Protocol)** A standards based first-hop routing protocol that provides redundancy with a virtual router elected as the master.

**vSmart** The brains of the SD-WAN architecture, which provides routing, enforces policy, and enforces segmentation.

**VSS (Virtual Switching System)** A Cisco technology that allows certain Cisco switches to bond together as a single virtual switch.

**VSS (Virtual Switching System)**   A Cisco technology that converts two physical switches into one logical switch.

**VTP (Virtual Trunking Protocol)**   A Cisco-proprietary protocol that reduces the administration in a switched network.

**window size**   The upper limit of frames that can be transmitted without a return acknowledgment.

**WoL (Wake on LAN)**   A feature that allows a network administrator to remotely power up sleeping machines.

**XML (Extensible Markup Language)**   A markup language similar to HTML that was designed to store and transport data.

**YANG (Yet Another Next Generation)**   A data modeling language used to describe the data for network configuration protocols.

# Index

# D

# F

# G

# H

# J

# K - L

# S

# V

# W

# REGISTER YOUR PRODUCT at CiscoPress.com/register
## Access Additional Benefits and SAVE 35% on Your Next Purchase

- Download available product updates.
- Access bonus material when applicable.
- Receive exclusive offers on new editions and related products.
  (Just check the box to hear from us when setting up your account.)
- Get a coupon for 35% for your next purchase, valid for 30 days.
  Your code will be available in your Cisco Press cart. (You will also find
  it in the Manage Codes section of your account page.)

Registration benefits vary by product. Benefits will be listed on your account page
under Registered Products.

---

**CiscoPress.com – Learning Solutions for Self-Paced Study, Enterprise, and the Classroom**
Cisco Press is the Cisco Systems authorized book publisher of Cisco networking technology,
Cisco certification self-study, and Cisco Networking Academy Program materials.

At **CiscoPress.com** you can

- Shop our books, eBooks, software, and video training.
- Take advantage of our special offers and promotions (ciscopress.com/promotions).
- Sign up for special offers and content newsletters (ciscopress.com/newsletters).
- Read free articles, exam profiles, and blogs by information technology experts.
- Access thousands of free chapters and video lessons.

**Connect with Cisco Press – Visit CiscoPress.com/community**
Learn about Cisco Press community events and programs.

# Cisco Press